Journalism for Democracy

Journalism for Democracy

Géraldine Muhlmann

Translated by Jean Birrell

polity

Liberté • Égalité • Fraternité
RÉPUBLIQUE FRANÇAISE

This book is supported by the French Ministry of Foreign Affairs, as part of the Burgess programme run by the Cultural Department of the French Embassy in London (www.frenchbooknews.com)

Ouvrage publié avec le concours du Ministère français de la Culture – Centre national du livre

Published with the assistance of the French Ministry of Culture – National Centre for the Book

Polity Press
65 Bridge Street
Cambridge CB2 1UR, UK

Polity Press
350 Main Street
Malden, MA 02148, USA

ISBN-13: 978-0-7456-4472-1
ISBN-13: 978-0-7456-4473-8(pb)

A catalogue record for this book is available from the British Library.

Typeset in 10.5 on 12 pt Plantin
by Toppan Best-set Premedia Limited
Printed and bound in Great Britain by MPG Books Group Limited, Bodmin, Cornwall

The telling of factual truth comprehends much more than the daily information supplied by journalists, though without them we should never find our bearings in an ever-changing world and, in the most literal sense, would never know where we are.

Hannah Arendt, 'Truth and politics'

Brecht's line – that the party has a thousand eyes while the individual has but two – is as false as any bromide ever. A dissenter's exact imagination can see more than a thousand eyes peering through the same pink spectacles.

Theodore W. Adorno, *Negative Dialectics*

Contents

Acknowledgements

This book has benefited enormously from discussions over many years with Miguel Abensour, to whom I once again express my deep gratitude.

I was also greatly helped by many conversations with Anne-Sophie Menasseyre at the time of publication of the first version of this book, for which I offer my thanks.

Introduction

A plague on all journalists! Denounced on all sides as a shameful trade, the profession is accused of selling out to the powerful and of presenting a superficial, biased and misleading picture of the world. Occasionally, behind the condemnation, one can detect a desire for reform, a feeling that an activity that consists of looking at the present, and making what it sees available to all, is important for the health of a democracy, and that it is high time it is taken seriously. Too often, however, we get no further than the well-worn formulas of the historic battle for freedom of expression – much loved by journalists as a defence against their critics. The question of the political meaning of the practice of journalism is scarcely tackled. That of what an 'ideal journalism' might be is rarely posed. Yet some foundation is surely needed on which to base the expressions of anger felt in the face of 'real journalism'. A constant onslaught is not without its virtues, but it hardly amounts to an informed critique of the issues, a critique worthy of the name.

It is true, of course, that sociologists have made journalism a subject of study, and that thanks to them we have a better understanding of this professional milieu and of the rules and constraints under which it operates. But sociologists analyse journalism just as they analyse any other milieu. They dissect it according to general analytical principles: who are the actors? How do they interact? How is the journalistic 'product' created? What are the rules of the 'media field'? The question of what journalism could be, or should try to be, is not addressed. The sociology that sometimes claims to be 'critical' is not worthy of the name, or at any rate not in the sense given to this word by the thinkers of the first Frankfurt School (Horkheimer, Adorno), and which required, as they said, more 'theoretical imagination'.[1] A certain positivism still dominant in the social sciences often prevents them from freely interrogating their subject or integrating it into a normative, free and fruitful thinking. 'Real journalism' has no more secrets for us, but we do not always know which ideal-critique to draw on when we condemn it. The sociologists keep their judgements on the meaning of the practice of journalism to themselves, or else give vent to them in articles or opinion columns that stand *alongside* their 'scientific' work. And their judgements, it must be said, are often remarkably hostile, based on the conviction that the gaze of the journalist, unlike that of the sociologist, is doomed to remain on the surface of things, remote from the 'truth' of the social; in short, erroneous.

It might be thought that, in a world seemingly enamoured of disciplinary divisions, it would be the philosophers who would consider the political implications of journalism, who would give it meaning and lay the foundations for a serious critique. Sadly, they often find it difficult to free themselves from an ontological contempt for that *everyday* that is the daily bread of journalists, but from which they, for their part, feel they need to distance themselves in order to attain – once again – the 'truth' of things, or the 'being'. One senses that, beyond the conjunctural irritations in the face of what our newspapers, radio and television provide, it is journalism *itself* that is despised: even when it is 'good', nothing can be expected of it; it gets everything wrong, it lacks rigour, it is without interest. What purpose would be served, therefore, by spending time pondering what it could be if it was 'good'?

Studies have revealed the depth of the repulsion for the present in the philosophical tradition. Stéphane Haber has explored what he calls the '*presentophobe*' (or *presentofuge*) reflex in the history of philosophy, which explains, in particular, the original hostility of philosophy towards the social sciences, which often choose their subjects of study from the present.[2] The slowness with which the historical sciences have turned to the present testifies to the same reflex, and also to the prestige it has long drawn from the fact of being a gaze distanced in time. Strangest of all is the way that the social sciences, in constructing themselves in this hostile context, have in a way repeated with regard to journalism the *presentophobe* reflex from which they themselves have suffered at the hands of philosophy and history. Haber has shown how the arrival of the present as a subject of study in the social sciences has been accompanied by a more subtle reinvestment in the original *presentophobe* reflex: alongside the present deemed worthy of scientific study there has often remained a certain devalorized present – what Haber calls the 'immediate present', or 'the actual' – and this is the province of journalists.[3]

There are, of course, some dissenters from these views. In any case, the *presentophobe* reflex is primarily characteristic of the French sociological tradition, and less strong elsewhere. France is a country where disciplinary identities seem particularly fraught, constantly demanding an 'other' in order to affirm themselves, and frequently making this 'other' the journalist. The sociologists of the Chicago School, who often, like Robert E. Park, came from the world of journalism, did not see the continuity between journalism and sociology as in any way taboo – and they produced the first serious studies of the popular press that had emerged at the end of the nineteenth century, evidence that they saw it as a subject worthy of serious consideration. French sociologists, by contrast, echoing the concept of sociology of Emile Durkheim, have never ceased to construct their practice both as a 'science', wholly at odds with the journalistic gaze, and as an academic discipline, cut off from the world of journalism. I believe, in particular, that the criticisms of the world of journalism formulated in recent years by Pierre Bourdieu, which I will discuss later in this book, need to be located within this historical French context.

France is home to another deep division, stronger there than elsewhere: that between the writer and the journalist. Once again the United States provides a good example of a more relaxed attitude to issues of identity. This was visible in New York at the end of the nineteenth century, among a body of reporters that included future sociologists like Robert E. Park and reporter-writers like Stephen Crane. Urban reportage gave rise to and brought together literary and sociological approaches, without the need to make clear differentiations between journalists, writers and sociologists.[4] It was also visible in the emergence in the 1960s and 1970s of the New Journalism and the Nonfiction Novel, a movement of writer-journalists who set out actively to destroy the artificial frontier between the writing of fiction and reportage.[5] It is true that French journalism has historically always been open to the world of writers, but it is a mistake to assume that this openness has meant the absence of tensions and the end of frontiers.[6] Far from it. For example – to choose a writer who can hardly be suspected of a principled hatred of journalism – the great French naturalist writer Emile Zola has some similarities to Stephen Crane. Zola may have described himself, in spite of his unease, as 'for and with the press',[7] he may have led the French delegation to the first International Congress of journalists in London in 1893, he may even have shown interest in some talented reporters, but it is nevertheless clear that the signs of recognition he accorded them remained distant; they were certainly not such as to question the frontiers between 'true' literature and literary reportage. It is hardly surprising, in this context, that the construction of the identity of the French journalistic milieu, in particular through its professionalization, should finally have been achieved by an emancipation from the reference to literature, which had been more intimidating, even paralysing, than rewarding. So much so that, a few years later, it was journalists who reproached Albert Londres for having 'introduced into *Le Matin* the microbe of literature'.[8] A few individuals may have switched backwards and forwards between literature and journalism, but France has never experienced as radical a challenge to the frontiers as, for example, has the United States.

Journalism has remained in France the 'other' of both the social sciences and philosophy and of literature. Such tensions surrounding identity and such a liking for institutions, which have always been at the expense of journalism, can be summed up by a metaphor borrowed from Wolf Lepenies.[9] He tells a story that speaks volumes as to the battles fought by French sociology in the early 1900s to get itself admitted into the established university disciplines. A goal of symbolic importance was the erection of a statue representing sociology to stand alongside those of Pasteur (science) and Victor Hugo (literature), which occupied, and still occupy, a place of honour in the Sorbonne. Thanks to the efforts of Emile Durkheim, a bust of Auguste Comte was erected in 1902 to the glory of sociology; but it was placed, not inside the Sorbonne but outside, in the Place – a half-victory, heavy with innuendo. One may well wonder whether this third statue has ever been tempted to assert its identity by resorting to those very practices from which it had itself suffered, that is, recalling that there are some who are even more external to the established disciplines than it. The journalist is the other about whom everyone is agreed. The journalist is someone who lacks even the right to a statue, a devastating blow in a country so devoted to them.

This temptation of contempt is not, however, confined to the emblematic case of France. Too preoccupied, in the case of the social sciences, with proclaiming the 'scientific' nature of their activities or, in that of philosophy, with proclaiming the 'ontological' profundity of their enquiries, all are often alike in finding it difficult to take journalism seriously. In fact they seem scarcely to be cured of what Michel Foucault pejoratively called the cult of the 'hidden', which leads to contempt for ordinary, quotidian gazes, those gazes which, like that of the journalist, are content to 'make visible that which is visible'.[10] The stately swans, sure of their own identity and nobility, do not deign to engage in a real dialogue with the ugly duckling. Instead they dissect it learnedly as an object wholly external to them, constantly use it to define themselves – 'we don't do journalism!' or 'let's leave journalistic considerations out of this' – but avoid questioning it in a way that would risk revealing its own nobility, different from theirs, or providing it with the tools to formulate its ideas. Such disdain for a practice they see as poorly equipped for the quest for 'truth', poor, that is, from the *epistemological* point of view, enables them to avoid engaging in a *political* questioning, in which journalism would certainly appear richer, and in which those who asked the questions would be forced to think more deeply about their own research methods.

Prosaically formulated – which does not imply a 'functionalist' bias – such political questioning would come down to this: what purpose is served by journalism in a democracy? And what underlying conception of democracy or of 'ideal journalism' can serve as a basis from which to critique 'real journalism'? Plenty of polemical articles and satirical writing half raise such questions, or conceal, sometimes without realizing it, certain representations which serve as cursory responses. But a certain vagueness generally persists, a difficulty in addressing the problem as such, in daring to go down certain dangerous paths.

Why dangerous? Because the difficult question which a coherent critique of journalism inevitably comes up against is this: does criticism of journalism not, in the last analysis, amount to criticism of democracy itself? Is it not democracy that is the real target when people start bemoaning the mediocrity of our journalists?

For some legendary denigrators of journalism this was clearly the case, nor was there any reason to be secretive or defensive about it. When Balzac, for example, lambasted the arrogant journalistic milieu, he believed that it was the very principle of a public bourgeois space in which opinions and gazes were exchanged that ensured a sad fall from the values of the old aristocracy. One first taste of the glory to be won on this deceitful stage was all that was needed for a man like Lucien de Rubempré to abandon the authenticity of the 'true' writer. The real problem, for Balzac, was the triumph of the principle of 'publicity' – everything is subject to the collective gaze – which heralded a democracy that sullied everything it touched.

Few critics today would adopt this sort of 'aristocratism', or any anti-democratic elitism, though it is apparent in certain formulations even so. Nevertheless, it is surely right to believe that a serious critique of journalism cannot avoid the problem. Rather, it must face it head on, it must recognize what is at issue and the risks of its positions; that is, it ought to know how far it is ready to accept an element of anti-democratism or, to be more precise, of democratic despair. Rather than retreat, having scarcely ventured onto this tricky terrain, thanks to a democratism too frightened of being caught in the act of criticizing democracy, a critique of journalism would do better to pose the problem clearly. It would then be forced to ask whether to be a democrat is necessarily to remain a stranger to the temptation of despair or whether, on the contrary, this temptation is not likely to be fruitful for a rigorous and lucid reflection on democracy. In other words, it would accept democratic unease as a way of embracing the democratic ideal.

That said, caution is needed. There is a certain type of criticism, made in the hurly-burly of daily life, when we feel irritated by, bemoan or rage against journalism, that can take us onto dangerous territory. And here and there, in certain criticisms of journalism, a more or less conscious seriously anti-democratic hostility can emerge. This is understandable, since any criticism of journalism must at some point face up to the problem of democracy itself, and be ready to criticize it, too. This is the real problem, and, in a way, it is at the heart of my book. My aim is to formulate an acceptable critical position, one that remains committed to democracy in spite of the anxieties about journalism and even the anger it can arouse, but also one that does not lapse into a democratic naivety – the naivety that consists of systematically lauding the role of the journalist without recognizing its limitations.

How are we to define the 'ideal journalism'? Only from this position on a knife-edge can we hope to provide some satisfactory answers to this question. On the one hand, those who despair of both journalism and democracy have long ago abandoned the attempt. On the other, the most enthusiastic democrats, those at risk of 'naivety', who believe in journalism as a space for interchange in the service of the plurality of opinions, and regard the failings of 'real journalism' as no more than ills susceptible of reform (by greater freedom of expression, more openness in the journalistic profession, less censorship and self-censorship), tend to be reticent on the question of the 'ideal journalism'. They let it be understood that it exists, and that it really is 'ideal', but they rarely develop these ideas, and less so in France than in the Anglo-Saxon world. The American debate on Public Journalism or 'civic journalism' over the last twenty years is evidence of a desire to ask the question, whatever one thinks of the replies, either practical or theoretical.[11] Anglo-American work on the philosophical sources of the principle of freedom of expression,[12] and on the cultural and political issues of 'information' and 'communication',[13] offers precious analytical tools. It may still be possible to add to the palette of tools necessary to a serious consideration of the ideals of journalism, and this is what my book aims to do.

I will start by embracing the 'enthusiastic' democratic position and taking it as far as it will go. What are the philosophical foundations of the belief in the virtues of 'the public' and in the political importance of the figure of the spectator? To do this I need to discuss the key concepts which justify the most wholehearted commitment to journalistic practice and the desire constantly to improve it, that is, the conviction that it can be pushed towards an 'ideal' that is itself clearly defined. In this context I will return to one of the most important theoretical sources for this enthusiasm for the figure of the spectator: the thought of Immanuel Kant. I will try to define the representation of the ideal spectator to which it leads, in other words to derive from it an ideal-critique for journalism. By demonstrating a link between Kant and Baudelaire, I will show that this ideal-critique has much in common with the Baudelairean figure of the flâneur. This will be my first ideal-critique, the first step on the journey I will make in this book.

Then, having taken the enthusiastic position, product of the Enlightenment and expertly formulated by Kant, as far as it will go, I will take the risky step of entering into a dialogue with those who despair of democracy, those who are without this Kantian confidence in the figure of the spectator. This will involve discussing the ideas of those who make a more structural critique of the ills of democracy, of which even the most 'reformed' journalism is inevitably part. I will need to rework the ideal-critique previously formulated, but this time giving due weight to the deeper anxieties about democracy, seen as a false plurality and as source of a structural homogeneity of gazes, against which journalism can do nothing, which it is more likely to confirm, or to fix. It is in this uncomfortable context, this dialogue with Marx and with the sociology of crowds and publics, that I will formulate my arguments: does a role for the journalist still exist, given this un-naive approach to democracy, and this uncompromising point of view? A role that is meaningful, in spite of everything? An 'ideal' role, which makes it possible to think about the way in which 'real' journalists perform – or do not perform – it, but which will no longer relate to an 'ideal', that is, idealized, vision of democracy?

The problem, once we have left Kantism behind, is this: democracy is not the marvellous plurality painted in glowing colours by the most enthusiastic democrats. But is there space, nevertheless, between this confidence, blind to the dominations which permeate democratic space, and the hateful condemnation that abandons journalism and democracy to their irremediable mediocrity, for a consideration of the political issues of journalism in a democracy and the construction of an ideal-critique of journalism? I believe there is such a space. My reworking of the original ideal-critique into a second, and then a third, ideal-critique, as my argument develops, will be based on and will also consolidate this belief. I hope to show that there is something worth saving in journalism, in spite of the dissatisfactions and the anxieties which are perhaps, in truth, inherent to a serious and clear-headed commitment to democracy.

In an article published in 1981,[14] the historian and sociologist Christopher Lasch bemoaned the way in which the profound and radical critiques of the media and mass culture formulated in the 1950s and 1960s had produced such a massive swing of the pendulum. Fearful of questioning a sacrosanct democracy, he argued, some on the Left seemed to have decided to adopt a principled enthusiasm with regard to the modern media,[15] which, he believed, simplified the nature of the problems and ultimately destroyed any critical perspective. Lasch correctly emphasized that democratic vigilance should not take the form simply of critical inhibition. This inhibition exists, it seems to me, in spite of the anathemas regularly launched against the media, which are, in the end, abortive. Howls of rage are no substitute for a meaningful critique; a diffused anger, which never penetrates to the essence of things, that is, the difficult problem of democracy, is no doubt a more comfortable position.

Lasch is a good example of a thinker who is aware of the risks of the critique, yet does not evade them. He is no stranger to the temptation of despair. This theme is central to his study of the journalist Lincoln Steffens, luminary of the American muckraking movement of the early twentieth century.[16] Lasch shows how despair is constantly surfacing in the itinerary of Steffens – the feeling that journalism, prisoner of the expectations of its public, is unable truly to enlighten that public about the evils of its age, in which it ultimately participates.[17] Lasch shows himself to be fairly despairing, ending his article of 1981 with an appeal to look elsewhere than the media for the means for change – in particular to civic associations and less 'visible' battles. He shows that there is no critical thinking about journalism, in the name of a demanding conception of democracy, that does not experience the temptation to throw in the towel, that is, a fierce longing to close the newspapers, switch off the television and the radio – and these days the computer – and search for 'another stage', on which the 'real' conflicts by which a democracy lives and grows are played out.

This is the problem that has bedevilled all critical thinking about journalism: what if the media is a place where, by its very nature, the conflictuality and plurality that permeate the social world are stifled, submerged in a unified, homogenized and deceptive vision? What if nothing can be expected of journalism except this imprisonment of the democratic life in dominant representations that ignore conflict, diversity and marginality? We may well feel tempted to despair! But my book is based on the assumption that this cannot be the last word.

The most resigned, in their hatred of journalism, are not immune to the volte-face described, with grim humour, by Isaac Bashevis Singer in the case of his father, a man who detested newspapers and valued only study and prayer:

> Father said that the newspapers were full of blasphemy and heresy. He said that to start the day by reading the papers was like eating poison for

> breakfast. But as the armies fought around the towns and villages where we came from and the Tsar's uncle, Nikolai Nikolaevich, ordered the Jews driven out of those towns and even took Jews as hostage and sent them to Siberia, Father started to glance into the papers, too – not the first thing in the morning but later in the day, after praying and studying.[18]

Some days it pays to read the papers! In other words, whatever one thinks, to make a complete break with the sort of community that is the political community may be no easier than to break with other sorts of community (family, religious, spiritual). Reading the paper is a *mise au monde*,[19] that is, it places one in a relationship with a totality that is greater than the individual, while at the same time giving the individual a place. This experience of political belonging is something it is hard wholly to reject. Though it may often be when worse threatens that those who want nothing to do with politics are trapped by it, like Singer's father, there are plenty of less dramatic examples of this particular schizophrenia; one need only think of those ferocious scoffers who nevertheless continue to buy their newspaper every morning!

Like it or not, journalism is a fundamental mediation between the individual and the community. One may believe that it distorts this link, that it oversimplifies it and standardizes it and that it creates a 'common' that is artificial and violent for many individuals, but it remains the case that to turn one's back on the problem is not a solution. That would be to abandon the question of democracy, to settle on a definitive judgement on this eternally frustrating, standardizing system in which freedom of expression is only 'formal' (to use the vocabulary of Marx), leading to the crushing of the plurality of the actors. I am naive enough to think, with all due respect to Noam Chomsky, that the *New York Times* and *Pravda* are not exactly the same thing;[20] to be more precise, that if standardization spoils democracy, especially through the journalism that is its new king, there are different ways of creating a 'common', and that the way of the democracies deserves a rather more sustained analysis. It may well be that we need to cure ourselves of an idealized vision of democracy as a marvellous conflictual plurality, orchestrated by journalists, but it is still the case that the act of bringing together the democratic community in 'common' media representations does not necessarily kill off all conflictuality. Lastly, it is perhaps at this point that a reflection on a 'de-idealized' democracy becomes truly important: how can democracy be both unifying and conflictual? And how can these two processes be imbricated in the gaze of the journalist at the world?

I hope that my book will show that a critique of journalism will gain from addressing questions of this type. Of course, I will need to prepare the ground. I will first explain my own dissatisfaction with current critiques of journalism, which are often confused and lacking in coherence or any serious consideration of their implications. I will then gradually lay the foundations on which a productive critical questioning of 'real journalism' can be based. By navigating between the most enthusiastic (Kantian) position and the most uneasy positions (Marx and his concept of 'ideology', but also those who fear that modern 'publics' will inevitably become intolerant 'crowds'), I will arrive at a final ideal-critique, which will consider journalism as a project for a 'conflictual unifying' of the political community.

My main concerns here are the philosophical and political aspects of the ideal-critiques that I will in turn examine and develop, and their implications and the representations of democracy they assume. In this sense, my book is a *theoretical* essay on the practice of journalism. I should at this point explain that this book started life as the first part of a more general study of journalism. In this sense, my book is a *theoretical* essay on the practice of journalism. It was completed by a second, a study of journalistic practices and content since the invention of modern journalism in the mid-nineteenth century; this is the basis of another book, *A Political History of Journalism*, first published in France in 2004 (reprinted in 2006) and translated and published by Polity in 2008.[21] I would like to say here what a great pleasure it is for me to see both volumes appear in English with the same publisher and the same translator, Jean Birrell, to whom I express my warm thanks, as this brings out their complementarity and the unity of the intellectual project which inspired them. This dates back to my doctoral thesis, 'Le Regard du journaliste en démocratie. Conditions et enjeux de 1880 à nos jours', supervised by Professor Miguel Abensour.[22]

It goes without saying that in writing these two books I have seen them as distinct, each constituting its own world and each able to be read without reference to the other. It is still possible, however, that the reader of the earlier book, *A Political History of Journalism*, might feel the need for a deeper theoretical exploration, and that the reader of the present book might wish to see some of my analyses related to more concrete journalistic examples. I would like, therefore, to spell out more clearly the connection between them.

For me, it has always been essential to work by relating empirical analysis (drawing on the material bequeathed by the history of journalism, that is, on concrete journalistic writing) and theoretical analysis (a conceptual elaboration). The concept of 'ideal journalism' that I try to construct here has thus involved a consideration of the history of 'real' journalism, and it led, in *A Political History of Journalism*, to a veritable 'proposal' for the reading of the journalistic tradition. Which is why, from time to time, as my argument develops, I have referred to this earlier book. The 'ideal' that consists of 'unifying' while at the same time 'creating conflict' has left its mark on journalism itself. In the earlier book I identified some major 'figures' who put these two acts into practice in their journalistic writing, giving priority either to the act of unifying (the model I called the witness–ambassador) or to that of injecting conflict, or decentring (the model I called the decentrer). And it was while working concretely on the history of journalism that I developed this 'ideal', an ideal whose theoretical implications seemed to me both complex and fascinating. I try in the present book to explore these implications more deeply.

Any separation of empirical studies from a more theoretical reflection on the issues they raise and their presuppositions is inevitably artificial. An examination of the methodological options used by the former often makes one aware that they relate to major questions of political philosophy, which only an excessively scientistic credo would wish to be forgotten. It is the aim of this book to examine closely the tools with which we understand, and with which we could understand, journalism, in order to construct a way of interrogating it that is aware of the conceptions of democracy that it assumes and confirms.

1

Critiquing journalism: a difficult exercise

Critiques of journalism come thick and fast. Though they sometimes seem to be repeating themselves, they are not all saying the same thing. I cannot, of course, discuss each of them in detail. In general, however, they often seem to me to be prisoners of schemas that are an impediment to critical thinking. This abortive character, despite the vehemence, and in some cases the violence, of the onslaught, suggests that there is a need to consider the possible bases for a new critical approach. The spadework I propose to undertake in this first chapter will prepare the ground for the definition of a 'critical path' which will try to clear a way through, without denying, the obstacles inherent to a critique of journalism.

1. The public: hostage to journalists

Journalists in the service of the powerful

A first category of critiques denounces journalism as a profession which imposes biased and distorted points of view, as compared with the shifting opinions and gazes which would freely circulate in public space, if only it was not controlled by the media. It is generally connivance within the profession with those wielding power in the political and/or economic sphere that is targeted by this critique; thus it demonstrates how journalists provide the powerful with the means to impose their world view on the public.

The accusation of connivance is often convincing, and it is supported by conclusive and shocking examples. It is a necessary criticism, and it rightly denounces practices which stifle the plurality of points of view and sap journalistic independence. The problem with this sort of critique, however, is its tendency to stick to a schema that conceals a certain naivety with regard to the 'public'. In order to be clear and crisp, and unhesitatingly identify the 'baddies', it tends to represent the public as innocent victim, taken hostage by a profession. This latent schema also renders problematic its relation to Marxism, which it often proclaims, in particular when it takes over the concept of 'ideology' developed by Marx and Engels in 1843–5. As we will see, however, the complexity of this founding concept bears little relation to the way the word is used by the 'neo-Marxists'.

The emblematic figure in this first category of critiques is without doubt Noam Chomsky. In his book of 1988, written with Edward S. Herman, Chomsky analysed the American media and showed that 'the observable pattern of indignant campaigns and suppressions, of shading and emphasis, and of selection of context, premises, and general agenda, is highly functional for the established power and responsive to the needs of the government and major power groups'.[1] The dependence of the media on the business world (especially for advertising revenues), on the government[2] and more generally on influential people, who are important sources of information, produces a series of uniform and reverential representations.

This diagnosis, elaborated by Chomsky in his many works on the media, has found obvious echoes in France in the anger of Serge Halimi, a *Le Monde diplomatique* journalist and author, in 1997, of a short book with the title *The New Watchdogs*.[3] Adapting an expression used by the writer Paul Nizan, in the 1930s, to criticize an elite, especially an academic elite, barricaded behind a narrow vision of scholarship and thought,[4] Halimi denounced the majority of French journalists as the contemporary 'watchdogs' of power, both economic and political; he accused them of practising what he called a 'journalism of reverence'. This criticism has been repeated in France by others, often close to *Le Monde diplomatique*, including members of the organization Acrimed (Action-Critique-Médias), which is internet-based, and the film director Pierre Carles, whose *Pas Vu Pas Pris* ('Not Seen, Not Captured') appeared in 1999. This way of using the word 'watchdog' is very different from the way it is used in the Anglo-Saxon tradition, where the 'watchdog journalist' is, on the contrary, someone who harbours an aggressive mistrust of the powerful, especially those with political power. Such journalists may have the faults of their radicality,[5] but they at least 'watch over' professional ethical principles in the face of the influence of those in power. These contradictory usages of the same word can achieve an almost comic effect, as when Serge Halimi evokes, by contrast with the journalistic practices he observes in France, the model of Bob Woodward and Carl Bernstein in the Watergate affair, that is, precisely what the United States regards as 'watchdog journalism'.[6]

The reference to the journalism of the Watergate affair reveals the extent to which, behind this official neo-Marxism, there lies, in reality, a fairly simple schema, which is very effective for the punchiness of the critique: that of the innocent public and wicked journalists, the former taken hostage by the latter. Nor is this unilateral conception of domination and this tendency to idealize the public, a victim that needs to be liberated from the yoke of the powerful, unknown in the Chomskyan critique.

It is a schema which has strongly 'liberal' implications. It supposes that a public space truly liberated from the censorship and the biases imposed from outside by a clique of the powerful would no longer be subject to any domination that led to homogeneity in the representations exchanged. The assault on the public's plurality of points of view is seen as exogenous, the result of a constraint that is in some way external, which clamps down on a violated public space; it is the act of the powerful and of their intermediaries, that is, the journalists. The public is not envisaged as an entity that is itself impure, permeated by endogenous dominations which have a 'homogenizing' effect on the representations exchanged there.

Thus the 'ideology' that is denounced does not implicate the public. The public suffers it; it is imposed on the public. And the public must be liberated. The latent fantasy here, which is eminently respectable, and encouraged by some major episodes in the history of western democracies, is that of a heroic journalist who will succeed in liberating the public from the powers that be.

A hero to liberate the public!

This great myth has been frequently illustrated. The most recent and perhaps most successful example is the 1999 film by Michael Mann, *The Insider*, which portrays real-life events which took place in 1996 within the editorial team of the highly regarded CBS television network series *60 Minutes*.

The reporter Lowell Bergman (played by Al Pacino), producer of *60 Minutes*, has received the 'confession' of Jeffrey Wigand (Russell Crowe). Wigand was a former vice-president of the tobacco company Brown & Williamson, a chemist of high standing, once head of research and development within the company, who had eventually been sacked by his employers. Wigand breaks the confidentiality agreement which bound him to his former employers and, in front of the *60 Minutes* cameras, tells what he knows, that is, the precise nature of the additives used by the tobacco companies to speed up the absorption of nicotine and increase the satisfaction experienced: they had an ammoniac base which was damaging to the nervous system. Wigand had alerted his former employers to the proven harmfulness of a new product recently used by the company, but had met with an outright refusal to stop its use, which would have adversely affected sales. It was these strained relations with his superiors that had led to his dismissal.

The journalist Bergman appears as a 'hero' in the sense we have just defined, that is, he incarnates the public against the powerful. This gives the film great dramatic power. When Wigand is still hesitating, before finally agreeing to testify to *60 Minutes*, Bergman talks to him about the easing of his conscience that will ensue and also about the power of public opinion. Once you have entered 'the court of public opinion', he says, it will decide. Once you have been seen by thirty million people, nothing will ever be the same. 'And that's the power you have, my friend.' Bergman then had to fight against his own editor-in-chief, who refused for a long time to broadcast the interview, under pressure from CBS, which had been threatened by the tobacco firms with a costly lawsuit if they went ahead. This was indeed a heroic battle fought by a single journalist against a veritable conglomerate of the 'powerful'; and a battle that was eventually won. There is certainly some bitterness – which adds to the film's interest and depth – in the film's denouement, visible in particular in the doubtful question Bergman puts to his wife when she congratulates him on his 'victory': 'What did I win?' But the film also admirably describes a certain heroic model of the 'good' journalist, who serves the interests of the public against the powerful – of a public that is also ideal, seeking the truth being kept from it, as worthy as its hero.

This model is frequently implicit in my first category of critiques of journalism: the denunciations of connivance with the powerful. But, by placing such confidence in the notion of the public, these critics cannot, without contradicting themselves or destroying the very concepts they employ, proclaim a neo-Marxism, as they often do; in this pseudo-Marxism, virtually nothing of Marx and his concept of ideology remains.

A confused use of the term 'ideology'

The word 'ideology' is primarily used by Chomsky and Herman to describe certain specific aspects of the world view transmitted by the media. The expression 'the ideology of anticommunism', for example, is used to indicate the hatred of Communism which permeates the American media discourse.[7] However, it is clear that it is the whole media discourse, described as a discourse to justify economic domination, which these writers see as 'ideology', echoing the Marxian concept. They make implicit reference to the definition of this concept given by Marx and Engels in *The German Ideology*: 'ideology' is constituted by the 'ruling ideas' of an epoch, which 'are nothing more than the ideal expression of the dominant material relations', or 'the dominant material relations grasped as ideas; hence of the relations which make the one class the ruling one, therefore the ideas of its dominance'.[8]

The critiques considered here stop well short of the implications of the concept of ideology in Marx. Whereas Marx and Engels came to have a deep distrust of the public space of opinions and representations,[9] these critiques seem rather to preserve the notion of 'public' and, as a result, the simple 'journalists vs. public' schema, the former as malevolent as the latter are innocent. It is as if the public, constrained and stifled, seeks only to express its neglected point of view; as if all that is needed is to lift the lid clamped down by the powerful and their accomplices, the media; as if there is a 'non-ideology' which is waiting only to be liberated. This is all very much simpler than in the analysis of ideology in Marx.

Domination in the realm of ideas, as evoked in *The German Ideology*, applies not only to the expression of these ideas, but to their very production: 'The class which has the means of material production at its disposal, consequently also controls the means of mental production, so that the ideas of those who lack the means of mental production are on the whole subject to it.'[10] Ideology does not simply prevent other existing world views from being expressed; it prevents any other world view from being developed, like an invisible straitjacket that restricts the field of vision in general. This phenomenon means that every sort of belief must be suspect as 'ideology', including those which think they are rebellious. Even the status of economically dominated is not enough to guarantee a position outside ideology. How, then, can one believe that an entire public is un-ideologized, constrained by a few, waiting its moment? The concept of ideology in Marx *implicates* the public; it applies to all the representations and ideas that circulate in a society. The realm of ideas is affected, according to Marx, by a sort of 'delayed action' in relation to the material situation. That is, the reversal of a particular hegemonic view of the world can begin to happen only when the material reversal of the corresponding material domination is already taking place.[11] So there isn't really a public ready to express clearly other ideas than those of the ideology, before the material reversal of the economic domination corresponding to this ideology.

Every time that contemporary critiques insist on the arbitrariness of public sentiment faced with the dominant thinking imposed on it by the media, they are diverging from the conception of ideology developed by Marx; they imagine a public that is already saved, outside ideology, which is aberrant in the Marxian vision of the social world. It is true that, in Marx, ideology is the product of particular interests *which pass themselves off as* common. But this illusion extends to the public itself. Whereas the Marxian notion of ideology ought to lead to a blurring of the simple divide between the ideas of those who produce news and the ideas of those who are 'subjected' to it, journalistic domination is conceived of in contemporary critiques simply as a barrier to the expression of the ideas of the public – of which, happily, certain heroic journalists remain the representatives.

In any case, how can journalists emerge from the 'system' and become heroic? This question is hardly addressed by these critiques. Is it enough for them to be the 'dominated' of the profession? How exactly do they distance themselves from the ideological contexts? Here too we are far from the complexity of Marx's thinking on ways of escaping from ideology. Perhaps the only difference between contemporary neo-Marxism and the American myth of a combative journalism is the belief of the former that what determines this heroism is the fact of being professionally, and hence 'materially', dominated; whereas in, for example, *The Insider*, the heroic journalist is a former student of Marcuse, but hardly one of the 'dominated' of the profession. Such 'materialism' in explaining the genesis of heroism or dissidence is hardly Marxism. There is no identification of an ideology in the Marxian sense, but rather, within a liberal, almost caricatured vision, an identification of external constraints which are imposed on the public and which provoke an ardent desire to be rid of them.

The problem with this category of critiques

The problems posed by this category of critiques of journalism are revealed by this confused use of the Marxian term 'ideology'. In a sense, they want to have the advantages of the basic schema which is their keystone, the 'innocent public/evil journalists' schema, without the disadvantages.

This basic schema underpinning the critique has the advantage of giving it a crispness, linked to the clarity of the target, and also the security of an undiluted democratism. The evils are easily identified – journalists in the service of the powerful – and this assumes a remedy that is itself clear – a journalism that severs this incestuous link with the powerful. This critique never sullies the good name of the public but, on the contrary, permanently sings its praises, and claims to be acting in its name; it is thus by its very nature a hymn to democracy, to a free public space, laudable in itself, which needs only to be released from the exogenous dominations that imprison it. These particular critiques run no risk of slipping into a critique of democracy.

Yet this advantage has a corresponding disadvantage, that is, an inability to question in any depth the evil that is denounced and, as a result, perhaps a superficiality, a failure to understand the possible structural causes of journalistic 'wrongdoing'. It is complicit and subservient individuals who are accused, not any mechanisms that might lie behind individual cases. It is never envisaged that the public might be implicated in the construction of the bias to which it is subject; which works well as a guarantee of 'democratism', but is less conducive to a serious investigation of the mechanisms by which journalistic content is decided. The notion of 'ideology' gives a semblance of a more structural analysis, referring back to an 'economism' – those with economic power dominate all of us. But in fact, continuing to spare the public (which is, after all, also an economic actor), and in this totally unfaithful to Marx, it limits the investigation of the structural causes of the journalistic 'product'.

These inadequacies in the analysis of the mechanisms of journalistic *production* are often matched by a simplism in understanding the *reception* of journalism. The rhetoric of 'manipulation' (of the people by the media) often prevails, revealing, once again, a reductive, even false, use of the Marxian concept of ideology. For Marx, there was no public 'manipulated' by the ideology of the dominant. There was a complex development of this ideology, which involved the whole functioning of society. It was the state of the 'infrastructure', that is, of the system of economic production, which determined the content of the ideology of the moment, a content which was imposed on all alike. It should also be emphasized that the notion of manipulation by the media, though frequent in the discourse, remains unproven by works on the reception of the media messages. This is not to say, of course, that the public is in a state of permanent revolt against the messages it receives. Reception is a complex question of the sociology of publics, bringing together phenomena of resistance and of (variable) receptiveness to influence.[12] The word 'manipulation' is far from doing justice to this complexity. In many respects, it makes it possible to avoid reflecting in depth on the nature of the dominations operating in public space.

In short, faced with this first category of critiques of journalism, it needs to be emphasized that you cannot have your cake and eat it. You cannot parade an irreproachable democratism and a vibrant, focused critique of journalists, deemed solely responsible for the evils they inflict on their innocent audience, and at the same time borrow a vocabulary, that of ideology, which would normally – if not trivialized in this way – complicate the analysis of the causes of the journalistic biases that are denounced, sully the purity of the public and topple the over-simple schema and triumphant democratism on which the argument is based. To try to win on every front is inevitably to misrepresent something at some point, and in this particular case, what is most often misrepresented is the depth of the analysis and the affiliation to Marx.

One might imagine that the critiques which take an opposite, more 'structural' path from the outset, and which constitute our second category, would demonstrate these same advantages and disadvantages, but the other way round. Their analysis might be more profound, with a readiness to see the public as implicated in the evils denounced, but the downside would be, by contrast with the first category of critiques, both a dilution of the target – who is ultimately responsible for all this journalistic mediocrity? – and, through the attacks on the principle of 'publicity', a questioning of democracy. This is an uncomfortable position, which is why these critiques, too, are prone to incoherences and volte-faces, often reverting to the more comfortable schema of innocent public/sinning journalists, in which these critiques cannot really believe. To them also, we might say that it is impossible to have your cake and eat it.

2. Journalists: hostages to the public

Over and beyond the 'corruption of persons', the 'structural corruption' of the media field (Pierre Bourdieu)

Certain contemporary critiques of journalism aim to go beyond the simple schema of an (innocent) public manipulated by journalists complicit with those in power. They seek to make an in-depth analysis of the mechanisms that lead to the choice of journalistic content, and they are readier to implicate the public. In this sense, their approach is certainly more deserving than the previous one of being described as Marxian, even if it does not necessarily take the same paths. One of the most important figures in recent years in this second category of critiques is Pierre Bourdieu.

Although mutual friendships exist between Bourdieu and certain individuals in the first category,[13] and although intellectual links continue to be forged between all these types of critique, they should not be confused. There are in Bourdieu arguments which appear to reveal serious reservations with regard to the critiques of the first category. For example, in this extract from *On Television and Journalism*:

> I even think that scandals such as the furor over the deeds and misdeeds of one or another television news personality, or the exorbitant salaries of certain producers, divert attention from the main point. Individual corruption only masks the structural corruption (should we even talk about corruption in this case?) that operates on the game as a whole through mechanisms such as competition for market share. This is what I want to examine.[14]

Bourdieu is even openly mistrustful of the 'half-baked version of materialism, associated with Marxism' that 'condemns without shedding light anywhere and ultimately explains nothing',[15] a formula which may well be aimed at Noam Chomsky (in passing, the fact of being 'associated with Marxism' does not prevent a blindness to the complexity of the analyses of Marx, which Bourdieu certainly knows).

For Bourdieu, it is important to look closely at the way journalists work and at the constraints their practices reveal. Of course they differ according to the place each actor occupies in the 'journalistic field'; and of course there are the dominated and dominant in the field, the external signs of which – salary level, but also social circle of 'connivance' – vary, all of which has implications for their work. However, these very categories (dominated, dominant) depend on structural constraints, which relate to the logics of the field, and which apply to all, *the dominant included*. The dominant are simply those who have most successfully understood and internalized the constraints of the field. Thus, in a way, the dominant are also dominated. Bourdieu even says:

> But the further you get in the analysis of a given milieu, the more likely you are to let individuals off the hook (which doesn't mean justifying everything that happens). And the more you understand how things work, the more you come to understand that the people involved are manipulated, as much as they manipulate. They manipulate even more effectively the more they are themselves manipulated and the more unconscious they are of this.[16]

In other words, the faults cannot easily be apportioned nor the remedies conceived on a simple voluntarist model – of the type 'let us change our practices, let us put ourselves at the service of the public and not of those with power'. An analysis of what Bourdieu says above about the nature of the 'structural corruption' suggests that many factors influence the logics of the journalistic field, *especially the public*. After all, what is the race for audience share if not a permanent desire to woo the public? The inclusion of the public in an analysis of the constraints which weigh on the work of journalists is particularly clear in the work of a writer much influenced by Bourdieu, Patrick

Champagne, in his book *Faire l'opinion* ('Making Opinion', 1990). He explains that 'the mode of domination has changed; subjection to those in power has been replaced by subjection to the impersonal and anonymous laws of the economic market, which take the objective form of the audience ratings which the directors of the chain ensure are displayed in television studios'.[17] Champagne recalls in particular the expression 'dictatorship of the public' used by a journalist to mark the difference between the current situation and the old 'dictatorship of the authorities', a diagnosis he seems to accept.[18] This is a very different approach to that of the critiques of journalism in our first category. The 'journalistic field' is a space of encounters and tensions between diverse demands, which clearly bring into play the two poles of the journalist/public relationship. When Bourdieu blames 'the pressure to get things out in a hurry' to which the journalistic world is subject on the importance of audience ratings,[19] or when he describes the journalist's imperative to chose what he calls 'omnibus' facts, facts that 'interest everybody',[20] the public is certainly implicated in the development of journalistic content. How can we not conclude that it is the public itself – which by definition 'looks', hence demands things that are 'apparent' – which explains or at least contributes to the journalistic concentration on 'what appears'?

In fact Bourdieu applies to journalistic practices the formula of Berkeley: 'To be is to be perceived' (*Esse est percipi*).[21] This applies even beyond the – extreme – case of television. Even the written press, Bourdieu says, which 'names', has this role of 'showing',[22] and moves, therefore, in a world of apparent objects (or at least of objects that can appear, after a little investigation). Journalism is thus limited to a type of thinking that is closely dependent on *visualization*, which, according to Bourdieu, does violence to reality, which has many dimensions that are not susceptible to being revealed to the observer in this way. In order to 'show', journalism accentuates, in an extreme and sometimes purely artificial manner, what can be seen. To 'show' a social movement, for example, journalism seeks out faces, representatives and leaders. Like others, Bourdieu emphasizes the extent to which the media, mechanisms for making visible, end up by affecting reality itself; social movements are often one step ahead of the journalistic demand and so provide the media with something visible from the start. Daniel Cornu had already pointed out that the Chinese students in Tiananmen Square, Beijing, in the spring of 1989, 'carried banners with inscriptions in English, for the benefit of the international audience for television news programmes'.[23] This dictatorship of 'seeing' and its effects on reality were described nearly forty years ago in an article by Pierre Nora.[24]

However Bourdieu himself attacks this primacy of 'seeing' in such a drastic manner that he ends up questioning the notion of 'public' itself. He not only asks how journalism can rethink the way it puts into practice its need for visibility, but attacks this need itself. But it is difficult to see how journalism can do away with it without doing away with itself, and along with it this space effectively devoted to 'seeing' together, a space historically instituted and protected by freedom of expression, where points of view and gazes are exchanged. Good or bad, journalism cannot escape the constraint that consists of seeing and showing, which relates to the very position of spectator which it shares with its readers. If this is the constraint that Bourdieu is denouncing, one can say that it is, in a way, the 'public' which takes journalists hostage in his analysis, rather than the other way round; and that it is therefore ultimately the public that is the target of his critique. Bourdieu may be right to think that the more one seeks to reach a wider public, the more these constraints intensify; but it is clear that they are already there when the public is small, because of the sole fact that *journalism has to provide a spectacle*. The real problem in Bourdieu's approach is thus 'publicity' as such, by its very nature greedy for visibility.

A certain distaste for public space

The epistemological, even ontological – as the reference to Berkeley suggests – tone of Bourdieu's critique of journalism thus implies a certain distaste for public space, as incapable of 'touching' social verities because it is subject to the primacy of 'seeing'. In *On Television*, Bourdieu opposes that which *is seen* of the real and that which *is the essence* of this real, an essence which, it seems, inevitably remains hidden from view. This opposition turns, consequently, into an opposition between the journalist, tethered by nature to a space where the point is to see and to show, and sociology, which touches other things than what is seen. Bourdieu here repeats a central motif of his *The Craft of Sociology*. In it he had already opposed 'perception' and 'science', 'spontaneous sociology' and scientific sociology, and urged the sociologist to make a 'rupture' analogous to the transition from 'daily life' to the 'laboratory' in the natural sciences, even though this was more difficult to achieve in the social sciences.[25]

Tethered to 'seeing', the journalist is the great creator of 'emptiness'. It will be noted how the ontological vocabulary permeates Bourdieu's writing, especially in his attacks on one of journalism's favourite foods, the *fait divers*, that is, 'sensational news' or 'human interest stories'. The *fait divers* is denounced as 'empty', as 'nothing or almost nothing',[26] in fact as not existing. It is once again clear that it is public space itself which, at a deeper level, creates 'emptiness'. When one examines Bourdieu's other references to what, like the *fait divers*, is 'empty', it emerges that many exchanges, forms of communication between individuals and perhaps even communication as such are all subject to this condemnation: 'People talk so much about the weather in day-to-day life because it's a subject that cannot cause trouble. Unless you're on vacation and talking with a farmer who needs rain, the weather is the absolutely ideal *soft* subject.'[27] In short, 'fullness', for Bourdieu, corresponds to the conflictual, whereas emptiness is what serves the minimal consensus necessary to social intercourse. This explains the importance of the *fait divers* to the avoidance of conflicts that are too 'full': 'Human interest stories create a political vacuum. They depoliticize and reduce what goes on in the world to the level of anecdote or scandal.'[28]

Bourdieu seems to leave open the possibility of a 'full' communication – which one imagines would be 'his' ideal public space. But the problem is that much of what he says actually makes this project contradictory. If the 'full' is the conflictual, it is likely that it is by definition a threat to socialization. Yet socialization seems to be a necessary condition for the existence of a public space, that is, of a relatively peaceful exchange of views. In fact the categories of 'full' and 'empty' as they are defined here – the more the conflictual comes to the surface, the more the 'empty' fills with content – suggest rather an inability, inherent to public space, that site of exchanges, requiring a minimum of socialization, to touch the 'full', the essence and the truth of social relations. Far removed from any glorification, most of all Kantian, of public space, Bourdieu belongs to a quite other theoretical universe, which is spontaneously sceptical regarding this space, either hypocritical or policed. In any case, is he only denying that he himself is part of such a theoretical universe?

Admittedly, Bourdieu avoids one of the traditional positions of hostility to public space, which he himself analysed in his book on Heidegger:[29] that of simple contempt for the quotidian as site of the 'inauthentic', as an obstacle on the path of 'being'. Yet Bourdieu seems to accord an ontological status to the quotidian, as a sort of being of the empty or of nothing. But he refuses quotidian activities access to their own being. In order truly to grasp what is the quotidian, the banal, the ordinary, in order to grasp the being of the empty, one still needs to be an expert in being, that is, a sociologist or an artist, who here appear together as the opposing models to the journalist:

> There is nothing more difficult to convey than reality in all its ordinariness. Flaubert was fond of saying that it takes a lot of hard work to portray

> mediocrity. Sociologists run into this problem all the time: How can we make the ordinary extraordinary and evoke ordinariness in such a way that people will see just how extraordinary it is?[30]

Thus the retreat of the scholar or the artist from an ordinary life, busy with inessentials, is not exactly a contemptuous flight, but rather a search for the very essence of this ordinariness, this mélange of empty. It is still the case, however, that this retreat requires a break with natural perception, especially with the immediacy of seeing, blind by nature. If the *fait divers* is the focus of Bourdieu's anger, it is because it is precisely what the everyday *offers to be seen*, hence what is the opposite of its deep essence. The *fait divers* is the *spectacular* manifestation of the quotidian; it is what *gives the effect* of it, the impression or feeling of it. This is precisely, according to Bourdieu, what the sociologist should go beyond.

Thus, at a deeper level, Bourdieu's critique of journalism is an attack on the position of the spectator, hence on the very notion of public. So it is hardly surprising that the recommendations laid out at the end of the book, for the benefit of the fields of knowledge, which are urged to strengthen their 'autonomy' – 'crucial to scientific progress against the growing power of television'[31] – sound like an injunction *to remain hidden*. The latent dangers of the isolation of each field are never evoked, although Bourdieu dwells at length on the political danger associated with excessive openness.[32] Even politicians are urged to adopt this sort of self-preservation against permanent visibility, since Bourdieu denounces that 'perverse form of direct democracy' which is encouraged by media pressure and which destroys 'the usual buffers (not necessarily democratic) against these pressures' that 'are normally linked to the relative autonomy of the political field.'[33] In short, political practice, too, seems to be evaluated as a function of its capacity to 'know' (the social); if scholarly it can hope to touch the 'full'. It is essential, therefore, out of respect for the invisibility of the true, that it is able to conceal itself from the public gaze. It is still surprising that the obvious risks of such a position – invisible politics, the politics of specialists, politics without public control and without exposure to criticism – go unmentioned. Bourdieu is not worried that media invisibility, which he encourages, might lead to invisibility full stop; because what other means than the media does the public have at its disposal in order to *observe* their political representatives? Bourdieu does not say. For him, invisibility seems less of a risk than excessive visibility.

It is difficult, in this context, to see how journalism, tethered by nature to a place enamoured of visibility, can achieve any respectability. It is not 'bad' journalism that Bourdieu criticizes, but any kind of journalistic practice. We should have no illusions, therefore, regarding the reformist perspectives laid out in this little book, intended for the journalistic profession. In fact, looked at more closely, they amount, explicitly or not, to the death of journalistic practice. Look, for example, at what Bourdieu has to say about the methods of popularization in each field. Popularization is a gesture to make oneself visible, to publicize oneself, to put oneself on public view. Bourdieu is so distrustful of this idea of openness that some passages in his discussion are seriously aporetic. The question he puts in the mouth of Mallarmé goes unanswered:

> If the media today had existed in full force at the time [of Mallarmé], he would have wondered: 'Shall I appear on TV? How can I reconcile the exigency of "purity" inherent in scientific and intellectual work, which necessarily leads to esotericism, with the democratic interest in making these achievements available to the greatest number?'[34]

And when Bourdieu envisages, nevertheless, a process of popularization, it is from a perspective in which each field enjoys total mastery of its public appearances, and has total control over the process of 'esotericizing the esoteric'.[35] 'Producers in their little citadels', he says 'have to learn how to get out and fight collectively for optimum conditions of diffusion and for ownership of the relevant means of diffusion.'[36] It is necessary to prevent the heresy he calls 'heteronomy', which 'begins when someone who is not a mathematician intervenes to give an opinion about mathematics, or when someone who is not recognized as a historian (a historian who talks about history on television, for instance) gives an opinion about historians – and is listened to.'[37] Does this, concretely, leave a place for a 'journalist'? Surely it means that there will be no more journalists, and that the actors in each field will be the sole agents of their own opening up, or 'popularization'? If any journalists remain, it will be in a way that totally abolishes their exteriority with regard to the fields they observe and question; 'good' journalists will be at the mercy of the field in question, wholly controlled by the actors in that field, carrying out their wishes, asking the questions they tell them to ask.

This explains the dubious nature of the reference to Socrates to describe the attitude of the 'good' journalist: 'You put yourself at the service of someone with something important to say, someone whose words you want to hear and whose thoughts interest you, and you work to help get those words out.'[38] In fact, Bourdieu has kept only the third of the three metaphors used by Plato in *Meno* to define Socratic reasoning – the gadfly, the torpedo-fish and the midwife – which rather undermines his point. The role of the ideal 'Socratic' journalist in Bourdieu is not to provoke unexpected births, products of critical questioning, but to efface himself entirely in listening and to receive, unhurriedly, even passively, whatever child he is given. In fact this is to discount as far as possible the violence inherent in exposure to the gaze of another, even more of a public, a violence which is assumed by the Socratic attitude (Socrates violently drags his interlocutors from a theoretical sleep). It is also assumed, as we will see, by Kantian thinking on the principle of publicity (Kant never considered exposure to the critical public as something gentle or controllable). The complete and untruncated figure of Socrates is closer to this exposure to danger inherent in Kantian 'publicity' than it is to the docile midwife evoked by Bourdieu.[39] In fact all this only confirms Bourdieu's hostility to the idea of a public space where opinions and gazes are freely exchanged, not under the control of 'scholars'.

The difficulty of accepting the risk of anti-democratism

Bourdieu is aware that this hostility implies an anti-democratism; indeed he is explicit about the latent aristocratism of his positions:

> At the beginning . . . I claimed that television is not very favorable to the expression of thought, and I set up a negative connection between time pressures and thought. It's an old philosophical topic – take the opposition that Plato makes between the philosopher, who has time, and people in the *agora*, in public space, who are in a hurry and under pressure . . . It's a perspective that's clearly aristocratic, the viewpoint of a privileged person who has time and doesn't ask too many questions about the privileges that bestow this time. But this is not the place for that discussion.[40]

Thus the confession is followed by a fudge. We will never know more about it, which is a pity.

In general, Bourdieu gives the impression of refusing to confront the problem. He prefers a volte-face – the claim that his words are falsely 'elitist', that 'ordinary people' are really on his side and that they need to be liberated from their false representatives: 'In fact, I am defending the conditions necessary for the production and diffusion of the highest human creations . . . The audience rating system can and should be contested in the name of democracy.'[41]

The problem is that, in assuming that the 'public' measured by audience ratings is a journalistic construction, and that it bears no relation to the 'true public', Bourdieu is returning to a 'simple' opposition – wicked, manipulative journalists/innocent public, victims of this odious imposture – which is at odds with the tenor of his own argument. Suddenly, the journalistic field, its constraints and its logics, no longer expresses, as we had thought, and as his own analyses clearly suggest, the state of a public/journalists relationship implicating both partners; rather, it constitutes a one-way domination, wholly external to the public, constructed without it and at its expense.

This is a true volte-face on the part of Bourdieu in the face of the implications of his own arguments. It is a sort of ultimate strategy for rescuing the public, against the evidence of its implication in the problems journalism raises. In places, although he has struggled elsewhere to nuance and deepen his critique, Bourdieu relates the journalists' outlook solely to internal rivalries between them,[42] or to their simple and unilateral stupidity.[43] At the risk of contradicting himself, he presents journalism as a place of unilateral manipulation and censorship, where, for example, the decision on the way to organize a television line-up is wholly arbitrary.[44] He says:

> There is no discourse . . . and no action . . . that doesn't have to face this trial of journalistic selection in order to catch the public eye. The effect is censorship, which journalists practise without even being aware of it. They retain only the things capable of interesting them and 'keeping their attention', which means things that fit their categories and mental grid; and they reject as insignificant or remain indifferent to symbolic expressions that ought to reach the population as a whole.[45]

In fact, on closer examination, Bourdieu does not really pursue in these pages the stimulating but also slightly obscure idea, well worth developing, that the audience and the people or the 'real public' are two different entities. He simply suggests that the audience does not play the crucial role that is generally attributed to it and that he himself accords it elsewhere; the audience, he says, is ultimately a pretext, which the journalists themselves secretly scorn. The audience is thus no more than the name they give to their own wishes. It is clear that this runs counter to the complexity of his own analyses of the notion of 'field', and that it serves the simpler thesis to the effect that journalists decide everything in total 'freedom', in line with representations that never encounter the need to touch a particular public, since, in any case, the public 'follows along'. These are unexpected arguments coming from Bourdieu. They culminated in his address to the members of the International Council of the Museum of Television and Radio, on 11 October 1999, 'Masters of the world, are you masters of your own mastery?',[46] in which he offered a representation of their power – 'these very powerful people' – and of the power of their tools – 'means of manipulating or satisfying the primary impulses of the spectator' – which seems remote from the more complex thesis of 'manipulated manipulators' put forward in the extracts quoted above from his booklet *On Television*.

Bourdieu seems even to lapse into an idolization of the dominated of the profession, who are in tune with the public, although the complexity of his conception of domination restrains him. This sentence from *On Television* reveals his indecision:

> There are small fry, newcomers, subversives, pains-in-the-neck who struggle desperately to add some small difference to this enormous, homogenous mishmash imposed by the (vicious) circle of information circulating in a circle between people who – and this you can't forget – are all subject to audience ratings. Even network executives are ultimately slaves to the ratings.[47]

He begins with a simple opposition of the dominant and the dominated of the profession, the latter, like the unfortunate public, subjected to the yoke of the former; but then he returns to the more complex idea of a 'dictatorship of the public' in the form of ratings – the powerful themselves being the 'dominated' of the public. Thus sometimes he puts the emphasis on that diffuse domination, the ratings, responsibility for which it is difficult clearly to apportion, and which is a product of the general functioning of public space in which the public plays a part; but sometimes, as in his most aggressive writing on the journalistic profession, the ratings appear as a simple construction of the journalists themselves, and the public bears no guilt.

This indecision is hardly conducive to the clarity of his argument. Is the problem that the audience has some resemblances to the public, but that journalists do not *in practice* take account of this in their strategies? Or is it that journalists are obsessed with the audience, but that the audience bears no resemblance to the public? If the latter, if the audience is not the public, what exactly is it? What is the difference? We may suspect that this indecision is symptomatic of a reluctance to engage in a type of analysis which is, at bottom, damaging to the idea of democracy. In spite of an obvious hostility to democratic public space, something that makes his work a valuable and stimulating critical focus in the face of excessively optimistic theories, Bourdieu seems, even at the risk of contradicting himself, to wish to retain the idea of a 'real', pure public, which must be liberated from the yoke of the powerful.

But this deceives no one. If there is a thinking that includes clear anti-democratic elements, it is this. No one could claim that Bourdieu echoes the nostalgic desire of Habermas to rediscover a full and entire democracy, which would finally achieve the Kantian principle of publicity, that is, would create a critical 'publicity' instead of this distorted notion of 'publicity' – this 'publicity' deviation – which has been current since the end of the nineteenth century.[48] It is true that Bourdieu seems to share some of Habermas's ideas, as when he recalls how the old cultivated public was offended by the popular press and tried to resist it.[49] And his concluding remarks on the need to work for the advent of a true democracy might also be seen as to some extent echoing Habermas. In reality, however, there is a big difference between the two writers: the conception of the 'ideal' public in Bourdieu lacks the Kantian tone it has in Habermas. Whatever one thinks of the 'ideal' public of Habermas,[50] it is impossible to deny that he sees it as a faithful application of the Kantian principle of publicity – more faithful, Habermas believes, than the distortion of this principle in the great contemporary media spectacle. Whether his dream seems abstract or not, at least he claims to dream of a collective debate, in which everyone can take part, not only experts. Whereas, in Bourdieu, there is one point that is never questioned and that differentiates his position from the Kantian principle of publicity: while Kant implies that rationality is the product of a collective development, Bourdieu sticks to the idea that there are always, on any question, including those concerning political action, specialists and non-specialists. Even given the ideal of an educated public, initiated into various fields of knowledge, Bourdieu seems unwilling to yield on this point; specialists in these fields still have a better right to express their opinions than non-specialists.

Another way of saying this is that Bourdieu never clearly expresses the idea that there is a domain where one can *express an opinion* that is independent of learning, hence egalitarian. This follows, naturally, from the separation of society into 'fields', which means that public exchange is always conceived of in terms of 'entries' and 'exits' from fields; the Bourdieu model for the exchange of opinions always demands a 'fee' for right of entry to a discussion. He is emphatic that no one should engage in serious discussion with someone who is not in the same 'field' or who does not have the 'tools to decode' what they are saying.[51] The 'dream' of his he describes speaks volumes: 'A highly autonomous field, mathematics, for example, is one in which producers' sole consumers are their competitors, that is, individuals who could have made the discovery in question. (I dream of sociology becoming like this, but, unfortunately, everyone wants to get in on the act . . .).'[52] There is no space for a dialogue where the hierarchy, linked to differences of *competences*, on which Bourdieu always insists, often with good reason, is no longer respected.

The notion of an 'exit duty' – or a duty to share what one knows – does not in any way offset the rigour of the 'entry fee', since it is wholly conditional on these last requirements, that is, that the interlocutor should not be too external, that he should have the tools to decode and so on. The 'exit duty' is very conditional and not really a duty, in the sense of a categorical imperative, especially since it is for the 'producer' to know, in the 'field', and to judge if the necessary conditions are fulfilled for him to be able to share what he knows. One can easily imagine a situation where, even if all the means for controlling the 'popularization' were met, such a 'producer' might decide not to proceed if he judged that there was no one out there fit to receive his 'knowledge'.

This distrust of public space in Bourdieu is clearly not unrelated to the *epistemological* tone of his critique of journalism, which implies a fundamental disregard for the order of opinion as opposed to that of knowledge. His 'dreams' of a journalism that is at last a quality journalism, animating a public space that is also a quality public space, reveal this persistent low regard for the sphere of opinions:

> One could imagine – or dream – that journalists might agree to forget about audience ratings for once and refuse to open their talk shows to political leaders known for their xenophobia. Further, they could agree not to broadcast what these characters say. (This would be infinitely more effective than all the so-called refutations put together.)[53]

This is a dream in which 'good' journalists have a normative function as regards opinions, and receive their norms from an expert, an expert in what is, or is not, effective. Briefed by knowledgeable people, at their service, without real exteriority in relation to them, they carry out the informed regulation of the order of opinion. In the ideal world of Bourdieu, everything that is profane – the journalist in particular and opinion in general – is thus under control.

The volte-faces and the recurrences of attacks on a powerful and harmful profession, one that manipulates the public and impedes true democracy, cannot efface the anti-democratic tone of Bourdieu's critique of journalism. To emphasize this is in some ways to praise him because this is also what gives depth to his critique and differentiates it from those of the first category I identified above. One can only regret that the implications of his arguments are not fully accepted – in which they resemble the critiques of the first category, equally hesitant and disinclined to stick to their guns.

The problems with the second category of critiques

How can Bourdieu's volte-faces, like the twists and turns referred to above in connection with the first category of critiques, be seen as other than signs of unease and of the desire to win on all counts – that of the depth of a structural analysis of the failings of democratic public space and that of 'democratism'?

Certainly, it is uncomfortable to confront the problem of the public's involvement in the genesis of journalistic content. According to one specialist in the American media, Michael Schudson, the reluctance to implicate the public – hence, in a way, fully to espouse the second category of critiques – is a very general phenomenon in the current condemnations of journalists. Schudson explains that the discourses on the media have great difficulty in representing the media or the news in general as a 'cultural system',[54] which would assume bilateral relations between journalists and public. This in itself provides a possible explanation: perhaps what is feared is precisely the victory of a wholly cultural – one might almost say 'culturalizing' – resignation in the face of the media discourse? In the absence of a pure victim and a clear aggressor, would it still be possible to designate this media discourse as a discourse of domination, to be fought against? Would there not be a risk of slipping into a more diffuse critique of democracy, which would be both less invigorating, in the absence of a clear target, and politically less comfortable?

Perhaps we have here the reason for the predilection, emphasized by Schudson, for the notion of 'ideology' among critics of the media. Not staying true to the Marxian concept, it allows them to think in terms of a unilateral power relation of journalists over the public, and in this way to designate a clear enemy. For Schudson, this notion of ideology is an obvious impediment to a sophisticated understanding of the media world, because there is a pressing need finally to recognize the news as 'a social and cultural institution far more complicated than anything one could reduce to an articulate political ideology'.[55] But the reluctance to adopt this 'complicated' cultural approach, and the preference for a 'simple' reading in terms of ideology – though very far from the (complicated) Marxian concept of ideology – is easily understood in the light of Schudson's analysis. To conceive of the news in terms of culture (product of the journalists/public system) rather than of power (of the journalists over the public) is inevitably to make the domination less clear, and the emancipation also. In particular, the cultural approach suggests the need to think an emancipation of the public from itself, and not only from journalists, which is considerably more complicated.

Nevertheless, Schudson does not see all critiques of journalism as equally remote from an analysis of the news in terms of culture. Some, he says, are very far from this from the outset: those that denounce in journalism a 'political bias', that is, a singular group with a singular view of the world, out of touch with the rest of society. Other approaches, however, have the potential to come closer to it: those that observe in journalism a 'professional bias', that is, professional practices, conditions of work, that produce, often without those concerned realizing it, a biased view of the world. These two categories are fairly close to the categories I have defined above. According to Schudson, only the second, which thinks in terms of the 'professional biases' of journalism, is capable of incorporating a complex 'cultural' approach. The first category, in which he includes the work of Noam Chomsky, remains a prisoner of the simplistic notion of 'ideology'.

What my discussion of the work of Bourdieu has shown, however, is that even an approach which is remote from the simplism of the condemnation of the 'political biases', and which explores the 'professional biases' in all their complexity, finds it difficult to follow this argument through. It is still drawn to the simplistic representation of an innocent public 'manipulated' by a clique of journalists in the service of the powerful. It is easy to understand why: reverting to this schema makes it possible to escape its inconveniences, that is, avoid the risk of implicating the public in a sombre diagnosis and hence erode confidence in democracy.

3. Two poles, two risks: what next?

The debate on Public Journalism

Critiques of journalism are caught between two poles, both uncomfortable, which explains their shifts and their tendency to confusion. On the one hand, the schema of the innocent public/guilty journalists lends itself to a lively and focused attack, but fails to question the responsibility of the public for the mediocrity of the journalistic products it denounces. On the other, the public is implicated in the critique, is perhaps even the ultimate cause of unease, but the risk of deviating into an anti-democratic position leads to obvious wavering.

This polarity keeps emerging in debates on journalism, like a structure quick to resurface however new the form assumed by the debate. Let us take the recent example of the Public Journalism movement, initially an American phenomenon, which questioned traditional journalism and proposed 'remedies'.

The idea of Public Journalism was born around 1989, in the context of what studies of the period claimed was a crisis of American democracy,[56] that is, a loss of confidence in the political representatives and various elites, a decline in sales of newspapers and questions about citizenship. At this period many journalists of the written press, joined by colleagues in the audiovisual media, figures from the academic world and a range of foundations and supporters, initiated a debate on the future of the journalistic profession. It was a public debate, conducted through seminars and conferences held all over the country. The idea behind this project was that, like other American elites, journalists had become increasingly remote from the central interests of citizens. Their way of covering political and social life seemed to be seriously out of touch with the 'citizens' agenda', the concrete interests of the people and of the public. The method adopted to remedy this situation was to listen to the citizens, and to listen in a way that was often organized, since the newspapers themselves began to arrange public debates in order to understand better what it was about certain subjects that interested people. These debates began to determine the 'angles' of various articles in the daily press. Certain pages were reserved for 'Public Journalism', and the articles either were simple syntheses of these citizens' debates, at which journalists had been present, or provided information closely linked to the questions aired at these debates. In other words, the journalists began to rethink their role in close association with a *public conversation*, which preceded their own work, which they had often instigated, and which was further stimulated by their articles. In the years that followed, the growth, in both the United States and Europe, of television programmes calling on 'ordinary citizens' to address politicians directly, and, more recently, the appearance of internet blogs and an 'interactive' journalism, in which professionals engage in a conversation with non-professionals, can all be considered an extension of Public Journalism. In any case, these practices have continued the latter's questioning of traditional journalism.

Yet this questioning has not escaped the schemas which threaten all critiques of journalism. The supporters of Public Journalism were unable to avoid a certain idealization of the public (or publics), as compared with a journalistic profession they believed to be too closed in on itself and ultimately responsible for the low esteem in which it was held. This idealization certainly contributed to the clarity of the critique and the liveliness of the debate, less so to the quality of thinking about the evils denounced or the remedies to be adopted.

Yet Public Journalism had been ambitious. It had proclaimed its desire to achieve a total paradigm shift in relation to traditional journalism and, in particular, to transform the conception of 'the public' (readership, audience). To use the vocabulary of Cole Campbell, editor-in-chief of the *Virginian-Pilot*, an emblematic newspaper in the Public Journalism movement, journalists needed to stop treating readers as clients receiving a professional service in order to obtain information, or simply as spectators seeking good stories; they should instead consider them as actors, 'people who have a stake in the news, who want to see the possibilities behind often troubling developments, who want to participate in solving shared problems'.[57] Campbell called this 'a conversational model', which would make it possible, by inventing a 'deliberative democracy', to transcend the current crisis of representative democracy.[58]

The theoretical reference points of the founders and supporters of the Public Journalism movement, in particular Jay Rosen, confirmed this idea of a paradigm shift. In particular, they evoked the figure of John Dewey, author, in1927, of *The Public and its Problems*.[59] Let us look briefly at this theoretical background.

This book of Dewey's had sparked a major debate with another great thinker on democracy, Walter Lippmann, the author most famously of *Public Opinion* (1922) and *The Phantom Public* (1925). As James W. Carey explained, in a book published in 1989 that has become a classic of the sociology of communication, *Communication as Culture*,[60] Lippmann and Dewey were the 'fathers' of two different traditions in the sociology of the media and in the history of theories of democracy. Lippmann incarnated the most classical approach to the media, which he saw as essentially a tool for the (more or less effective) 'transmission' of material which existed in raw form in 'reality'. He was part of the late nineteenth-century paradigm (the Progressive Era) which had given birth to the modern press, that is, in the words of Michael Schudson, the 'trustee model'.[61] According to this model, a public trusts journalists to go and 'see' in its place, and report impartial news, that is, the news that any witness of good faith would have reported. In my earlier book, *A Political History of Journalism*, I spoke of the figure of the 'witness-ambassador', a figure that is essential to an understanding of the political, social and narrative issues in the appearance of the 'reporter'. The reporter, who became increasingly central to the American press from the end of the nineteenth century, and a pillar of the modern conception of journalism, expresses, in the way he or she works and writes, a valorization of tangible experience: reporters are on-the-spot *witnesses* and not commentators from afar. This valorization of tangible experience appears as a guarantee of the 'truth' of whatever is recounted, and by this fact a guarantee that the implicit mandate entered into with the public – the mandate to provide it with an account acceptable to all, the account that anyone could have given if they had been put in the position of witness – will be respected. It is because they are *witnesses* that they can be good *ambassadors*; and because they are *ambassadors* and must honour this mandate, that they must be *witnesses*.

Lippmann never abandoned this figure, or model, but he came to make very high demands of it, and sometimes revealed a slightly despairing attitude of resignation, because he recognized its limitations.[62] Lippmann feared that the public was not capable of grasping all the issues at stake in the problems reported by journalists, and, worse, that the journalists, under the influence of their public, would have an increasingly biased, simplified and distorted point of view. He often expressed great distrust of the notion of 'public', source of bias for the journalist. He never ceased to denounce the shameful blunders that were common in the press because it donned the same blinkers as its public, and was unable, without making a huge effort, to take them off.[63]

But he believed it was possible to create safeguards. Epistemological certainties, leavened with positivism, ought to enable journalists to keep a distance between them and their readers and to become reliable 'reporters', independent of the pressures exerted on them by the curiosity of the public. He also formulated clear requirements regarding journalism and, in particular, its central figure, the reporter: the highest possible degree of factual accuracy, a permanent search for the truth. In a way, Lippmann constantly reaffirmed the 'witness' against certain deviations of the 'ambassador'.

Dewey vigorously attacked these views. He agreed with Lippmann that there was a gulf between the public and its 'representatives' and the various experts who contributed to political decisions, a gulf which obviously raised questions regarding journalists as 'mediators'. But he found Lippmann's response inadequate, since he was content to deepen the gulf and to put journalists on the same plane as the experts, remote from the questions of the public. Lippmann had not changed the paradigm. As a result, failing to offer a new way of thinking democracy, his critique fell into the anti-democratic temptation. Dewey, for his part, wanted to abandon the model of representative democracy, which had revealed its limitations, in favour of the model of a participatory democracy; this would mean changing the very conception of the public, making it an actor instead of a simple receiver, capable of itself creating a 'common culture' and thus of becoming what he called the 'Great Community'. Dewey inspired a 'cultural' approach to the media, which saw media output as the expression of collective rituals, in which the public participated.

The Deweyan ethos which permeated Public Journalism won him support among some adherents of the cultural approach to the media, such as James W. Carey.[64] And, with patrons such as this, the movement could give the impression of avoiding the twin pitfalls of any critique of journalism, that is, idealization of the public or else a certain anti-democratic distaste for it. For Dewey wanted to abandon the model itself, a model structured by a confrontation between 'the elites' and the people-spectator (or 'public'). He was clear that, without a complete paradigm shift, critical thinking would always founder on these reefs; Lippmann had fallen foul of one of them, the anti-democratic risk.

Dewey, it might be retorted, had succumbed to the other temptation, that of idealizing the public, but this is perhaps a reproach better directed against his new disciples than against Dewey himself. This, at least, is the opinion of Michael Schudson, expressed in an article perhaps made all the harsher by the way he exonerates Dewey from his criticisms of Public Journalism, thus suggesting that the movement had seriously misunderstood its inspirer.[65] According to Schudson, there had been no paradigm shift, whatever was claimed. In fact this was the problem. To correct the failings of representative democracy and remedy the crisis of confidence in the journalistic profession, Public Journalism had actually revived that which had been most conservative in the ideas of the Progressive Era and, one might add, that which had been most naive. What Schudson saw as 'conservative' was leaving the central role to professional journalists, in the absence of a new pact or greater closeness to the people. It was journalists, the professionals, who were central to the new configuration and who were still the mediators between the public and the authorities. It was they who inspired the debates, made the choices and so on. They renewed the pact, and perhaps even improved it, but it remained the same pact as before; the legitimacy of the journalistic function of mediator, of expert, was not seriously questioned. On this point, Schudson regarded Public Journalism as failing to match up not only to the lucidity of Lippmann, but even to the intuitions of Dewey, which, said Schudson, had been above all aporetic. They had diagnosed an evil for which Dewey did not have a clear remedy; his idea of revitalizing society was no grounds for thinking that he would, to this end, have put greater confidence in journalists than in the other elites.

Schudson emphasized in passing the confused nature of the references both to Dewey and to Tocqueville by the thinkers of Public Journalism, who invoked the idea of 'community' without specifying what they understood by it in their own day. They paid insufficient attention to the risks that the debate would be biased by interests capable of seizing power in these spaces for local democracy. The localism that characterizes Public Journalism, said Schudson, promised domination by cliques and the tyranny of 'neighbourhood'.[66] He was uneasy about this search for 'community', which he considered potentially oppressive for the individual.[67] It amounted, he said, to a clear communitarian thematic and, worse, one that was insufficiently thought through.

The charge of 'conservatism' in Public Journalism is harsh. However, it must at least be accepted that, of the ideals of the Progressive Era,

Public Journalism seemed to adopt the most naive, in particular trust in the public as a value. For Public Journalism, the public ultimately decides what is the 'right' way of conceiving a problem. In this sense, Public Journalism is remote from the deep crises experienced by some great reporters in the role of 'witness-ambassador'. The muckraker Lincoln Steffens, for example, who was a master for Walter Lippmann (who was at one time his assistant), came in his own itinerary seriously to question the notion of public, which had been the very foundation of his journalistic commitment. The gravity of the problems he raised, as revealed in his autobiography, and the echoes of these torments in the work of Lippmann,[68] went well beyond the questioning characteristic of Public Journalism, which retained a fundamental confidence in the idea of public. Even Dewey, according to Schudson, was more profound and more serious in his reflection on the gulf between elites and public, and would hardly have been content with local community deliberations as a cure. Schudson is surely right when he claims that the New Journalism movement of the 1960s was far more fundamentally critical than Public Journalism of the 'trustee model', which the latter never really abandoned. In fact the New Journalism was an experience of writing and of reportage which mounted a serious challenge to the certainties of classic journalism and its faith in objectivity and in the clarity of the reality/fiction divide. It reintroduced, in an original and truly vertiginous manner, the question of the subjectivity of the reporter and of all points of view faced with a given situation. In writers like Norman Mailer this led to ideas about the eternal incommunicable or fundamental misunderstanding that prevented any definitive view of an event. The New Journalism denounced 'objective' journalism as new power and it wanted to destroy this assumption of power journalistically, by decentring those journalists who remained serene in their belief that they were at the centre, and by ever more dangerously decentring the point of view.[69] Alongside this, the crisis of journalism that Public Journalism claimed to support, so as to make it give birth to a new paradigm, seems pretty bland.

In fact Public Journalism had a tendency to think about the problems of journalism from within this double polarity, which was an impediment to real thinking: either you criticize the current situation by implicating the public, and thus risk lapsing into a degree of anti-democratic despair, or you propose a reform of journalistic practices in order to rediscover the vitality natural to the public, and thus risk idealizing it. Democratic naivety responds to anti-democratic temptation. It is this very naivety that was attacked, in its turn, by John Durham Peters.[70] He criticized in Public Journalism an ignorance, or at least a neglect, of four fundamental obstacles to deliberative democracy, four classic problems in democratic theory: (1) the scale of the community, which made the collective debate more or less possible and fluid; (2) the natural human tendency to want not to be constantly preoccupied with the community, but to think also of oneself; (3) the economic and technical conditions of the debate (he reproached Public Journalism for the poverty of its thinking on the subject of the economics of the media); and (4) the difficult question of knowing if there is a common faith to be reactivated, at the basis of a political community, or not, a question too quickly settled (positively) by Public Journalism. On this fourth point, Peters suggested that, in wanting to probe the deep faith placed in the public, Public Journalism was ultimately revealing a more naive and possibly more dangerous vision of this public than that of the journalism that claimed somehow to perform a labour of mediation between the authorities and the public. Peters, who confessed he had for a long time sided more with Dewey than with Lippmann, admitted to a change of mind; he had come to prefer Lippmann's idea – however sad – of a fundamental and probably irremediable mismatch between the democratic ideal and its concrete and always frustrating manifestations. In other words – not those of Peters – it is perhaps mistaken to seek democratic 'authenticity' in a system characterized by the impossibility of defining what the 'authentic' desires of the people are. Nothing is more conducive to deep and dangerous despair than to have held such high hopes. Or, this time in Peters's own words : 'it is better to take democracy as tragically flawed and yet still worthy of admiration'.[71]

The invitation to take account of the imperfections of democracy, and to recognize what one might call the impurity of the notion of 'public', is essential if we are to break out of the double polarity described above. There is probably no other way forward than to think about the 'public' in a way that is both less enthusiastic – less 'trusting', perhaps – and less despairing – less resigned and less blasé.

Rethinking the 'principle of publicity'

There is only one way to avoid these swings between distaste for the public and its idealization; that is, to develop another approach to the 'principle of publicity', in order to define more clearly the conditions in which the best can be got out of journalism. In this way one can avoid, in particular, that unspoken hatred, perhaps the other side of the coin to exaggerated hopes, which the philosopher Michel Foucault so often detected in critiques of journalism – critiques of which, as a result, he took a dim view.

In an interview with Christian Delacampagne for *Le Monde*, in April 1980, Foucault declared:

> there is an enormous curiosity, a need, a desire to know. People are always complaining that the mass media stuff people's heads up. There is a certain misanthropy in this idea. On the contrary, I believe that people react; the more one convinces them, the more they question things. The mind isn't made of soft wax. It's a reactive substance. And the desire to know more, and to know it more deeply and to know other things increases as one tries to stuff people's heads.

In other words, why complain about the application of the principle of publicity, through the proliferation of the media, if not because you are actually afraid of this principle? The critiques of journalism are surely simply imprisoned in the fear of its concrete application. Foucault continues with a hymn to curiosity, which encourages journalism to develop still further, against censorship and authorities of all kinds:

> The problem is to multiply the channels, the bridges, the means of information, the radio and television networks, the newspapers. Curiosity is a vice that has been stigmatized in turn by Christianity, by philosophy, and even by a certain conception of science. Curiosity is seen as futility. However, I like the word; it suggests something quite different to me. It evokes 'care'; it evokes the care one takes of what exists and what might exist; a sharpened sense of reality, but one that is never immobilized before it; a readiness to find what surrounds us strange and odd; a certain determination to throw off familiar ways of thought and to look at the same things in a different way; a passion for seizing what is happening now and what is disappearing; a lack of respect for the traditional hierarchies of what is important and fundamental.[72]

There may be some who consider that Foucault himself, in reaction, tends to lapse into an idealization of the public. Yet that would be to misunderstand the extent to which he was aware that he was dealing with something unpredictable, uncontrollable and probably frustrating. His comments on the text of Kant, 'What is Enlightenment?' (a text I will consider at some length in my next two chapters, when discussing Kant), reveal how Foucault recognized and welcomed the uncertainty of popular curiosity, far from being sure of the ideals it would serve (which probably reveals a major difference between the Kant of Foucault and the Kant of Habermas). This benevolence was not idealization. It opened up to scrutiny the concrete consequences of the principle of publicity, instead of blocking such scrutiny by *a priori* attacks which often expressed hatred of precisely what was most unexpected and most iconoclastic in curiosity. This Foucauldian benevolence is reminiscent of that of Robert E. Park. When he was writing his doctoral thesis, Park was if anything hostile to the flourishing popular press, but by the

1920s, at the Chicago School, he was arguing that there should be an end to 'moral' judgements, in order finally to free the way for a true scrutiny of this popular press – and as a result to refine, even invent, the criteria for judgement.[73]

Foucault believed that one should distrust 'scholarly' critiques of journalism, which express nostalgia or the wish for a public space controlled by learning, instead of the latter being constantly challenged by the former. He repeatedly condemned, in the name of curiosity, the position of the 'savant', or expert. In philosophy he denounced the cult of 'the hidden' (*l'être cachée*),[74] which made it possible to cut oneself off from ordinary gazes, by pretending to comprehend a world irreducible to the visible ordinary world; and he refused the status of 'sciences' to the human sciences, because it, too, introduced a rupture that legitimized contempt for profane gazes. His writings on the political function of the intellectual denounce a scientism which is a temptation all the stronger because we have entered the era of 'specific intellectuals'; this scientism, in the name of an ontological specificity of the subjects on which one works, amounts to placing the 'truth' with which one is concerned under a 'system of power'.[75] On the contrary, Foucault saw the labour of thinking about society as a prolongation of, not rupture with, the everyday gaze and ordinary visibility – a conception that is again close to that of Park. Foucault liked to describe the thinker as a 'diagnostician of the present':

> I would say briefly that the intellectual does not seem to me today really to have the role of speaking the truth, of speaking truths prophetic for the future. Perhaps the diagnostician of the present, as I was saying a moment ago, can try to help people to grasp what is happening, in precisely the spheres where the intellectual is competent. By the tiny gesture of shifting the gaze, he makes visible that which is visible, makes appear that which is so close, so immediate, so intimately linked to us that, because of this, we do not see it. His role is much closer to that which in the eighteenth century was called 'philosophy'.[76]

It is hardly surprising, therefore, that, in contrast to Bourdieu, Foucault is careful to build bridges between the thinker and the journalist, a figure he goes a long way to de-demonize. Significant here is his reflection – the exact opposite of the critique of Bourdieu discussed above – on the interest of the *fait divers*, beginning with those exposed by the media. He sees the thinker as a sort of gaze directed at society, but one that is in continuity with the gazes that from time to time appear in everyday life, and are expressed in the press. He developed this approach most notably in his comments on the 'Pierre Rivière affair'. Foucault had published the testimony of this nineteenth-century criminal,[77] which was later, in 1976, made into a film by René Allio. In an interview that same year, Foucault was asked:

> There is one of your expressions that Allio likes to quote in connection with this film; it is 'The miniscule grain of history'. With an event like that, in retrospect, has the grain not ceased to be miniscule? And Foucault replied : 'It's *Blow-up*,[78] if you like, a sort of phenomenon of explosion which happens in all enterprises of this sort as in everyday life. When you open your newspaper, you read, for example, that a man has killed his wife after a quarrel: it's simply everyday life which, at a given moment, after an accident, a detour, a tiny excess, became something huge, which will disappear as rapidly as a pricked balloon. That's what it was, the Rivière affair, and that's exactly what this film shows: an everyday life, a dispute about a field, some furniture, old clothes. The unconscious of history, that's what it is, it isn't a sort of great force, a life or death impulse. Our historical unconscious is made up of these millions, these billions, of tiny events which, little by little, like drops of rain, mark our bodies, our way of thinking, and then, by chance, one of these micro-events turns out to have left traces, and it can become a sort of monument, a book, a film.'[79]

Thus, the 'grain of history', a visible micro-event, but submerged in the middle of so many others, was a real issue for Foucault; the 'hidden' was not.

This directly opposite approach to that of Bourdieu is particularly worth emphasizing because, in Bourdieu's short book *On Television*, there is a passage which seems to echo certain words of Foucault on the subject of the mission of researchers, which is to make the fruits of their research available to everyone. In fact the analogy conceals a crucial difference. What Bourdieu says needs to be read while keeping in mind all the precautions with which he has surrounded 'popularization' and the 'exit duty':

> Researchers, and scholars in particular, have an obligation – and it may be especially urgent for the social sciences – to make the advances of research available to everyone. In Europe, at least, we are, as Edmund Husserl used to say, 'humanity's civil servants', paid by the government to make discoveries, either about the natural world or about the social world. It seems to me that part of our responsibility is to share what we have found.[80]

Compare this with what Foucault said in 1982:

> When newsmen ask me for information about my work, I consider that I have to accept. You see, we are paid by society, by the taxpayers, to work. And really I think that most of us try to do our work the best we

> can. I think it is quite normal that this work, as far as it is possible, is presented and made accessible to everybody. Naturally, a part of our work cannot be accessible to [just] anybody because it is too difficult. The institution I belong to in France (I don't belong to the university but the Collège de France) obliges its members to make public lectures, open to anyone who wants to attend, in which we have to explain our work. We are at once researchers and people who have to explain publicly our research. I think there is in this very old institution – it dates from the sixteenth century – something very interesting. The deep meaning is, I believe, very important. When a newsman comes and asks for information about my work, I try to provide it in the clearest way I can.[81]

We should note the extent to which this declaration of Foucault insists on the fact that the researcher is there to serve the journalist, and not the other way round. Foucault appears not to expect any 'ideal' public or any 'ideal' journalist to apply the principle of publicity fully and unconditionally; a publicity which, furthermore, fundamentally exposes researchers, which *confronts* them with their public. This may end in failure – incomprehension – but it seems it would then be for the thinker to try to explain things better. The idea of an 'entry fee' in this sphere could hardly be more alien to Foucault. He refused even the word 'teaching' to describe his activities, preferring to speak about 'acts carried out in public'.[82]

Thus the notion of public appears to be the basic problem in the risky exercise of critiquing journalism. Yet – or perhaps as a result – this problem is too often unexpressed. The public is idealized, or rejected, or both at once, in a strategy designed to avoid the problem it poses. It is difficult to understand the labour of journalism in its bond with the public, a bond of mutual influence in which responsibilities are shared. Far from preventing thinking about the role of journalism, this approach simply makes the task more complex. What exactly do we expect of journalists? That depends, first, on what can be hoped for from the principle of publicity. It is this problem that must be dealt with first. The answer will help us to define what journalists *could do* to help the principle of publicity to operate to the best advantage.

2

The notion of 'public', and what can be expected of it

The chief difficulty with the notion of 'public' is that it has historically appeared in that very polarity that is so awkward for us: either in enthusiasm or in disgust. From the beginning, it has been the subject of radical positions: the fervour of the Enlightenment, on the one hand, and Kantian enthusiasm in particular; aristocratic hatred, on the other, which for a long time, especially in France, associated freedom of expression and 'the newspapers' with the revolutionary barricades, themselves related to the spirit of the Enlightenment.

How are we to move on? We need first to understand how this situation came about, and this is what this chapter will try to explain.

1. The premises of the notion of 'public': liberal England in the seventeenth century

The premises of the notion of 'public' were set out in the very first defences of freedom of speech in the liberal England of the seventeenth century, among Puritans and then in Whig circles, in opposition to absolutist ideas such as those of Hobbes. In 1644 John Milton published *Areopagitica: A Speech for the Liberty of Unlicenc'd Printing*; soon after, the Lockian theory of individual liberties (1690), contemporary with the Bill of Rights, included a defence of freedom of speech – though less radical than that of Milton.

But these English texts of the seventeenth century defended freedom of speech in a way that did not yet employ all the arguments of the Age of Enlightenment. They saw it as one of the individual rights to be protected against any state intervention – one of those things which, according to Locke, were the 'property' of the individual.[1] It was part of a necessary respect for individual conscience, like religious freedom (freedom of worship), with which it was strongly linked from the beginning. These rights of conscience seemed to be an extension of the right to the integrity of the body and property of the individual, defining an external boundary which the state should not cross. It was a liberty assumed 'against' the state, and in this sense 'negative', saying to the state: 'Here, you will not enter.'

The Age of Enlightenment brought a new and more participatory approach to freedom of speech. It saw it as necessary to the development of a more rational politics of the state. The Kantian argument, in particular, was that when there was freedom of speech in 'civil society', a new sociability was created, an interchange of varied points of view and a dynamic that constituted the 'public'. Kant believed that the ideas and opinions exchanged within this public would be increasingly 'rational', and he argued that this rationalizing trend was good for the state, as long as it, too, wished to engage in an enlightened and increasingly rational politics. This type of more 'participatory' argument for freedom of speech had only been hinted at in the previous century. The vision of freedom of speech offered by the thinkers of the seventeenth century had been primarily 'liberal', individual and even individualist (in the sense of defending the individual 'against' social and political power).

According to the jurist Eric Barendt,[2] an expert in freedom of speech within democratic juridical systems, only two of the four classic arguments in defence of this liberty were clearly formulated before the Enlightenment. Barendt sets out the four main arguments historically advanced in defence of freedom of speech. First, it is 'important to the discovery of truth'; second, it is 'an aspect of self-fulfilment'; third is the 'argument from citizen participation in a democracy'; fourth, freedom of speech squares with the exercise of a necessary 'suspicion of government'. This summary suggests a chiastic structure, since the first and third arguments are, put briefly, 'participatory', valorizing the individual conceived of as part of a collective, and in this way participating in the collective search for truth and just politics; whereas the second and fourth arguments derive more from the point of view of the single individual, conceived of independently of collective life and especially of the government, and to be protected against it.

Barendt is explicit that the second and fourth arguments correspond to a sort of 'liberal-individualist' vision of the individual, whose integrity must be protected against anything that might encroach on that individual's own domain, and more generally to an approach that distrusts all state intervention. These two arguments, he observes, are difficult to distinguish from the general libertarian thesis. The fourth argument is naturally 'negative', emphasizing the damaging effects of any regulation of opinions, in line with a liberal fear of state intervention. The third argument, by contrast, is essentially 'participatory', and owes a lot, according to Barendt, to the theories of Louis Brandeis (1856–1941), appointed Justice of the Supreme Court by Woodrow Wilson in 1916, and the philosopher Alexander Meiklejohn (1872–1964). It can be argued, however, that the debts are much earlier, corresponding to the participatory vision which developed in the Age of Enlightenment. As for the first argument, it is not, says Barendt, concerned with the purely individual search for the truth. Rather it claims that the truth gains by being searched for collectively, in a wholly free exchange of ideas, a belief that found a typically American formulation in the concept known as the 'marketplace of ideas'.[3]

To what extent had this participatory approach of the first and third arguments already been articulated by writers before the Age of Enlightenment? Barendt suggests that the first argument had been used by John Milton in 1644; on this point, however, I share the doubts of another expert on the philosophical foundations of freedom of speech, John Durham Peters, who believes that Milton poses the question of truth in very different terms from the later participatory approach of the Enlightenment, of John Stuart Mill and of the theory of the marketplace of ideas.[4] In Milton the argument is strongly religious – Puritan – which poses the question of truth from an essentially individual point of view, that is, from the point of view of conscience and the necessity of confronting it with bad ideas as well as good. Peters emphasizes the importance of not reading *Areopagitica* anachronistically; those who find in it a theory of public space as a free exchange of points of view, from which the best and most rational inevitably emerge, are mistaken.[5] Milton, says Peters, even stops short of the liberal 'Whig' argument that freedom of speech is part of the whole array of civil liberties which the state must be made to respect.[6] It may be argued, nevertheless, that this Puritan approach, focused on the question of conscience, and the 'Whig' defence of what properly belongs to the individual against the public authorities, are sufficiently linked, theoretically and historically, for them to be seen as part of a great pre-Enlightenment moment, a liberal moment, before the major 'participatory' arguments of the eighteenth century; before, that is, the development of the notion of 'public'.[7]

The necessity of confronting conscience with evil: John Milton

Milton's argument puts great emphasis on the fact that censorship 'paralyses' thinking. It blocks it and prevents it from advancing, which, incidentally, makes it less able to resist the influence of bad ideas, which will in any case continue to circulate. He quotes by way of example a certain Dionysius Alexandrinus, 'a person of great name in the Church for piety and learning', about AD 240, who was in the habit of confounding heretics 'by being conversant in their Books'. To one objector he replied, doing no more, says Milton, than quoting 'a vision sent from God': 'Read any books what ever come to thy hands, for thou art sufficient both to judge aright, and to examine each matter.'[8] Milton later writes:

> Since therefore the knowledge and survay of vice is in this world so necessary to the constituting of human vertue, and the scanning of error to the confirmation of truth, how can we move safely, and with lesse danger scout into the regions of sin and falsity than by reading all manner of tractats, and hearing all manner of reason? And this is the benefit of books promiscuously read.[9]

It is true that the metaphor of the trial, a metaphor that would be dear to Kant (public space functioning in Kant as a trial of reason), is already present in Milton. But in Milton it is a trial of conscience, which, in solitude, ought to be able to confront everything, including evil and bad opinions, in order to overcome them and purify itself.[10]

John Durham Peters shows that Milton's comments are in reality part of a veritable theory of redemption, which is achieved by the experience of the abyss: the abyss prompts in the conscience a capacity to face up to it and 'redeem' it: 'good via evil', in the words of Peters. This involves a re-reading of original sin. For Milton, it was necessary to have experience of it in order to save oneself. Peters quotes the comment of John Carey to the effect that, if Milton had been in Adam's place, he would have picked the apple and would then have written a pamphlet justifying himself.[11] Peters notes that, in essence, all this is closer to the Nietzschean principle: 'what does not kill me, makes me stronger'.[12] More generally, Milton, with these ideas of the abyss and of redemption, has more in common with the Romantics – who were inspired by him – than with the rationalism of the Enlightenment. He is part of, and revived, a long tradition in the history of religious, political and aesthetic thought of 'abyss-redeemers', of saviours seeking a way out of the abyss, inevitably fascinated by Satan because one had to meet him in order to triumph over him.[13] In passing, Peters notes that this figure still exists in the concept of press freedom. In 2002, for example, there were some who defended the idea of circulating the video of the decapitation of kidnapped journalist Daniel Pearl by his captors, available on the internet, in accord with the necessity of every one of us having an 'instructive' confrontation with evil.[14] And Louis Brandeis himself said that 'Sunlight is the best disinfectant.'[15]

Milton's argument is thus somewhat remote from the notion of 'public' in the Enlightenment sense, even if his text sometimes touches on this issue, as, for example, when he emphasized that Christ himself preached in public, and made the possibility of being refuted a criterion for the truth of his preaching;[16] or when he described an active public, capable of creating conflict and of emerging from it closer to the truth, hence immune to manipulation, contrary to the scornful vision held by the censors of 'the people' as 'an untaught and irreligious gadding rout'.[17] Milton could sometimes say 'we' and speak of 'the Nation', of which he had a dynamic evolutional vision; for it, he dreamed of something very different from a beatific contemplation of fixed truths: 'The light which we have gain'd, was giv'n us, not to be ever staring on, but by it to discover onward things more remote from our knowledge.'[18] There are hints of many Enlightenment themes here – beginning with that of 'light', and the insistence on movement, human progress, the opposite of the fixity of the censors. In the same vein he later wrote: 'I see in my mind a noble and puissant Nation rousing herself like a strong man after sleep, and shaking her invincible locks.'[19]

Nevertheless, it would be going too far to project all the arguments of the eighteenth century onto this Puritan text. John Locke, too, stopped short of the arguments of the Enlightenment.

The beginnings of the idea of public opinion in Locke

We should first be clear that the defence of freedom of speech in Locke is less radical than in Milton. In his *Essay Concerning Toleration* of 1667, Locke is clear that there should be limits to the freedom to express one's opinions. It may be that a man cannot stop believing what he believes, but it is still justified to prohibit him, in certain cases, from *publishing* what he believes.[20] The risk, which the government must take into account, is that such expression may have politically dangerous consequences, for example the appearance of factions likely to destabilize the government.[21] Similarly, there should be no toleration for those who are enemies of toleration, an argument in whose name Locke, in his *Essay Concerning Toleration*, opposed freedom of worship for papists.[22] It was this same argument which, in his *Letter Concerning Toleration* of 1674 (which is not fundamentally different in ethos from the *Essay*), led him to consider that certain opinions could be banished from the community, in particular atheist opinions.[23] It may be that Locke said this only out of prudence, without necessarily believing it, but it still has to be recognized that these texts, as they stand, express only a *limited* defence of freedom of speech.

But this was already a lot, compared with the positions of the absolutist monarchists such as Hobbes, author in 1651 of the *Leviathan*, to which the *Second Treatise of Civil Government* was a direct response. In the *Leviathan*, the subject has neither the right to resist sovereign law nor the right to comment on it. Hobbes may have accepted that the individual, at the moment of his own execution, has no alternative but to resist, and that he can hardly 'obey' as he mounts the scaffold, because it is contrary to his natural right (that is, to seek every means for his own survival), but Hobbes nevertheless legitimized this execution by the sovereign, if it was his will; the sovereign could not tolerate the principle of this resistance without endangering his own raison d'être, that is, public order. As for the individual liberty to express disagreement without active disobedience, it seemed, in all logic, that it was again for the sovereign and him alone to rule on its appropriateness. And the least that can be said is that Hobbes had little sympathy for 'protests', as is shown by this extract from chapter 18 of the *Leviathan*:

> because the major part hath by consenting voices declared a Soveraigne; he that dissented must now consent with the rest; that is, be contented to avow all the actions he shall do, or else justly be destroyed by the rest. For if he voluntarily entered into the Congregation of them that were assembled, he sufficiently declared thereby his will (and therefore tacitly covenanted) to stand to what the major part should ordayne: and therefore if he refuse to stand thereto, *or make Protestation against any of their Decrees*, he does contrary to his Covenant, and therefore unjustly. And whether he be of the Congregation, or not; and whether his consent be asked, or not, he must either submit to their decrees, or be left in the condition of warre he was in before; wherein he might without injustice be destroyed by any man whatsoever.[24]

It can be argued that Hobbes created, in his system, an 'author' and an 'actor', but not a 'spectator'. In chapter 16 of the *Leviathan* he explains that the principle of the contract is to establish a representative who will be like an 'actor' whose acts can be imputed to those represented, hence 'authors'. This mediation, this artifice that is representation, allows the people to possess a unity, a 'face'. They need to be represented, according to Hobbes, because they cannot be spontaneously present, present in person; they are, in their natural state, simply a multitude without unity. To be a 'person', you have to put on the 'mask' of an actor – and Hobbes is here playing on the dual meaning of the Latin word *persona*, that is, 'person' and 'mask'. The people-author must then accept all the acts of their representative, the sovereign-actor, unless he undermines their security and thus repudiates the very principle of the contract made between them. However, it is clear that this breach of contract, when it happens, happens *in fact*; it is the *fact* of the imminent danger of death that ends the pact. Hobbes is hardly envisaging a daily public debate within the people-author regarding the actions of the sovereign-actor, in order to consider if he is acting properly and perhaps ultimately decide on the breach. In other words, the people is never established as a 'spectator' of its 'actor'. Hobbes introduces an actor–author pair, but the figure of the spectator, who observes, judges, deliberates and so on, has no place in his conception of representation.

It is, however, something very much along these lines that is suggested by Locke. For him, the principle of representation involves surveillance by the represented of their representatives. He rejects a system in which one can 'ask' for nothing, as he says in a passage in his *Second Treatise* which is implicitly aimed at Hobbes.[25] To use an exclusively Hobbesian vocabulary, Locke believes that the 'author', the people, exists before the mediation of the representation and beyond it. When the people designates its representative, its 'actor', it lays down from the outset much stricter conditions; it can change them if it believes it has been betrayed (right of resistance) and it never ceases to *watch* this actor playing his role as actor, judging and *supervising* him. In particular, any decision to break the contract is taken in this space of judgement, discussion and critical observation, which Locke, contrary to Hobbes, allows to the represented. A judgement has to be made, obviously, to decide whether resistance is justified: 'for this operates not till the inconvenience is so great, that the majority feel it, and are weary of it, and find a necessity to have it amended'.[26]

In this sense, the notion of 'public opinion', so characteristic of the eighteenth century, makes a timid appearance in the work of Locke. It is put, for example, into the mouth of his adversaries, and notably of a possible Hobbesian interlocutor who might be offended by his defence of the right of resistance:

> To this perhaps it will be said, that the people being ignorant, and always discontented, to lay the foundation of government in the unsteady opinion and uncertain humour of the people, is to expose it to certain ruin; and no government will be able long to subsist, if the people may set up a new legislative, whenever they take offence at the old one.[27]

And this is Locke's response to the objection, a response which touches on precisely this notion of *opinion*, something he believed to be generally less fickle and less enterprising than his objector claimed:

> To this I answer, Quite the contrary. People are not so easily got out of their old forms, as some are apt to suggest. They are hardly to be

> prevailed with to amend the acknowledged faults in the frame they have been accustomed to. And if there be any original defects, or adventitious ones introduced by time, or corruption; it is not an easy thing to get them changed, even when all the world sees there is an opportunity for it.[28]

In Locke there is a real intuition of what public opinion is.

However, it is far from being a theorization as developed as that which was proposed in the Age of Enlightenment. The theme of the 'surveillance' of the representatives, especially by the free press, assumed much greater importance in later liberals, such as Benjamin Constant. In Locke the space for opinion was thought of only as the prolongation of that inner space where individual conscience communed with itself. There is nothing to suggest, as in Kant, that the collective development of a judgement had a special value, perhaps greater than that of a purely individual judgement. Significantly, Locke's text keeps wavering, in the search for criteria that would legitimate the decision to engage in resistance. Sometimes he suggests that there must be the agreement of many consciences (but exactly how many?), sometimes that the judgement of one single, isolated conscience is enough on its own to justify resistance. Locke sometimes locates the right of resistance in 'the people' (§222), sometimes in 'the body of the people' (§242), sometimes in 'the community' (§243) and sometimes in individual conscience itself, as in paragraph 241, where he poses the question 'who shall be judge?' followed by 'God in heaven is judge. He alone . . . is judge of the right. But every man is judge for himself'; which refers back to the Protestant conception of conscience as the sole mediation with God. This paragraph echoes an earlier one, paragraph 168, where Locke had already raised the question of evaluating a possible abuse of power by the representatives, either legislative or executive, and replied: 'The people have no other remedy in this, as in all other cases where they have no judge on earth, but to appeal to heaven.'[29] Here it is clearly the 'people', but one senses, in another formulation in the same paragraph – 'it being out of a man's power so to submit himself to another' – that the individual conscience, too, has this right on its own. This is in any case made explicit in paragraph 210, when he says: 'how can a man any more hinder himself from being persuaded in his own mind, which way things are going; or from casting about how to save himself'.

Thus Locke develops, against Hobbes, the figure of the citizen-spectator. Did he also develop that of the people-public? Not yet, or at least not in the terms of Kant. There are only hints of this notion in the first defences of freedom of speech in the seventeenth century, and when freedom of speech was introduced in England at the end of that century it was far from complete. The Bill of Rights of 1689, fruit of the Glorious Revolution, consecrated the right of all subjects to petition the king (article five) and freedom of speech for all members in Parliament (article eight). Censorship before publication was to cease. But if there was a clash between freedom of speech and the representatives of the legislative body, the English judges of the eighteenth century did not preserve the former at any price, so journalists lost many lawsuits against parliamentarians. Nor did this legislative body, so well protected by English judges, refrain from passing harsh legislation on the subject of the freedom of the press throughout the eighteenth century and still early in the nineteenth century.

Liberal principles demanded more, as some disciples of Locke never ceased to point out. They included the authors of the celebrated *Cato's Letters*, published in the English and American press between 1720 and 1723, under the pseudonym 'Cato' (the real authors were John Trenchard and Thomas Gordon), which defended a more radical conception of freedom of speech and which inspired the American Founding Fathers. Nevertheless, from the eighteenth century on, European thinking on the subject of the freedom of the press drew its inspiration from other sources than strictly liberal arguments. When, in 1784, responding to a question put to its readers by a Berlin newspaper, Immanuel Kant suggested to King Frederick II of Prussia that he might, as a good *Aufklärer* ('Enlightener'), grant freedom of speech to his people, he put at the heart of his text a quite new idea: that of the *public* as seat of reason.

2. Kant and the principle of publicity (*Offentlichkeit*)

Kant's 'An answer to the question: "What is Enlightenment?"' appeared, five years before the French Revolution, in the *Berlinischer Monatschrift*. It expresses, in the most enthusiastic terms, confidence in the idea of the people who will become a 'public'. It describes all the promise this idea holds out; it praises the plurality of this people-public, which Kant never doubted, as long as it was allowed freedom of expression; it describes a dynamic of progress towards ever more rational judgement; it is a hymn to curiosity and to the figure of the citizen-spectator. And it offers a first theoretical model for thinking journalism.

When individuals become 'spectators' of themselves: the birth of another stage

Kant's text begins by defining the Enlightenment as a state of immaturity and an apprenticeship in autonomous thinking. To emerge from this, he said, was difficult, and few individuals were capable of it. A collectivity, on the other hand, could achieve it more quickly than a number of isolated individuals: 'only a few, by cultivating their own minds, have succeeded in freeing themselves from immaturity and in continuing boldly on their way. There is more chance of an entire public enlightening itself. This is indeed almost inevitable, if only the public concerned is left in freedom.'[30] In other words, it is not necessary for every one of the subjects who constitute the public to have already emerged from immaturity for a people to be granted the right to free speech – the right to constitute a public – since it is by the very fact of granting this right that one speeds up, and even guarantees, the arrival of Enlightenment. This argument amounted, for the benefit of Frederick II, to the following injunction: give them freedom of speech, they will become wise. No need to wait until they are wise; it is by kick-starting the process of the public exchange of points of view that a rationality will emerge, from which you, the emperor, have everything to gain.

The reason for this phenomenon is the dynamic set in motion by a free public exchange of opinions: 'For there will always be a few who think for themselves, even among those appointed as guardians of the common mass. Such guardians, once they have themselves thrown off the yoke of immaturity, will disseminate the spirit of rational respect for personal value and for the duty of all men to think for themselves.'[31] The central idea of the text, therefore, is that 'the public use of . . . reason' is superior to its strictly private use. This public use of reason is 'the use that anyone as a scholar makes of reason before the entire literate world'.[32] In other words, there is a sort of division of each individual into two: an actor, in his social role, with the constraints this implies, and alongside him, as it were, a spectator, who observes what he does, he and all the others – this is what is meant by the expression 'as a scholar'– and who also exposes his gaze to the others, in short observes and is observed. And one may expect from this, from this observation that is itself observed, an increase in rationality.

In fact 'An answer to the question: "What is Enlightenment?"' is a very concrete description of this new stage which will be instituted, alongside the stage of actions, when a regime introduces freedom of speech: that is, the stage where the individuals, doubled up as spectators of themselves, converse, exchange and work at developing a correct judgement. Kant is emphatic that this really is a different stage, which does not immediately disrupt the first. Thus, 'as actors', dare I say, the individuals are expected to obey; it is on the other stage, that of opinions, that, in parallel, 'as scholars', they can challenge the roles they play:

> It would be very harmful if an officer receiving an order from his superiors were to quibble openly, while on duty, about the appropriateness or usefulness of the order in question. He must simply obey. But he cannot be reasonably banned from making observations *as a man of learning* on the errors in military service, and from submitting these to his public for judgment.[33]

The same is true of the citizen who believes the rise in taxes is too high. As a taxpayer, he has to pay what he owes without argument, but 'the same citizen does not contravene his civil obligations if, *as a learned individual*, he publicly voices his thoughts on the impropriety or even injustice of such fiscal measures'. Likewise, 'a clergyman is bound to instruct his pupils and his congregation in accordance with the doctrines of the church he serves', but '*as a scholar* he is completely free, as well as obliged to impart to the public all his carefully considered, well-intentioned thoughts on the mistaken aspects of those doctrines'.[34]

The creation of a space for opinions *alongside* the sphere of actions means that, for Kant, *Aufklärung*, in politics, does not consist of immediate action but is a long process born of the public exchange of *gazes* directed at the sphere of action. It is only after the public debate that, if necessary, that is, if it seems rational, a particular opinion can be put into practice and find an outlet in the space for action. In religious matters, for example:

> The newly established order would continue to exist, until public insight into the nature of such matters had progressed and proved itself to the point where, by general consent (if not unanimously), a proposal could be submitted to the crown. This would seek to protect the congregations who had, for instance, agreed to alter their religious establishment in accordance with their own notions of what higher insight is, but would try not to obstruct those who wanted to let things remain as before.[35]

This implies, in a sense, that, for Kant, the 'true' place of politics – of rational politics – is not immediate action, but action *put on display*. The actors enter politics by becoming both actors *observed* (that is, actors in the theatrical sense of the term) and spectators observing the other actors. If it is not observed, not put on display, action seems doomed to irrationality; it is as if pre-political. The most important stage is that constituted by the public, because it is there that the reforms that will later be applied on the stage of actions are decided.

This is how Kant celebrated the notion of 'public' in this founding text. It is not difficult, of course, to identify the flaws that would be seized on by critics of this celebration. It is still necessary to be sure that all the action can be put on display or made visible in this way; that the distancing brought about by the introduction of the spectator is not the source of a structural bias, which will prevent a 'true' understanding of what is taking place; and that the collective debate is not, in essence, given its situation, a place of debates that are false, out of touch, even blind to the reality of what it is that should be debated. Well before the observations of Bourdieu on the limits of the desire to see, inherent in this stage of politics conceived as stage of a spectacle, the Marxian critique pointed to the blind spots which characterize a stage not only distinct from the true stage of history, praxis, but largely determined by the state of the dominations within this praxis; structurally, for Marx, the political gaze is biased and blind to what determines it.

To accept the Kantian paradigm is effectively to accept what is implicit in it and later denounced by its critics, that is, that the gazes directed at the stage of opinions are not wholly blind and that, on the contrary, it is on this stage that rationality can emerge. This is, in effect, the basic presupposition of a theoretical world for which the notion of public, and the public exchange of opinions and gazes, has meaning and value: the position of spectator should be valorized, seen as a plus, not a minus, as compared with the actor tied to his actions. Hannah Arendt wrote that Kant shared a conception, 'as old as the hills', to the effect that 'only the spectator but never the actor knows what it is all about'.[36] Kant believed that the spectator had the advantage over the actors of being able to 'discover a meaning in the course taken by events, a meaning that the actors ignored',[37] by reason of the distance and disinterestedness inherent to his contemplative position: 'The existential ground for [the spectator's] insight [is] his disinterestedness, his nonparticipation, his noninvolvement.'[38]

Long live the plurality of gazes and opinions!

So, Kant celebrates the spectator. Does this mean that all spectators are equally worthy? Is there, in Kant, a theory of the 'good' spectator? To reply to this question, we need to remember that the principle of publicity assumes that just or rational judgement is never the act of an isolated spectator, but rather of a plurality of spectators. Take, for example, this extract from *The Conflict of the Faculties*, in which Kant discusses the reasons which make it possible to believe that the French Revolution was a step forward in human history. The criterion is not the judgement of this or that observer, but that of all the spectators. Kant writes:

> But I maintain that this revolution has aroused in the hearts and desires of all spectators who are not themselves caught up in it a sympathy which borders almost on enthusiasm, although the very utterance of this sympathy was fraught with danger. It cannot therefore have been caused by anything other than a moral disposition within the human race.[39]

As Michel Foucault has correctly emphasized, 'what is important in the revolution is not the revolution itself, it is what happened in the minds of those who did not make it or who were not, at any rate, the principal actors; it is the relationship they themselves had with this revolution of which they were not the active agents'.[40] It is thus 'the revolution as spectacle, and not as gesticulation, as focus of enthusiasm for those who were present, and not as principle of upheaval for those who participated'.[41] We may note that it is a *collective* spectacle.

This is why Arendt emphasizes the complexity of Kant's thinking on the subject of the spectator. On the one hand, she observes, as noted above, the valorization of the spectator is part of a long tradition; on the other, Kant made a radical break with this tradition, which had a natural tendency to assume the superiority of some spectators over others, and did not require the former, who were often philosophers, to submit to the test of 'publicity'. Arendt quotes from a letter of Kant that is a veritable invitation to a never-ending debate with constantly shifting interlocutors, and a systematic search for the 'just' judgement, defined here as 'impartiality', as a consequence of an intersubjective exchange: 'I entertain the hope that by thus viewing my judgments impartially from the standpoint of others some third view that will improve upon my previous insight may be obtainable.'[42] Of which Arendt observes, 'one sees that impartiality is obtained by taking the viewpoints of others into account; impartiality is not the result of some higher standpoint that would then actually settle the dispute by being altogether above the melée'.[43] Kant's attachment to the idea of a collective working-out of rationality in political matters, according to Arendt, spills over more generally into his conception of the value of a labour of reflection; 'publicity' is the best guide, and Arendt cites as proof the importance Kant attached to 'popularising' his works, less from a desire simply to pass them on than to submit them to a salutary test.[44]

However, if it is a plurality of spectators, exchanging their points of view, which collectively develops the just political judgement, Arendt believes that Kantism also implies a reflection on the 'good' spectator, conceived precisely as someone open to the plurality in which he is immersed. She thinks that Kant thought political judgement in an analogous manner to aesthetic judgement, even claiming that the first part of Kant's *Critique of the Power of Judgment*, which contains a theory of aesthetic judgement, or judgement of taste, 'contains perhaps the greatest and most original aspect of Kant's political philosophy'.[45] In his *Critique of the Power of Judgment*, Kant defines taste as a sense of aesthetic 'justice' that is attained when the spectator makes contact with a plurality of possible spectators. Taste corresponds to the '*sensus communis*', that is, 'the idea of a communal sense', also defined as;

> a faculty for judging that in its reflection takes account (*a priori*) of everyone else's way of representing in thought, in order, as it were to hold its judgment up to human reason as a whole and thereby avoid the illusion which, from subjective private conditions that could easily be held to be objective, would have a detrimental influence on the judgment.[46]

The judgement of taste does not necessarily demand an effective aesthetic discussion. Even if it is wholly internal, imaginary and mute, however, it implies a relationship with the points of view of others, a sort of intersubjective test, or what Kant calls the experience of 'enlarged mentality',[47] which is unconnected either to scientific reasoning (application of laws) or to the determination of the moral order (application of categorical imperatives). The 'good' spectator, in aesthetics, touches a very specific universality; a 'subjective' reality,[48] that is, is experienced in the form of a feeling common to all and 'universally communicable'.[49]

In so far as the short piece 'An answer to the question: "What is Enlightenment?" invites whoever wishes to judge in an enlightened manner to explain themselves publicly and to confront a plurality of points of view, it seems legitimate to see it as a reflection on political judgement as an opening up to a political 'communal sense', similar in essence to the aesthetic 'communal sense'. As Arendt says, Kant is concerned here, as in his analyses of taste, with 'a different way of thinking, for which it would not be enough to be in agreement with one's own self, but which consisted of being able to "think in the place of everybody else"',[50] which is in line with the definition of the 'enlarged mentality'. Like the man of taste, Kant seems to have considered the 'good' spectator in politics as whoever makes live within himself this plurality, this public debate; that is, he who, to find what is 'just', seeks within himself for a sort of collective assent – which he is always, of course, ready to test in a real public debate.[51]

A hymn to curiosity and an 'ideal-critique' of journalism

We may then ask, does this 'enlarged mentality', which implies a curiosity about every point of view and a capacity for constant self-distrust, perhaps define something like a journalistic attitude? This would be, of course, an 'ideal' journalism, unfailingly curious and anxious to vary the point of view, and making it possible to criticize the possible inadequacies of 'real' journalism.

A further point entitles us to believe that Kant was far from being hostile in principle to the figure of the journalist, though the task he assigned him was difficult and demanding. Kant never restricted the subjects in which the 'public' ought to be interested. There is no *a priori* hierarchy between important and less important things – an ontological hierarchy which would lead to a hierarchy of 'observers' and no doubt to contempt for the simple journalist. Kant says only that it is necessary 'to use reason publicly *in all matters*',[52] which suggests that the gaze ought *a priori* to leave nothing out. Everything concerns it, including the most immediately quotidian. According to Michel Foucault, it is on this point that Kant's text is most revolutionary. Foucault wrote: 'The question which seems to me to appear for the first time in this text of Kant is the question of the present, the question of actuality: what is happening today? What is happening now? And what is this "now" within which we are this one and that one; and what defines the moment in which I write?'[53]

This valorization of actuality, what Foucault also calls this 'will to "heroize" the present',[54] derives from the liberating impulse which permeates Kant's text, the desire for humanity to emerge from the 'state of immaturity', in short, for everyone to 'think for themselves'. For Kant, this liberation could only be achieved by a decision marked by resolution and courage; hence the use of the imperatives: 'Sapere aude! Have the courage to use your own understanding.'[55] This imperative incorporates by nature a valorization of the present of the interlocutors. Reason *now!* says the Kantian text. Thus, together with the appeal to use reason, there is, as Foucault says, an appeal to think *today*, hence to think about one's own relationship with today, and hence also to think about this 'today' in the freest possible manner, rejecting all pre-existing and unexamined categories. There is nothing that says *a priori* what is essential and important and what is not, since the whole point is to construct, through collective debate, the criteria for the essential and the important. An *a priori* ontological value is accorded to everything that constitutes actuality. This is probably why Foucault's formula 'heroize the present', used in the English version of his text on Kant, finds its counterpart, in the French version for the *Magazine littéraire*, in the expression 'ontology of the present'.[56] And because it is for collective thought that Kant is appealing, his injunction, according to Foucault, boils down to this: to define – even invent

– collectively the 'we' that we are today.[57] Thus *Aufklärung* is 'a period which itself formulates its own device, its own precept, and which says what it has to do, both in relation to the general history of thought and in relation to its present and to the forms of knowledge, learning, ignorance and illusion in which it can recognize its historical situation'.[58]

Thus Kant invites gazes of all sorts to express themselves and expose themselves, flouting categories which *a priori* confine 'actuality'. He opens up to a boundless curiosity, which seems very favourable to the figure of the journalist. Foucault notes that Kant himself, when he examines his own times, offers an unexpected gaze, attentive to 'small things'. Foucault is referring to the second dissertation of *The Conflict of the Faculties*, where Kant proposes to seek in his own times signs that human beings are caught up in permanent progress, that is, an occurrence that is 'recollective, demonstrative and prognostic' of this progress. Kant warns his readers that this 'occurrence' does not involve 'any of those momentous deeds or misdeeds of men which make small in their eyes what was formerly great or make great what was formerly small, and which cause ancient and illustrious states to vanish as if by magic, and others to arise in their place as if from the bowels of the earth. No, it has nothing to do with all this.' From which Foucault concludes that the *Aufklärung* is also a break with everything that was 'traditional' in the previous gaze, as when he seeks 'the proofs of progress or of non-progress of the human race in the overthrow of empires, in the great catastrophes by which the best-established states disappear, in the reversals of fortune which lay low established governments and make new ones appear'.[59] According to Foucault, Kant is here calling for the gaze to be inventive, curious about everything, even small things ('much less grandiose and much less perceptible events'),[60] a gaze that escapes the established categories and disciplines. If 'publicity' is the only tool for *choosing* from between the plurality of gazes, it also supposes an unprecedented encouragement of such a plurality.

In which case it is inconceivable to draw from Kant's text any condescension towards journalism. On the contrary, it is an enthusiastic text, which lauds the position of the exposed spectator, of the 'observer observed', and which in this way celebrates journalistic practice. This celebration allows and even strongly encourages dissatisfaction with regard to 'real' journalism, but from a very specific critical perspective; it judges it in terms of that boundless curiosity which it poses as an ideal-critique. It is a strongly democratic position, which 'believes' in journalism, and dreams of it finally serving the plurality that constitutes public democratic space.

3. French Enlightenment and American Enlightenment

Other sources for the idea of 'public': Adam Smith and his influence on the American Founding Fathers

It should be remembered that this Kantian principle of publicity echoes other themes common in the political and aesthetic thought of the eighteenth century. Many works before Kant had laid particular emphasis on this domain of intersubjectivity, in which important values were developed. First were some publications of the Scottish Enlightenment. For Adam Smith (1723–90) it was from intersubjective relations that morality itself emerged, which he then related to 'sentiments'. His *Theory of Moral Sentiments* (1759) was part of the Scottish thinking of the eighteenth century which rejected the cold artificialism and contractualism of the English thinkers of the century before (Hobbes and Locke); Smith believed in the 'natural gregariousness' of mankind.[61] And Hume, like Smith, believed in the capacity for empathy which, by force of habit, created moral markers for individuals. In fact this Scottish thinking is one of the first great theories of 'communication'.

In Smith, intersubjectivity or communication was a true source of norms, because, in particular, of what he called the figure of the 'impartial spectator': every individual who contemplated another individual and 'empathized' with him wondered, at the same time, how he himself should react to the feelings of that other and their manifestations; thus Smith invented an internal figure of the 'impartial spectator', who dictated his conduct, or at least laid down moral markers for it.[62]

John Durham Peters notes that the thinking of Smith has often been compared to the Kantian principle of publicity.[63] Above all, however, Smith and the Scottish Enlightenment in general were a major influence on the thinking of the American Founding Fathers. This was true, in particular, of James Madison, to whom is owed the First Amendment, emblem of the American conception of free speech. The First Amendment declared, in 1791, that 'Congress shall make no law respecting an establishment of religion, or prohibiting the free exercise thereof; or abridging the freedom of speech, or of the press; or the right of the people peaceably to assemble, and to petition the government for a redress of grievances.' For Madison and this American conception, as Peters observes, the 'public' is also elevated into a fundamental value, superior to all the constituted powers, including the legislature.[64]

The First Amendment was part of a more radical conception of freedom of speech than that in France, where this freedom should not be above the law in this way, as we will see. It can be argued, therefore, that, while the Age of Enlightenment celebrated the notion of 'public', it gave rise to two different 'lines', the French and the American, more or less radical in the degree of freedom they intended to allow this public. In both cases, nevertheless, the strictly liberal arguments of the seventeenth century were left behind in favour of a more profound reflection on the notion of public.

For the American Founding Fathers, the decisive factor was the strict limit imposed (by the law) on the freedom of the press in England at the beginning of the eighteenth century. They wanted to make a radical break with this by putting freedom of speech above the law, which was in accord with their analysis of the notion of public. Here, the press trial known as 'the Zenger Case', in 1735, in the colony of New York, played a crucial role. John Peter Zenger was an immigrant of German origin and editor of the *New York Weekly Journal*. He published a series of articles hostile to the governor of the colony, who had him tried for 'seditious libel'. The court eventually acquitted Zenger, in a verdict widely regarded as a decisive step in the history of the freedom of the press. We should note that among the works published by Zenger was *Cato's Letters*.[65]

However, there is scarcely a passage in the *Federalist Papers* specifically devoted to the freedom of the press; and the same is true of the American Constitution. Andrew Hamilton even expressed the view, in *Federalist* no. 84, that there was no need to declare the freedom of the press – it was enough that the Constitution had not given the government any power to control it; he relied on the 'public' to safeguard this freedom and prevent the government from restricting it. The Constitution was perceived as what had been granted to the government in terms of powers, and there was no need to mention anything else, as long as the people were vigilant. Madison, too, principal drafter of the Constitution and the Bill of Rights, was sometimes reticent on the question of the press. Admittedly he formulated with great clarity the fundamental problem of democracies, that is, public opinion, and, as a result, relied heavily on the press. Thus in *Federalist* no. 10 he wrote that the principal danger in a democracy was constituted by 'factions' and that, to counter this, there must be institutional checks and balances and a vigilant public opinion; a role for the press is implied here, even if it is not made more explicit. Later, in 1791, that is, after the adoption of the Bill of Rights, Madison was to write in his correspondence that every good citizen was 'a sentinel over the rights for the people', which assumes they express their opinions publicly. In this same text, however, he revealed his unease, fearing that the free press might abuse its power, that it might serve factions and commit libels.

It was probably Jefferson, ambassador in France when the *Federalist Papers* appeared, who, of all the Founding Fathers, was the one most interested in the question of the press, so much so that he has been called the newspapers' 'best friend'.[66] In 1787 he had said in a letter that he would prefer newspapers without a government to a government without newspapers. In fact, according to J. H. Altschull, Jefferson seems to have been seriously torn between a real desire to limit the freedom of the press so that it could be held to account in case of false facts, and, at the same time, a need to emphasize that no one should be punished for words alone, and that any intervention in the sphere of press freedom had its dangers. Jefferson may not always have been totally coherent, as Altschull observes, but his hesitations also reveal the extent to which he saw the press as a vital issue, on which his ideas continued to evolve.

The radical American conception of free speech was in reality to be shaped in concrete terms by the actions of the Supreme Court.[67] Throughout the nineteenth and twentieth centuries, the Court's case law redefined the crimes and offences which the old English common law had established with regard to freedom of speech. It imposed stricter limits on them, as in its decision in *Cantwell v. Connecticut* (1940), which defined the notion of 'breach of the peace'. A sub-category of the latter, the notion of 'improper language', was also restricted by the decision in *Chaplinsky v. New Hampshire* (1942), which created an exception to tolerance only in the case of insults, and 'fighting words' (a category which was increasingly limited in the case law of subsequent decades). In its case law after *Sullivan v. New York Times* (1964), the Court also limited libel to the existence of 'actual malice', in order to avoid the dissuasive effect which libel in the traditional interpretation (responsibility for risk) had had on newspapers, encouraging them not to publish certain things when they feared pecuniary damages above what they could afford. In general, in the case law of the Supreme Court on the First Amendment, liberty was the rule and control the exception, and the Court insisted that the latter be 'content neutral'.[68]

The French conception of public space

In 1789 the French Revolutionaries believed freedom of speech to be a principle which should, nevertheless, be controlled by the law, like religious liberty. Article 10 of the Declaration of the Rights of Man and of the Citizen states: 'No one may be disturbed on account of his opinions, even religious ones, as long as the manifestation of such opinions does not interfere with the established Law and Order'; to which Article 11 adds: 'The free communication of ideas and of opinions is one of the most precious rights of man. Any citizen may therefore speak, write and publish freely, except what is tantamount to the abuse of this liberty in the cases determined by Law.'

This difference between the American and the French ethos, which is expressed in the relationship to the law – the French considering nothing to be above it, not even freedom of conscience – owes much to the influence in France of Jean-Jacques Rousseau (1712–78). This is a point that needs further discussion, given that Rousseau is sometimes seen as one of the philosophical sources of freedom of speech.

Rousseau instituted the people as legislative power – without representatives, hence in an ideal world, or a very strictly controlled one.[69] His conception of sovereignty was absolutist; this was his Hobbesian heritage, even if Rousseau differed fundamentally from Hobbes in that he transferred sovereignty to the *people*.[70] So, the law, in Rousseau, as long as it respected the conditions he laid down for its development – that is, corresponded to the 'general will' – could not be limited in any way.

It was necessary, obviously, for the law to respect the very precise conditions which ensured that it really did express the 'general will': it must be 'general in its object as well as its essence', which means, according to chapter 4 of book 2 of the *Social Contract*, that 'it must both come from all and apply to all'. A double generality, then, of the object and of the essence of this will: every one must have participated in the vote, and the objects to which it applies must concern 'all'. But if this is the case – and the problem is clearly knowing how to be sure that the 'general will' is expressed, purged of any 'particular' concern – then no principle above the law is recognized. As in Hobbes and Bodin, the law can do and undo in total freedom; it is the fundamental freedom of peoples that they should not be bound, not even by their earlier 'general wills'. Similarly, the idea of a right of resistance to the law, which clearly existed for Rousseau if the law has not been developed in the conditions of the general will, disappears if the conditions of the general will are satisfied, as is the case in the system founded by the *Social Contract*. This explains the draconian character of chapter 7 of book 1: 'whoever refuses to obey the general will shall be compelled to do so by the whole body. This means nothing less than that he will be forced to be free.'

This firmness is based on the assurance that whoever resists does so only in the name of a 'particular will' and that he is duly punished in the name of the 'general will'. Conversely, if the law corresponds not to the general will, but to the victory of some particular interests, Rousseau has no difficulty in acknowledging a right of rebellion. The real problem is that, contrary to the right of resistance in Locke, who opened up a space for evaluation within each conscience and between many consciences (should it be exercised? is it really the last resort?), in Rousseau the question of obedience is settled from the outset, in binary mode, with no grey areas: the law is, or is not, the product of the general will, and from this derives the behaviour – disobedient or obedient – that should be adopted.

The question then arises, does the prohibition on resisting the general will in deeds apply also to purely verbal expressions of disagreement? It is even more pertinent in that Rousseau saw as one of the conditions of access to the general will the fact that *all* consciences express themselves, which ought to make it sensitive to expressions of disagreement, even marginal, as possible signs that the law had not taken sufficient account of the general will. Here some clarifications are necessary.

First, we need to understand the way in which Rousseau intended the law to be developed. The deliberation he advocated has little in common with the Kantian conception of the principle of publicity and shows signs of deep hostility to the notion of 'public opinion'. Deliberation is certainly essential for Rousseau; it produces something like an alchemy within the people. One Rousseau specialist, Blaise Bachofen, even detects the idea of a 'prodigy', linked to a 'decisional mechanism':[71] the public debate allows a confrontation between various points of view, often still 'particular', and in this way the progressive elevation towards the general, towards the perception of a 'common'. It is this labour of deliberation that should be understood behind Rousseau's description of the elaboration of the law in chapter 6 of book 2 of the *Social Contract*: but when the whole people decrees for the whole people, it is considering only itself; and if a relation is then formed, it is between two aspects of the entire object, without there being any division of the whole. In that case the matter about which the decree is made is, like the decreeing will, general. This act is what I call a law.'

However, this debate is strictly controlled. First there has to be the mediation of the 'Legislator', that person who helps the people to perceive a question correctly and to consider it at a general level, beyond situations involving particular wills – that is, the person who 'teaches the people what it wants';[72] the debate must also take place in specific conditions, in a sort of ideal purity, which reveals Rousseau's distrust of the most concrete and freest forms of intersubjective communication. He is much more uneasy than Kant in the face of the risk that the marvellous alchemy of the public debate might be biased by rhetorical and factious seizures of power, by which particular interests are able to pass themselves off as general. He even dreams of a debate without 'communication', as in this passage from chapter 3 of book 2 of the *Social Contract*: 'If, when the people, being furnished with adequate information, held its deliberations, the citizens had no communication one with another, the grand total of the small differences would always give the general will, and the decision would always be good.' If this is not absurd, it means a debate in very specific conditions and, in particular, a ban on contacts between people outside this context. It is difficult to believe that such an arrangement would not, even so, result in a restriction of freedom of speech.

Another Rousseau expert, Bruno Bernardi, emphasizes the fact that the general will is something quite different from 'public opinion':

> the essential point is that public opinion is not the general will . . . public opinion is a general sentiment, it is not the result of a generalisation of the will or of the understanding required by determining what is the general will. Opinion is here the opposite of public debate: it proceeds neither from the process of determining the will nor from recognition of the common good. Public opinion is even, in a sense, an anti-model of the general will.[73]

Public opinion is the result of partial associations of particular interests. The problem, for Rousseau, is to establish the conditions for an authentic public debate, and this is also the task of the Legislator: to bring about what Rousseau calls 'public enlightenment', the purpose of which, as is emphasized by Bernardi, is to 'enlighten the general will'.[74] This is clear in the passage in book 2 of the *Social Contract* which concludes chapter 6 ('The Law') and prepares the ground for chapter 7 ('The Legislator'): 'The individuals see the good they reject; the public wills the good it does not see. All are equally in need of guidance. The former must be compelled to bring their wills into conformity with their reason; the latter must be taught to know what they want.' This is effectively to restrict the process that should lead to the emergence of the general will with a rigour that clearly distances Rousseau from the winds of freedom that blow on the Kantian principle of 'publicity'.[75]

There is another problem: that of the possibility of an individual disagreement with a law, a disagreement persisting after the promulgation of that law. Rousseau's answer is in part Hobbesian, that is, to leave to the individual conscience the sphere in which the law has no interest; this sphere, which Hobbes called the 'silence of the law' (*Leviathan*, chapter 21), and which it is for the sovereign alone to define (which means he can increase or reduce this sphere by changing the law as he wishes), appears in chapter 4 of book 2 of the *Social Contract*. But Rousseau needs to provide a more developed answer than Hobbes, because he makes more of a point of the individual conscience. Robert Derathé recalls this sentence from the *Nouvelle Héloise*: 'Never does [conscience] mislead a soul that consults it sincerely' (part three, letter

18).[76] Does this imply that the conscience always has the right to express itself, even when it is against a law voted by the general will? How does Rousseau deal with the problem of possible conflicts between the law, expression of the general will, and an individual conscience?

In fact Rousseau believed that this sort of purely individual 'liberty', in conflict with the general will, was not a true liberty. As we have seen with regard to the right of resistance, which he rejected, for Rousseau, if there really was a conflict between a conscience and the general will, there could only be liberty, true liberty, on the side of the latter; the rebellious conscience is simply in thrall to its narrow focus on its particular interest. The Rousseauist tour de force is to redefine the liberty of the opponent as servitude, and the law that constrains as liberty. In other words, he refused to contemplate the eventuality of a *real* conflict between the general will and a *free* conscience – because the conscience that opposed the general will could not really be free. There is no reason why this Rousseauist argument, so strongly against the 'liberty' of the liberals, which he transformed into servitude, opposed to the true liberty that consisted of obeying a law born of the general will, was any less applicable to freedom of speech than to the freedom to oppose in deeds. In any case, once again, we can be sure that whoever decides on the appropriateness of allowing greater or lesser freedom of speech to all, and especially to those who oppose the laws, will be, in the Rousseauist system, the sovereign and the law.

Thus, there is no 'absolute' principle of freedom of speech which comes before and above the law in the *Social Contract*; the law retained the right to restrict free speech. Which is exactly what it says in Article 11 of the Declaration of the Rights of Man and of the Citizen.

That said, the Rousseauism of the Revolutionaries greatly changed the thinking of Rousseau. Under the influence of Sieyès, in particular, the principle of representation on the legislature, which Rousseau held in such contempt, was rehabilitated. A strict Rousseauist might consider that, having changed an element so essential to the Rousseauist system, one could hardly retain the absolutism of the law: if the law is no longer made by the people itself, but by its representatives, is it still acceptable to reject all opposition to it? It is precisely because, in Rousseau's system, the law was the product of a collective enterprise, in which every one had been able to express themselves, in specific conditions that assured an authentic debate, that he could conclude that any liberty subsequently exercised against the law was not a true liberty. Essentially, he saw this pseudo-liberty as the weak arm which remained to the people when it was not they who exercised sovereignty directly, the pitiable right of opposition that devolved on it in the sort of liberal thinking enamoured of the representative principle. Nor was this enough for Rousseau; he wanted to change the very exercise of power by truly attributing it to the people, without representation. It was on this basis that he believed that the liberal tools of opposition no longer made sense. But if there was a return to the representative system, the whole context of Rousseau's thinking was altered.

This objection is well founded. We are still left with the problem of what happens to the liberties of the liberals in systems which, like Rousseauism, seek to break with liberal thought. If it is true that Article 11 misrepresents Rousseau, it is equally true that an un-misrepresented Rousseau has little to contribute to the debate on freedom of speech. It is not, it has to be accepted, a Rousseauist subject. This may be because, historically, it has primarily been of interest to thinkers concerned with the representative principle, that is, thinkers at peace with this principle, who seek only ways of making it work best for those represented.

In any case, if the notion of 'public', so dear to the Enlightenment, was of less interest to Rousseau than is sometimes claimed, it was of very great interest to the liberal thinkers of the early nineteenth century. They understood the value of this new principle of 'publicity' in enriching the whole English tradition of the seventeenth and eighteenth centuries, all those ideas on representative government which they valued and developed. This is particularly the case with Benjamin Constant, who reveals the difference between the liberalism of before the Enlightenment and the liberalism of after. He certainly appreciated the value of this new notion of 'public', as a modern way of participating in politics.

Constant defended freedom of the press as the necessary complement to the 'defensive' character of classic liberalism, as the 'participatory' dimension which was lacking in a liberal thinking primarily focused on the protection of the private sphere. As Stephen Holmes has emphasized, Constant understood that 'private rights are endangered by excessive privatization; individual experience cannot survive without some form of citizen involvement'.[77] In particular, he believed that the experience of Bonapartism, so catastrophic for individual liberties, had been the consequence of a retreat of the French people from politics, of apathy linked to disillusionment in the face of the course taken by the Revolution. It was this that he wanted to remedy. From the liberal point of view, however, it was obvious that this civic participation could not go against the modern attachment to the independent enjoyment of the private sphere, which led, in particular, to the delegation of political tasks to representatives. Constant was affected by the Rousseauist desire for participation, but he rejected the Rousseauist solution as pure nostalgia for the Ancients. What he wanted to find were forms of participation that were truly *modern*.

Freedom of speech and a free press proved fertile ground for Constant. Individuals, he claimed, should have, as regards their representatives, 'a right of control and supervision by expressing their opinions'.[78] In this he was more explicit than, for example, Locke. Freedom of speech, in Constant, was in part a new emphasis which gave the classic liberal themes a new resonance; they now sounded more Kantian and less negative on the subject of political participation. In effect, says Stephen Holmes, he 'questions the association of liberalism with a hysterical fear of civic activism'.[79] Constant was also responding to Rousseau; liberalism, he showed, by defending 'political liberty', was not a complete stranger to 'public affairs', or to 'our right to share in political power' or to the 'desire to broaden our knowledge and develop our faculties'.[80]

In a way, Constant was trying to correct certain characteristics of French democracy by drawing on what were, after all, strong points in its history; the Enlightenment breeze had undeniably consecrated journalism as a key element in democracy. The growth of newspapers had spectacularly accelerated well before the recognition in law of freedom of speech. Constant was by no means the only one to be angry that the Revolution, by reintroducing censorship, had caused these green shoots to wither.

4. The denunciation of the naiveties of the notion of 'public': the problem of the domination of the 'homogenous' in democracy

So the notion of public was formulated historically, in democratic enthusiasm. It soon came up against hatred and mistrust. How could one believe, concretely, in the notion of the people as a marvellous plurality? And how could one believe that, whatever the faults of 'real' journalism, it could still be reformed, that is, believe in the ideal of a journalism in the service of this plurality? It was not long before the notion of 'public' was criticized for its naivety, its simplism and a latent myth of innocence which made it more attractive but also illusory.

The public as 'crowd', or the total condemnation of journalism (Gustave Le Bon)

The position representing the clearest and most extreme contempt for democratic public space is perhaps that of Gustave Le Bon, whose *The Crowd: A Study of the Popular Mind*, published in 1895, devotes several pages to a venomous attack on the journalism of his day. In fact what Le Bon represented in France was simply the culmination of a whole counter-revolutionary and anti-democratic mindset, for which the newspapers had for a century been a prime target, so closely were they associated with the memory of the barricades.

Not only had the outstanding figures of the French Revolution been prolific journalists, acting 'through' the newspapers, but they had frequently commented on this journalistic practice, and on its role and its implications. Camille Desmoulins spoke of the 'revolutionary torrent', to describe which the historian must take up a new pen, the 'rapid and breathless' pen of the journalist.[81] Brissot, back from America for the newly convened Estates General and founder of the *Patriote français*, confided in his friend Piéton: 'It is with the newspapers that the Revolution happened in America.'[82] Loustalot, editor of the *Révolutions de Paris*, according to Desmoulins, 'never stopped repeating this maxim of an English writer: If the freedom of the press existed in a country where the most absolute despotism concentrated all power in a single hand, it would be enough on its own to act as a counter-balance'; to which Desmoulins added, 'The experience of our revolution has shown the truth of this maxim.'[83]

The Revolutionaries described this new press, a radical departure from the traditional publications, as a gaze turned 'outwards', out towards this new power that came from the exterior. In his painting of 1791, *le Serment du Jeu de Paume*, David showed the traditional publicist Barère among the deputies, and, in the top right corner, Marat, who is writing for *l'Ami du Peuple*; he stands against the wall, turning his back on the room, facing what was happening *outside*.[84] Newspapers were frequently seen as that which made it possible to understand by looking at, while also participating in, this mélange of disorderly conflictuality and the creation of a new political community. The motif of the 'torrent' in Desmoulins encapsulates both these ideas. Two specialists in Revolutionary journalism have shown how Desmoulins offered a double symbolism, two 'stages', 'that of the riot and that of the festival, that of fratricidal strife and that of happy reunions, that of conflict and that of harmony; 23 and 25 June, 14 and 17 July, and 5 and 6 October'.[85] The press, in short, celebrated a 'we' as well as a conflictual tearing apart. To be more precise, it celebrated this 'we' only by showing how it was created in rioting, chaos and a generalized conflictuality. The journalists liked to see themselves as an 'I' central to the constitution of the 'we'. Historians have noted just how few publications gave prominence to the 'word of the subject';[86] rather there was an abundance of the rhetoric in which the journalists presented themselves as 'delegates of the public', 'friends of the people' or 'eyes of the public',[87] representatives of a 'community without visible presence'.[88] We should also remember the importance of public readings of the newspapers,[89] which added significantly to the community of readers, blurring the frontier between the invisible and the visible community, and ultimately strengthening the feeling of a 'we'. The superiority of the newspaper over the book, said Brissot, was because it 'rapidly enlightens a mass of men, whose ideas react simultaneously'.[90] The idea that journalism was written with a new 'ink', which embraced the immediate present and thus, unlike the dry ink of books, had a liveliness and a collectivity about it – the metaphor of the blood of the people was not far away – was later to be a key theme of Jules Vallès, perhaps the most faithful heir to the conception of the newspaper held by the Revolutionaries of 1789.[91]

The French nineteenth century continued to be haunted by this danger – or for others, this virtue – of the free press, which constantly prepared for, stimulated and accompanied the democratic revolution. It was haunted, in other words, by the fear – or the fascination – of the street. The increasingly harsh legislation which punctuated the century was clearly linked to this anxiety. The Ultra camp, under the minister Villèle, was behind the extremely stringent press law of 1822. Going back on the liberal gains of the Charter of 1814 and the press law of 1819 (owed to the Comte de Serre), this law restored prior authorization and the possibility of censorship, creating the 'offence of opinion' and the right to punish a newspaper for its 'ethos'.

Benjamin Constant liked to bring the Ultras face to face with their contradictions, claiming that their intransigence actually nurtured that which they held in contempt. In fact, after the Martignac interlude, the ordinances of Charles X of 1830, one of which explicitly targeted the freedom of the press, played a significant role in provoking the revolutionary events of the Three Glorious Days. But the triumph of this (very Kantian) idea that the people become a 'public' might be the best protection against the people as 'crowd', that freedom of speech might actually neutralize the risk of revolution, was a long time coming. It was all the longer in that the lessons of history are not always clear. The revolutionary events of 1848 seemed to many observers to have been prepared for rather than delayed by the growth of the press since 1830 (unchecked by the legislation of the July Monarchy even if it had never been completely liberal). The memory of the seventy days of the Commune, which saw the birth of dozens of newspapers, did little to mollify the more conservative, who still existed even in the ranks of the republicans of the Third Republic. This is why the debate on the freedom of the press in France remained heated for so long, certainly until the law of 1881 and even beyond.

Le Bon was a figure in the counter-revolutionary Right at the end of the nineteenth century, whose theory of crowds had a major impact, long after his death. His concept of 'crowd' cannot but appear as the exact opposite of the Kantian idea of the 'public'. The symmetry is near-perfect. Against the democratic enthusiasm that surrounds the principle of publicity, Le Bon incarnated the radical anti-democratic position. He swept aside all the hopes placed in plurality, that fine plurality that would, according to Kant, bring ever more rationality. In Le Bon the 'public' is denounced as simply a 'crowd', not physically admittedly, but a crowd nevertheless in its essential characteristics: behaviour motivated exclusively by affects and impulses, lacking rationality, without space for any sort of plurality.

For Le Bon, the crowd was an anonymous force, which unified different individuals by denying their differences, creating over and above them an entity destructive of the foundations of civilization. It is obvious that the underlying, anxiety-inducing image for Le Bon was the revolutionary crowd. Nevertheless, what is fundamental in his concept of the crowd is that it went beyond the phenomenon of the active crowd, visible in the street – that is, the crowd in the most common sense of the word. On the one hand, when Le Bon spoke of this physical, active crowd, he kept referring to its less visible features, its representations, its feelings and its 'ideas', thus emphasizing that it was not simply something that could be seen. On the other, he believed that this invisible psychological dimension was so crucial that a crowd could exist even without any physically visible manifestation. And the classic example of an invisible crowd, for him, was the newspaper-reading 'public'.

Thus the 'crowd' in Le Bon is a concept related primarily to psychological phenomena, which had, or did not have, physical manifestations. This was well understood by Robert E. Park, in the sections he devoted to Le Bon in his university dissertation of 1904, 'The crowd and the public'. He wrote:

> A number of individuals gathered in a square constitutes a crowd in Le Bon's sense only when it possesses a certain psychological nature. On the other hand, an entire nation can be a crowd in the psychological sense, without any visible gathering of people. Thus it is the psychological conditions rather than the spatial relationships of individuals which form the essential content of the concept 'crowd'.[92]

These 'psychological conditions' consisted of an inability to accept diversity, in whatever form it took, and in particular to imagine *many* things. The crowd can never retain many ideas, nor even a single idea which is too complex, that is, has several dimensions. 'Whatever the ideas suggested to crowds they can only exercise effective influence on condition that they assume a very absolute, uncompromising and simple shape. They present themselves then in the guise of images.'[93] Thus the crowd simplified or drained of vitality the ideas it adopted, often at the price of their transformation.[94]

Le Bon regarded crowds as that which triumphed when 'the collective soul' of a people went astray. Each people had a 'collective soul' which expressed intentions that were as much psychological as biological, and were thus related to the characteristics of its 'race'.[95] However, this soul, especially under the influence of the prevailing egalitarian ideas and the disorder they produced in the life of a people, might experience a moment of 'going astray'.[96] Democratization was one of these upheavals which made the 'psychological species' that are peoples experience 'regressive transformations the consequence of which was an often very rapid destruction. Peoples spend long centuries acquiring a certain mental constitution and they sometimes lose it in a very short time.'[97] What succeeded to the feeling by a people of its 'soul' or its 'race' was the anarchy of crowds: 'While our ancient beliefs are tottering and disappearing, while the old pillars of society are giving way one by one, the power of the crowd is the only force that nothing menaces, and of which the prestige is continually on the increase. The age we are about to enter will in truth be the ERA OF CROWDS.'[98] The crowd was the consequence of the loss of control by an elite, that 'small intellectual aristocracy' which had until then 'created and directed' civilizations.[99] And nothing but an elite could eventually counteract this destructive power, although Le Bon was pessimistic on this point.

The privilege of complexity was exclusively reserved to the individual, or to a few exceptional individuals – that is, according to Le Bon, to those who were the guardians of the 'race' of a people. Le Bon did not envisage any group in any sense intermediary between the individual and this odious crowd which denied the individual and endangered the 'race'. Thus exceptional individuals – the elite – did not constitute a united group, something like a public in the Kantian meaning of the word. They were each, individually, in a relationship with this entity that constituted the substance of a people, its profound identity, the 'race', but there was no inter-individual communication between them in which something like a new collective thinking could emerge. Thus Le Bon's ideas are wholly alien to anything that was specific in the notion of 'public', in relation to this fusional group that is the crowd. The 'publics', whatever they are, are nothing but crowds; beginning, of course, with the readerships of newspapers, which were expanding as he wrote.

Admittedly, the public which got its news from the press had the appearance of allowing the circulation of varied opinions. But if the public was a particularly capricious crowd, which constantly changed its 'idea', it was still a crowd, that is, a unity which could scarcely have more than one idea at a time. Thus, while Le Bon spoke, in particular to characterize the readers of newspapers, of 'changeable opinions', which were, he said, 'greater in number than they ever were', he emphasized the very short lifespan of these opinions. The governments of 'the present age', he claimed, as a result, always faced not a blank space where many opinions were exchanged, but a scene in which a few dominant opinions of the moment stood out: this was 'the opinion of crowds'. It is why, when Le Bon accused the press and the government of giving in to the public or to public 'opinion', instead of directing it – as an elite worthy of the name should – he was explicit that what they were yielding to was to 'the power of crowds'. This plural, 'the crowds', is highly significant. In fact diversity was not tolerable in the crowd, so it quickly caused it to fracture into one or more other crowds. This plural is the exact opposite of a recognition of the plurality of opinions in the Kantian meaning of the term, which implied an exchange; here it is the plural of juxtaposition and hermeticism.[100]

The crowds which are the 'publics' may differ a little from the preceding crowds, those which had occupied the street; the press had created crowds that were more changeable and less visible than before. But they were still crowds. Le Bon completely rejected the specificity of the shift to the 'spectacle' which was so important for Kant. Le Bon did not recognize any specificity in the groups of spectators as compared with the groups of actors which were the active crowds. In fact, in rejecting the notion of 'public' in favour of that of 'crowd', he wrote off all Kant's thinking on dividing a people into two and putting it on two stages: that of actions and that of gazes. Kant expected this division would lead to the development of a judgement that respected the plurality of points of view, the gradual construction of the correct point of view, and then the utilization of its practical consequences. This was the best way of preventing the people from becoming a great power acting blindly and of helping it to become a rich and self-conscious plurality. Le Bon's concept of 'crowd' made it possible to abandon the whole of this Kantian position at a stroke. The people that turned into a 'public' was no more than a fixed, blind, unconscious block – exactly what it was when it was an 'active' people. Whereas, in Kant, the plurality of the spectators enabled them to perceive themselves more clearly as a plurality of actors, in Le Bon, the homogeneity of the public which observed was substantially of the same contemptible nature as that of the people who acted.

It is obvious that the condemnation is here so blanket and so definitive, and so explicitly anti-democratic, that journalism simply ceases to be a subject for open critical debate. There is no point thinking about what it could be, when all it can be, by definition, is crowd fodder. Any intelligent, 'elitist' argument knew it had no need to resort to 'journalism', that is, publicize itself, because it would inevitably be simplified and destroyed. 'Publicized' as it was by its nature, journalism would become a shameful simplistic product, in which no hopes could be placed. Just as the public democratic space was crushed by the concept of the crowd, removed from any sophisticated, nuanced thinking, journalism was definitively condemned as mediocre; it contained nothing worthy of reflection. Le Bonism was a deliberate, proclaimed desertion of public space.

What can we learn from this encounter – without dialogue – between Kantism and Le Bonism? Essentially, that it fossilized critical thinking on the subject of journalism. It suited a latent bipolar structure, which is still damaging to current thinking on journalism, even if Le Bonism today generally lacks disciples. It is a sort of spectre at the feast, a sneaking temptation that is scarcely realized, rejected as soon as espoused; hence the volte-faces we described above. Essentially, everything is simplified. On the one hand, criticism of the public is inhibited by the spectre of Le Bonism. But is there no way of engaging in a critique of this notion of 'public' without going to the extreme of Le Bon's desertion of public space? Or without falling into this anti-democratic contempt? On the other hand, and conversely, anyone who trusts the idea of 'public' risks ridicule. Yet the myth of the innocent and marvellous public is, as I will show, inadequate as a way of summarizing Kant. Kantism did not fail to see the public as dangerous and difficult to control. Nor is it necessarily naive to believe that journalism is capable of 'reform', that it can be drawn into greater curiosity. What is there to stop us imagining a reformer at the end of his resources, on the edge of despair, who fights a constant battle against the imperfections of 'real journalism', who complains about a curiosity that is constantly truncated and perpetually timid, who even sometimes comes to think that there may be something deeply tainted in democratic public space . . . but who, because he stays true to this critique, refuses to desert and flee to 'another stage'? As we will see, it is Karl Kraus I am thinking of here. Lastly, rather than naivety, we should speak of courage: the courage to stand firm, to refuse to yield to the temptation to desert, to persist in making public space a place to be reformed, instead of turning away. It is this courage, it seems to me, that emerges from the Kantism of Foucault.

Is it possible, then, to reject sterile bipolarity in favour of the search for a middle way, one which will truly liberate critical thinking on journalism? To leave behind the strictly Kantian world, to accede to structural critiques of the idea of 'public', which see a structural homogeneity in it, and insuperable difficulties, and yet at the same time to retain a core of Kantism which prevents a retreat into simple anti-democratism, and precludes a complete desertion of public space by becoming fossilized in a position of contempt?

It may be possible to do justice to the unease and refuse Kantism's over-serene enthusiasm without abandoning all the requirements of the Kantian principle of publicity.

Tocquevillean unease

What is needed, in a way, is to inject a little Tocquevillean unease into thinking on the idea of public. Tocqueville (1805–59) called into question the Kantian belief that the free exchange of opinions led almost naturally to a progressive rationalization of these opinions. He questioned the dynamic that was supposed to lead to a rational 'common' emerging from plurality. This dynamic is also present in the works of the French Revolutionaries, so confident that the press would be able to perform two opposing functions: accompany and even intensify the conflict under way, *and at the same time* bring about the unity of a people, a unity based on reason.

This idea of the public as both plural and one was precisely what Tocqueville called into question in his observations on American democracy. For him, the damaging consequences of modern individualism lay both in a paucity of ties between individuals – not enough unity – and a staggering uniformity – not enough plurality.[101] Individualism both isolated the individual and fuelled a herd instinct, a standardizing temptation most strikingly illustrated by the phenomenon of public opinion, that mass where everyone was alone and where everyone was like everyone else ('differences of opinion' in America, he noted, 'are quite subtle').[102] Tocqueville tried to find a way of neutralizing as far as was possible this double evil, in which the press was obviously complicit.

It is clear that for Tocqueville the press was both the ill and the remedy. In this regard, his thinking corresponds to the approach I described above, a desire to criticize without 'deserting', to identify the evils of public space without jettisoning the principle of publicity. For

Tocqueville, the press was an obvious complement to the associative life he wished to stimulate; 'hardly any democratic association can do without a newspaper', he wrote.[103] In fact the readership of a newspaper was itself referred to as a sort of association: 'a newspaper always represents an association of which its regular readers make up the membership'.[104] Which is to say that Tocqueville's thinking about the press was essentially ambivalent: the press was one of the main symptoms of the democratic disease, and at the same time one of its remedies. This is why *Democracy in America* is both a critique of public opinion and a eulogy of the press.

The ambivalence is apparent in his first discussion of the freedom of the press in the first volume of his book: 'I confess I do not accord to press freedom', he wrote, 'that entire and instantaneous affection one grants to things which are supremely good by their very nature. My affection for it stems more from my regard for the evils it prevents rather than from the benefits it produces';[105] and later in the same chapter, 'In America, as in France, the press has the same extraordinary power, such a strange mixture of good and evil that, without its presence, freedom could not thrive and with its presence good order could hardly survive.'[106] One feels he is resigning himself, without any great enthusiasm, to treat the evil by means of this good-evil, and that the real problem lies here, in the transition from the press-as-symptom to the press-as-cure. The Tocquevillean way of observing the role of the press thus belongs to that middle way that I referred to above, uneasy but refusing to abandon ship.

However, in the case of Tocqueville, we need to be aware that the temptation to resort to less 'modern' weapons in order to cure the ills of democratic modernity is strong, perhaps even stronger than his search, both ambivalent and fruitful, for remedies actually in the symptoms of the democratic disease. The importance of religion in Tocquevillean thinking is undeniable, and it represents all it contains that is most nostalgic, traditional and pre-modern, even anti-modern. It is of particular interest to note that the problem of religious belief is posed in Tocqueville with regard to those, dare I say, lesser beliefs generated by public opinion, hence particularly by the press; which is why the press and public opinion are generally unreliable remedies, which do not entirely succeed in allaying the unease of the democrat. Religion is the last refuge of belief.

This point is especially clear at the end of the chapter on press freedom in volume 1 of *Democracy in America* (part 2, chapter 3: 'The freedom of the press in the United States'). Tocqueville explains that there are three 'distinct and often successive' states of human intelligence. The first is that of firm belief, though often through lack of deep thought; it is impossible not to think here of the state of immaturity evoked by Kant, a moment of tradition, before the modern emancipation of the individual, which came about, according to Kant, through freedom of speech and the principle of publicity. All the more so in that the second state is that of the freedom of the press. But Tocqueville did not believe that this produced a deeper belief. All the press taught was how to change one's beliefs often. In fact it is a cause of unease in the democrat, for whom the acme, the third state, is 'widespread doubt and mistrust', in which, having changed beliefs so often and been made only too aware of their relativity, people end up clinging to some of them, but out of an ill-at-ease and ill-thought-out obstinacy ('All the social theories having been challenged and defeated in their turn, all those who had adopted one of them stick to it, not so much because they are convinced of its excellence, but because they are unsure that a better one exists'). Here Tocqueville clearly articulates the failure of Kantian enthusiasm: no deep knowledge can be expected of this state. He is scarcely more convinced of the collective spread of rationality, which, on the contrary, he says, will be confined to an elite: 'Only a very small number of men will ever be blessed with the attainment of this other kind of deliberate and self-confident conviction born of knowledge and arising from the very heart of agitation and doubt.' It is here that, in the hierarchy of Tocquevillean values, the superiority of religious belief triumphs, in fact tradition triumphs, over modern remedies. Because, at the end of the day, 'it has been noted that in centuries of religious fervor, men sometimes changed beliefs, whereas in centuries of skepticism, each man hung on to his own'. A mind-numbing mechanism for doubt, rather than the virtuous Kantian dynamic! And the end, furthermore, of the fruitful mobility of opinion, ultimately replaced by the incarnation of fixity itself: material interest: 'When abstract opinions are in doubt, men end up hanging on to their instincts and material interests alone which are much more obvious, tangible and permanent than opinions.' This, ultimately, is what happens 'when the freedom of the press prevails'. The age of religion was, in the end, less rigid.[107]

If this is not anti-modern nostalgia, what is? Tocqueville reveals that his strongest attachment is to the beliefs that are most solid and also least susceptible to being diverted into a fixation on material interests alone, that is, religious beliefs, which have an authentic transcendence as compared with material life. He achieves the remarkable feat of concluding his chapter on the freedom of the press with remarks that are as anti-Kantian as it is possible to imagine.

In a recent book, Agnès Antoine has emphasized that, of all the remedies for democratic excess, religion is the most important, because it is the only one that really urges individuals to 'detach themselves from the visible reality'.[108] It is significant, therefore, that the civic morality lauded by Tocqueville finds an essential support in religious transcendence; this enables it to play its role to the full; it gives to this morality the content without which it risks lacking the totally transcendent dimension of the values to be affirmed. Like Stephen Holmes,[109] Antoine notes the extent to which Tocqueville differentiates himself from Constant and retains many more links with Rousseauist pre-romanticism – it, too, tinged with nostalgia and anti-modernism. One might also point to the nostalgia for the values of the *ancien régime* in Tocqueville's praise of the associative life and intermediary bodies. Certainly it also includes a reflection on truly modern political participation, with, in particular, an analysis of the notion of 'parties'. But Tocqueville also seeks for something which resembles the conception of 'community' and notably of 'corporation' in the *ancien régime* sense.[110]

The Tocquevillean approach clearly articulates the unease caused by the notion of 'public', but it goes further: it seriously questions the democratic project itself, and some aspects of his thinking reveal serious reservations. This is why, to the extent that I myself wish to locate the critique of the notion of public within this democratic project and take full account of the unease, but without falling into the anti-democratic temptation so well analysed by Michel Foucault, I believe it is necessary to remain cautious with regard to Tocqueville.

How to critique journalism while remaining attached to democracy?

How, then, should we proceed? How can we introduce the problem of the homogeneity of the public, the problem of this structural domination of 'the homogenous' at its heart, without permanently discrediting public democratic space? Because would this not be to attack the very basis of the hopes Kant placed in public space? And to wreck any project for a serious reflection on an 'ideal' journalism?

We need to try to define exactly what it is that is 'naive' in Kantism. It is not the idea that the public is a 'good' or an 'innocent' entity – an idea too simple to be Kantian. Nor is it the certainty that reform will triumph over the obstacles to 'publicity' – Kant was content, in itself no small thing, to claim that reform was *possible*. What is 'naive' is *this very idea that reform is possible*, that what stifles plurality, in public space, is not structural. Journalism *can* aspire to an ideal of respecting and stimulating a plurality of points of view – this makes sense; the labour of boundless curiosity it promotes is not a hollow duty but, like all Kantian obligations, a *possible* aspiration. It is here that we may admit to a reservation, and ask if this 'ideal gaze', which puts itself at the service of the plurality of points of view and breathes life into public space, is not perhaps a delusion, enabling us to forget that this space, if it is to be common, requires a structural limitation of diversity. The most unbridled curiosity is surely subject, despite its best intentions, to the homogeneity that is a constituent element of public space.

Finally, the 'naivety' denounced here relates back to the very peaceful and very serene conception of the 'common' that is implicit in the Kantian conception of public: this 'common' is constructed in plural interchange, and constantly reconstructed, through the challenges presented to it by new gazes, relayed by the 'ideal' journalism. But how can we be sure that this 'common' is not in fact a domination that stifles anything that differs from it and reproduces itself in the perpetuation of this suffocation?

To preserve a Kantian core we need to recognize that a degree of homogeneity is structural to every public, reflected by journalism, but also maintained by it, without necessarily preparing for or contributing to the position of contempt for public space. This is perfectly possible. The question 'what can journalism be?' can make sense even in a non-Kantian theoretical universe, where the plurality of the points of view exchanged in public space remains imperfect. The Kantian ideal of an infinitely curious gaze, enamoured of diversity, can be reinterpreted in the context of an approach more sensitive to the structural dominations which inevitably restrict this curiosity. But this ideal will mean we no longer search for a marvellous plurality of points of view, but for a reduction in homogeneity; which is less ambitious but probably more realistic.

What the ensuing discussion will seek, bit by bit, to 'complicate' is the Kantian articulation between the political trend to inject diversity and that to create something 'common'. In Kant there is, in a sense, no problem: the 'ideal' spectator, in politics as in aesthetics, is open to the diversity of things in order to contribute to the development of a correct judgement, that is, one that is *commonly* valid. The 'common' is thus endlessly redefined, enriched by the most curious gazes, and this in serene fashion. It is this serenity of the debate that becomes impossible for those who see the public space of points of view as a space affected by structural dominations. For them, the 'common' is inevitably more restricting; it impedes the curious search for diversity, it prohibits a perfect plurality of gazes. In this case, the peaceful Kantian common/plurality pair turns into a more fraught pair: domination/resistance. The problem is no longer that of giving life to a plurality that is assumed to be acquired and that allows a constant enrichment of the common; it is rather to preserve the possibility of conflict in an imperfectly plural space, where the 'common' always has within it an element of domination.

In other words, on the one hand, the desire for *plurality* is replaced by that for *conflict*, a desire both more modest and more combative: even to introduce a different point of view is a struggle. On the other, the aim of redefining the 'common' is not abandoned, but it can be attained only through a painful struggle, in conflict, and without it ever being possible to be sure that, in challenging one domination, one is not helping to create a new domination.

This change of universe with regard to Kantism thus entails major theoretical shifts. But it does not kill off the Kantian questions. It does not put an end to the problem of the 'good' spectator, or, in so doing, to that of the 'ideal' journalism. It does not lead to a desertion of the public space of gazes and opinions, in spite of its imperfectly plural character, revealed in contrast with Kantian enthusiasm. The main problem is now to know how the 'good' spectator can forge something 'common' on the basis of the least domination possible and of maximum respect for the conflictuality of points of view – in short, by doing as little as possible to 'crush' this conflictuality, even stimulating it, although the overriding concern is to unify and create a bond within the public. Conflict becomes a key element in this approach: how can the dynamic of the 'public' preserve, in spite of the demand to create a 'we', an important element of conflict and the permanent possibility of challenging the 'we'?

Essentially, this problem relates to the democratic difficulty itself. Is democracy not the very system that seeks to create a political community in which the 'common' crushes conflictuality, even ceases to be nourished by it? This approach is an essential axis in, for example, the work of Nicole Loraux on the Athenian city. Even if what the Greeks called *stasis* (division, conflict) was frequently masked by the official Athenian discourses on 'community', and has continued, according to Loraux, to be neglected by many specialists in the Greek world, the fact is that '*stasis* [was] congenital to Greek political existence' and the very essence of the democracy which Athens tried to create.[111]

At the same time, Loraux finds in Athens an original and repeated refusal to recognize this 'essence'. The ancient city, she argues, was characterized by a 'fundamental denial: the denial of conflict as the law of politics and life in the city. Anything is preferable to recognizing that in the city power rests in the hands of one group, even if this group constitutes a large numerical majority.'[112] And it is this refusal, unfortunately, that we Moderns have mainly remembered: 'It would be fruitful to consider the ways in which modern representations of the political have retained this logic. But we might also ask why there is such a consensus to make consensus the bond of politics. Or, in other words, what it is that makes the choice of consensus seem incontrovertible?'[113] These words are central to her thesis: what Loraux restores to the centre of Greek democracy, by returning conflict to its place, and by liberating the repressed of the Athenian city, is a sharper sense of domination. This is how she interprets the refusal: 'Anything is preferable to recognizing that in the city power rests in the hands of one group, even if this group constitutes a large numerical majority': the reality of Athenian power was a domination by some that was constantly denied.

For Nicole Loraux, to see democracy as the consensual, peaceful construction of the 'common', accepting a true plurality of points of view, is to fantasize it. The specificity of democracy, as compared with other systems, is simply to *give conflict a chance*; and so to expose the domination to its challenge. In which case, the only 'common' known to democracy is that which is forged in conflict: 'what separates also forms a strangely powerful bond', writes Loraux.[114] She pushes her theory of democratic conflict a long way, since she sees it as a paradoxical unifying principle: *stasis*, she says, is 'the cement of the community'.[115] There is no need, however, to go so far in the theorization of the virtues attributed to conflict; it is enough, to do justice to the specificity of democracy, to state that it welcomes conflict without disintegrating. Such a statement is content to grasp an enigma that is difficult to resolve. It even leads to this enigma being made into a sort of paradigm of democracy, an essence, which can be incarnated in a variety of ways, of which the Athenian way is only one.

It is in terms of 'enigma' – 'enigma of politics' – that C. Lefort and M. Gauchet defined the democratic system, in an article written in 1971.[116] Democracy, they claimed, marries conflict and unity; it achieves, in a way, an impossible alliance. But how? In fact in the way they refer to it, they suggest a certain 'resolution' of the democratic enigma. They write:

> The inaugural gesture on which the democratic system is based consists of recognising the legitimacy of conflict in society. Democracy, in other words, is necessarily contemporary with the age in which the class war became identifiable as such. But by giving conflict its expression at the level of the open competition for power, it provided it with a *symbolic* issue, which deflected the threat of disintegration which, if given free rein, would inevitably have hung over the community.[117]

They themselves underline the most important word here: democracy organizes a '*symbolic* issue' for the conflict which permeates it, which is why it does not disintegrate. This is not the place for a detailed discussion of the meaning of the word 'symbolic' for these two writers. Nevertheless, we may perceive that the fundamental issue is that of the possibility of *representing* conflict. This, clearly, is the key to the enigma.

The staging of conflict on the agora – *making it visible* – was a major characteristic of the Athenian city. With the appearance of modern states, it can reasonably be argued that the renaissance of democracy required the reinvention of politics as the subject of a collective spectacle, that is, as a stage visible from another stage: that where the people makes itself a public. This is what Kant did, in a break from a modern political philosophy which had long paid little attention to the figure of the spectator and even less to that of *the spectators*, that is, the people-public. We have noted this absence in Hobbes, in spite of his liking for theatrical metaphors (author/actor). Kant's novel valorization of the figure of the spectator in politics – though admittedly hinted at in Locke – is what led Hannah Arendt to say that Kant in many ways revived the Greek political heritage.[118] What is certain, in any case, is that the theatrical metaphor as a way of conceiving politics makes very much more sense in Kant than in Hobbes.

The democratic idea seems to require a collective site of observation, where points of view are exchanged, not directly, but in actions; where conflicts are *represented* and *acted out*. In general, Lefort and Gauchet believe that democratic institutions *act* social conflict, and in this way, far from resolving it, or abolishing it, they allow it to be seen and to proceed without causing the community to fragment.

Of modern democratic institutions, there is one that is particularly adapted to this need to act out, to represent and to make visible, one that can be specifically defined as an institution devoted to collective 'seeing': journalism. My hypothesis is that journalism could be the institution which would enable modern democracy to achieve its impossible marriage, its alliance of unity and conflict. It is now journalism that constitutes this space for collective 'seeing'.

Athens had made each individual (male and not a slave) both a fully committed political *actor* and a *spectator* of himself and of others. It had defined political action as a speech that happened in a space of 'spectacle', open to all, where it had to *demonstrate* its relevance. Modern politics, defined by the state/civil society separation, has broken the actor–spectator unity; by inventing the state, it has invented, to adopt Hobbesian terminology, the distinction between the *actor* and the *author*, and then, taking its time, it has also rediscovered, with Kant, the figure of the *spectator*. Ideally, according to the Kantian principle of publicity, each individual ought now and then to become a spectator, that is, take up his pen and write 'as a man of learning'; but it is clear that the function of observing the government and society has been gradually delegated to official spectators, that is, journalists. The press (and then the media in general) may enable each person to be a spectator, but it nevertheless orchestrates the collective 'seeing'; it is now down to it to see and to make everyone see. Thus modern politics has created three 'personages', this time distinct: the actor (the state), the author (the people) and the spectator (the journalist), who between them create new relationships.

There is no point bemoaning this. It is more useful to reflect on what these relationships ought to be if modernity is to re-enact, in its own fashion, the process that is constitutive of democracy, that is, a process of conflict that is endlessly played out but that does not lead to fragmentation. In other words, angry condemnation of journalism makes no sense, if not that of renouncing democracy; enthusiasm on principle makes no sense either, as it sacralizes more than it reflects on the role of these new 'pupils' of democracy, which is what journalists now are, in every sense of the word. This is how things are. Whether we like it or not, journalists have become the 'eyes' of the political community and also, as a result, something precious and fragile, to be 'protected', because it is they who breathe life into the space of gazes, that is, who can offer democracy the 'symbolic issue' which will enable it to achieve its enigmatic essence. We ought to be demanding when we define the implications of such a role, but we cannot deny that this role has devolved on them.

These spectators who are the journalists must assist the political community both to make conflictuality live within it and to create a common within it. It is because they open up a space for the gaze, for representation, that they may perhaps envisage carrying out these two contradictory acts at the same time. It is because they offer the people the possibility of being a *public*, in other words, because they establish another stage than that of real conflicts, a stage where one watches and where one debates while being, in spite of everything, *together* in doing so, that they can achieve this enigmatic alliance of conflict and integration.

This was intuitively understood by the press of the French Revolution, which never ceased to claim precisely this mix of generalized conflict and new unity which gripped the French people, a double trend which the press both sensed and at the same time helped to activate. It is clear, however, that the press could think things in this way only because it itself was a stage of *representations*, a stage on which conflict was transfigured, put into words, images and symbols. To be able to give rise to, while it is happening, and in its very disorder, the feeling of a 'we', conflict needs to *represent itself*, to act itself, to put itself on stage before a public and to offer itself to gazes. The Revolutionary press admirably understood that this role had devolved on it, and that it was crucial. It created the stage where the people could see themselves, and be a public; it made a new sort of conflictuality happen, one that did not lead to fragmentation, but, on the contrary, produced a new sort of unity (the unity of a people watching its own conflicts). The Revolution thus gave a real and original role to the spectator, or, to be more accurate, to the assembly of spectators, to the *public* – the only personage, ultimately, which had access to the enigmatic truth of this new community, democracy, conflictual and one at the same time, or, to adopt the terminology of Antoine de Baecque, the great Body made up of a multiplicity of bodies.[119]

The idea of public was born in enthusiasm, but it could spread and develop only in a more troubled context. How, if one rejects the Kantian myth of a marvellous plurality causing the common spontaneously to appear, can the public best realize, in itself, the marriage of unity and conflict? How can journalism help to activate these two trends – apparently contradictory but both essential to democracy? What sort of 'ideal journalism' does this assume? I have identified a first definition of 'ideal journalism' – to be more precise, a first 'ideal-critique' – on the basis of Kantism; it needs to be further refined. But how can I rework this ideal-critique, given that I have chosen to leave Kantism behind while retaining a Kantian core? What other non-Kantian theoretical universes can help to reformulate the ideal-critique of journalism?

I will first return to Kant and spell out the journalistic ideal suggested by this Kantian hymn to curiosity; this will be my first 'ideal-critique' (Chapter 3). I will then correct this ideal-critique, ridding it of its 'naivety' and introducing the problem of domination and of structural constraints; in other words, think in a more complex way the interaction between unity and conflict. I will discuss the theoretical universes, first of Marx (my second 'ideal-critique', Chapter 4), then of the sociology of publics, from Gabriel Tarde to the Chicago School, that is, Robert E. Park and Helen M. Hughes (my third 'ideal-critique', Chapter 5).

3

A first ideal-critique: the journalist-flâneur

If we confine ourselves to the Kantian universe, and to that enthusiastic hymn to curiosity, 'An answer to the question: "What is Enlightenment?"', precisely what ideal-critique for the journalist emerges? I need to start here, before I can proceed to correct and redevelop the ideal-critique that I will define.

So, what exactly does it mean to put journalism at the service of the plurality of opinions and gazes? How can we be more specific about this aim of an all-embracing curiosity, a total, bold liberation of the journalistic gaze?

1. Varying the gaze

From Kant to Baudelaire: the 'attitude of modernity'

Michel Foucault has shown, in his discussion of Kant's 'An answer to the question: "What is Enlightenment?"', that the principle of 'publicity' implies a recognition of 'actuality', broadly defined, as a subject worthy of observation and analysis, and also a hymn to curiosity. Far from a principled contempt for the activity of journalism, Foucault suggests that we should consider an 'ideal' journalism as a labour to vary the gaze, and as being permanently open to novelty and diversity. He goes on to suggest a similarity between this attitude on the part of the Kantian spectator and the attitude of the modern painter, as defined by Baudelaire: 'It seems to me', he wrote, 'that we may recognize [in Kant] a point of departure: the outline of what one might call the attitude of modernity . . . To characterize briefly this attitude of modernity, I shall take an almost indispensable example, namely, Baudelaire; for his consciousness of modernity is widely recognized as one of the most acute in the nineteenth century.'[1]

In his article of 1863, 'The painter of modern life', Baudelaire had distinguished the modern artist, for whom the model is Constantin Guys (referred to only by his initials, 'M. C. G.', or just 'M. G.'), from the traditional artist, by his ability to make himself master of the most anodyne of subjects, the least noble of his day. The modern artist is an alchemist, who turns mud into gold – to borrow an expression used by Baudelaire with regard to one of his works, *Les Fleurs du mal* ('*The Flowers of Evil*'). He makes something beautiful out of something ugly, something eternal out of banality and ephemerality. To define his attitude, Baudelaire coined the neologism 'modernity'; the 'attitude of modernity', he said, is 'to extract from fashion whatever element it may contain of poetry within history, to distil the eternal from the transitory',[2] and then, 'By modernity, I mean the ephemeral, the fugitive, the contingent, the half of art whose other half is the eternal and the immutable.'[3]

In this comparison of Kant and Baudelaire, we detect in Michel Foucault, as also in Hannah Arendt, the desire to understand the spectator in politics by analogy with the aesthetic figure of the spectator. When Kant said that it was necessary to put oneself in the position of the observer, which one did 'as a scholar', and share this gaze with others, he was not lauding a *scholarly* gaze. He was calling for one that was curious, full of 'taste', accepting no *a priori* ontology for classifying the essential and the inessential – a gaze which readily evokes, observes Foucault, the liberty of the modern artist.

That said, Foucault notes that it was still a rigorous and a demanding gaze; a gaze that laboured. This is why, in this discussion, Foucault is reluctant to recognize, behind the 'attitude of modernity', the figure of the – very Baudelairean – flâneur, which seemed to him insufficiently rigorous. 'The attitude of modernity', he wrote:

> does not treat the passing moment as sacred in order to try to maintain or perpetuate it. It certainly does not involve harvesting it as a fleeting or interesting curiosity. That would be what Baudelaire would call the posture of the flâneur. The flâneur, the idle, strolling spectator, is satisfied to keep his eyes open, to pay attention and to build up a storehouse of memories. In opposition to the flâneur, Baudelaire describes the man of modernity.

Therefore, he goes on, 'Let us make no mistake, Constantin Guys is not a flâneur; what makes him the modern painter par excellence in Baudelaire's eyes is that, just when the whole world is falling asleep, he begins to work, and he transfigures that world'.[4] Foucault was largely basing himself on one passage, in fact the only one, in Baudelaire's article of 1863 which suggests a difference between 'flânerie' and the 'attitude of modernity':

> And so away he [M. G.] goes, hurrying or searching. But searching for what? Be very sure that this man, such as I have depicted him – this solitary, gifted with an active imagination, ceaselessly journeying across *the great human desert* – has an aim loftier than that of a mere flâneur, an aim more general, something other than the fugitive pleasure of circumstance. He is looking for that quality which you must allow me to call '*modernity*'; for I know of no better word to express the idea I have in mind.[5]

We may note, in this passage, that Baudelaire endows his artist with an *active* imagination, which appears to relate to the idea of a will, of rigorous effort, the opposite of the relaxed attitude and passivity which characterize the flâneur. In his comments, Foucault is constantly emphasizing this deliberate dimension of the attitude of modernity, even asserting that 'the deliberate attitude of modernity is tied to an indispensable asceticism. To be modern is not to accept oneself as one is in the flux of the passing moments; it is to take oneself as an object of a complex and difficult elaboration: what Baudelaire, in the vocabulary of his day, calls *dandysme*.'[6]

One can understand the concern that led Foucault to write like this. It derived from his deep knowledge of Kantism, and in particular the Kantian aesthetic. For Kant, the politically 'correct' gaze, like the correct aesthetic gaze, was one that ceaselessly examined itself, that put itself to the test, that watched itself watching. It was this that gave it its rigour. This can be seen, in the Kantian aesthetic, in the relationship between 'genius' and 'taste'. For Kant, the man of taste had within himself his possible detractors, and he developed his judgement in contact with them (this was the 'enlarged mentality'). The artist who created, who invented by deploying 'genius', was, according to Kant, permanently testing himself in this way, as if, even before being a creator, he had to be a man of taste, a good critic of art; his inventiveness, or his 'genius', remained subject to his 'taste'. Thus, whether in art appreciation or art creation, Kant rejected the possibility of an easy, passive glance; even inspired by genius, this glance had to be part of the gaze of the man of taste, hence engage in that rigorous labour of putting oneself to the test which characterized 'taste'. This line of thought relates to a certain 'classicism' in Kant, obvious in paragraph 50 of the *Critique of the Power of Judgment*, where he clearly places 'genius', the power of invention, after 'taste':

> Taste, like the power of judgment in general, is the discipline (or corrective) of genius, clipping its wings and making it well behaved or polished;

> but at the same time it gives genius guidance as to where and how far it should extend itself if it is to remain purposive . . . Thus if anything must be sacrificed in the conflict of the two properties in one product, it must rather be on the side of genius.[7]

If we apply these aesthetic categories to the figure of the spectator in politics, we get this: it is not enough to be 'a genius', that is, to produce a new gaze – new, for example, in its subject matter, taken from a novel actuality – or to produce a pertinent gaze; a gaze gets its pertinence from its ability to stand up to public exposure, hence its ability to reveal 'taste' in politics. Thus Kant's gaze at the French Revolution may be 'new', but this novelty does not guarantee its correctness; it is, as has been said, the collective enthusiasm, the collective sharing of this new gaze, that gives it its pertinence.

It is true that this requirement of Kant that the inventor – of a work or of a gaze – should never be free from the constraints of taste, in short, Kant's classicism, suggests we should remain cautious with regard to the – hardly rigorous – figure of the flâneur. One can understand that this figure may lack, as Foucault observed, a certain 'asceticism'. The flâneur is inventive, certainly, that is, curious, but he is perhaps not sufficiently demanding with regard to his own visual 'creations' to fit the Kantian definition of the good spectator in politics. At least Foucault seems to think so, when, to justify his comparison between Kant and Baudelaire, he is quick to separate Baudelaire from this model of the flâneur, deemed to be too superficial, too passive, too given over to visual distraction.

Yet this position is difficult to accept in its entirety. Foucault was the first to read Kant other than through this prism of strict classicism. Even if taste, which is defined at the outset as the virtue of entering into the 'common' (the 'enlarged mentality'), comes first in relation to the genius which opens up an indeterminate breach, nevertheless the 'common', in the Kantian aesthetic, is not a concept, something objective and fixed; it is a common *sentiment*, which exists only if it is experienced – in every sense of the word 'experience', it seems to me. The same is true of Kant's political thinking, as Foucault so ably showed: the 'common' only has meaning if it is experienced as such. It must, therefore, be permanently challenged. 'Publicity' puts the 'common' permanently under fire; it prevents it from becoming fixed; it exposes it to a variety of gazes which guarantee that it is forever being renewed. This is why the essential political virtue to emerge from this short work of Kant is, as Foucault himself emphasized, curiosity. When Foucault praises an 'ascetic' vision of the attitude of modernity, he seems to be drawing back a little from his total defence of curiosity, where complete freedom, even fantasy, has little to do with asceticism. The end of this text is, in essence, very un-Foucauldian.

Above all, however, it is so un-Baudelairean! For one sentence, quoted by Foucault, in which Baudelaire differentiates flânerie, that very ordinary curiosity, from the attitude of modernity, how many others are there where he establishes a connection? Contrary to what Foucault says, Baudelaire anchors the attitude of modernity in the most ordinary curiosity, and he protects it, in reality, from any excessive voluntarism, *a fortiori* 'ascetic'. In fact Baudelaire accepts much more than Foucault in these few lines the double dimension of the gaze of the modern artist: his activity, his work, his rigour and his ability to transfigure *and* his nonchalance, his passivity, his childlike stupor and his unchecked flânerie. The figure of the dandy, furthermore, which relates back to an attitude of control and will, is not unreservedly celebrated in this article of 1863. Baudelaire is more 'complicated', dare I say, than Michel Foucault's reading of him; and he is ultimately faithful to that hymn to curiosity which the same Foucault liked to sing, faithful to Kant. In short, Foucault is right to draw comparisons between Kant and Baudelaire, but he could have gone further. The Kantian injunction permanently to invent the gaze at the present, which Foucault brings out so well in his discussion, does not seem to me to be seriously betrayed by the 'passive' dimension of Baudelairean flânerie. On the contrary, this element of passivity is also present in Kantian thinking about the gaze in politics, precisely because the analogy exists with the *aesthetic* gaze – because, in short, Kant thinks the position of the spectator in politics as the contemplation of a fully fledged *spectacle*, giving rise to sentiments and emotions that are not wholly under control. Kant invites the spectator to catch hold of actuality in an 'inspired' receptiveness, inventive by its very passivity, and *at the same time* Kant enjoins him to experience his gaze by exposing it in its turn to the gazes of everyone else; in other words, by making it part of the collective search for 'taste' in politics.

We need, therefore, to take to its conclusion the line of thought started by Foucault, and recognize that it is probably a person as complex as the Baudelairean flâneur, active and passive at the same time, that best realizes the model of the Kantian spectator, anchored in an aesthetic.

A gaze both active and passive

Contrary to what Foucault says, the attitude of modernity is far from exclusively active or deliberate in Baudelaire, and the modern artist is not, in consequence, so sharply distinguished from the flâneur.[8] It is 'curiosity', says Baudelaire, that is 'the mainspring of his genius', and it is undeniable that this curiosity has a passive dimension, an abandon, which Walter Benjamin would later call a tendency to 'intropathy' with everything that the gaze encounters.

The very expressions 'man of the world' or 'man of the crowd', which Baudelaire uses to characterize Constantin Guys, suppose a capacity for abandon: he mingles 'through the medium of thought, in the turmoil of thought that surrounds him', and his passion is '*to become one flesh with the crowd*'. He truly captures the world around, which he reflects. The modern artist resembles in this the child or the convalescent, two figures which, for Baudelaire, retained this sensitivity to the singular world, this 'genius for which no aspect of life has become *stale*'. The child – possessed of the 'genius of childhood', inventive – is closely associated with the theme of intoxication, which supposes a loss of control, of oneself and of one's gaze: 'The child sees everything in a state of newness; he is always *drunk*.' Thus the artist, far from inspecting the world with a keen gaze, abandons himself, steps out of himself. This is surely the prime meaning of the 'ecstasy' to which Baudelaire refers: 'It is by this deep and joyful curiosity that we may explain the fixed and animally ecstatic gaze of a child confronted with something *new*.'

And then, having evoked the modern artist in his guise of man of the world, man of the crowd, a child and a convalescent, Baudelaire unhesitatingly dares the characterization that causes Foucault, oddly, to recoil: he speaks of him as a 'perfect flâneur'. The expression supposes, once again, something like a capacity for abandon, a passivity; indeed it comes just after his reference to the passion of the artist to 'become one flesh with the crowd'. Baudelaire wrote: 'For the perfect flâneur, for the passionate spectator, it is an immense joy to set up house in the heart of the multitude, amid the ebb and flow of movement, in the midst of the fugitive and the infinite.' There is in this modern artist a real enjoyment of limitless variety: 'He delights in fine carriages and proud horses, the dazzling smartness of the grooms, the expertness of the footmen, the sinuous gait of the women, the beauty of the children, happy to be alive and nicely dressed – in a word, he delights in universal life.'

It is clear that the intensity of the gaze of this artist – Baudelaire speaks of his 'burning glance' – is not owed exclusively to an *activity*, generating its own strength; it is also because this eye *reflects* the surrounding world, because it is full of it, because it is enthralled, that it is intense. M. C. G. is a 'lover of universal life'; he 'enters into the crowd as though it were an immense reservoir of electrical energy', comparable to 'a mirror as vast as the crowd itself, or to a kaleidoscope gifted with consciousness, responding to each one of its movements and reproducing the multiplicity of life and the flickering grace of all the elements of life'. His gaze reflects the multiplicity which surrounds him and into which he loves to merge. It is to his childlike or animal receptivity, too, that the modern artist owes this uncommon gaze.

We need, therefore, to think the labour of extracting the eternal from the transitory, a labour Foucault likens to the Kantian 'critique', in the context of passivity, the childlike or animal receptivity that Baudelaire liked to describe. Of course, this receptivity supposes a certain activity *at the same time*; no sooner has Baudelaire described the gaze of M. G. as a sort of mirror reflecting the world than he refers to his 'eagle eye' – an expression which assumes an element of control, and even a certain desire to inspect and analyse in detail, without being totally overcome by the enjoyment of the spectacle:

> If a fashion or the cut of a garment has been slightly modified, if bows and curls have been supplanted by cockades, if *bavolets* have been enlarged and chignons have dropped a fraction towards the nape of the neck, if waists have been raised and skirts have become fuller, be very sure that his eagle eye will already have spotted it from however great a distance. A regiment passes, on its way, as it may be, to the ends of the earth, tossing into the air of the boulevards its trumpet-calls as winged and stirring as hope; and in an instant Monsieur G. will already have seen, examined and analysed the bearing and external aspect of that company.

What Baudelaire seems to want to show, in essence, is that the curious gaze of M. G. contains both things at the same time, a wholly passive receptivity and an 'active' desire to analyse. The expression 'passionate spectator' juxtaposes these two aspects, the word 'spectator' evoking the active labour of rigorous inspection, the 'passion' passive abandon. The richness of Baudelaire's text lies precisely in this *mix of passivity and activity*, of distraction and perception, of abandon and elaboration, which he shows in the 'attitude of modernity'. When you really think about it, this mix seems inherent to the very notion of 'gaze'. Each of the meanings has the characteristic of combining a passive and an active dimension, which makes a variety of attitudes possible, sometimes differentiated by the language – 'see' and 'look at', 'hear' and 'listen to'. The injunction to be 'active' never entirely nullifies the passive dimension of the meaning in question – far from it – and this explains the always slightly strange nature of expressions such as 'opens his eyes' – an injunction to become receptive, activity aiming at passivity itself.

It is obvious that Baudelaire rejected everything that might reduce the gaze of the modern artist to one or other of these two dimensions. In the article discussed here, he is less favourable to dandyism than

Foucault claims, precisely because he fears that the dandy is a figure too active and not sufficiently passive, not receptive enough, too blasé, and hence too distant from the childlike genius 'for which no aspect of life has become stale'.

> I might perhaps call him [M. C. G.] a dandy, and I should have several good reasons for that; for the word 'dandy' implies a quintessence of character and a subtle understanding of the entire moral mechanism of this world; with another part of his nature, however, the dandy aspires to insensitivity, and it is in this that Monsieur G. dominated as he is by an insatiable passion – for seeing and feeling – parts company decisively with dandyism. '*Amabem amare*,' said St Augustine. 'I am passionately in love with passion,' Monsieur G. might well echo. The dandy is blasé, or pretends to be so, for reasons of policy and caste. Monsieur G. has a horror of blasé people.

We see, once again, the use of the word 'passion', which refers, by definition, to the notion of passivity and is lacking in the dandy. This misunderstanding with regard to the dandy, more valorized in Foucault's reading of Baudelaire than in the text itself (at least this particular text), reveals very clearly the tenor of Foucault's reading: of the two aspects of the 'attitude of modernity', receptivity and selectivity, openness and criticism, passivity and activity, he plays down the former in favour of the latter. It is all the more unfortunate in that so many texts of Foucault lavish praise on curiosity in both its dimensions, ultimately forging a stronger bond, although not explicit, between the Kantian defence of the spectator open to plurality and the 'active-passive' flânerie of Baudelaire.

Flânerie as a journalistic ideal: its implications

Thus Baudelairean flânerie may help us to clarify the ideal-critique of journalism which I am attempting to develop on the basis of the Kantian principle of publicity. We need first, however, to be clear what this means: the only acceptable criticisms of 'real' journalism, in this context, are those which denounce it for insufficient or 'bad' flânerie. In other words, much of what is found exasperating in 'real' journalism, the flitting from one subject to another, the constantly shifting gaze, the 'zapping' or the 'flânerie', will no longer be invoked here. In short, the most talked-about failings of journalism are now assumed by its ideal.

This still leaves the field open for many criticisms of real journalism, in particular for those which denounce its systematic introduction of bias, which confine the gaze. However, for these critiques to remain true to the ideal I am defining here, they have to see these biases as faults due to an *insufficient flânerie*; the flânerie – the varying of the gaze, the protection and stimulation of the plurality of points of view – has to be implicit as a remedy for these biases. In short, there is no question here of *seeing flânerie itself as a bias*. Such a critique would belong to a different theoretical universe from the one in which I am operating; it would involve a more profound and more structural questioning of the position of the spectator in politics, hence of the public space in which points of view and gazes are exchanged. The only criticisms admissible here are those that denounce biases in this exchange, and the types of 'fixities' imposed by a journalism that is *insufficiently flâneur*.

We are far removed, therefore, from critiques of journalism as such, denounced as a superficial, inauthentic, 'zapping' etc. activity. This is only natural, given that I am deliberately locating myself in a theoretical universe viscerally attached to the principle of publicity, consequently welcoming towards the figure of the journalist, that person who directs his or her gaze at actuality and exposes this gaze to others on a public stage. I will not be reproaching journalists for being flâneurs here; in fact, I would wish them to be rather more so. Journalism, here, cures itself, by multiplying its sites of expression and by the desire to attain its ideal: an unbridled curiosity, a perfect flânerie.

This benevolence in principle towards the journalist-flâneur establishes a crucial divide within the various critiques of journalism. The most odious of them, those that contain, as Foucault observed, a deep hostility towards curiosity and a persistent fear of the principle of publicity, and, consequently, a latent anti-democratism, detest the figure of the flâneur. And what they denounce, in the person of the journalist, is not the 'insufficient' flâneur – the one who is bad at it, or who should be more of one – but the very fact that he is 'simply' a flâneur – superficial, incapable of an 'authentic' relationship with things, a disregarder of disciplinary and/or ontological frontiers. The figure of the flâneur is deeply subversive for those whose aim is to protect certain sacred places from the unrestricted gaze, and who are consequently horrified by the sort of journalist who pokes his or her nose into everything. By making this figure central to my discussion, I am very clearly differentiating myself from those critiques which attack the very principle of journalism. I aim to construct an ideal-critique that is firmly attached to the Kantian principle of publicity.

It is a source of some annoyance to find that these conceptually important distinctions are little respected by certain critical discourses on journalism. It is not unknown, for example, for them to cite, without realizing it, in support of an absolutely traditional denunciation of journalism as a superficial, inauthentic and intolerably 'flâneur' gaze, great lovers of flânerie, whose critique of journalism is necessarily more complex and less malicious. This confusion of genres is most common in the use sometimes made of Walter Benjamin. To interpret his criticisms of the popular press as a condemnation of journalism as a cult of superficiality, as 'inauthenticity' etc., is to forget that there is no more radical challenge to notions of 'depth' and 'authenticity' than in a thinker like Benjamin, and, conversely, that the figure of the flâneur was very dear to him. In other words, to make his critique of popular journalism – which certainly exists – serve a wholly 'traditional' condemnation of journalism as a regrettably inauthentic relationship to events could hardly be more anti-Benjaminian.[9] Benjamin was not Heidegger, disgusted by the everyday, seeking a process that would leave behind the 'inauthenticity' of the ordinary gaze and reveal the 'being' of things. On the contrary, the Benjaminian theme of the loss of 'aura' in the modern age contains a serious critique of the category of authenticity,[10] whether in art or in philosophy, and leads, consequently, in a delightfully subversive way, and one completely alien to the serious Heideggerean, to a blurring of the frontiers between the modern artist, the modern thinker and . . . the journalist.

This is so to such a point that Benjamin, though a critic of the journalism of his age, should probably also be understood as a critic of many of the 'traditional' critiques of journalism; of all those which, sure of the rock on which they stand, trot out an outdated and arrogant opposition between journalist and irreproachable philosophers and artists, deemed able to establish an 'authentic' relationship to the event. For Benjamin, there was not, or was no longer, a secure distance between a model of authenticity and the inauthentic popular press. The gaze of the modern artist, whose nature Benjamin tried to define, and which has many analogies with Baudelairean flânerie, is no longer protected by an indestructible wall (the privilege of 'authenticity', access to the 'aura') from its odious adversary, the journalist. It itself labours in a context of 'loss of aura'. In this sense, it is dangerously close to what it criticizes. Perhaps it simply defines the good flâneur – 'ideal' journalist? – by contrast with that bad or inadequate flâneur, that is, the 'real' journalist denounced; the distance, we see, is small.

Just as Benjamin is sometimes read in a way unsuited to the complexity of his arguments, a person like Karl Kraus, legendary for his merciless criticisms of the Viennese popular press in the first decades of the twentieth century, is frequently oversimplified. The vehemence of his criticism seems to justify ignoring the ambivalence inherent to his character. Yet it is this very ambivalence that gives his work its interest, its richness and its originality compared with the traditional postures of condemnation of journalistic inauthenticity. If he fascinated Benjamin, it was precisely because of what Benjamin called, in his essay on Kraus,[11] the 'demon' in him, referring to an ambiguous proximity on the part of this denouncer of the press to the object of his wrath. For Kraus, as for Benjamin, there was no possibility of flight into a clearly defined, protected space outside journalism. Kraus made visible a sort of condemnation of modernity to journalism, which made his battle against journalism much more complex than is often claimed. He is more like a touching Sisyphus, rolling his boulder up the mountain of journalism, than a proud thinker, confident he has reached the summit of the mountain and contemplating the journalist as a contemptible 'other'.

Thus Benjamin and Kraus, angered though they both were by 'real' journalism, nevertheless remained strangers to the traditional opposition between the journalist and those claiming 'authenticity', 'depth' or 'essence'. Benjamin and Kraus counteracted the smugness of those who claimed to speak on the basis of 'another stage' than that of journalism. They insisted on, they even theorized, the point that, in any case, there is not, there is no longer, another place. Thus they remained faithful to the principle of publicity. How, for example, can one not see the deep passion for public space that characterizes Kraus? Of course, such exasperation, in their gazes at journalism, encourages the idea that they were nevertheless a long way from Kantian enthusiasm. This may be so, but they ultimately convey the impression that it is by realizing the Kantian project, by taking to its logical conclusion his thinking on the 'ideal' spectator, and by precisely defining the person towards whom it leads, a flâneur, that it will be cured of its element of naivety. If one stands firm so far, if one accepts this so imperfect, so ambivalent and so exasperating person, one can then claim truly to have accepted the implications of the principle of publicity, without naivety and without cosiness; to be 'vaccinated' against the temptation to flee to another stage than that imperfect and frustrating stage where gazes and opinions are publicly exchanged. One is then a democrat *in spite of everything*. In essence, Benjamin and Kraus have already indicated what needs to be retained of Kantism, even if we follow him, further than they did, into the critique of democratic space and journalism: the concern not to break with it, *in spite of everything*. Flânerie is still the best we can do. We can denounce its inadequacies yet again – they were the first to do so; we can experience the exasperation that makes one want to break with it – they knew all about that sort of despair – but we will not break with it.

So it is with Benjamin and Kraus – and first with Benjamin, an acute commentator on Baudelaire – that I will try to clarify this ideal-critique of the journalist–flâneur. I will not gloss over the ambivalences and the frustrating, even exasperating, character of flânerie. This, it seems, is the price that has to be paid if we are to remain truly and lucidly faithful to the hymn Kant sang to the glory of the present, of public space and of curiosity.

2. An ambiguous and frustrating ideal

Rebellion and conformism: the ambiguity of the flâneur (Walter Benjamin)

When Walter Benjamin (1892–1940) discusses the figure of the flâneur, in his studies of Baudelaire of 1938–9, he presents him in all his ambivalence. There is no question of celebrating Baudelaire as a perfect model. He is an artistic model, but it is his very 'impurity' that makes any watertight barrier between the artist and the journalist impossible. In this sense, we are presented with an ideal that is both artistic and journalistic: the ideal of a spectator whose curiosity mingles activity and passivity, and whose gaze varies, in a permanent openness to all that is new. Like Baudelaire, Benjamin does not hesitate to expose all that can be criticized in this model, and all that is exasperating. Yes of course the flâneur can be regarded as a false lover of plurality! Yes of course his enjoyment of multiplicity can be suspected of merely repeating, by changing objects, an enjoyment of the same, that is, of an only too constant, 'homogeneous' and conformist gaze, in spite of seeming permanently to contest every norm. Benjamin never ceases to present us with a rebellious conformist, a curious man oscillating between true subversion and untroubling docility: flânerie can be the worst of things and the best of things; it is fundamentally ambivalent.

The flâneur is the eponymous subject of part two of Benjamin's *The Paris of the Second Empire in Baudelaire* (1938). In fact in part one, 'La Bohème', he had already laid down several markers for an approach to this personage. When the word 'flâneur' is first used, right at the end of part one, Benjamin signals the ambiguity: 'Baudelaire knew what the true situation of the man of letters was: he goes to the marketplace as a *flâneur*, supposedly to take a look at it, but in reality to find a buyer.'[12] Thus the flâneur appears from the outset as a dual personality, his behaviour that of a 'neutral' observer, but his intentions venal. This at once makes it possible to signal a break with a more traditional representation of the artist, that is, as he who lives only for beauty and despises the market. The flâneur participates in the capitalism he observes. He is implicated in the very subject of what constitutes his revolt.

The revolt of the modern artist against the society that surrounds him is not, therefore, 'pure'. More generally, this theme of the suspect and ambiguous revolt is constantly evoked in part one of the book. Baudelaire, Benjamin declares, could have taken as his own the statement of Flaubert: 'In all politics there is only one thing that I understand, revolt'; it is still necessary, however, to appreciate the deeply ambiguous nature of the Baudelairean revolt. It resembles the revolt that characterized 'Bohemia', which he drew on Marx to define: Bohemia is the milieu of professional conspirators and provocateurs, easily roused to indignation but of doubtful effectiveness as revolutionaries. The person of the ragpicker, one of the figures with whom the conspirator likes to identify, only deepened this ambiguity: 'A ragpicker cannot, of course be part of [Bohemia],' wrote Benjamin, 'but from the littérateur to the professional conspirator, everyone who belonged to [Bohemia] could recognize a bit of himself in the ragpicker. Each person was in a more or less obscure state of revolt against society and faced a more or less precarious future.'[13] The conspirator thus identified with the most perfect representative of the 'lumpenproletariat', who lived off the debris of the market system and was himself a sort of debris. Revolt was thus incarnated in the weakest person, the one most alienated from the system, which is what gave it its ambivalence. It is not far from the rebel to the docile alienated. The boundary is almost imperceptible.

A few pages later, still in part one, Benjamin compares a member of this Bohemia, a conspirator, Blanqui, to Satan.[14] But this particular Satan is less a figure of 'pure' evil than a figure of duplicity, ambiguity and impurity. 'Baudelaire was thoroughly familiar with this dual aspect of Satan. To him, Satan spoke not only for the upper crust but for the lower classes as well.'[15] In other words, he who dances to the tune of revolt also dances to the tune of the established order. Yet again, opposites meet.[16]

Likened to a variety of persons, such as the rag-and-bone man and the conspirator, who gradually define the figure of the flâneur, the Baudelairean artist is deeply ambiguous. It is clear that Baudelaire's break with the proponents of art for art's sake tends in the direction of this ambiguity in the art he now defends. Modern art condemned to be useful – this effectively implies that it produces no beauty that does not originate in actuality and that does not, in its own way, eventually return to it. Not only does the artist labour 'inside', and not safely aside, but what he produces remains caught up in the world he observes, his works being, for example, part of a market. The 'utility' of art gives a dimension of 'prostitution' even to the labour that seeks to be revolutionary – indeed revolutionary effectiveness even explicitly demands an element of prostitution: the work must be 'used'. Benjamin recalls here

Baudelaire's comment on Lamartine: 'a bit whorish, a bit prostituted'.[17] And Baudelaire, he recalls, compares himself, in 'The Venal Muse', to a whore: 'I who sell my thought and who want to be an author'.[18]

This venality corresponds explicitly, for Benjamin, to a *flirtation with the world of journalism*; modern writers are condemned to frequent this world of feuilletons that he describes at length. In fact what the modern writer has lost is his exteriority in relation to society, and hence his 'purity', which gives rise only to a little vain nostalgia – the 'puerile utopia of the school of *l'art pour l'art*', says Benjamin.[19] His home has become the boulevard,[20] his brother, the journalist, his reader, the man of curiosity, and his mirror, the harlot. The list of persons associated with the modern artist continues to grow.

This ends part one of *The Paris of the Second Empire*, which sets the scene for a deeper exploration of the ambivalence of flânerie. Flânerie is the attitude which, in a sense, synthesizes all the persons he has evoked. The ambivalence quickly emerges in part two, when Benjamin describes the relationship of the flâneur to the street. Flânerie as discovery of the street is an expression of freedom and a rejection of bourgeois conformism – a freedom that is threatened by the spread of Haussmannian urbanism, which spells danger for the alleyways. But this anti-bourgeois spirit of freedom is counterbalanced by a question: is there not, all the same, something bourgeois in the attitude of the flâneur? Benjamin writes: 'The street becomes a dwelling for the flâneur; he is as much at home among the façades of houses as a citizen is in his four walls.'[21] Doubts arise: perhaps the anti-bourgeois revolt conceals an only-too-bourgeois projection of the interior onto the exterior, which makes the street a familiar apartment, and not in any way the scene of a disturbing disorientation? Once again, the rebel may conceal a conformist. And once again, it is the attitude of the journalist that best illustrates this ambiguous flânerie.

This is because, says Benjamin, the feuilleton-writers have made the street their home. They scour the streets for types and physiologies, to be classified and ranked, just as one restores order to an apartment. They are flâneurs who reveal the most bourgeois aspects of flânerie. Benjamin's prose leaves no doubt as to the identification he intends between the flânerie of the modern artist and 'the device of the feuilleton'.[22] Far from being opposed to flânerie, as a bourgeois deviation from it, the feuilleton makes it possible to emphasize that flânerie itself is an ambiguous model; it, too, is tempted to list types and track individuals, to rank them, and so achieve a fantasy of control.

Ultimately, it is the attitude of the detective that shows through in the evocation of the flâneur and the journalist: 'In times of terror, when everyone is something of a conspirator, everybody will be in a situation where he has to play detective. Strolling gives him the best prospects of doing so.'[23] In the Baudelairean world, this figure of the detective connects with the heritage of Edgar Allan Poe, by whom Baudelaire was fascinated. And, as Benjamin emphasizes, the fantasy that permeates the imagination of Poe is that of the investigation, police or journalistic.[24]

But Baudelaire is not Edgar Allan Poe, it might be said, and in fact he liberated flânerie from the influences that had made it veer towards a fantasy of control and a wholly bourgeois mastery of the street. 'Baudelaire', says Benjamin, 'wrote no detective story because, given the structure of his instincts, it was impossible for him to identify with the detective.'[25] In fact Baudelairean flânerie had something within it that put an end to the desire to seize on types and track individuals in the crowd, and which may therefore have restored a more subversive tone. It seems to imply the impossibility of possessing what it touches. The flâneur of Baudelaire immediately loses what he grasps. Benjamin's discussion of the poem 'À une passante' ('To a passer-by') emphasizes this aspect of flânerie: no sooner has she been singled out from the crowd by the gaze of the poet than the passer-by merges back into it. Benjamin goes so far as to say that the crowd is the real subject of the poem.[26] Thus this sonnet illustrates the failure of the detective, because she who is seen is quickly lost. The poet photographs her, but loses the photograph. There is in Baudelaire, Benjamin seems to be saying, a pleasure in the uncontrolled, or a pleasure in loss, which follows the fleeting pleasure of the capture, and this seems to allow Baudelairean flânerie to escape the trap of classification and control which haunted the world of Poe.

It is true, furthermore, that the world of Poe, made up of person-types, who rob the crowd of its diversity, is actually a nightmare for Baudelaire. This nightmare is portrayed in one of his poems, 'Les Sept vieillards' ('The seven old men'), which Benjamin discussed in a lecture in May 1939. This poem, he argued, shows the world from the standpoint of the detective who establishes types, who ranks and classifies individuals; it is ultimately a world in which all individuals, like clowns, are moved by reflexes, without their own singularity or charm; above all, it is a world in which *flânerie has become impossible.*[27] Diversity is 'controlled', it is one, and predictable, but sterile for the gaze, and flânerie has disappeared. The search for types, classification and the institution of order are relegated to the status of harrowing nightmare, which is death to flânerie; this is tantamount to saying that the true Baudelairean flânerie, as long as it is not corrupted, is actually something quite different – even the very opposite. It thus also recovers something more subversive, even if this subversion seems fragile and precarious: how long will the flâneur resist the mass society, which tends to crush the picturesque diversity in which he moves? The Baudelairean flâneur is a person on the way out.

That said, removed from one pitfall – the gaze of the controller, the feuilleton-writer and the detective – and so shown as more rebellious and more subversive, Baudelairean flânerie comes up against another pitfall, the very opposite, which also in its way damps down subversion. If flânerie contains a pleasure in the uncontrolled, is there not a risk, if it goes too far in this direction, that it will be no more than a pure enjoyment of diversity, a passive and complacent fusion with its many subjects, a fascinated fragmentation of the gaze, a loss of self in what Benjamin calls 'intropathic intoxication'?[29] This is another way for the flâneur to lose his subversive power, not this time by revealing a desire to control and classify, but by abandoning himself totally to 'the intoxication of the commodity around which surges the stream of customers',[28] by practising an intoxicating 'empathy' with everything that is merchandise – for example with the prostitute. Like the prostitute, he yields to the rule of merchandise, he uses it, celebrates it. He does not rebel, he joins in; we should remember that, in 'Central Park', Benjamin says of prostitution that it 'opens up the possibility of a mythical communion with the masses'.[30] This makes flânerie suspect once again: what if the flâneur is no more than a victim of modernity, hypnotized by department stores, a stroller not so much rebellious as complacent, receptive but not critical, a passive passer-by?

One has the impression that the flâneur is constantly encountering pitfalls which belie the rebellious element he carries within him. Either his gaze is too controlling, or it is not controlling enough. The subversion he incarnates demands an almost untenable happy medium. And this happy medium relates to a powerful fantasy in the aesthetic world of Baudelaire, well described by Jean-Pierre Richard.[31] Richard shows that Baudelaire was always trapped between two opposing fears: on the one hand, fear of aridity and sterility; on the other, the opposite fear of an overabundant multiplicity, teeming like the vermin on decomposing bodies. This explains his predilection for translucent substances, such as *glass*, or for the ambiguity of *mist*, which let something show through, but not too much, so avoiding both the splenetic anxiety of opacity (the blocked horizon, 'a muddy black sky') and the terror of an equally sterile perfect transparency (the too clear well, the 'azure sky'). According to Richard, fruitfulness, for Baudelaire, implies a 'very human mixture of expansiveness and reticence';[32] which is why, as much as aridity and the 'fossilised', he fears overabundance, the expansion that submerges, the morbid fertility illustrated by the poem 'Une Charogne' ('A carcass'). In the same spirit as these observations of

Jean-Pierre Richard on the Baudelairean aesthetic, we may say, in terms of the comments of Benjamin, that the flâneur hesitates between two pitfalls: on the one hand, the hyperactive gaze of the controller, who controls more than he receives; on the other, the purely passive gaze which receives without control, to the point of submersion, infinite empathy with its subjects. These two pitfalls can also be defined as the figures, respectively, of the *detective* and the *badaud*.[33] In the light of Benjamin's remarks, these two possibilities define, it is clear, two failures, two temptations fatal to flânerie. Flânerie requires a carefully measured combination of control and abandon, of activity and passivity. The flâneur must be part detective and part onlooker, but never only one of these. He is all the more ambivalent in that his two constituent parts are actually his two worst enemies.

In part three of his *Paris of the Second Empire* Benjamin evokes other Baudelairean figures, the 'dispossessed', the apache, the ragpicker and the dandy, and it is at first sight not easy to say if they are quite different from the person of the flâneur or simply variants of him. At one point Benjamin declares that these are all 'so many roles' of this modern hero.[34] In any case each of these roles seems tinged with an ambivalence analogous to that concealed in the flâneur. As we have already seen in the case of the ragpicker, one is never sure towards which dimension of this mixture of rebel and victim, the active or the passive, he will ultimately incline. This is true also of the dandy. In 'The painter of modern life', as we have seen, Baudelaire 'drew' him towards the pole of control and activity – which prevents him from being sufficiently receptive or passive to be an ideal figure. But Baudelaire also emphasizes the dandy's closeness to the other pole, that of uncritical complacency, of fascinated and scarcely rebellious enjoyment, when he recalls the historical origins of the dandy: for the English, the dandy was the perfect merchant, who registered the tremors of the market and reacted without displaying his reactions.[35] A worshipper of the market, in short – although the fact that he does not reveal his emotions puts him closer, nevertheless, to a figure of control. There is ambiguity at every turn.

The flâneur is thus a singular model, caught between two poles, and it is sometimes difficult to see how he can escape. His gaze must be active-passive, without veering either into purely 'controlling' activity (the detective, the inquisitor of modernity) or, on the contrary, into purely passive abandon, complacent intropathic vertigo (the hypnotized consumer of the big stores, the *badaud*). It is not by chance that these two pitfalls epitomize precisely the faults most frequently held against journalism: voyeuristic investigation (the model of the detective), mesmerized entertainment (without critical distance, like the *badaud*). Benjamin never denied that in describing the person of the flâneur he was describing a sort of journalist. What is most interesting, however, is that the model described here is very similar to what betrays it; if the various characteristics are unevenly balanced, the flâneur veers towards enemy figures. The ambivalence of the model signals just how easy it is to fail in seeking to attain it. Or, put another way, based on such an equivocal and fragile model, the critique of 'real' journalism is very far indeed from a position of tranquil assurance.

From the worst to the best, a journalism of the shock

A critique of 'real' journalism is necessarily complex if the ideal itself is complex. Such a critique is undeniably present in Benjamin. His text of 1939, *Some Motifs in Baudelaire*, has a eulogy of Karl Kraus towards the end:

> If it were the intention of the press to have the reader assimilate the information it supplies as part of his own experience, it would not achieve its purpose. But its intention is just the opposite, and it is achieved: to isolate what happens from the realm in which it could affect the experience of the reader. The principles of journalistic information (freshness of news, brevity, comprehensibility, and, above all, lack of connection between the individual news items) contribute as much to this as does the make-up of the pages and the paper's style. (Karl Kraus never tired of demonstrating the great extent to which the linguistic usage of newspapers paralysed the imagination of their readers.)[36]

If one were to read these words out of context, without any knowledge of Benjamin, one might think that he is defending the idea of a true 'experience' of events and of the world, against the denaturing of experience in which the press participates. But this would be to misinterpret him. For Benjamin, this real 'experience', which he calls *Erfahrung*, is abolished by modernity itself. The journalistic gaze may 'contribute' to this loss of experience, but it only contributes. The fault, if there is one, lies elsewhere. Above all, it is inconceivable to demand a remedy – let us not even think of asking the press to be this remedy.

This idea, that the 'loss of experience' (*Erfahrung*) is the very characteristic of modernity, is developed in some detail in *Some Motifs in Baudelaire*, with reference, in particular, to the Freudian notions of trauma and defence: the gaze of the modern man is presented as a protected gaze, which is no longer touched by what it observes. Whereas in experience (*Erfahrung*), the gaze accedes to the 'aura' of things – it 'is returned'[37] – which makes it an authentic or 'auratic' experience, modernity is characterized by the development of a protection against reality. The relationship to things is now no longer the sensation of various *shocks*, which the consciousness seeks to absorb, and to incorporate into what Benjamin calls a 'lived experience' (*Erlebnis*). This 'lived experience' (*Erlebnis*) is very different in nature, therefore, from *Erfahrung*; it is the screen which separates the consciousness from the authentic or 'auratic' experience.[38]

There was no question, for Benjamin, of indulging in the nostalgic desire for a restoration of *Erfahrung*, in an age when all that remained was *Erlebnis*. At a general level, his thinking takes note of this loss. His ideas about modern art, for example, may encourage us to see it as a project to puncture the screens of *Erlebnis*, to acknowledge a true 'shock', but this was not in the hope of bringing about a new *Erfahrung*. Benjamin's interest in the aesthetic of shock, already visible in *The Work of Art in the Age of Mechanical Reproduction* (1936), where he salutes the 'shock effect' of the work of the Dadaists,[39] is most clearly revealed in his discussions of Baudelaire. In *Some Motifs in Baudelaire* Benjamin presents him as the very incarnation of this 'aesthetic of shock', citing, in particular, the Baudelairean motif of the duel with psychological defences, which ends in their defeat and victory for the shock, and produces in the artist a 'fright' which Benjamin compares to the fright of psychotics.[40] But we need to be clear that this shock, which blows holes in *Erlebnis*, is not in any way a rescue of the aura, or an authentic, that is auratic, experience (*Erfahrung*). For Benjamin, the shock was something very different from a rescue or a miraculous resurgence of *Erfahrung*. He presents it rather as the traumatic realization that there are no more rescues, that it is hopeless, that the loss of experience is irremediable.

This is the meaning of the passage Benjamin devotes to Proust and Baudelaire in *Some Motifs in Baudelaire*. He brings out a dimension common to both writers: the search for something 'immemorial' buried in the protective consciousness. In Proust, the involuntary memory makes possible an ultimate rescue of the aura, and in this sense Proust maintains a foothold in tradition.[41] But Baudelaire, unlike Proust, has no truck with the aura, and so incarnates the true modern artist, reduced to an aesthetic of shock. Admittedly, Baudelaire experienced rare auratic moments, such as the peaceful moments of *The Flowers of Evil*, the free and almost miraculous games of correspondences, explicitly compared by Benjamin to Proustian miracles of involuntary memory.[42] But they are rare; they are 'festive days', when there is an 'encounter with an earlier life',[43] precious access to a buried aura. Above all, they are clearly not the moments of shock evoked by Benjamin elsewhere; they are far more peaceful and far more gentle. The aesthetic of shock relates to something different. It is symptomatic of 'the incomparably more elemental and powerful counterforces that Baudelaire faced'.[44] In fact, no sooner has Benjamin evoked the correspondences than he insists that they are in no way essential: 'the *Fleurs du mal* would not be what it is if all it contained were this success. It is unique because it is able to wrest from the inefficacy of the same consolation, the breakdown of the same fervour, the failure of the same effort, poems that are in no way inferior to those in which the *correspondences* celebrate their triumphs.'[45] Commenting on a line in the poem 'Le Goût du néant' ('The taste for nothingness'), 'Adorable spring has lost its fragrance!', he emphasizes the extent to which the lost paradise is, in Baudelaire, definitively lost: 'The word *perdu* [lost] acknowledges the present state of collapse of that experience which he once shared.'[46] It is both the aura that is lost, and also the capacity to turn it into experience, that is, *Erfahrung*.

Thus art can no longer save anything; all it can do is express 'measureless desolation'.[47] If it touches a beauty, it is a splenetic beauty.[48] The aesthetic of shock no longer has anything to do with an auratic rescue. This explains Benjamin's emphasis on the Baudelairean motif of the loss of the *power to look*. Whereas the aura was defined as 'investing [something] with the ability to look at us in return' (attracting the gaze and responding to it),[49] 'what is involved here is that the expectation roused by the look of the human eye is not fulfilled. Baudelaire describes eyes of which one is inclined to say that they have lost their ability to look.'[50] The shock does not now produce a sudden emergence of the aura, but poetically and despairingly reveals loss and emptiness. The opposition between the shock and the auratic rescue is perhaps nowhere so clear in the work of Benjamin as in his brief piece, 'A propos de quelques motifs baudelairiens': 'The poet invokes eyes which have lost the power to look. Thus the price of beauty and of modern experience is determined: the destruction of the aura by the sensation of shock.'[51] This throws light in particular on the passages in which Benjamin emphasizes the notably un-visual character of Baudelaire's poetry.[52] In other words, the shock is the opposite of a sudden appearance of images and visions. He says that there is now nothing, no longer anything, to see, that the eyes no longer see, that *Erfahrung* and the aura are definitively lost.

This despair, this aesthetic of the shock which 'touches' nothing, is eminently applicable to the person of the flâneur, who is precisely a person thrown into modernity and its shocks, at best capable – this is his art, what makes him different – of recreating them without protection, without a screen, by undoing the labour of creating 'defences' performed by consciousness. The flâneur shows the failings of *Erlebnis*, 'lived experience', but he 'gains' no real experience, no *Erfahrung*. The Benjaminian understanding of flânerie as an experience of shock is particularly clear in 'A propos de quelques motifs baudelairiens', where he says: 'The eminently modern experience of shock would be the norm for Baudelairean poetry. In the image of the fencer, Baudelaire, who, as a flaneur, had been accustomed to rub shoulders with the crowds in the street, identifies with the man who parries shocks.'[53]

It is true that Benjamin is not always clear on these questions, sometimes reverting to a less despairing approach to the flâneur. At the end of *Some Motifs in Baudelaire*, for example, he seems to regard the flâneur rather as a person from before the triumph of despair, still deluded by an illusion from which Baudelaire has recovered.[54] That said, even if the flâneur is only on the edge of modern art, on the edge of despair and a keen sense of loss, on the edge of a true aesthetic of shock, this does not in any way alter Benjamin's fundamental theme: the flâneur is in no way a rescuer of the aura or of *Erfahrung*. At best he creates a little *Erlebnis*, 'lived experience'; but this does not give him any advantage in acceding to lost authentic experience.

It has to be recognized that this critique of the press as an institution which prevents *Erfahrung* is, to say the least, complicated, given that there is no longer any *Erfahrung* to restore – since the flâneur himself, figure of the modern artist, or figure standing just on the threshold of modern art, saves nothing of the sort. One can even take the 'complexity' a step further. When Benjamin writes of modern information as a series of 'shocks' administered to individuals, is he not describing something remarkably close to the modern aesthetic of the shock?

> Of the countless movements of switching, inserting, pressing, and the like, the 'snapping' of the photographer has had the greatest consequences. A touch of the finger now sufficed to fix an event for an unlimited period of time. The camera gave the moment a posthumous shock, as it were. Tactile experiences of this kind were joined by optic ones, such as are supplied by the advertising pages of a newspaper or the traffic of a big city. Moving through this traffic involves the individual in a series of shocks and collisions. At dangerous crossings, nervous impulses flow through him in rapid succession, like the energy from a battery.[55]

It has to be admitted that this description draws a strange comparison between journalism and modern forms of art, photography in particular, which are arts of shock. The traditional opposition between art and journalism is then thoroughly confused, as also is the critique of journalism; after all, what the press does seems not to be significantly different from what one may dream of doing, when one is an artist. The worst is close to the best.

From Benjamin's point of view, there is an obvious irony in seeing modern art as close to modern journalism, the latter using the most typical tools of the former (photography, film and now video). This irony is, of course, to be related to the fierce criticism of the notion of authenticity, for which Benjamin laid down markers, and which would later be followed up by Adorno. But it also has important implications for a consideration of journalism. Far from expecting that journalism will 'protect' its recipients, that it will soften the shocks, that it will create *Erlebnis*, 'lived experience', Benjamin seems primarily interested in what is generally held against it, that is, its tendency to operate through shocks. It needs to be emphasized that, no more than he dreams of the restoration of a lost *Erfahrung*, Benjamin has any liking for its modern substitute, *Erlebnis*, the 'lived experience' that constantly manufactures protections against shock. The press may deserve to be criticized, from a Benjaminian point of view, but this is because it participates in the creation of an illusory *Erlebnis*, not because it administers, or would (ideally) administer, *real shocks*. And on this point, Benjamin seems very faithful to Baudelaire himself. As Pierre Pachet observes in his study of 'Baudelairean politics', far from criticizing strong sensations, and the 'shocks' administered by the contemporary press in reporting the most sensational *faits divers*, Baudelaire felt a 'passionate interest' in the news provided by these papers and was amazed by the strange 'protection' of so many readers, who seemed scarcely to be affected by them.[56]

A text that is particularly revealing with regard to Benjamin's reservations about the notion of 'lived experience' is *The Storyteller* (1936). It is also a fundamental text for understanding his ideas on journalism. In it Benjamin revisits the theme of the loss of aura and the end of *Erfahrung* when he describes, in the age of modernity, the disappearance of the figure of the 'storyteller', that is, the person who tells stories aloud to others. 'The art of storytelling is coming to an end', he writes; that is, we now lack 'the ability to share experiences'. There is no longer a collective experience, a common knowledge, hence *Erfahrung*: 'Experience has fallen in value.'[57] Benjamin says that the two persons who have been substituted for the old figure of the storyteller are the novelist and the journalist. Both work in this context of loss of *Erfahrung*, creating a poor *Erlebnis*, wholly individualized, narrowed down to the individual. They are two complementary persons, and Benjamin spares neither of them. The novelist, 'in his isolation', is no more than a pale imitation of the old storyteller, and addresses a reader who is also isolated. There is an evident sadness in Benjamin's description of this phenomenon, 'the secular productive forces' which have 'gradually removed narrative from the realm of living speech' and confined it to literature.[58] The novel, he adds, 'gives evidence of the profound perplexity of the living'.[59] As for the journalist, he tries, vaguely, to give individuals the feeling that they live in a common world. The press gives them a collective knowledge, but it bears no relation to the collective experience (*Erfahrung*) created by the old narrator and his stories of the world: 'Every morning brings us news from across the globe, yet we are poor in noteworthy stories. This is because nowadays no event comes to us without already being shot through with explanations. In other words, by now almost nothing that happens benefits storytelling; almost everything benefits information.'[60]

We should not conclude, therefore, that Benjamin is praising the novelist *against* the journalist. He pairs the two of them in order to show their common failure to rediscover the figure of the storyteller, who had told stories for everyone and thus put a collective experience on display. It is clear that the 'shock' that Benjamin expects from the modern artist is a shock that reveals this common failure, refusing to accept, in particular, what literature has become: a world of in-turned individuals, a practice which cultivates the bourgeois value par excellence: *Erlebnis*. The press is not, therefore, as in more traditional approaches, the target that incarnates modern 'mediocrity'. The press is one symptom of the modern malaise, the novel is another. And once again Benjamin does not advocate in reaction any (impossible) restoration; he seeks the artist who will make people see this, see this modern emptiness.

One might ask if, of these two modern figures, the novelist and the journalist, it is not still the latter that the modern artist, flâneur and poet, most resembles. Because, in many respects, is it not the novelist who is more the 'champion' of *Erlebnis* than the journalist? The novel has made 'lived experience' its chosen terrain. And its readers are ready 'to devour it', Benjamin tells us, that is, are ready to make it completely their own;[61] it is made for this, intimate words which enter into a singular intimacy. There is more strangeness in the content of journalism, and greater distance. It is still, of course, something that we can devour, 'media-phages' as we all now are, constructing our own 'experience' with these anonymous destinies which fill the pages of our newspapers and our television screens. Admittedly, journalism is also an institution that protects us by providing us with its news, and it thus helps us to make it our own. But, in another sense, the notion of 'shock' is also highly journalistic; it is not by chance that Benjamin puts such emphasis on it; perhaps journalism too has this power to prevent the serene creation of a 'lived experience', of upsetting *Erlebnis.*

It goes without saying that the aesthetic of shock is a perspective that 'speaks' to the novelist also. The novel is not destined to remain in a state of modern complacency with regard to 'lived experience'; it, too, can make its rebellion against what it is reduced to, and aim to shock. But what is perhaps most unexpected is that this text of Benjamin also has much to say to *journalism*, for which the notion of 'shock' has real meaning – to the point where it is often for its very aptitude to 'shock' that it is criticized. Benjamin's thinking on the aesthetic of shock, a central characteristic of modern art and ultimate aim of the flâneur, may therefore be a very fruitful ideal-critique for thinking about journalistic practice today.

Further, this idea that journalistic curiosity, taken to its logical extreme – that is, pushed to the limits of the visible, in the permanent search for the new, improbable point of view – ultimately results in an almost aesthetic search for the 'shock' is an idea that is not unknown to certain reporters as they think about their own activities. It haunts in particular the journalism of war, confronted with an otherness that it has to try to see and to make seen, avoiding stereotypes, daring to open its eyes to everything. For Michael Herr, for example, who was sent to Vietnam for the magazine *Esquire* in 1967–8, the problem was how permanently to breach his own natural defences, those which, he said, were inherent to the gaze. How to de-protect the gaze, how to act to make this war truly enter the eyes of the journalist, piercing the screens? This obsession was central to his articles at the time and also later in his book *Dispatches*, published after an interval of some years.[62] Herr shows very clearly that it is the possibility of a real shock that he was seeking in Vietnam, fighting a constant battle with himself – against the 'lived experience' which prevents trauma.[63]

In my final chapter I will discuss this problem of journalistic writing more fully. What can it 'do', for example, to return to the public the shock par excellence, the confrontation with violence? Here I am still developing my first ideal-critique, all the implications and possibly inadequacies of which I need to explore. What my discussion of Benjamin has made it possible to observe is the extent to which the Baudelairean figure of the flâneur helps to think journalism in a critical, but also a concrete and constructive, manner, far from abandoning it to a more conventional contempt. The Benjaminian critique of the press is anchored in a thinking which refuses to imprison journalists in a traditional opposition between them and the artist or the philosopher, but which, on the contrary, sees them as clearly being close to these two other persons. I believe that this reflection on flânerie is a natural culmination of the Kantian thesis, as Michel Foucault already hinted when he suggested a proximity between Kant and Baudelaire. The flâneur fleshes out the Kantian ideal of an infinitely curious spectator. He does not prevent criticism of 'real' journalism, but on condition it refuses what I have called the simple desertion of democratic public space. This space in which gazes are exchanged and in which curiosity is given free rein is all there is; there are no longer other places to which one can flee, and from which one can serenely despise journalism and its impurity and 'inauthenticity'.

3. Fruitless exasperation: Karl Kraus as a modern Sisyphus

This accusation of 'inauthenticity' was clearly born of exasperation. Benjamin keeps demonstrating this, even in the portrait he paints of the flâneur, an ambivalent and frustrating figure. In fact exasperation is a possible variant of the critical position I am trying to define. It is fully justified by the principle of publicity; it is perhaps even a sign of its clear-sighted adoption. The ideal-critique of the journalist as flâneur can then accommodate a figure on the edge of despair, refusing, in spite of everything, to desert that place where journalism operates, the public space of points of view, even if it means considering this place as a condemnation. This extreme figure is incarnated, it seems to me, in Karl Kraus (1874–1936), Viennese intellectual and founder, in 1899, of the journal *Die Fackel* ('The Torch'), who continued, right up to his death, to denounce the press of his day with extraordinary vehemence. In fact, in spite of this vehemence, I believe that his critique of journalism, as in the case of Benjamin (who was fascinated by Kraus), was more complex and more tormented than a simple appeal for the restoration of 'authenticity'.

This may seem surprising. Did not Kraus present himself as the tireless critic of 'inauthenticity', most obviously manifested in what he called 'journalese'? The Krausian critique of journalism was part of a reflection on language, a reflection in which the content of a thought was closely linked to the way in which it was formulated. To Kraus, the laziness and the barbarisms of journalistic jargon were symptoms of a decadence of western thought. He believed that it was the prose of Heinrich Heine that was responsible for the hateful journalese, because Heine had imported into Germany a conception of language that was Latin, in particular French, that is, ornamental.[64] Kraus accused Heine, as Benjamin observed, of infecting the German language with the 'chronic sickness' of 'inauthenticity'.[65] Over and above his many campaigns against the corruption of the Viennese press, which made sheep's eyes at the powerful instead of serving the public, it was the very idea of publicity that Kraus found exasperating; it involved a loss of authenticity, it sullied the language. In his article on Heine, Kraus said: 'To write a feuilleton is to curl locks on a bald pate – but the public likes these curls better than a lion's mane of thought.'[66]

In which case, Kraus's fight against the 'journalese' of the press might well be understood, in Benjamin's phrase, as a 'liberation of language',[67] a salvaging of the authentic. There is no doubt that many Krausians believed, at the time, that this critique of journalism would lead to a world in which language was finally purified – we should perhaps say 'Adamic', a Benjaminian adjective for the original lost language – that is, to a restoration of authenticity. Concretely, Kraus put the journalists he criticized on display; he quoted from them at length in his journal *Die Fackel*, or he declaimed their words in public. He wanted in this way to expose the vanity of this language, and to reveal its emptiness and pretension. The acoustic test, in particular, was fundamental for Kraus, which followed from his conception of language as intended to be heard. The theatrical presentation of his enemies was another typically Krausian procedure. For example, in his monumental play *The Last Days of Mankind*, he ridiculed the journalist Alice Schalek, who had written reportages from the front in the 1914–18 war. Kraus denounced her voyeuristic search for 'real-life experience', and in particular her complacency in describing her own, shamefully comfortable, experiences with an officer who had entertained her lavishly.[68] It was above all the way in which she *spoke* that Kraus set out to demonstrate in this play. His theatre can be seen as another version of his usual 'acoustic tests'.[69]

It should be noted, further, that Kraus and Benjamin had in common the fact that, if they had still believed in the possibility of rescuing the aura, they would have located it more readily in the acoustic sphere than in the visual order. In Benjamin, the sense of sight seems to have been definitively lost, although he is admittedly often less peremptory with regard to the other senses. Indeed it even sometimes seems that, for Benjamin, the problem of modernity stemmed primarily from its having led to 'a markedly greater emphasis on the use of the eyes than on that of the ears'.[70] Hearing was certainly a special sense for the young Benjamin; and if an ultimate place of auratic rescue had had to survive, for him it would certainly have been language, in its sonorous dimension. This can be seen in his articles on language,[71] although it should be remembered that they are much earlier than his more pessimistic writings on Baudelaire, in which the theme of loss seems to dominate. In general, Benjamin's last texts on Baudelaire announce the end of the hopes placed in *all the senses*. Like the sense of hearing, the sense of smell was probably also special, the sense that had been central to the recovery of the past by the involuntary Proustian memory; this only adds a more despairing tone to the line of Baudelaire which, according to Benjamin, expressed the theme of irremediable loss: 'Spring, the Beloved, has lost its scent!' Even the senses that had perhaps represented the last hope had now faded.

This theme of loss seems also to have been very Krausian. The fierce anger of Kraus in the face of journalistic inauthenticity was clearly heavy with despair as to the possibility of salvaging any vestige of authenticity. As in Baudelaire and Benjamin, the Krausian paradise was a lost paradise. And in Kraus, too, this theme of loss gave his critique of journalism a fundamental ambivalence: what if journalism was merely a symptom of modernity as a whole being doomed to inauthenticity? But then, what value has a critique of inauthenticity that fails to attack something more solid? Perhaps the critique of journalism itself was in crisis?

This crisis is admirably described by Elias Canetti, who was a disciple of Kraus until breaking all ties with him. In a piece on Kraus, Canetti analysed the weapon of quotation and repetition which Kraus used, in his denunciation of journalese, so as to demonstrate what he, Canetti, called 'literality' – that way of repeating the words 'until they say something quite different from what they meant before'.[72] Canetti begins by describing the Krausian ideal in terms which might suggest a restored purity: 'His concern was this: a sentence that cannot be improved, that is without imperfection, without a flaw, without a misplaced comma – one sentence follows another, one fragment follows another, forming a Great Wall of China.'[73] But he then added (my emphasis): 'The assemblage is everywhere of high quality, one could at no point be mistaken as to its character, but *no one knows what it actually encloses. Behind this wall, there is no kingdom, it is itself the kingdom, all the life of the kingdom that may have existed has passed into it, into its manufacture.*'[74] We are here given a key: it is a sort of admission that perhaps the acoustic critique, the repetition of sentences, leads nowhere but to itself. Language may be a wall which does not delimit any kingdom. Kraus is then, as Canetti said, a 'unique solitary custodian',[75] who has no palace, no marvellous world, in the name of which to do what he does. For Canetti this discovery marked the end of his fascination with Kraus, because in this pious solitude Canetti detected, as well as despair, the danger of a dictatorial stance: 'I think that it is the feeling of unease born of the sight of this wall and the desolate aspect of the desert on either side of it that gradually aroused my anger against Kraus.'[76] In fact it is clear that the labour of destruction acquired an arbitrariness while becoming essentially total (there was nothing left to save).

Benjamin, too, enlarged upon this conclusion. But he is less sweeping in his judgement of Kraus. Canetti's text is one of rupture; that of Benjamin is much more under its spell. He examined all the consequences of this loss of the kingdom. In particular he explored the theme of Kraus's own vulnerability, which derived from this loss. The Krausian project of destruction implied a self-destruction, too, because what could resist this general suspicion of inauthenticity? Krausian exasperation was accompanied by a feeling of participating in the fault: the enemy was everywhere, including within oneself. Perhaps nothing could be saved, not even oneself. To say this using Kraus's own images, there was perhaps no child to be made with language, and certainly no man to give it this impossible child.[77]

We may note that Kraus himself talks of his 'satanic impulse',[78] which explains the comments of Benjamin, who gave the subtitle 'Demon' to the second part of his article on Kraus. Benjamin discusses at some length the theme of unmasking, so frequently employed by Kraus in dealing with his enemies – quoting from them so that their repeated words end up by unmasking them – but which should also, Benjamin believed, be understood as an unmasking of the self. The passage is a little obscure, admittedly, but it seems to me to indicate something important that distances Kraus from a classic, simple hatred of journalism: 'ambiguity, the demon, is manifest: self-expression and unmasking merge in it as self-unmasking'.[79] Benjamin goes on to emphasize the theme of the guilt of Kraus, who, in order to unmask, had to speak the same language as that which he unmasked – 'journalism', quoting from it over and over again. Benjamin put his finger on the fundamental ambiguity of the weapon of quotation, which necessarily consists of imitating the enemy: 'he imitates his subjects in order to insert the crowbar of his hate into the finest joints of their posture'.[80] And, a little later: 'His passion for imitating them is at the same time the expression of the struggle against this implication, and also the cause and the result of that ever-watchful guilty conscience in which alone the demon is in his element.'[81]

We rediscover here the ambivalence we detected in flânerie as ideal-critique, in particular the closeness between the ideal and what it denounces. When Kraus put journalists on show he gave them the same treatment as that they applied to the world; his critique was not without its analogies with the principle of *publicity*, the Kantian making of a spectacle. When Benjamin hailed Kraus as a great 'satirist' at the end of his essay, he used a word which linked him to the figure of the journalist, far from establishing the traditional contrast between the journalist and his critic.[82] Benjamin may not have explicitly called Kraus a 'flâneur', but he used in regard to him expressions such as 'subversive dilettantism',[83] and he compared him to Baudelaire: 'This is a poetic, martial angel with a foil in his hand, as only Baudelaire knew him.'[84] In other words, flâneur or not, a satirist at all events, Kraus perhaps exercised such fascination because, like Baudelaire, he remained ambivalent, so close to what he rebelled against, for ever deprived of 'paradise'.

Krausian exasperation was thus a dead end. There was no other stage than the exasperating stage of journalism. In his article with the title 'Apocalypse', the most triumphant formulas are in the imperfect tense – 'I wanted to de-journalize language'[85] – and what gradually emerges is the theme of powerlessness, or, once again, that of being doomed to journalism: 'It becomes increasingly painful to me to figure in the newsagents, in sad little bits, alongside humorous papers which appeal to the customer through their mishmash of pointless revelations.'[86] So there he was, still in this place and in no other, for ever! These lines let it be seen that he had no other weapon than that against which he fought – a magazine, *Die Fackel*. Further on, Kraus firmly rejects the perspective of a flight from reality: 'Just as it is stupid to want to join the flight from reality of the readers of the Viennese newspapers, it is honest to put them from time to time at the base of the wall.'[87] His desire to recreate was irrevocably chained to a need to destroy, to the point where one wonders if it could ever succeed. 'Neither to seek reality nor to flee it, but to recreate it, create it in the time where one destroys it', he said, with undeniable ambiguity.[88]

A piece by Kraus from before the First World War – which was in future to serve as backdrop to all the Krausian fantasies on the theme of catastrophe – expands, with delicious ambiguity, on the metaphor of loss.[89] In 'The beaver coat', Kraus tells the following story. He had mislaid (had stolen?) a fur-trimmed overcoat (his dress coat, his best coat, his status symbol?). He was left with nothing, not even a suspicion as to the thief. And suddenly, he who had been viewed with indifference, he who had been quietly invisible when he had been richly attired, became the main topic of conversation in Vienna and the recipient of every mark of sympathy. The newspapers were full of it, the cafés and the gossip hummed with it. Kraus read in the paper that a journalist had managed to speak to the thief – which conjured up the possibility of a degree of collusion between the thief and the press. This whole world of the inauthentic seemed to be deeply interested, in every sense of the word, by and in this theft or loss. Here he was, then, his tranquillity (his 'art for art's sake'?) gone. Kraus tried to defend himself, but in vain: 'I realised that there was no road back.' What 'situation' was he now to seek? What place was he to fight for, in the here and now? 'I decided to withdraw from private life. But I still had one hope left: By publishing a new book I might manage to make the Viennese forget me.' What are we supposed to make of this? Perhaps that there is a place, in the full glare of publicity, which resembles this lost tranquillity, this invisibility which leaves every one indifferent. It is a place of solitude, hence of critical distance, but it is still a public place, not a nostalgic retreat into the sweet, private isolation that is lost for ever.

At the same time, however, Kraus never ceased to say how fragile this new place was. He himself might be lost in his turn, and the rebel might finally be subsumed into what outraged him. In another article, also written in 1909, 'The world of posters',[90] he begins by saying once again which his place is. It is not among the great works of art or in the libraries and museums, it is in the street, listening to the 'noises of the day', everything that aroused a childlike curiosity, most of all, advertising posters. This is truly a text on flânerie, but with a significant dimension of revolt against the citadels of 'art for art's sake'. It ends, however, on a vertiginous note: the man who gazes at posters is engulfed by posters, he is himself lost. Suddenly,

> there is a cacophony of voices: I can no longer tell the products apart; a hundred grotesque faces appear and a hundred cries can be heard. I can make out only advice like 'Cook with gas!' 'Wash with air!' 'Bathe at home!' And since life is surging around my bed of pain in such profusion, offering all the conveniences and all the automatic joys that can be obtained at this point in time, a gun dealer notices I no longer know what is going on and drowns out the din with his own slogan: 'Be your own murderer!'

The flâneur, critic of the journalism of his day, perishes by means of the very subjects that interest him as a flâneur, subjects that are just as 'journalistic'. The flâneur, who wants to be the 'ideal' journalist, spends so much time in the company of the 'bad' journalist that he is swallowed up, destroying himself. The frightening ambiguity of the Krausian position is clear. It was a futile anger, a despair which lacked even the advantage of preserving the break with what had been its cause.

It was a despair which never lifted. Kraus could not even present himself as tragic victim of an execrated and deserted scene – 'publicity'. There is nothing in Kraus to evoke the position of the accursed poet or the misunderstood philosopher, labouring on another stage, that of eternity, far from the cruelty of reality and 'publicity'. That was all too traditional and conventional for Kraus, as it was for Benjamin. Sadly, there was no other stage. Sadly, journalism did not offer the option of its calm repudiation. The victim so resembles his executioner that he is forced permanently to fight on the same ground, so as to assert his difference. This constant battle sharply differentiates the attitude of Kraus from, for example, the despair of Spengler, as Jacques Bouveresse has shown. In an article comparing these two thinkers, Bouveresse emphasizes the refusal of Kraus to accept the inevitable. 'According to Spengler,' he writes:

> European humanity had to want what was, in any case, going to happen to it, or want nothing at all. Faced with the threat of decline and final

> catastrophe, the attitude of Kraus was clearly at the opposite pole from the Stoic, or pseudo-Stoic, pathos and so-called 'wisdom' which accepted the inevitable. His point of view was diametrically opposed to the flight into the inhuman advocated and practised by Spengler. It was, as ever, that of indignation and rebellion, that is, that of victims already resigned and virtually doomed.[91]

Kraus never stopped fighting, though well aware of the futility of his fight. This probably makes him an absurd rather than a tragic figure; there is something of a Sisyphus about him.

In any case, it seems to me that this complexity hardly justifies the identification with Kraus made, at times quite unscrupulously, by Bourdieu in his intervention at the colloquium 'L'Actualité de Karl Kraus' in 1999.[92] Bourdieu refers to the 'common features' shared by his review *Actes de la Recherche en sciences sociales* and *Die Fackel*: 'by the fact of pasting a document, a photo or an extract from an article into an analytical text, one completely changes the status both of the text and the document; what was the subject of a rather absent-minded reading can suddenly take on an astonishing, even scandalous appearance.' Bourdieu seems to be comparing the methods of Kraus to his own sociological labour of the 'objectification' of the words of journalists, emphasizing in passing that he arouses their hatred in the same way as the prestigious Viennese intellectual. Would Pierre Bourdieu be the Karl Kraus of today?

In fact Bourdieu is aware he cannot push this identification too far. Indeed he establishes a distance between himself and Kraus when he emphasizes that the Krausian critique of journalism remains highly 'journalistic' in its method, because it consists of employing against journalism journalism's own tools: 'quotation and juxtaposition have the effect of turning against the journalists a practice they engage in on a daily basis'. Bourdieu also acknowledges the individual, and hence extremely disturbing, nature of Kraus's attacks. For Bourdieu, this, too, is a journalistic method, which he rejects. He believes that personal attacks are a diversion at the expense of what is essential, that is, grasping the structural causes which explain the ills of journalism. So, though sympathetic to Krausian irritation and revolt, Bourdieu still notes the difference between them and his own attitude: 'The fact that I recognize K. Kraus is probably linked to an affinity of temperament . . . but the weakness of K. Kraus – and of every intemperate critic – is that he does not have a good grasp of structures; he sees their effects, he puts his finger on them, but without, for the most part, understanding the principle behind them.' The distinction is made even clearer a few lines later, when Bourdieu establishes a difference between a 'critical' attitude (that of Kraus) and an 'informed' attitude (his own).

Did Bourdieu write about Kraus with the intention both of paying him tribute and of asserting that, when all is said and done, he, Bourdieu, was not Kraus? This seems to be the case. Nevertheless, even if the praise of Kraus is restricted to an 'affinity of temperament', and not to an affinity of method, the conclusions Bourdieu draws are still not, in the end, true to Kraus. Bourdieu seems to envisage a hierarchy of critiques of journalism. There is a need, he effectively says, in the arena of journalism, for Krauses who fight and denounce; but what ought to anchor their critique, and inform it, is an understanding of the structural causes, which only sociology can provide. So Krausian fighters ought, in a sense, to fight under the aegis of the sociologist; they should be simply the sociologist's strong right arm. Bourdieu is not opposed to 'a veritable deontology of action (or of combat) in and by which journalists would denounce in Krausian fashion, as journalists, the journalists who are destroying the profession of journalist'. But the true battle takes place on another stage, that of sociological analysis: there is a superior and non-journalistic point of view, of another 'nature' than that of journalism, which explains everything. There is a kingdom, that of the sociologists and the sociologists' truths.

In short, Krauses are needed, but guided by Bourdieu. And there's the rub. Because what sort of Kraus is this, who will fight and who will criticize under the guidance of someone sure of himself, outside the arena, master of a kingdom sealed off from despised public space – is he a sociologist as Bourdieu intends? Did Kraus, in his struggle, have an assured direction and a certain paradise which determined his fight? No, he did not. Bourdieu's reading completely misses the complexity of the personality of Kraus, who fought, certainly, but without aspiring either to authenticity or to truth, without a clear perspective, but nevertheless without abandoning the place. What has become of the Krausian anguish at resembling what he criticized, the 'satanic impulse' inherent to a critique which has no kingdom to build? Could there be, lastly, a clearer admission that the figure of Karl Kraus, in spite of the 'affinity of temperament' it awakes in him, remains even so wholly alien to Pierre Bourdieu?

The refusal of Kraus to break with the place of exasperation prevents him, it seems to me, from being taken over by the more structural critics of public space who seek 'another stage'. Kraus remains, in a way, faithful to the Kantian principle of publicity *in spite of everything*. In spite of his exasperation, and his feeling of entering imperfect, 'inauthentic' terrains, he remained a journalist, he revealed himself in public, he made 'publicity' his only place. We may believe, as a result, that he continued to search for an 'ideal' journalism, infinitely curious, enamoured of variety, in fact a 'flâneur' journalism. Simply, he surrounds the figure of the flâneur with a permanent anger and dissatisfaction; he draws him towards the battle, he makes him a fighting confrontational figure. This dimension is not entirely absent from the Baudelairean figure of the flâneur, as we have seen, but it is radicalized by the great Krausian Sisyphus. One senses that in Kraus plurality is never achieved, that he is going to have a hard battle, and even that it will always be a prospect more than a reality. Kraus is forever on the point of giving up, without giving up.

Essentially, Kraus makes it possible to transform the Kantian project of plurality in public space into an issue of resistance, of fighting against dominations. Kant never thinks the 'common' norm, the one which the public establishes by its plural exchanges, as a potential 'contraction', as a future threat to plurality itself, in short, as a possible domination. In the Benjaminian, and also Krausian, figure of the flâneur, there is, in contrast, unease. The flâneur defends tooth and nail a threatened diversity; he battles against a potentially violent 'common'; he 'saves' forgotten points of view;[93] he defies the established norms; he makes curiosity a permanent battle. The words of Miguel Abensour, in an article devoted to Benjamin and Adorno, 'Le Choix du petit', help us to appreciate the implications of such an attitude: he describes

> a posture which is formed inside a polemical choice, an insurrection of the will, a refusal come from the body, from frayed nerves which oppose being conscripted; a posture also in the sense of a situation, a position alongside the detail, the miniscule, what is taken to be derisory, where there probably enters a moment of fantasy, but which cannot be reduced to this. A conversion, a refinement of the gaze which demands that credit is given to qualities previously seen as secondary; in short, an attempt at another experience of the world.[94]

After all, there is nothing to stop one from pulling Kantism in the direction of this restless and combative attitude. This might be to lose democratic enthusiasm, but it would retain, nevertheless, the attachment to democracy. It would be a position on the extreme edge that was defined by Kraus.

Perhaps the ideal of the journalist-flâneur should be pulled even more explicitly towards an ideal of the conflictual journalist. It is in this direction that it leads, seeming to build a bridge with ideas of domination and resistance. Concretely, to serve plurality is above all to fight to defend those gazes crushed by the dominant gaze. It is to reintroduce conflict with regard to the dominant point of view. It is to resist. Is it not possible, therefore, to retain a 'Kantian core', that is, the attachment, come what may, to the principle of publicity, but take on board a non-Kantian thought, which detects structural dominations in democratic public space and seeks ways of resisting them? To build on Kant, in short, by increasingly less 'naive' thought on the subject of plurality, disposed to rework the Kantian ideal to serve plurality as above all a need to confront this 'homogeneity' which tends increasingly to prevail?

Perhaps we need to build this bridge between, on the one hand, the Kantian attachment to curiosity and the liberation of the gaze and, on the other, certain thinkers on domination. The condition being that they *do not contemplate the renunciation of public space* – which, sadly, is often the case. Despairing, yes; in flight, no. Perhaps against all expectations, Marx escapes this temptation to desert. He offers a highly stimulating model for thinking about the methods of resistance, within public space, to the phenomena of domination that he calls 'ideology'. Marx will therefore be the next stage in our journey, as I develop the first ideal-critique of the journalist-flâneur into a second ideal-critique, that of the conflictual journalist.

4

A second ideal-critique: the conflictual journalist

At first sight, Marx's thinking seems to cast the whole idea of public space into total disrepute: what can be hoped for from a space wholly in the grip of ideology? Addicted to 'seeing', the public is, in reality, according to Marx, afflicted by a structural blindness, because this 'seeing' is subject to structures which reflect the material domination of the moment, and hence confirm it. Ideology serves to smooth over the differences, the gulf and the struggle between dominant and dominated. It allows circulation within a common space, but it is a 'common' that does not accept any real conflictuality. It prevents any point of view that is truly challenging to the current domination in society from being made to emerge, or being made visible. Ideology functions as a 'mask'; it 'euphemizes' in a way that is necessary to the existence of a common space of 'seeing'.

At the same time, certain commentators have shown how this structural character of ideology, according to Marx and Engels, resists facile attacks or simple contempt. Ideology is also what *constitutes*, what makes possible, the public space of exchanges. It is probable that no public space is possible without it – at least as things are, that is, as long as society remains riven by deep-rooted conflicts and a class struggle. This aspect is brought out in particular by Paul Ricoeur in his *Lectures on Ideology and Utopia*: 'The very extension of the concept of ideology acts as a progressive legitimation and justification of the concept itself.'[1]

The real problem is to know *what is to be done* with this structural homogeneity. It might be said that this concept of ideology makes possible two attitudes, both of which are obstacles to a fruitful reflection on journalism. The first is that of contempt and flight to another stage – that of social conflicts, of struggles *lived* since they cannot be *seen* in public space. This is perhaps also the position of the scholar who flees the blind gaze that operates in public space in order to seek to touch the materiality of the social by labouring elsewhere, in the isolation of a study. With all due respect to certain Marxisms, I do not believe that Marx authorizes us to think a flight of this dual nature. Neither the blind and mute social struggle, cut off from any collective search for visibility, nor the scholarly analysis, cut off from any collective gaze, is a definitive solution in his work, though they may have proved fleeting temptations. The second attitude is that of resignation, pure and simple. This means not deserting the public exchange of gazes, but expecting nothing from it, even, at a pinch, surrendering to that almost 'positive' dimension of the concept of ideology, that is, seeing it as a factor constitutive of public space. In this case too, however, there is ultimately little more to be said: journalism is perceived as a labour of integration, of fabrication of the 'common', of repetition of a domination, without room for manoeuvre, that is, without its being possible to make a particular demand of it, an 'ideal-critique'.

It seems to me that it is because Marx avoids either of these two attitudes that he makes an ideal-critique of journalism possible. This is a claim I need to justify in some detail. It is given immediate support by a number of factors. First is the fact that, throughout his life, Marx continued to write for the newspapers, even after he had developed the concept of ideology, in 1844–5, that is, after he had lost the journalistic – Kantian? – enthusiasms of his youth. In particular, he wrote for the *New York Daily Tribune* from 1851 to 1862, providing well-informed analyses of topics such as the opinion of the British elites on the subject of the Civil War. For someone supposed to despise the public exchange of points of view, he spent a very long time going over the press with a fine-tooth comb and dissecting the opposing arguments in the public debate! Second, as numerous specialists in Marx have demonstrated, his thinking implies a dynamic rather than a fixed conception of ideological domination. The space of ideas and gazes may always be behindhand in relation to the material stage – that of relations of production or 'infrastructure', true motor of history – but it still moves and it shows signs of an infrastructural change in progress; perhaps even those most immediately visible, since it is on a stage exposed to gazes that they appear. This makes it an interesting space to study. One sign of this is the research field born in the 1960s, initially Marxist in inspiration, known as Cultural Studies, devoted to studying the representations or 'cultures' of the working class. Two of its founding fathers, Edward Thompson and Raymond Williams, came from within the Marxist sphere of influence; this was not so in the case of a third great figure in Cultural Studies, Richard Hoggart, but his *The Uses of Literacy*, published in 1957, prompted an important debate within

Marxism. Cultural Studies tried to understand how, in the representations of the different classes, and in particular of the more economically dominated, mechanisms of resistance to ideology emerged. Far from thinking that these 'resistant' cultures defined a closed world, cut off from the public space in which ideology ruled, these works constantly demonstrated that, on the contrary, they were constructed on the basis of the dominant representations, especially those of the media. Since the 1980s, in particular, Cultural Studies has given rise to major works on the problem of the reception of media messages, suggesting that resistance developed, in a sense, on the same ground as ideology, initially feeding on it.

There are good reasons, therefore, for thinking that the Marxian theory of ideology did not definitively discredit the space of representations, but rather that it encourages us to look for phenomena of resistance within that space. As suggested in reference to Cultural Studies, this interest in the space of representations has so far led mostly to work on the *reception* of media content. We should also ask whether Marx has anything to tell us about the *production* of journalism, about ways of practising it. In other words, how can journalists, although they labour on the stage of ideology, and aspire to remain visible on that stage, introduce a little 'play' – like the 'play' of a door on its hinges – in relation to ideology? How can resistance operate in the gaze of the journalist?

It is clear that this interrogation is significantly different from the Kantian or Baudelairean demand to produce the most curious gaze possible. There is no question here of celebrating a journalism in the service of a true plurality, since we no longer really believe in this plurality, or at least not in the same way. In the Marxian theoretical universe, resistance introduces, at best, a little play with regard to the ideological domination. It emerges against a backdrop of a homogeneity that is structural to public space, perhaps even to some extent participates in it – because the break, according to Marx, cannot come about through an event on the stage of representations alone. It must come from elsewhere. It is to a different ideal-critique of journalism from that inspired by Kant that Marxism leads us here. Nevertheless, this new ideal-critique, which I need to describe in more detail, keeps something of its predecessor. It improves and corrects it, rather than radically rejecting it (as, for example, did Le Bon). It keeps in common with it a real respect for this public space in spite of its imperfections, which are now admitted. It reinterprets the Kantian aspiration for a journalism in the service of plurality by formulating the desire for a journalism of resistance, which would open a breach in the ideology, while operating within it. In short, it rejects the concept of 'plurality' which underlies the Kantian ideal-critique, preferring the concepts of 'domination' and 'resistance', but it does not abandon the desire to think about an ideal-critique of journalism; nor does it abandon the idea that this practice retains meaning and importance even in a public space that is admittedly imperfect.

What is interesting, in this return to Marx, is thus a trend that is by no means common in the history of ideas. With his concept of ideology, Marx produced one of the most virulent critiques of democratic public space, and yet there is in Marx no simple desertion of a space that is so vulnerable to criticism. He does not veer into a hatred of journalism, that hatred which, according to Foucault, serves as a rallying point for the enemies of the Kantian principle of publicity. The relationship of Marx to journalism is more complex, more troubled and most of all richer than that of outright hatred. It is this complexity that I will explore in this chapter.

When Marx belonged to the movement known as the Young Hegelians of the Left, in 1842–3, he became deeply involved in the practice of journalism; his battle against censorship even had overtly Kantian overtones. The intellectual crisis of 1843, which led Marx into a radical questioning of public space, should be understood against the background of this enthusiasm of his youth. The question for us is, what conclusions did Marx draw from this crisis? Journalism seems to have remained important to him, even once the concept of ideology was in place. One cannot but be surprised to find, as emphasized by Maximilien Rubel, that Marx, at a time when his theoretical itinerary suggests that the press had become no more for him than an ideology of despair, acted in a way which shows that he had renounced none of his youthful writings on the political importance of the press. 'In 1851', writes Rubel, 'when he had for some years been deeply involved in the workers' movement, Marx published a collection of his writings including the essay on Prussian censorship that had appeared in the *Anekdota*, and part of the critique of the debates of the Prussian Diet on the press, that is, two liberal manifestos dating from 1842.'[2] It seems that, for the mature Marx, criticism of the press, favoured vehicle of ideology, did not mean reneging on his earlier commitment on behalf of press freedom; nor did it prevent him from continuing to expose himself to and in the press, that is, from confronting ideology on its own ground. Concretely, however, how did Marx envisage the practice of journalism? And how did he himself practise it? To answer these questions I need to retrace the main stages in his relationship with journalism.

1. The journalism of the young Karl Marx (1842–3)

Kantian motifs

After his doctoral thesis of 1841, Marx, who had abandoned all hope of a university career, threw himself into journalism. He joined the editorial team of the *Rheinische Zeitung*, becoming its editor in October 1842. There he fought a fierce battle, with his pen, against Prussian censorship. Until the middle of 1843, when the paper was eventually banned, he wrote on many subjects, including the political role of the press.

These articles of his youth are full of Kantian motifs. While supporters of censorship defended it by the fallacious need for a search for a truth that was 'serious and modest', Marx accused it of being, on the contrary, a 'means of guarding against the truth'.[3] In his comments on the Sixth Rhine Province Assembly, he set up a wholly Kantian opposition between imposed external constraints (censorship), which produced only sterile servitude, and the sole constraint that was valid, the one which freedom rationally imposed on itself: a sort of internal censorship which required, as a preliminary, total freedom. 'The essence of the free press', he wrote:

> is the characterful, rational, moral essence of freedom. The character of the censored press is the characterless monster of unfreedom; it is a civilised monster, a perfumed abortion. Or does it still need to be proved that freedom of the press is in accord with the essence of the press, whereas censorship contradicts it? Is it not self-evident that external barriers to a spiritual life are not part of the inner nature of this life, that they deny this life and do not affirm it?[4]

He went on, using a very Kantian vocabulary: 'The true censorship, based on the very essence of freedom of the press, is *criticism*. This is the tribunal which freedom of the press gives rise to of itself.'[5]

These themes culminate in the metaphor of 'the eye of a people's soul', or that of the 'mirror', which give a cathartic connotation to this defence of the free press:

> The free press is the ubiquitous vigilant eye of a people's soul, the embodiment of a people's faith in itself . . . It is a people's frank confession to itself, and the redeeming power of confession is well known. It is the spiritual mirror in which a people can see itself, and self-examination is the first condition of wisdom . . . It is the ideal world which always wells up out of the real world and flows back into it with ever greater spiritual riches and renews its soul.[6]

We rediscover here the Kantian motif of the dual personality of the actor-spectator: the people acts politically by beginning to observe itself, by making itself the spectator of itself.

It is still in a very Kantian fashion that Marx asserts that intellectuals ought to expose themselves to criticism, reject isolation and take part in the public debate. Similarly, just as it is a good thing for the 'material struggle', the 'struggle of flesh and blood' and the 'struggle of need, desire, empiricism' to be transformed, through the press, into an 'ideological struggle', a 'struggle of minds' and a 'struggle of theory, of reason, of form',[7] so it is essential that specialists in ideas make contact with the material world, the 'real world of their day', by engaging with the newspapers:

> Philosophy, especially German philosophy, has an urge for isolation, for systematic seclusion, for dispassionate self-examination which from the start places it in estranged contrast to . . . the newspapers . . . Since every true philosophy is the intellectual quintessence of its time, the time must come when philosophy not only internally by its content, but also externally through its form, comes into contact and interaction with the real world of its day. Philosophy then ceases to be a particular system in relation to other particular systems, it becomes philosophy in general in relation to the world, it becomes the philosophy of the contemporary world.[8]

What is interesting in this passage is the way it creates a distinct impression, even if no name is mentioned, that it has a target, and not just any old target: a too 'isolated' philosopher, defender of the 'esotericism' of philosophy? A philosopher who would defend censorship? It is surely Hegel. As Maximilien Rubel says, it is hard to imagine that Marx was not conscious of delivering, in his defence of the freedom of the press:

> a very harsh condemnation of anti-liberalism, which the philosopher of the Prussian state [Hegel] had flaunted in his *Elements of a Philosophy of Right*, approving of 'those laws and ordinances, as upheld by the police, which prevent and punish [the] excesses of free public opinion', notably freedom of the press. No one had better than Hegel formulated the theory of the elite and of the 'bureaucracy of esoteric knowledge', which the monarchical state, idealised by its philosopher, could not do without, and which Marx criticised so vehemently in his essay.[9]

Yet Hegel had actually posited the present as the necessary field for philosophy. Nevertheless, one senses here that the radicality of the way Marx took up this Hegelian theme of the 'present', this need to 'think the contemporary world', was an attack on the master himself. Marx suggests that it is not enough to take the present as the *content* of philosophy; there has to be a *manifestation* – journalistic, it seems – of philosophy itself, that is, a real contact with this present. He seems to believe that one cannot seriously set oneself the task of thinking the present without truly espousing it, without immersing oneself in it to the point of losing one's system and one's solitude. It was necessary, therefore, to link the Hegelian theme of the present to the Kantian principle of publicity. The philosopher of the present had to embrace public exposure.

It is my view that all this was aimed at Hegel, adding to the deep ambivalence of the Young Left Hegelians, to whom Marx belonged, with regard to Hegel's ideas. 'It was still and it was already no longer Hegelianism', says Rubel.[10] This is how Bernard Groethuysen, in an article of 1923, summarized the position of the Young Hegelians: 'Locating themselves at the very heart of the philosophy of Hegel, they drew the true conclusions that Hegel himself dared not develop.'[11] But where exactly, on the question of the present, did Hegelianism go wrong? In what way did it fail to keep its promises? And how did the accusations against Hegel lead the Young Hegelians of the Left to make journalism a real political and philosophical issue?

Thinking the present: improving on Hegel

Hegel, it is true, gave philosophy the present as its subject matter. In fact he demonstrated the necessity of a confrontation of the consciousness with what is external to it – 'positivity' or 'the historical element'. This confrontation led first to contradiction, then to the dialectical resolution of this contradiction: reconciliation. For Hegel this external element, this 'positivity', was constituted by that which was *present* in the consciousness, which *presented* itself to it. Thus the Hegelian conception of the present played on the richness of the concept: the present is first of all 'presence'.

It was the Moderns, said Hegel, who had made the present world 'present' in their minds: 'the present (*vorhanden*) world was again present to man as worthy of the interests of mind'.[12] Hegel explained this historical discovery of the present as present (in the mind) by his philosophy of history. The linked development of the history of rationality (especially philosophy) and of 'real' history (itself always moving towards greater rationality) had led to this modern concentration on the present. The present appeared as that point at which the real passed from an already rational state, understood as such, that is, the past, to a future not yet realized and not yet understood as rational. The Moderns had understood that there was in the present something that was not yet rational but was in the process of becoming so; to think the present was thus to accompany the very movement of the real towards greater rationality – in fact the task of the philosopher. To use the vocabulary of Alexandre Koyré, the *direction* of philosophical thinking was to think the *direction* taken by the 'now'.[13] This theme was most notably developed by Hegel in his preface to *Philosophy of Right*.

That said – and it was into this breach that the Young Hegelians rushed – if the consciousness is in a position to comprehend the present in the present, it cannot *think* it completely in perfect simultaneity with this present. This is the meaning of the Hegelian metaphor of the owl of Minerva, which 'begins its flight only with the onset of dusk':[14] to think the present requires a step back. This is the reason for the ambiguity of the often-cited words of Hegel on the newspapers: 'The morning reading of the newspaper is a kind of realistic morning prayer.'[15] Reading the newspaper is certainly considered, in this aphorism, a prime subject for thinking, for that thinking which has as its ultimate aim its reconciliation with the present world. But to say this is also to say just how far *thinking is different from the newspaper*. The thinker of the present is not a journalist, but someone who, through the concept, seeks to separate the wheat from the chaff in journalistic writing, the rational – or the 'direction', to use the word of Alexandre Koyré – from the irrational. The preface to the *Philosophy of Right* suggests quite clearly that the issue, for the philosopher, is a choice, a selection, in this present, in order to extricate the 'core' from the 'covering' that surrounds it. I will quote the passage in full, to show just how strongly Hegel criticizes those philosophers who, by sometimes allowing themselves to express their present opinions on the present, like journalists, had forgotten that philosophy was not journalism:

> For since the rational, which is synonymous with the Idea, becomes actual by entering into external existence, it emerges in an infinite wealth of forms, appearances, and shapes and surrounds its core with a brightly coloured covering in which consciousness at first resides, but which only the concept can penetrate in order to find the inner pulse, and detect its continued beat even within the external shapes. But the infinitely varied circumstances which take shape within this externality as the essence manifests itself within it, this infinite material and its organisation, are not the subject-matter of philosophy. To deal with them would be to interfere in things with which philosophy has no concern, and it can save itself the trouble of giving advice on the subject. Plato could well have refrained from recommending nurses never to stand still with children but to keep rocking them in their arms; and Fichte likewise need not have perfected his passport regulations to the point of 'constructing', as the expression ran, the requirement that the passports of suspected persons

> should carry not only their personal description but also their painted likeness.[16]

In other words, in this present, there is the essential and the inessential, the interior and the exterior, truth and opinion, what is of interest to philosophy and what is of interest to journalism.

The consequence of this – also implicit in Hegel's mockery of opinions and of 'giving advice' on subjects that are, after all, of some importance to living together – is a sort of split, in Hegel, between thinking the present and the principle of publicity. The latter seems not to need to be applied to the former, which is thus not in any way 'public'. The philosopher who thinks the present has no need to expose himself to the public, on a stage where he will be confronted by other ideas about the present, and possibly challenged. The thinking of the present remains confined to the philosopher's study. This is what led Hannah Arendt to the harsh judgement that Hegelianism was a step backwards as regards Kantism and the Enlightenment: 'the mentality of the Enlightenment, on the highest level, did not last for long, and it may best be illustrated by contrasting it with the attitudes of the next generation, well represented by the young Hegel'.[17] Arendt then quotes words of Hegel which emphasize the necessary 'esotericism' of philosophy, since it is 'not made for the mob nor is it capable of being prepared for the mob'.[18]

Admittedly, some commentators reject an interpretation of the metaphor of the owl of Minerva which refers wholly, that is, exclusively, to a solitary attitude, without public manifestation and without political consequences. Jacques d'Hondt, for example, says: 'Restored to its context, compared with other expressions of its author's thinking, the image of the owl of Minerva, though it has a tragic, even melancholic dimension, and perhaps also, but only to a small degree, a quietist dimension, nevertheless conceals a profound revolutionary significance.'[19] The despairing character of this image, which d'Hondt correctly emphasizes, probably justifies giving it a dimension of revolt – despairing and futile, it must be said. But the word 'revolutionary' may seem a trifle excessive for an image which, as d'Hondt himself admits, implies a deep distaste for public life. This very despair tends towards a radical exit from politics, as shown by this passage from the *Lectures on the History of Philosophy*, which d'Hondt himself quotes: 'It is like this among almost all peoples, philosophy only makes its appearance when public life no longer satisfies and ceases to interest people, when the citizen can no longer take part in the administration of the state.'[20] Such a conception of philosophy hardly encourages an attempt to penetrate the socio-political realities which are the stuff of public life, as d'Hondt recognizes: 'I repeat, what leaves much to be desired, in Hegel, is his analysis of present social reality, even though it was one of his ultimate aims.'[21]

The unkept promise of Hegelianism is this: having put the present at the heart of his philosophy, Hegel ultimately described a thinker of the present in retreat from this present. His step back in time – 'the owl of Minerva begins its flight only with the onset of dusk' – is the counterpart of a sort of geographical step back; he flees the public stage, the very place where you are immersed in the collective present, where you 'are there'. The opposition between the thinker of the present (the isolated philosopher) and the journalist (the exposed public man) is ultimately only reinforced. This is something of a regression in relation to the path marked out by Kant, for whom, as Foucault has so well shown, the injunction to think the present was intrinsically linked to the injunction to do so in public. With Hegel, there reappeared a rift, in the present, between the 'true' present, studied by some, the philosophers, and the inessential actuality of the public stage. Just as the Kantian refusal to choose in the present between the essential and the inessential, the authentic and the inauthentic, or the fundamental and the frivolous implies the public character of all thinking of the present (the selection and the criticism are *public*), so, conversely, the return to an 'ontologizing' or 'essentialist' approach makes it possible to abstract the true 'thinker of the present', that is, the 'thinker of the 'true present', from the public stage.

An extended comment by Joachim Ritter, in his *Hegel and the French Revolution*, helps to clarify the relationship between Hegel and journalism. To regard the reading of the newspapers as philosophically interesting is one thing; to think the proximity of the journalist and the philosopher is another, which Hegel does not do. Ritter emphasizes that the praise for journalism that some commentators have detected behind the Hegelian interest in the present should be attributed not to Hegel but to his disciples – who rejected this Hegelian choice, in the present, between the essential and the inessential, and consequently this dichotomy between philosophy and journalism. Ritter writes:

> Beyer justifiably stresses the philosophical significance of publicist activity for Hegel; but, on the other hand, he ascribes a function to Hegel's publicist activity in relation to his philosophy which it first acquires for his critics . . . Hegel himself always saw his true goal to lie in philosophy and academic teaching, not only during his Bamberg activity, but also in his school post in Nurmberg.[22]

Ritter then refers to a letter from Hegel of this period in which he explains his decision to undertake some journalistic activities. The letter leaves us in no doubt as to the contempt Hegel felt for journalism, but it also provides a key to his conception of what was 'public'. The main argument in Hegel's eyes for accepting the invitation he had received from a newspaper to write for it was that 'this work leaves some time for me to sustain my scientific work further, whereas any position but a teaching post would restrict me much more in this'. That is, what mattered most to Hegel was his scientific work. Yet this is followed by a sort of political somersault: 'What counts against it is that . . . as seductive as independent isolation is, everybody must maintain a connection with the state, and must work on its behalf. The satisfaction one thinks one finds in private work is after all deceptive and insufficient.' His misgivings about seeking refuge in private life are not allayed by the fact that a little journalism would allow him to engage in a 'public' activity. The true public, for Hegel, was the service of the state, that is, a teaching post, or some other official position. He did not consider his journalistic activity a truly 'public' activity, strange though this may seem: 'I will not really be leading a private life, for no one is more of a public man than a journalist; and moreover, literary labours are precisely public, though neither, to be sure, is a public function.'[23] In other words, though he had some misgivings about shutting himself away in his private life, writing in isolation, they would not be allayed by the pseudo-public activity of the journalist. The true 'public', for Hegel, was the state. To be of the 'public' was to be employed by the state, not to remain in that space 'alongside' the state which was that of opinions (public space in the Kantian meaning of the term). This way of reducing the 'public' to the state was wholly in accord, of course, with his defence of state censorship against freedom of the press, that falsely 'public' freedom.

The Young Hegelians of the Left and journalism

Contrary to their master, the Left Hegelians, to whom Marx belonged until his break with them in 1844, interpreted in a radical fashion the Hegelian requirement for a confrontation between consciousness and the 'positivity' that 'presented' itself to it. In particular, this radical challenge was expressed in a rejection of the solitary contemplative position, towards which Hegel had oriented the thinking of the present. This is not to say that they rejected the actual principle of distinguishing, in the present, between an essential and an inessential, or between the core and the covering. What they criticized was the nature of the relationship Hegel had established with this present in order to operate this 'selection', that is, a *speculative* relationship. The consequence of this speculation was that the thinker of the present was doomed to fail in his attempt, because he could only think this present afterwards; thus the present was never apprehended except as the past. The only relationship to the present which could keep its promise, they believed, was a *practical* relationship.

To think the present, strictly speaking, therefore, was to do it. This is why the philosophy of the present was ultimately a wholly practical philosophy, an active philosophy, a philosophy being realized. Miguel Abensour has written of the Left Hegelians: 'Their work consisted . . . of bringing out the real question by which philosophy was to be measured after Hegel, that of its realisation.'[24] One of the chief inspirers of their movement, August von Cieszkowski, wrote, in his *Prolegomena to Historiosophy* (1838): 'The future fate of philosophy in general is to be practical philosophy or, to put it better, the *philosophy of praxis*, whose most concrete effect on life and social relations is the development of *truth in concrete activity*.'[25]

This inevitably leads to a certain rehabilitation of the 'covering': the distinction between the superficial and the profound, clear in the contemplative posture, is certainly much fuzzier for the actor. You have to act in the uncongenial circumstances of this present, in order to realize in it a rationality which cannot be grasped except in the very act of realizing it. This post-Hegelian rehabilitation of the actual in the widest possible sense has been emphasized most notably by Karl Löwith. In transforming the relationship to the present into a practical relationship, he says, Young Hegelianism broke with a certain Hegelian contempt for the ordinary, for the 'small events of daily life', for practical issues as broadly defined.[26] From which we may deduce that it challenged the Hegelian hierarchy between the thinker of the present – an isolated observer, standing back – and the journalist – close, even acting on the stage of the actors. The critique of the position of the former, in the name of the need for a practical relationship with the present, carries within it the rehabilitation of the latter.

The criticism of the speculative position of Hegel is compelling, in particular in the work of another of the great inspirers of the Young Hegelians, Ludwig Feuerbach. In his *Provisional Theses for the Reformation of Philosophy* (1842) and the *Principles of the Philosophy of the Future* (1843), Feuerbach denounced the orientation of Hegel's philosophy towards the past and the wholly illusory 'reduction', through thought, of the contradictions of the real world. Failing to experience these contradictions practically, in their tangible texture, the thinker 'reduced' them by a thought that remained abstract. According to Feuerbach, Hegelianism had made its task easier by not confronting a positivity that was truly external to the concept: 'Thought posits being as counterposed to itself, but still *within itself*',[27] hence Hegel was unable to '*overcome the contradiction of thought and being*'.[28] Feuerbach denounced the 'theological' character of Hegelian thought,[29] which derived from this implicit faith in the radical non-exteriority of being in relation to thinking. Hegelianism was doomed, therefore, to be no more than a 'philosophy of identity',[30] since the claim to grasp the concrete through the concept was a promise not kept: 'the *concrete* is turned into a *predicate of thought*'.[31] In a way, Feuerbach took literally the Hegelian demand to turn thought towards the non-philosophical, towards what was external to it and towards what was not yet rational. However, he accuses Hegel of not having thought through this demand, which, in Feuerbach, was expressed in a sensualism: the non-philosophical is grasped in a tangible or 'practical' relationship, which was banished when the position was – as in Hegel's – exclusively speculative.

One sees how this throws light on the passages in which the young Marx, in 1842–3, praised the ability of the press to transform material conflicts into conflicts of ideas, that is, to link the two worlds, the 'real' and the 'ideal'. The press, he seems to be saying, succeeded precisely where Hegel had failed, because it was in tangible contact with the real, because it was born in and of it. In remaining a solitary eye, Hegel was unable to encounter the materiality of the present, in contrast to journalism, that 'eye of a people', that philosophy realized.

And yet, this privileging of journalism – the only 'seeing' that touches the present – posed problems even within the thinking of Feuerbach and the Young Hegelians. How was the press in closer contact with tangible reality when, after all, it, too, was only 'seeing' and not 'doing'? It might even be asked whether their hymn to 'doing', in a purely practical relationship to the world, did not mean cutting this 'doing' off from any possibility of 'seeing'. Were they not, in the end, advocating the total abandonment of contemplation and of any 'seeing', in the name of a plunge into practice alone? Perhaps the ideal of the 'realization' of philosophy was simply an ideal its destruction?

Young Hegelianism seemed, it is true, to reject the possibility of such a rift. The aim was not to abolish 'seeing' in the name of 'doing', but to situate 'seeing' as close as possible to practice, to seek, in a sense, their perfect simultaneity. But this came at a price, even a gamble: it had to be *possible* for there to be, in the practical moment itself, an outpouring of philosophical seeing. So, like Kierkegaard, to whom Löwith keeps comparing them, or like Nietzsche, the Young Hegelians were fascinated by 'the moment'.[32] It alone made possible the miraculous simultaneity of seeing (in the sense of philosophical contemplation) and doing. 'Practical philosophy' was thus a quest for those moments when the actor *sees himself acting*.

Yet it was precisely this, surely, that gave the practice of journalism its appeal. The undeniable interest of the Young Hegelians in journalism was in fact linked to this search for the point of contact between seeing and doing. Arnold Ruge is one of the most obvious examples of a writer who, week in, week out, was alert to the 'spirit of the age' in the newspapers and magazines to which he contributed. The 'radical historicization of the spirit'[33] in which Ruge engaged made philosophy, in a sense, 'journalistic', that is, doomed to a provisional actuality. Ruge fully accepted this comparison of philosophy to journalism. Admittedly, one might point to the time lag which threatens the journalist no less than the isolated thinker, but it still had to be accepted that it was a lesser threat in journalism – it was even what it was sometimes criticized for. In fact the very thing that is usually disliked in journalism, and particularly disliked in the thought of Hegel, that is, the urgency, the closeness to the actors and the events, became particularly attractive for a thinking which, like that of the Young Hegelians, aimed at maximum coincidence between seeing and doing. It may be said that the Young Hegelians, against the master, restored a sort of truth of immediacy.[34]

However, to be able to think, through journalism, the point of contact between contemplation and action, it was still necessary to believe in the existence of such a point. But what if action, the practical relationship to the world that was so highly valued by the Young Hegelians, was a blind and mute relationship, which produced no vision, no moment of introspective lucidity? What if action created no space, in its proximity, which was not already a betrayal of what it is? And if all the journalistic observations which accompanied action were inevitably behindhand, missing the invisible and inexpressible heart of this action, and little different, therefore, from the 'abstraction' of isolated thinking?

We touch here, certainly, on a difficult area for the Young Hegelians. In putting such high value on practice, and assuming the exteriority of this practice in relation to thinking, they inevitably risked making it unobservable, incomprehensible and unknowable by a *gaze*. Certain texts of Feuerbach can even be read as a determined effort to avoid this trap, by constantly reducing the sensible and the practical to the order of communication and intersubjectivity, that is, an order in which this practice is immediately collectively observable, susceptible to a communal gaze and commentary. The sensible, for Feuerbach, did not confine the individual within a silent, non-introspective and unshareable relationship.[35] Thus the aim, for the contemplative activities, of which the labour of opinion and gaze, on the public stage, was one, was to remain part of the order of the tangible, to be located in an extension of practical experience. When he spoke about reforming philosophy, Feuerbach, like the Young Hegelians in general, did not want to substitute the actor for the thinker, but to make the thinker *also and always an actor*, that is, to establish a *simultaneity of practice and theory*:

> To philosophise, do not separate the philosopher from the man; just be a man who thinks; do not think as a thinker, that is, within a faculty detached from the totality of the real human being, and isolated for oneself; think as a living and real being, exposed to the revivifying and refreshing waves of the ocean of the world.[36]

Once again, everything was done to make this simultaneity possible, by avoiding making practice a closed order, resistant to the introduction of introspection.

And yet, what, in the end, were Feuerbach and the Young Hegelians advocating if not a curiously Kantian actor/spectator division, without breaking the link between the two orders? Certainly, their eager concern for the concrete and the tangible made more problematical than in Kant the hope placed in the stage of the spectators, in the public space of points of view and opinions: abstraction was always threatening, that is, the break with 'real', tangible, practical problems. They were more vigilant, perhaps, and more uneasy. But the aim was that of a collective 'seeing' which accompanied the 'doing' at the very moment that it happened – an aim which they themselves believed might best be realized in journalism.

The journalism of Arnold Ruge, for example, claimed to achieve concrete results, to touch and even to transform the real world. He criticized the 'liberal' conception of freedom of speech, which he believed made the public space of opinions an abstract space, cut off from the real world. In 1843 he called the liberals of his day 'petit bourgeois', because they believed that freedom of the press was a 'gift' from the king, and that they were going to solve all problems without concretely questioning social and political conditions, in particular the foundations of the monarchical system itself.[37] The freedom of speech he defended was of a very different type. Anchored in tangible problems, it was part of what he called – echoing the 'reform of consciousness' of Feuerbach – a 'conversion of political consciousness'. His journalism implied a position as a spectator who did not take pleasure in the spectacle, but came up against the battles of the actors; one of his criticisms of the liberals was that they failed 'to make us leave the state of spectator'.

So Young Hegelianism may have been Kantian, but, as Arnold Ruge's criticisms of the liberals suggests, it is still impossible to talk of a simple return to Kant. If the Kantian public space of opinions was rehabilitated against the speculative Hegelian position, it was a space whose connection with the 'real world' still needed to be preserved, as if it risked being undermined. The way in which Marx himself insisted on this connection, so exceptionally achieved by the press, injected a significant dose of Feuerbachism into his Kantism. And it was to precisely this sensitive issue that Marx would return in the next few years in order to call a halt to Young Hegelian enthusiasms, beginning with his own. The crisis of 1843 can be understood, in Marx's itinerary, as the realization of an irremediable disconnection between the public space of opinions and the world of *praxis*.

2. The crisis of 1843: towards a radical critique of public space

The obsession with the concrete

In the weeks he spent in Kreuznach, during the summer of 1843, Marx began to distance himself from the Young Hegelian movement. Above all, however, he seems to have been engaged in a radicalization of certain Feuerbachian–Rugian themes; that is, he did not break with the core of Young Hegelian thinking. In fact what characterizes Marx's writing at the end of 1843 is a veritable *obsession with the concrete*, visible both in his letter to Ruge of September of that year and in two articles published in the *Annales franco-allemandes* in February 1844, 'On the Jewish question' and 'Contribution to the critique of Hegel's Philosophy of Law'. The connection between the world of 'ideas' – of which the public space of opinions and also, to be more precise, journalism were part – and the world of 'real' struggles became a major issue.

The letter to Ruge of September 1843 emphasizes the need to practise a philosophy in contact with 'real struggles', a necessary condition if it was to deserve the name of 'criticism of politics'.[38] Marx's aim was still, however, to create a 'critical philosophy', which articulated theory and practice, true to the projects of Young Hegelianism. The obsession with the concrete is equally clear in 'On the Jewish question'. Marx launches into a critique of bourgeois freedoms, which he calls 'formal', unfitted to receive a real material content for those who were socially dominated. Here too, the break with the past is not total. It is apparent that, of all the political freedoms Marx attacked, freedom of speech, the one he had defended so strongly in his youth, was not as strongly criticized as the others. On the contrary, he denounces the hypocrisy of the revolutionaries who had made good use of this press freedom (claiming it de facto and then 'declaring' it in Article 11 of the

Declaration of the Rights of Man and of the Citizen), only then to suppress it. He also denounced the hypocrisy of the Constitution of 1793, Article 122 of which guarantees the '*liberté indéfinie de la presse*' ('unlimited freedom of the press'), but then adds '*la liberté de la presse ne doit pas être permise lorsqu'elle compromet la liberté publique*' ('freedom of the press should not be permitted when it endangers public liberty'); which means, says Marx, that, in practice, 'freedom of the press is totally destroyed'.[39] Thus, contrary to other freedoms, that of the press seems not to be sufficiently 'formal' for the bourgeoisie to defend it to the bitter end – which, conversely, justified Marx himself in continuing to defend it to the bitter end.

It is in his Introduction to the 'Contribution to the critique of Hegel's Philosophy of Law' that Marx took a further step, which led him to challenge the abstraction inherent to the debates that take place in public space. He also, for the first time, clearly differentiates two spaces: that of the 'previous form of German political consciousness' and that of 'praxis': 'the criticism of speculative philosophy of right strays, not into itself, but into problems which there is only one means of solving – practice'.[40]

Nevertheless, in much of this article, as in this particular statement, it may be said that Marx remains true to the Feuerbachian requirement to construct a way of thinking which, unlike the Hegelian philosophy of law, 'abstract extravagant thinking' of a state which itself makes 'abstraction of real man',[41] deals with concrete, practical problems.[42] His aim, once again, is a critical thinking anchored in the tangible, which will not, therefore, be 'passion of the head', but 'the head of passion'.[43] And the attitudes to which this critical thinking leads appear as a veritable journalistic programme, wholly worthy of the ambitions of Young Hegelianism. He asks the critical thinker – who is clearly conceived of as a *public* person – to practise 'indignation', 'denunciation' and the almost pictorial description of every sphere of society, including its '*partie honteuse* (shameful part)'.[44] Here, Marx still retains the very 'Young Hegelian' desire for a 'seeing' that would accompany the concrete struggles and thus produce the 'consciousness of pressure'.[45]

However, something else emerges in this article: the idea that criticism 'strays, not into itself, but into problems which there is only one means of solving' – that is, praxis – evokes, all in all, an impotence of this criticism in the face of the concrete with which it deals, because, in spite of this contact, it seems it must give way before praxis alone. It is towards the end of the article that he makes his fiercest attack on the concept of public space, denouncing political attitudes in general, that is, those attitudes which affect only the relations between the state and its 'public' (civil society, spectator of the state); they appear, all their energy notwithstanding, doomed to remain cut off from 'real struggles'. Marx vehemently attacks the idea of political emancipation, which he calls 'partial emancipation' because it is the act of a 'part of civil society'.[46] He believed that the political upheavals which take place in this space – regime changes as a result of a protest, political revolutions – were necessarily limited. One part of civil society assumed power at the expense of another, and that was all; there was little real practical effect, because this 'political emancipation' left 'the pillars of the house standing'.[47] The deep underlying reason was the 'mediocrity' of the classes: 'every class, once it begins the struggle against the class above it, is involved in the struggle against the class below it'.[48] The only instances when the pillars shook seemed to be the rare cases when the part of civil society which toppled the existing political order succeeded in winning unusually broad support, that is, in appealing beyond the existing 'public' to the very people that were excluded from the public – the non-public, in a way. Thus this part of civil society (or of the public), even if it was only a small part of the public, drew its strength from the fact that 'it fraternizes and merges with society in general'.[49] In other words, it was not so much its powers of persuasion within public space, the 'public' impact of the indignation it conveyed, as the fact that this indignation made contact with those excluded from the 'public' – the 'people' – which ultimately enabled it 'to overthrow all relations in which man is debased'.[50] 'The weapon of criticism', which in general cannot replace 'criticism of the weapon',[51] can thus exceptionally lead to it, but in this case, it is due less to the aura of this criticism within public space than to its capacity to touch the people excluded from this public space. Nevertheless, such a thing is rare and not all nations, it seems, are equally predisposed to it. France, for example, was an exceptional country for Marx, where criticism, in the space of opinions, sometimes succeeded in touching the real people, and where political 'revolutions' seemed less quickly threatened by the brake constituted by the 'mediocrity' of the classes.[52] If I have understood this correctly, however, the mediocrity of class is the most natural accompaniment of political emancipation, the latter having little, even no, practical effect (simply the replacement of one domination by another).

These passages anticipate the later discussion in *The German Ideology* of the substitution, in history, of one dominant class for another, each imposing its mark on the world of the ideas and representations which circulate in public space. Public space, whatever happened in it, was thus a place which exercised a domination over the rest of the people. Here, Marx discredits the shifts of opinion, indignation and calls for change which shake public space, and which in fact produce conflicts that are in some way 'euphemized' or policed. The world of newspapers was a prime target here.[53]

So for the first time Marx began to develop the idea that the only way to emerge from this history of successive dominations was to rely on the totally dominated, who had suffered the 'absolute wrong', that is, been excluded from this public space, outside politics. This exclusion from participation was the guarantee that there was no 'mediocrity' of the dominated 'visible' in public space, who remained caught up in the game of successive reversals of domination without abolishing the domination that this space of itself exercised on those it excluded. Total exclusion was the guarantee of the overthrow of the structure of public space itself: the state/civil society pair. By that fact, however, it also became unattainable. Marx was seeking a politically 'invisible', perhaps even an undefined, class since its interests are not clear, nor are represented in public space. This was the paradox to which he was led: he was seeking *a class which is not a class*.[54]

This paradoxical, unattainable character of the proletariat (class/non-class) hints at the problems which become clearer on reading *The German Ideology*: what is a class which does not express itself politically as a class, in the public space of opinions? Can it possess class-consciousness without first possessing a way of being political? Can it be a class if it does not have this class-consciousness, the 'consciousness of oppression'? At the same time, this distancing from the place of politics, from the public space of opinions, where only classes with particular interests express themselves, is precisely what guarantees that this non-class will be the motor of real change, that it will be as close as possible to the concrete – to this suffering that is *undefined*, not formulated, not defined by the public expression of a class standpoint which would inevitably betray it, euphemize it and make it more 'abstract'. Marx was well and truly caught in a paradox. He was effectively seeking a class which would have none of the faults of the 'mediocre' classes, with their well-formulated, indeed too well-formulated, interests, that is, well represented, too well represented, in public space. He was seeking a 'non-class'.

What is essential in all this for my argument is that, for the first time, Marx envisaged that it might be necessary to leave the public space of opinions in order to find something good, something that would make 'the pillars of the house' tremble; for the first time he expressed doubts as to what, in reality, ideas or even a highly 'critical' journalism could achieve, because the fact of happening in the public space of points of view, the fact of being part of it, might well, structurally, block their access to the concrete.

The 'masses' at the gates of public space

It was not until the second half of 1844 that Marx's thinking on the autonomy of the social in relation to the political clarified. A major text here, which directly poses the question of *what journalism can do*, is the article of August 1844 in *Vorwärts!* ('Forward!'), in which Marx quarrelled with Arnold Ruge.

Ruge, in an article signed 'A Prussian', had expressed anger at the near-total lack of response in Germany to a workers' revolt in Silesia. True to the journalistic enthusiasms of the Young Hegelians, Ruge expressed indignation and made visible and placed on the public or political stage a social issue that had been left in obscurity. He *wished* this revolt to be perceived in a different way – in particular by the king, whose scant interest in social reform he deplored – and he explained the general indifference by the lack of political culture in Germany, which it was his duty to remedy as far as he could by his pen. Marx replied to Ruge, in this article of August 1844, that he no longer believed in this 'voluntarist' position (let us alert public opinion! let us sound off in the newspapers!): 'The more one-sided and, therefore, the more perfected the political mind is, the more does it believe in the omnipotence of the will, the more it is blind to the natural and spiritual limits of the will, and the more incapable is it therefore of discovering the source of social ills.'[55]

This criticism by Marx is precise about the issue: it was *visibility*. 'The political mind', to which the Young Hegelian thinker aspired and hoped to accede, in particular through the practice of journalism, is decried as blindness. There is a sort of mask, he says, induced by the use of the category of the will. This criticism is all the harsher in that Young Hegelianism prided itself on a politically lucid thought, of which the guarantee was, in effect, the substitution, for abstract speculative reason, of the faculty of the will.[56] According to Marx, he who has 'political understanding', the individual who wants to see and to see well, is, by his very situation, condemned to abstraction. Because the wish to observe, to denounce and to understand signals that one is oneself in a position to exit from the lived, concrete domination, hence that one misrepresents it, that one only apprehends it in an abstract manner. 'That *social distress* produces *political* understanding is so incorrect that, on the contrary, what is correct is the opposite: *social well-being* produces *political* understanding. *Political* understanding is a spiritualist, and is given to him who already has, to him who is already comfortably situated.'[57] In short, Marx severs the links which the Young Hegelians had established between seeing and doing: to want to see is necessarily to emerge from the concrete, from the practical, from the 'real'. It seems that there is increasingly less choice. Either you go in for the real, concrete, painful struggle, without the possibility of political expression, or you go in for political expression, a symptom of a lack of anchorage in this real struggle. There is in this text, furthermore, an explicit opposition between 'political understanding' and 'social instinct'.[58]

So 'political understanding' produces blind abstractions, of which one example is the category of 'mass', dear to the Young Hegelians, including Ruge, and denounced here by Marx. The masses were all those who do not 'see' as he who has political understanding does, that is, who do not share his enlightened, progressive, 'voluntary' view. Thus Ruge, in the article attacked here by Marx, failed to distinguish 'the different categories contained in the expression "German society": the Government, the bourgeoisie, the press and, finally, the workers themselves. These are the different masses with which we are concerned here. The "Prussian" lumps all these masses together and, from his lofty stand, passes sentence on them en bloc.'[59] In actual fact, the 'masses' at whom the 'Prussian' pointed the finger only revealed the extent of his own blindness.[60]

It is clear that, to Marx, even the king, even the indifferent bourgeoisie, were less blind than the man of 'political understanding' who 'sees' – thinks he sees, wants to see, does not see – the importance of this revolt. They, at least, were anchored in praxis, which gave them a place and determined their behaviour. They made no pretence of seeking out a place from which they could see, so did not lay themselves open to this special sort of blindness. Conversely, Marx criticized the idea that some bourgeoisies (such as the English bourgeoisie) were more lucid or enlightened, less blind or indifferent, than others. It was the order of praxis alone – its relations with the proletariat, its 'needs' – which gave a certain, very relative, visibility to one's situation within this praxis. Marx thus discredited the 'politics' so vaunted by the Young Hegelians as the place where lucid points of view, detached from the social, were constructed. The man of 'political understanding', not anchored, even seeking not to be anchored, sees even less than the rest.[61]

Marx seems even to cut off the social – the 'lived' or 'acted' struggles – from the political, where a community tries to see the real together and to discuss it. 'But do not all uprisings', he writes, 'without exception, break out in a *disastrous isolation of man from the community*? Does not *every* uprising necessarily presuppose isolation? Would the 1789 revolution have taken place without the disastrous isolation of French citizens from the community? It was intended precisely to abolish this isolation.'[62] So, while waiting for this to happen, the revolt took place on a stage of political invisibility, which was more of a non-stage, where everything, from the standpoint of the political stage, resembled an unformed 'mass'.

Was there no place left from which one could observe this praxis? The article against Arnold Ruge seems sometimes to propose, as the only alternative to 'political understanding', to 'playing . . . the schoolmaster',[63] or to 'phraseology'[64] (a term valued by Marx well before Kraus!), the position of the scholar and theoretician. Was this a return to Hegel? Marx claims, for example, that if 'the "Prussian" were to adopt the correct standpoint', he would 'find that not one of the French and English workers' uprisings had such a theoretical and conscious character as the uprisings of the Silesian weavers'.[65] Yet this path, which is not without its contradictions of the rejection of the contemplative posture which permeates his writings of this period, seems less pronounced than another path, further developed in *The German Ideology* and formalized in the celebrated Eleventh Thesis on Feuerbach ('The philosophers have only *interpreted* the world in various ways; the point is to *change* it'): the search for an exclusively practical position.

Ideological chatter, silent masses

The German Ideology, written in 1844–5, is the culmination of this challenge to the public space of 'political opinions'. This time, the break with Young Hegelianism is total, since Feuerbach himself is accused of having held what was, ultimately, an abstract, contemplative, insufficiently practical vision of the 'tangible'. No Young Hegelian was spared the accusation of 'phrases',[66] which implied, however good their intentions, an inability to 'deal with' the 'real' struggles.

The concept of ideology enables us to clarify the meaning of this word 'phrases'. As already observed,[67] it referred to a domination not only in the *expression* but in the very *production* of thoughts, which immediately poses the problem of whether, in such an analytical framework, it is possible to envisage a thought that would *not* be ideological. The domain of representations in general, and hence the public space in which they are exchanged, seems to suffer from a time lag in relation to the developments within the praxis; you can only begin to break with ideology when the domination which corresponds to it on the economic plane is in the process of dying out, that is, precisely when this ideology ceases to be one. In spite of the specificity of its nature, this 'time lag' is not without echoes of that attributed by the Young Hegelians to the Hegelian contemplative posture ('only when the shades of night are gathering'). But while the Young Hegelians still preserved a place for a gaze truly synchronized with practice (that is, journalism), Marx was now refusing to the world of ideas, including that constituted by the press, any other condition than that of preserving the status quo, until a practical or material overthrow emerged.[68]

Finally, Marx denounced the fundamental illusion which Feuerbach left untouched: he had continued to believe that it was possible for contemplative thought – subject to certain conditions – to perform this labour of apprehending tangible exteriority. For the Marx of *The German Ideology* it seems that no contemplative posture, even that which remained in contact with the practical, could do this without lying in its turn. The only thing that made it possible to apprehend tangible exteriority was praxis.[69]

And this praxis now appears totally autonomous in relation to the world of representations, discourses etc. What Marx opposed to ideological chatter was precisely this 'mass' misunderstood by the 'politically understanding', and which they wrongly thought of as passive matter, waiting to be informed by political ideas. For Marx, the 'mass' was active by the very fact of its theoretical virginity, which he treated to a veritable eulogy:

> The real, practical dissolution of these phrases, the removal of these notions from the consciousness of men, will, as we have already said, be effected by altered circumstances, not by theoretical deductions. For the mass of men, i.e., the proletariat, these theoretical notions do not exist and hence do not require to be dissolved, and if this mass ever had any theoretical notions, e.g., religion, these have now long been dissolved by circumstances.[70]

The Feuerbachian theme of the 'transformation of consciousnesses' was abandoned in favour of the 'transformation of circumstances'. It was no longer enough to think differently; it was necessary to seek out a place where, apparently, what mattered was not thinking but acting. The only ideological traces which remained in the 'mass' were those which the dominant class had left it; but historical 'circumstances' would end up by cleansing it of and emancipating it from these dominant representations.

In which case, as Etienne Balibar has shown, the concept of 'mass' in *The German Ideology* repeats the same paradoxes, enigmas and perhaps aporias as the theme of class/non-class in the 'Contribution to the critique of Hegel's Philosophy of Law'.[71] The concept of 'mass' makes it possible, in its turn, like the concept of 'non-class', to retain all the generosity of class without its mediocrity; that is, to think a group at war with *the*, universally understood, domination, not seeking to promote only its own petty class interest. It is the guarantee of its real effectiveness, but it is also what Balibar calls its constitutive ambivalence. It fails to develop, in the course of its practical emancipation, any particular class point of view, which would risk making it a future dominant class, imposing its own ideology. No specific *political* identity is attributed to this mass, in the sense of an identity that would make it visible in the public space of representations – precisely because this world of representations is discredited as ideological.[72]

It seems that the Marx of *The German Ideology* considers that the practical transformation of the world is possible without there being, previously or even simultaneously, a theoretical representation of this transformation. This has an inevitable consequence: the mass has no need, according to Marx, to be or to become a *public*. Here the rupture with Kantism is complete. It seems that praxis requires no gaze at the self, no spectacle, no mirror. Mirrors are a waste of time, they salute the status quo, they confirm the dominations in place. They no longer have the cathartic and *effective* function Marx had detected in 1842. Thus the glorification of the 'mass' in *The German Ideology* is the exact counterpart of the abandonment of the concept of 'public': it is precisely because it *is not* an observing and chattering public that it is the motor of history.

It is difficult, in the light of this theoretical evolution on the part of Marx, to see how journalism, attached by definition to the public space of opinions, could have any interest. But this is to forget the concern of Marx to respond to the difficulties posed by his own analytical framework. In fact the idea of an absolute gulf between, on the one hand, public or political space, chattering and seeking to 'see' the social, and, on the other, praxis, silent and blind, operating in a 'real world' which requires no search for visibility, is not Marx's last word. For Marx, journalism was doomed to remain an issue.

3. Journalism, an ongoing problem: Marx as conflictual journalist

Finding a vantage point

To cut the 'real world', praxis, off from any search for visibility on itself would be to put total confidence in 'the social instinct' and, above all, to dismiss at a stroke the problem of class-consciousness. Marx was clearly not willing to do this. So he had to return to the question of the link between the political stage – public space – and the social stage – the other stage, that of social struggles.

The Communist Manifesto, published in 1847, is already evidence of this. Marx and Engels began, certainly, by locating the struggle of the proletariat on a trajectory imposed by the development of material conditions alone (industrial growth), without apparent need for any 'consciousness' of its historical situation. Nevertheless, there was a shift. The first proletarian unions were regarded as preliminaries, as 'riots'; they would lead to a second stage, which would be political: 'Every class struggle is a political struggle.' And, Marx and Engels continued, for this to happen, it was necessary for proletarians to organize 'into a class, and, consequently into a political party'.[73] It seems that the aporia of the class/non-class schema has now been abandoned in favour of the need to become a true 'class', politically defined, having a representation of itself, hence a discourse in political space. As a result, says Etienne Balibar, 'it is clearly no longer a case of representing the revolutionary proletariat as situated beyond any existence as a class, in a mass of de-individualized individuals, as *The German Ideology* would have it'.[74]

However, while this advance seems to resolve some difficulties, it creates others, which are simply echoes of earlier problems. It should not be the case that accession to political existence involved the formulation of a world view which was no more than a potential ideology; nor should the historical specificity of the proletariat – it is the last class, the class that does not aim particularly to impose its domination, but finally to go beyond the class struggle – be written off. Balibar also argues that, while marking a step forward, *The Communist Manifesto* reveals 'a full-blown contradiction'; that is, 'how do we think a politics without a political ideology, without a discourse on the state, or the future state, or the future of the state (were this future its disappearance)?'[75] The real problem was now this: whereas the need for the proletariat to possess a political 'standpoint' of its own, which could also be called 'class-consciousness', had been of no importance, it is now accepted, but on one condition: that of recognizing its specificity in relation to the other class points of view, those which are marked by the ideological domination of the moment, and which, when they fight against, or believe they are fighting against, this are only new potential ideologies.

Whether this problem is soluble or not, it represents, I repeat, a break with the approach which had made praxis a 'stage' radically autonomous in relation to that stage of spectacle and discourse which is the political stage. I am here in agreement with those heterodox Marxists of the 1920s, such as Karl Korsch and the young Georg Lukacs, who rejected the 'orthodox' Marxist interpretation to the effect that praxis only needed to be guided by some theoretical reflection, by some 'point of view'. It was essentially the very idea of a 'social instinct' irreducible to any conscious thought that Korsch was combating when he accused the so-called 'orthodox' Marxists of confusing the thinking of Marx with a banal materialism.[76] In the name of the need for a theoretical moment, and even of a Marxian defence of philosophy, Korsch was particularly critical of the hasty reading of the Eleventh Thesis on Feuerbach by the 'orthodox' Marxists: 'This does not mean, as the epigones imagine, that all philosophy is shown to be mere fantasy. It only expresses a categorical rejection of all theory, philosophical or scientific, that is not *at the same time* practice.'[77]

The Feuerbachian, and more broadly Young Hegelian, tenor of these words is striking. In emphasizing the persistence in Marx of the idea of a dialectical complementarity of theory and praxis, which sharply differentiated Marxism from classic materialism, Korsch is suggesting that Marx may not have broken with the demands dear to the Young Hegelians, even if he accused them of having failed to honour them. The question of the articulation between seeing and doing had not, he is saying, disappeared from Marx's writings after *The German Ideology*. This is what the young Georg Lukacs also tried to emphasize in his *History and Class Consciousness* (1923), showing the dual process of Marxism as he understood it; the practical struggle *and* the advent of a certain form of 'visibility' (theoretical), the two things being linked: 'It was necessary for the proletariat to be born for social reality to become fully conscious. The reason for this is that the discovery of the class-outlook of the proletariat provided a vantage point from which to survey the whole of society.'[78] Whether one agrees with Lukacs or not with regard to the *comprehensive* nature of this visibility, what is most striking here is the insistence on the question of *visibility* – that is, a theoretical question. A special, dialectical articulation between theory and practice needs to be established, each guiding the other, or, to be more precise, each criticizing the other. Praxis presupposes and is nourished by points of view on the social premises of a theoretical reflection, but it never stops putting them to the test and thus correcting, renewing and expanding them; new theoretical perspectives are created, which begin to nourish praxis, before, in their turn, being put to the test by this praxis, corrected, and so on.[79] According to this reading, there remained in Marx the desire for the gaze and action to go together, which makes it possible gradually to define the place both of the revolutionary struggle and of visibility.

And yet, this rehabilitation of a labour of 'seeing', of a theory that accompanies practice, could very well admit of, without implying, a rehabilitation of the public space of opinions. After all, there is nothing to say that the gaze that is rehabilitated here as an accompaniment to the practical struggle develops within the public space of gazes. The visibility in question here could very well be sought wholly outside public or political space, in a more 'protected' sphere. This gaze might then have nothing 'journalistic' about it – knowing that such a description requires there to be public exposure. This hypothesis is probably implicit in the readings which consider Marxian theory as a scientific point of view, totally at odds with the ideologized exchanges in public space. For these (notably Althuserian) readings, Marx does not renounce all theorizing, but the gaze he proposes is radically new, at last scientific, and in total discontinuity with ideological points of view. Certain passages support this hypothesis. When, in the article against Ruge in *Vorwärts!*, Marx claimed that if 'the "Prussian" were to adopt the correct standpoint', he would 'find that not one of the French and English workers' uprisings had such a *theoretical* and *conscious* character as the uprisings of the Silesian weavers',[80] he seems to be calling on Ruge to move on to the correct theoretical point of view, the latter seeming to be at odds with all the sorts of points of view habitually exchanged in public space. Similarly, the reference in *The German Ideology* to the need for a 'study of actuality' is surely a pointer towards a specific place of theory or of 'vision', at odds with public space – in short towards a science that would have no connection with ideology and that would have no need publicly to confront the latter, but be wholly outside it. 'One has to "leave philosophy aside"', wrote Marx, denouncing it here as ideology, 'one has to leap out of it and devote oneself like an ordinary man to the study of actuality . . . philosophy and the study of the actual world have the same relation to one another as onanism and sexual love.'[81] The 'study of actuality' is thus performed as 'an ordinary man'; but nothing says that it should be performed as a *public* man. Perhaps Marx is here advocating a science of the 'ordinary man' which would develop in total separation from the exchange of points of view in public (or political) space.

I have no wish here to enter into a debate which has so troubled Marxism, especially in France. I need emphasize only that, in the hypothesis of a Marxian invitation to a purely scientific gaze, thus a gaze totally at odds with the public space of (ideological) opinions, that is, in a schema in which science and ideology are radically opposed, there is good reason to think that journalism would have little value, since it is by definition bound up with public space, hence with the very place of ideology. But for Georg Lukacs, a scientific conception of 'theory' is a way of getting round the difficulties inherent to the dialectical complementarity of theory and practice. Because, in the certainty of doing 'science', there is a refusal to think visibility as a perspective, which is constructed gradually, dialectically, on the basis of partial gazes, in the progressive revelation of their blind points – that is, their ideological elements – as a result of the double process of theory and practice. Lukacs's *History and Class Consciousness* is in this regard a critique of any Marxism that presents itself as sure of already being in possession of the 'total' point of view – it is open to the accusation, in the vocabulary of Lukacs, of 'reification'. No one can ever be certain of being in the right place – in the right place for the struggle and the right place for 'seeing' properly, outside of ideology. This place is something to be sought for permanently, in a complementary dialectical labour of struggle and vision, and of theory and practice. No one can escape a permanent critique.[82]

As a result, visibility, far from establishing itself in total and immediate exteriority to ideology, conquers ideology by confronting it. The anchorage in praxis, struggle and militancy are certainly necessary to a fully self-critical gaze; they make it possible to show more things than a simple 'theoretical' confrontation with other gazes, that is, the 'Kantian' exchange of points of view. But this particular confrontation remains no less fruitful, even indispensable to the preservation of a certain theoretical freedom, which is precisely what Lukacs accuses the so-called 'orthodox' Marxists of wishing to limit by invoking the needs of praxis, needs that are assumed, never questioned, never 'thought'.

In this conception of Marxism, which I accept, journalism can then appear as the labour of this confrontation with ideology. Admittedly, journalism can only be the pure expression of ideology, but it *can* also hope to emancipate itself from the ideology of the interior, by an internal critique – since we are here accepting a schema in which the emancipation from ideology does not demand absolute discontinuity with it. It may even be able to incarnate the 'political moment' I referred to when discussing *The Communist Manifesto*, a moment which, in confronting ideology on its own ground, public space, constructs the point of view of the dominated, and through this its consciousness as a political class.

However, we should not ignore the limitations inherent to this conception of the critique of ideology happening *from the inside*. It has to be recognized that it risks going round in circles, in that it means envisaging a critique of ideology whose aim is access to the place from which this critique of ideology will at last be fully possible and relevant. Does this not require one to be already in the place at which one aims? The development of visibility seems to assume that this visibility is already there. Nevertheless, the gaze which Lukacs seeks to develop has a 'modesty' which is lacking in the gaze which proclaims itself 'scientific' from the beginning. It is ready to confront the ideology it criticizes; it even exposes itself to it. No doubt it can be perceived as not wholly accepting the *principle of publicity* (if points of view confront each other, reason will prevail . . .); no doubt it is ready for the dialogues of the deaf that will ensue from its confrontation with ideology. It remains, nevertheless, more under (public) control than the 'scientific' gaze which proclaims itself from the outset to be emancipated from ideology and feels no need to confront it. It may have few illusions about the public, but nor does it completely despise it. It fights against it, but from within.

Confronting ideology: Karl Marx on the American Civil War

In spite of the difficulties it poses, it seems that it is this labour of constructing a critical standpoint, won over, but developed in contact with, ideology, which is revealed by the journalism of Marx. I will consider here his articles on the United States, in particular those of 1861–2 on the Civil War, which appeared in the *New York Daily Tribune*.[83]

Marx had met the American journalist Charles A. Dana in Europe, in the summer of 1848. With his support, Marx became a regular contributor to the *New York Daily Tribune* in 1851, and he continued to write for this newspaper until early in 1862. It was an important daily paper, with a circulation of 200,000, selling at 2d a copy. Initially assisted by Engels, who even wrote most of the first articles, Marx practised his English and was able to write in this language by 1853. He submitted two articles a week, and was paid for each article published. From 1857, the *Tribune* commissioned only one article a week. With the outbreak of the Civil War, at the beginning of 1861, the paper axed all its foreign contributors with the exception of Marx, but published only eight articles of his that year, between 11 October and 25 December. Six of these dealt with the Civil War and its impact in England. His last article for the *Tribune* was published on 10 March 1862.[84]

The articles Marx wrote in 1861–2 broadly analyse the ideas, opinions and principles – especially legal – of the British elites on the subject of the Civil War; in other words, the ideology which dominated English public space. Marx quoted, discussed and dissected declarations and arguments heard in one place or another, especially in the press. His critique was essentially internal. He espoused the logic of the actors he evoked in order to bring out, suddenly, by means of a contradiction or flagrant incoherence, another latent logic, a dead angle, a hidden interest. He wanted to show how the ideological discourse sought to mask the real motives of the actors, which were economic. English anger against the North was in particular a response to the economic damage suffered by England's textile industry, due to the blockade imposed by the North on the export of cotton from the

Southern states. Sympathy for the Confederates was also fostered by the economic benefits to Great Britain of divisions in a potential rival. However, instead of treating the ideological discourses from the beginning as masks of little interest, Marx made them the focus of his journalistic attention. Instead of adopting a 'scientific' standpoint which would be, from the outset, outside ideology, Marx looked for the flaws internal to the ideology. He showed that the truth about what it was, and about the role it played, was obvious to anyone who took the trouble to follow the logic through – that is, until it fell apart of its own accord.

Marx thus embarked on a resistance to ideology *from within*, ready to beat it on its own ground. It could be said that he was a flâneur in ideology, that he sought with his gaze those things that ideology seemed to hide; its blind spots. And it was then, when he had put his finger on a flagrant incoherence, that the conflictual flâneur denounced it as a hidden domination. In other words, he was not a flâneur within a beautiful diversity of points of view, himself seeking to enrich this diversity by a boundless curiosity. It was rather that his curiosity enabled him to be alert to what was strangely homogeneous in the discourses he observed; and he dissected this homogeneity, so that it eventually appeared for what it was. It was in this way that he created a new gaze, a gaze which was able to grasp what dominated and could then oppose it.

I will take as my first example an article of 1861 in the *New York Daily Tribune*, dated 18 September but appearing on 11 October, with the title 'The American question in England'.[85] Here, Marx analyses in detail the British reluctance to align itself with the Union (North), 'which looks rather strange on the part of people affecting an utter horror of Slavery'. How, he asked, was this possible? It was against the most deeply held principles of the British nation! This ironic naivety conceals a method: first espouse the point of view of the enemy, listen to his arguments and denials, then unmask him.

Many leader-writers and influential persons tried to show, for example, that loyalty to the main principles was not, in fact, seriously betrayed, because the anti-slavery of the North was highly suspect. Marx took this argument totally seriously; he entered into its logic. Indeed he largely accepted it, since the claim that the issue of slavery was secondary in the war seemed to him correct. The abolition of slavery was not the main motive for the Northern struggle. But then, from within, he gradually picked holes in this logic. The anti-slavery of the North might well be dubious, so there was good reason to be cautious, but not so cautious, surely, as to forget that the Southerners were slavers without any qualms at all? How was it that the explicit slavery of the South had so far given rise to fewer reservations than the dubious anti-slavery of the North?

Yet here, too, he let the ideology speak; he let it defend itself and rehearse all its arguments. The Northerners might *appear* to be less pro-slavery, said some, but their attitude revealed, if in a more subtle and less explicit fashion, a point of view that was *in reality* similar to that of the Confederates on the question of slavery. How else could one interpret their many attempts to reach a compromise with the Southerners? Were these not an indication that the Northerners were ready to yield entirely to the Southerners on the question of slavery? Did this not make their pro-slavery almost as explicit as that of the Southerners?

Once again, Marx listened to the argument, acknowledged it, even accepted it. There had indeed been attempts to reach a compromise on the part of the Northerners, and they could certainly be interpreted in this way. But he then posed an awkward question: why did those who attached so much importance to these attempts never refer to the fact that they had failed? The structure of the article, which allowed ideology to respond in order to dissect its answer, nicely demonstrates Marx's journalistic method. It was not to mock from the beginning the defensive methods of an ideology all the more argumentative in that it was weak; it was to take them seriously, to understand how ideology surmounted the obstacle, in order finally to reveal the weakness of the process. The 'facts' which ideology quoted in its support revealed of themselves the inadequacy or the bias of the gaze which had selected them.

Another 'argument' much favoured by British leaders of opinion was to recall how ambiguous the Republicans of the North had been with regard to slavery *in the past*. Once again, Marx accepted the fact, this past ambiguity, and developed the line of argument which seemed to follow from it – until its absurdity was suddenly revealed for all to see:

> This is, in fact, a masterly piece of logic. Anti-Slavery England cannot sympathize with the North breaking down the withering influence of slaveocracy, because she cannot forget that the North, while bound by that influence, supported the slave-trade, mobbed the Abolitionists, and had its Democratic institutions tainted by the slavedriver's prejudices. She cannot sympathize with Mr. Lincoln's Administration, because she had to find fault with Mr. Buchanan's Administration. She must needs sullenly cavil at the present movement of the Northern resurrection, cheer up the Northern sympathizers with the slave-trade, branded in the Republican platform, and coquet with the Southern slaveocracy, setting up an empire of its own, because she cannot forget that the North of yesterday was not the North of to-day.

It is only at this point, when the absurdity has become patent, that Marx can finally argue that there is clearly something else motivating the actors than the 'logical' principles – in fact so short on logic – they invoke: 'The necessity of justifying its attitude by such pettifogging Old Bailey pleas proves more than anything else that the anti-Northern part of the English press is instigated by *hidden motives*,[86] too mean and dastardly to be openly avowed.' This reference to 'hidden motives' – the real motives, which derive from another stage than that of the discourse – appears at the end, not the beginning, of the discussion; it was the ideology itself, taken to its logical conclusion, which fell apart, pointing to some other factor to explain its incoherencies, at last laid bare. The external factors, far from having been posited at the beginning, as 'scientific' evidence, had emerged from within; the discourse, when analysed closely, had itself suggested exiting from the discourse in order to understand its own flaws.

Another article from the same period is particularly revealing with regard to this method of Marx. It is one of those he wrote on the *Trent* affair,[87] a political-legal-diplomatic incident which he dissected in a degree of detail which makes it impossible to regard him as someone who despised politics and public space; no detail, legal, strategic, cultural or psychological, escaped his analysis.

Let us briefly recall the principal events. On 13 May 1861 England declared its neutrality in a proclamation by Queen Victoria. This proclamation was in itself notably ambiguous, since it both signalled that England would not take the side of the Confederation (South) against the blockade imposed by the Union (North), and in effect recognized the Confederation as a belligerent power, in the same way as the Union. Besides, England had already established diplomatic relations with the Confederation, whose representative in London was William L. Yancey. In November 1861 the Confederation sent two diplomats to Europe, James M. Mason and John Slidell, to replace the Yancey delegation. Mason and Slidell embarked on a British ship, the *Trent*, from the port of Havana. On 8 November 1861 Captain Charles Wilkes, commanding a Northern ship, the *San Jacinto*, decided on his own responsibility to arrest the *Trent*, search it and take the two enemy diplomats prisoner. The outrage in England was so great that, as is generally agreed, the risk of a British intervention on the Confederate side was closer then than at any other point in the course of the war. In the end, the crisis subsided, the Union's minister of foreign affairs deciding to free the two diplomats, who landed on English soil at the end of January 1862.[88]

Marx analysed British indignation at the time of the arrest of the two diplomats in order to understand the logic behind it – once again, he was going to expose its contradictions, which the various lines of argument were unable to conceal. In particular, he showed how the incoherence of the statements of the English government at the beginning of the crisis – one day indignation, the next an effort to calm things down – was a consequence of the contradictions in which they were mired. At the strictly legal level, the attitude of the North was perfectly admissible: recognition of the Union and the Confederation as belligerent powers by England meant that it was itself subject to 'all the duties and inconveniences of a neutral in maritime warfare'. International law, in fact modelled on English law, authorized any belligerent power to search the ships of a neutral power in order to verify that they did not contain any goods or persons serving the enemy belligerent power, and to seize anything that seemed to fall into this category. Marx showed how the British press, even the most anti-Yankee, was forced to recognize this, even if there were some who argued that this legal rule had been established in 'circumstances very different from those which now occur'. He then examined how ideology had stymied itself: in the name of respect for its own legal principles, it was unable to give a legal dimension to its anger.

Yet it was necessary for the anger to be based on principles. Marx then noted the way in which the discourse of political indignation found a legal dimension after all – a piece of sleight of hand typical of the ideological discourse as Marx understood it. So the English crown lawyers ended up by accepting that the fault committed by the *San Jacinto* had been not one of substance, but one of form or procedure. Once again Marx listened to the arguments and even accepted them. But, in doing so – thus still using the same method – he put his finger on the hidden consequence, which was an embarrassment to the very people responsible for the argument; after all, the damage was much less if the legal fault was formal and not material. In which case, the legal argument could hardly do what it had initially been intended to: justify all the anger. The restitution demanded by England from the government of the Union could not be as great as the lawyers had attempted to argue when maintaining that the fault was material. So, at the end of the article, Marx advised the Northerners to take the British lawyers at their word, that is, to make public excuses but not to offer very substantial reparations; the Northerners had, after all, been well within their rights to act as they did, a few technical errors notwithstanding. In fact he advised them to reach a political or diplomatic settlement to this crisis as this was in their interests – it would hardly be to their advantage if an exasperated Great Britain entered the war against them; but they should avoid going to extremes, weakening or grovelling to those who had accused them of what was, after all, a very relative disregard for international law. Yet again Marx had shown the function of the ideological discourses, in particular of the legal principles, which was to try to provide a basis for an anger whose true causes were actually quite different.

The question remains, obviously, was Marx, by confronting ideology, really claiming to be able to overcome it? It should be made clear that Marx was not primarily addressing those whose discourses and arguments he was reporting, as he was writing for an American rather than an English audience. It seems unlikely that he was hoping to raise awareness among the English public.[89] The only public he seems truly to confront, and expose himself to, is the American public. It was to them alone that he appealed, directly and familiarly, apparently seeking to engage in a dialogue and exert influence, as when he wrote: 'Of one thing *you may be sure*, Palmerston wants a legal pretext for a war with the United States.'[90]

In essence, it is as if Marx needed interlocutors who were visibly out of step with the ideology he criticized, so that he could be open with them, seek their agreement and present himself as a participant in the ongoing debate, manifesting a desire to influence it. This does not imply that this public was without any ideology. What mattered was for it to have a different ideology from the one at issue in the debate, so as to make the criticisms at least audible, receivable and likely to be discussed by this new public. Even though the American public ought to prepare for the advent of a new ideology – which would need to be criticized in its turn, later, in front of another public – Marx went along with it for the time being. He helped it to take a step back from England, and to realize that the old European bourgeois ideology was finished, just as he would probably have supported the bourgeois 'public' on the eve of the French Revolution, as an expression of the class on which one had to pin one's hopes, even though this would in due course be the new ideology against which the struggle must in future be directed. The enthusiasm of Marx for the American public sometimes took an extreme form, since it was seemingly without any reservations that he described America, in one of his articles, as 'the only popular Government in the world'.[91] That said, Marx was not writing in total separation from the English public; he confronted it openly, on the basis of the very subjects it suggested to him. The American public and the English public stage were not hermetically sealed off from each other. But one senses that, though he may have confronted the English public, his purpose in doing so was not so much to influence it as to consolidate the gaze of a third party: that of the American public.

It is possible that not all of Marx's journalistic writings had equivalent status. Those for the *New York Daily Tribune* may have had a particular tone, since here Marx had some hopes of being heard. In this specific case, which may not be general, what we see is *truly public speech* – exposed and tested in public – and neither a solitary analysis, without hope of encounter, nor a learned disquisition, which might be 'publicized' by chance (for example for financial reasons), without expectation of any consequences for oneself or for others. In essence, the articles for the *Tribune* were not perhaps the *most journalistic* Marx wrote – that is, they were a real contribution to a public debate, expressing a point of view which, alongside and together with others, might help his interlocutors to come to a decision.

Marx's thought was thus in no way a serene search for 'another stage' than that of public space. Ideology was an enemy, certainly, but an enemy that must be confronted in order to see it more clearly. It was this search for visibility – an issue which remained central – that preoccupied Marx in his tireless journalistic activities. It would be simplistic, once again, to believe that, for Marx, the search to 'see' took place in the solitude of a study. Marx took on one public (American) in the very process of dissecting the ideology of another public (English). He laid himself open, in his labour of struggle or resistance; he was a 'flâneur' with and for others.

So he makes it possible for us to go beyond the ideal of the flâneur to an ideal of the conflictual journalist. With Marx, it is clear that the Kantian faith in the wonderful plurality of points of view, which the 'ideal' journalist should seek to serve, has been left behind. Only a 'core' of Kant has been retained, that is, the desire not, after all, to desert the public space he had criticized so harshly, after lauding it in his youth. Marx still 'believed' that something could be done in this space: no longer a peaceable varying of the gaze, but a battle against ideological domination.

Nevertheless, there is something left unsaid in the journalism of Marx, which I tried to bring out at the end of my discussion. In the act of resisting one public (English), he was obliged to constitute another (American). This raises questions which Marxism may not allow us fully to explore: is journalism not always a practice which, *at one and the same time*, detaches itself, produces a conflict and designates a 'them', *and also* integrates, establishes a 'common' and defines a 'we'? There is here a dual process, which the journalism of Marx only enables us to understand in part: the process of entering into conflict, of refusing, of confronting. The conflictual journalist is in reality only one of the two aspects of the journalist. Journalists are also, in their own way, engaged in creating a 'common' – certainly not the same as that against which they fight. We need to try to think these two processes at the same time, which may mean we have to abandon the strictly Marxian analytical framework, so that our discussion is not confined within a very narrow concept of ideology. We need to pose the question in a broader context.

That said, even from the Marxian standpoint, the double process performed by the journalist is pretty obvious, although implicit: journalism that is critical inevitably produces, in its own way, other representations, which operate in a common space, and are thus likely to participate in the creation of another ideology. It is impossible to escape this eventuality as long as there is class war, that is, as long as there exist material dominations which mean that the constitution of a 'common', at the level of representations, requires ideology.

But perhaps there are other theoretical universes which will enable us to think more precisely about the dual process that constitutes journalism, that is, *integrating and injecting conflict at the same time*. I propose now to turn to the sociology of publics. From the books of Gabriel Tarde to the works of the Chicago School of the first half of the twentieth century, those of Robert E. Park in particular, it has never ceased to respond to Gustave Le Bon and to that radical position which likens the 'public' to the 'crowd' and conclusively condemns journalism. The Chicago School has asked how far one can think a domination in the public, source of homogeneity in representations, while allowing the press a certain room for manoeuvre and hence responsibility. Can journalism, in spite of everything, help to inject an element of conflict into this public? Can it introduce some 'play' and in this way neutralize that which, in the public, corresponds to its most homogenizing impulse, the impulse most destructive of the plurality of points of view: the impulse of the 'crowd'?

At this point we leave the Marxian concept of ideology, though without forgetting the issues it raises: thinking a structural homogeneity in public space, which questions Kantian enthusiasm, but yet without abandoning all regard for this space. In the course of my argument I will imagine a dialogue between the sociology of Chicago and the more disturbing analyses of Roland Barthes on journalism as 'myth' – analyses which clearly nod towards the Marxian analytical framework. In short, I will try to define one last time the ideal-critique of journalism, in the form of a third ideal-critique which will be better than its two predecessors at enabling us to think journalism in a democracy in both its aspects, that is, as a sort of 'conflictual unifying' of the political community. This will mean correcting and improving on the two first ideal-critiques, not breaking with them. The journalist-flâneur took clearer shape in the conflictual journalist; this journalist will now be allocated an even more complex role, already implied in my earlier discussion, but as yet insufficiently explained.

5

A third ideal-critique: journalism as a 'conflictual unifying' of the democratic community

To define this third ideal-critique of journalism, we have to begin by accepting that journalism, whatever else it may do, produces a 'seeing in common', and so initiates a trend to *integrate* the political community. The question then becomes, does this trend allow an opportunity for conflict? In other words, can we, on this basis, think an 'ideal' journalism which *also* introduces conflictuality? And what would this mean?

In our discussion of the journalist-flâneur and the conflictual journalist, it has still not been possible to think this twofold trend. We need to take one further step.

1. Gabriel Tarde and an answer to Gustave Le Bon

From the 'age of crowds' to the 'age of publics'

To say that the public is something unified and 'integrated', in this rather homogeneous sense, and that journalism shares these characteristics, does not necessarily mean accepting Gustave Le Bon's contemptuous comparison of the public to a 'crowd'.[1] It can leave journalism with room for manoeuvre and open up possibilities for the public to escape this spectre of the crowd. It has been one of the main aims of the sociology of publics, and in particular of the work of Robert E. Park, to demonstrate this.

Some readers of Le Bon, however, had already rejected his analysis. The most important of these was Gabriel Tarde. Tarde was a total stranger to the Marxian theoretical universe, and his conceptualization ran along very different lines. Nevertheless, one can detect in it an analogous trend: an absence of Kantian enthusiasm, because Tarde, on the contrary, was anxious to define with precision the very specific homogeneity which characterizes publics, and, at the same time, an unequivocal rejection of the definitive condemnation of Le Bon. What concepts did Tarde develop, and in what way are they helpful to thinking the practice of journalism?

Tarde's articles, collected in 1901 in his book *Public Opinion and the Crowd*, were a direct response to Le Bon: 'Thus I cannot concede to a robust writer, Dr Le Bon, that our age is the "age of crowds". It is the age of the public or of publics, which is a very different matter.'[2] In rehabilitating the concept of 'public', against Le Bon, Tarde was probably revealing a certain attachment to the 'classic' actor/spectator distinction and aiming to restore all its specificity to the position of spectator. He returned to a distinction between the crowd, a physical and visible group, and the public, a group that was neither. The growth of the press had produced groups – readerships – which, because they were primarily concerned to see, rather than to do, could not be thought on the same model as the physical groups that were crowds. 'The psychology of crowds has been done; the psychology of the public remains to be done, understood in this other sense, that is, as a purely spiritual collectivity, as a scattering of individuals physically separated, whose cohesion is purely mental.'[3]

In fact readerships were for Tarde only emblematic instances of a more general mode of socialization, in which mutual observation, usually unconscious, the 'spectacle', played an essential role; this mode of socialization was *imitation*. It seems that, for Tarde, imitation only began to take place in the more developed social forms, which were probably the only ones to merit the description 'social'; at a certain stage of human evolution, social groups formed, no longer on the model of the 'crowd', which belonged to an earlier age,[4] but of the 'public'. It is difficult to tell whether Tarde considered that the crowd was a primitive social group, in which imitation existed, but in a very basic form, or whether this primitive nature made it a pre-social group, still without the minimal interpersonal communication – *conversation* – necessary for it to be possible to speak of imitation.[5] In any case, he perceived the public as a truly 'social' group, corresponding to an 'advance of civilisation',[6] because, unlike the silent crowd, it engaged in a conversation, assisted in this by the reading of newspapers.

The appearance of the press gave an unprecedented impulse to conversation, even more so than books, which did not deal with '*actual* questions simultaneously fascinating to all'.[7] Tarde saw the French Revolution as a crucial moment, the date of 'the true advent of journalism'.[8] Nevertheless, it was only with the revolution in the means of communication that the public came into its own; it was thus the nineteenth century that sounded the true death-knell of the 'age of crowds' and the beginning of the 'age of publics'.[9]

Inasmuch as conversation leads to imitation, it is difficult to conceive of the public as something marvellously plural. However, Tarde believed that the homogenization that operated through conversation was a very different phenomenon from the homogenization that prevailed among the individuals in a crowd. It was a dynamic, gradual, interactive process by which individual differences were reduced, whereas the crowd was created at once through the negation of these differences. This is how Tarde describes the imitation which happened through conversation:

> Take two persons, men or women, who pay a courtesy call and who engage in conversation; they carefully avoid the subjects where they risk being of different opinions; or, if they cannot escape the necessity of mentioning them, they conceal their opposition as far as possible; they even go so far as sometimes, in fact usually, sacrificing some of their ideas to preserve an atmosphere of harmony. Polite conversation can thus be regarded as a continuous and universal exercise of sociability, a unanimous and contagious effort to harmonise hearts and minds, and to erase or disguise their disagreements.[10]

The tie that binds the multiplicity of individuals who read the same newspaper is of the same type as that which is forged in a one-to-one conversation. There is, says Tarde, a 'relation of sympathy'[11] between each individual and the other readers.

It is clearly a powerful tie; it is also one of the reasons why individuals are interested in reading the newspapers. If I open a newspaper, says Tarde, if I begin to read and suddenly realize that it is several days old, 'it immediately loses its interest for me'. For him, 'this proves that our lively curiosity is the result of the unconscious illusion that our feelings are shared by a large number of people'.[12] This bond is also a fundamental factor in the work of journalists because, if the subjects they write about enter this common consciousness, they are assured of success, and it will be further strengthened by their work. Tarde believed, furthermore, that journalists were often far more conscious of this invisible bond than their readers.[13]

It is difficult to say if a journalist is able to create this invisible bond alone. In Tarde's discussion, the idea of journalists having an *influence* on their public is complex. It exists, certainly, but it is conditioned by a prior influence of the public on 'its' journalist, and its preferred channel of communication is the more general influence exerted by members of the public on each other. The reader feels as though influenced by a group, and not only by the journalist, even though it is the journalist who, by writing, gives this invisible group life. The real 'power' is then held by

> the consciousness of each one of them that this idea or this will is shared at the same moment by a large number of others. It is enough for [each of them] to know this, even without seeing these others, for them to be influenced by these others taken as a whole, and not only by the journalist, their common inspiration, who is himself invisible and unknown, and thus all the more fascinating.[14]

In fact what Tarde is describing, in his discussion of the relationship between journalists and their public, is that very process of conversation which creates homogeneity, but only as long as it goes on; it therefore requires to be permanently mutually engaged in, and constantly renewed. Some journalists prove to be better at this than others, and hence potentially more influential. In any case, this relationship is very different from that between the crowd and its leader, where there is no such room for manoeuvre. In the crowd the bond is made or is not made, there and then; it does not come about through conversation and it is ultimately less deep and less durable.[15]

Further, at any level, conversation operates on the basis of diversity. It gradually integrates differences, which it thus has to begin by encountering. This is why a public can go on expanding; it encounters otherness, then assimilates it. There is, it follows, a *dual* tendency in conversation: an opening up *and* a closing down, a diversification – different individuals make contact with each other – *and* a homogenization.[16] In the crowd, there are no such subtleties: at the slightest encounter with the different, the crowd rejects it or assimilates it completely. This is why Tarde believed that crowds were artificial entities, homogeneous only in appearance, ready to splinter at the least sign of difference (or of disagreement), whereas the homogeneity of a public is much deeper and more durable, because it is constructed and continues to be constructed.[17]

In short, Tarde was like Le Bon in thinking the unity of crowds and their intolerance, their unsuitability for any confrontation with difference, as a consequence of being rooted in affectivity. Starting from this common conviction, however, Tarde tried to show that publics achieved a unity on less affective bases. For Tarde, the crowd was animated by interests and desires rather than by ideas or beliefs (he spoke of 'faith') – and when there was a crowd that fell into this latter, minority category of believing, and not desiring, it was particularly dogmatic and intolerant.[18] This is why publics were better able to integrate differences, by taking the edge off them – always the dual tendency – something the crowd was unable to do. This dual tendency is visible again in the two adjectives Tarde used to think the effect of the newspaper: he wrote of the 'efficacy inherent to the newspaper, both solvent and regenerating at the same time',[19] then clarified his meaning by explaining that the press divided society not so much into interest groups as into ideas groups, and that these particular divisions were rifts that were less deep. 'The ideas and the passions may well froth when they clash, but they are still less irreconcilable than interests.'[20]

Thus the crowd can only incorporate or exclude on the spot, which aggravates social divisions, whereas the public, which smoothly integrates, produces social peace. 'If it so happened', hypothesizes Tarde,

> that all the newspapers were shut down and, with them, their publics, would not the population manifest a much stronger tendency than at present to gather in larger and denser audiences round the lecterns of professors, even the pulpits of preachers, to fill public places, cafés, clubs, salons and lecture halls, not to speak of theatres, and to behave everywhere more loudly? Only think of all the discussions in cafés, salons and clubs from which we are protected by the polemics of the press, a relatively inoffensive antidote.[21]

Even gatherings as anodyne as those evoked here are disparaged, so ever-present, it seems, is the spectre of the crowd. In fact the alternative to publics is either hermetic and conflictual crowds or equally hermetic isolated communities, the picturesque diversity of which leaves Tarde sceptical:

> In a small town, closed, let us suppose, to the reading of newspapers and lacking easy communication with the outside world, as under the *ancien régime*, one could talk away for ever, but the conversation, left to itself, would never rise above the level of gossip. Without the press, country gentlemen might well be great talkers, but they would talk of little else but hunting or genealogy, and the most eloquent of magistrates would speak of little but the law or shifts in competences, just as the officers of the German cavalry, according to Schopenhauer, speak only of women and horses.[22]

There was nothing to regret, therefore, certainly not the social unrest of this 'age of crowds', which was a consequence of their inability to integrate the different.

A sense of relief?

So Tarde 'defends', against Le Bon, the idea of public, while still approaching it with a notable lack of Kantian enthusiasm for plurality. He encourages us to reflect on the public in a dynamic, uncertain and open way. The public 'can' do many things that the crowd cannot; it is hardly marvellous Kantian plurality, but nor is it the immovable block of the crowd of Le Bon. What a 'good' journalism would be in this context, and what 'good' it might do the public, are questions that are opened up thanks to this fruitful analytical framework.

That said, Tarde's thinking, too, has its limitations with regard to these subjects. What impedes it more, perhaps, than one might have expected is a tone of resignation. So great is the relief at finding that the public has brought us out of the 'age of crowds' that it is difficult to ask any more of it. By overturning Le Bon while remaining a prisoner of his analytical framework (the crowd is something odious), there is a risk of putting too high a value on anything that breaks with the crowd, and then ending up in the same sterility of thinking as Le Bon, but the other way round: instead of pouring scorn on this structurally 'homogeneous' public space, one resigns oneself to it, in relief, and ultimately ceases to think this homogeneity as a *problem*, requiring that one ask *whether journalism can do something with it*. In other words, we no longer ask if it is still possible, on this basis, to think an ideal-critique of journalism.

In fact there is a way of reading Tarde that completely fossilizes his analyses. One can seek in him the cynical satisfaction of a conservative, happy to accord a people freedom of speech because its consequences will lead to a social pacification, and a smoothing over of conflicts, which are grounds for rejoicing. Far from the hopes of Kant, for whom the principle of publicity involved a historical trend of rationalization and reform, it is for Tarde primarily a way of inhibiting the most conflictual, and thus most destructive, social impulses. This amounts to reading Tarde as a digest of the arguments which made it possible, in France, to pass the law of 1881 on the freedom of the press. As Dominique Reynié has shown in his discussion of the parliamentary debates of that period,[23] the passing of this law owed much to the conservative arguments which presented it as a way of sublimating the violence of the crowd into a toned-down 'public' conflict, that is, of establishing a space for opinions separate from social space, and thus less dangerous. In fact in 1881 the deputies did everything they could – a perversion of the Kantian theme of 'doubling' – to make sure that the new scene of opinions was clearly cut off from the scene of actions. They demanded precise 'forms' for the expression of opinions in order to prevent an opinion from having any effect, from 'acting'. For example, this law 'authorized the free printing of a seditious song, but prohibited it from being sung in the street'.[24] It banned the street cry because 'it falls within the category of action, not opinion'.[25] Also banned were certain types of writing which acted too much, dare one say, like bills or posters.[26] The law was not without its attacks on certain types of content, but they were in the name of the same logic: certain opinions, either by their form or their content, should not spread beyond the sphere that was theirs. It prohibited, in an extraordinary phrase, 'active opinion'.[27] All these prohibitions reveal, of course, the hypocrisy of the law. However, they also reveal a logic close to certain analyses of Tarde: they relied on the calming effect, or 'solvent efficacy', of public conversation, so as to distance the spectre of the crowd, and were therefore careful, so as to guarantee this calming effect, to establish an order of opinion totally cut off from the order of action.

In fact it was the way Tarde's thought was rooted in the obsessions of Le Bon that gave it this reassured and reassuring aspect, and which risked closing down the critical analysis of the concept of public. Tarde tended to see the public first and foremost as what saves us from the crowd. His way of evoking a historic moment of 'progress' hardly encouraged critical unease with respect to publics. Even when he examined, after the transition from crowds to publics, that from publics to the mass public, he was unable to see this as anything other than a natural evolution. He could hardly be frightened *a priori* by this ever-expanding process of 'conversation', which pacified and integrated ever more: 'In spite of the divergences and the multiplicity of the publics coexisting and intermingled in a society, they seem to form one single, same public, by their partial agreement on several important points; and this is what is called Opinion, the political supremacy of which continues to increase.'[28] There is little fear in these words, more a hope of peace and 'social union'.[29]

It should be recognized, however, that Tarde himself was not always so serene. Many of his pages reveal a deep unease. What he feared was an increase in the power of journalists. Before the advent of a mass public, the power of journalists over their respective publics had already been considerable, although, as we have shown, ambivalent, in that it also required the journalist to submit to the general tastes of this public. Above all, however, the plurality of the publics constrained the power of each of them, imposing limits on it. If the publics merged into one, the power of the journalists would be further increased.[30] Admittedly, journalists must never forget to please, and were in this regard subject to certain implicit criteria; they needed to know how to vary their tactics so as to enthral a constantly shifting public, and to cultivate what was common rather than differences. If they were good at this, however, they had at their disposal a homogenized public of unprecedented size: 'It may be that [this development] increasingly enslaves mediocre journalists to the whims of their public, but, we may be sure, it increasingly subjects their enthralled public to the despotism of the great journalists.'[31] The risk, therefore, with the merging of the publics into one single, great, mass public was the increasing hold of the journalist over the reader, 'the one-newspaper man', who was particularly 'docile and credulous'. 'And this man', Tarde went on, 'is, at bottom, every one of us, or not far from it. This is the danger of the new times.'[32]

Yet Tarde's analytical framework did not enable him to offer a real conceptual outlet for this unease, for example by embarking on a discussion of the 'ideal' journalism that would enable this new era to protect itself against its possible demons. The reason for this incapacity in Tarde is his permanent obsession with the crowd; at least we are rid of it, he keeps reminding us. The mass public may have its disturbing aspects, but it is not a regression into a crowd – the 'psychological crowd' of Le Bon. It is something very different and, as a result, something which remains the downside of a gain – pacification, sociability – and so cannot be regretted. A thinking which at every point valorized unification and homogenization, natural effects of a 'communication' that was itself valorized, was incapable of truly integrating this final fear. In this conceptual framework, compared to the fear aroused by crowds, this new evil could only appear the lesser, since it at least had the advantage of delivering us from the former. In fact Tarde's thinking was blocked by his fixation on the public/crowd distinction, which was a product of his debate with Le Bon.

What was needed was for someone to take up the problem where Tarde had left off, that is, to face up to the problem of the uniformity of the public, unimpeded by the block created by the relief of having emerged from the age of crowds, and thus to free up critical thinking. This was, in many respects, what was done by the sociologists of the Chicago School.

2. The sociologists of Chicago (R. E. Park, H. M. Hughes) faced with the reality of an 'integrating' journalist

The risk of the public regressing into the crowd: the intellectual itinerary of R. E. Park

A discussion which takes as its reference point the crowd as defined by Le Bon risks getting no further than the definitive condemnation of a public that is no more than a 'crowd' or relief that the public is something fundamentally different from a crowd. It is this double impasse which Robert E. Park, an American who went to study in Germany, a former journalist and a future eminent sociologist, managed to avoid in his doctoral thesis of 1904 entitled 'Masse und Publikum'.

Park drew in this work both on earlier discussions of the subject of the crowd and the public and on the work of one of his principal masters, Georg Simmel, to construct a true critique of journalism. Siding with Tarde against Le Bon, he proposed a clear distinction between the public and the crowd. Unlike Tarde, however, he believed that the 'psychological crowd' of Le Bon continued to be an ever-present risk for the public. The problem for the journalist, therefore, was how to avoid this slippage, this regression of the public into the crowd. In thinking a sort of *crowd–public continuum*, Park raised important questions: what was it that encouraged the reversion to the crowd? How could it be avoided?

Park's views on these questions changed considerably during the course of his intellectual itinerary, though he eventually largely returned to his claims of 1904, as we will see. These questions never ceased to preoccupy him, which is why he is a major figure in the debate on journalism in a democracy. For Park, the problem was always to know how far the trend to institute something 'in common', for him fundamental to journalism, could go, while remaining a journalism worthy of the name – because, for him, journalism was something worthy. The problem was thus one of *limits*, which, in reality, led to that of the precise *nature* of the journalistic act of 'integrating'.

In his thesis of 1904 Park carefully distinguished the concept of public from that of crowd, but in order to articulate also, with great clarity, the anxiety that the mass press might make publics regress into crowds. The public, he said, was an association that respected individual singularities; the crowd was not. He called the unity which characterized a public a 'common consciousness', much more subtle and complex than the fusional 'common drive' which characterized the crowd, 'suppressing all purely individual impulses'.[33]

The difference between the two thus lay in the capacity of the public to be both *one* and *plural*, unlike the crowd, that enemy of plurality. This is essentially a fairly Kantian position, which owed much to a master of Park who had been a careful reader of Kant, Georg Simmel. It would be more accurate to say that it was the Simmelian theory of conflict that formed the backdrop to Park's thought on the public.[34] For Simmel conflict was a form of socialization. It integrated, it brought together, it created a tight-knit unity, beyond the division which it seemed at first sight to reveal. Such a theory made it possible to think the public, without difficulty, as both conflictual plurality and integrated unity, since it was the conflictuality that produced the unity. Armed with such a theory, the young Park was far removed from the ideas of Tarde on the public, which emphasized a homogeneity based on a *smoothing over of conflicts*. In fact, in this thesis of 1904, Park was highly critical of Tarde, unlike in his later writings.[35]

It is Simmel who was the real master here, not Tarde. Simmel promoted what was ultimately a very Kantian vision of the public, a space where the 'common' was constantly constructed and reconstructed through the plural, conflictual interchange of different points of view. In line with Simmel, Park made the importance of *opposition*, or *competition*, central to his analysis of the public. It was conflict itself, within the public, which produced its unity and its integration. Park also adopted the Simmelian theory of *objectification*: conflict, between two persons, as between a large number of individuals, eventually produces 'common objects', which have the same meaning for all. This is what makes possible, according to Simmel, the emergence in a society of common 'forms', beyond differences between points of view or subjective 'lived experiences'.[36] For Park, in a public, these common 'things', constructed through plural exchanges, were the 'facts'. Their existence was necessary for conflicts of interpretation, conflicts of 'values', to happen; and it did nothing to prevent the perpetuation of these conflicts of 'values': rather the opposite.[37] The objectification of the 'facts' was thus not an impediment to the plurality of points of view but, on the contrary, its condition; it was what both allowed it and organized it.

Thus the public is the association which, while being united, assures the widest possible plurality. The only thread which binds the individuals within it is this indispensable objectification of the 'facts', that is, the capacity to separate 'facts' from 'values'. It is this that opposes the public to the crowd, which is incapable of separating in this way the (common) 'facts' from the (plural) 'values'; the common objects of the individuals of a crowd are already 'values'. There is, therefore, a much greater uniformity of values in the crowd than in a public.

The real danger, for the Park of 1904, lay in the developments within the press which tended, on the contrary, to disseminate increasingly homogenized values and insidiously to transform the public into the 'psychological crowd' of Le Bon. The young academic denounced the damaging effects of commercial advertising but also the new forms of journalism: 'Modern journalism, which is supposed to instruct and direct public opinion by reporting and discussing events, usually turns out to be simply a mechanism for controlling collective attention.'[38]

All this supposes a fairly serene discussion of the unity that constitutes a public. The Simmelian heritage made it possible to trust in the capacity of a public to be one and diverse at the same time. It was perfectly logical, therefore, to ask that journalism be worthy of it. Park seems, at this point, not yet to have worried about the question of the effective capacity of a public to practise this distinction between 'facts' and 'values', which was the basis of his great tolerance towards the plurality of the 'values'. The 'public' of Park was almost as ideal as the plural public of Kant. Indeed it strongly resembled it. The discussion that took place within the public is described as a veritable intersubjective journey, respectful of the plurality of the meanings which the generally accepted 'facts' had for all, and leading, as in Kant, to the definition of a correct, 'supra-individual perspective'.[39] The mature Park was to change his views on mass journalism, because he was also to change his conception of the public as the reign of conflictual plurality. He lost his Simmel-inspired confidence in integration through conflict, and began increasingly to think integration *against* conflicts and, as a result, the public as a unity that may be from the outset less tolerant of plurality. The idea that the necessity of a public being *one* inevitably limited the plurality of the points of view which constituted it gradually emerged.

The first significant shift in his itinerary was the article of 1923, 'Natural history of the newspaper'.[40] In this article, Park distinguishes three stages in the history of journalism. The first was that of the earliest newspapers, at the level of the village, which he describes as 'devices for organizing gossip'.[41] This expression supposes that the 'gossip' existed before it was committed to writing; the newspapers recorded it on paper, simply giving it some order, in a way performing the function of a diary in individual lives. Modern urbanization transformed this situation: 'It is evident', he wrote, 'that a newspaper cannot do for a community of 1,000,000 inhabitants what the village did spontaneously for itself through the medium of gossip and personal contact.'[42] The role of the newspaper had to change; a second stage has appeared.

This second stage was that of the 'journal of opinion', in the large towns. In many respects this involved recreating, as far as possible, the conditions of the village, by dividing the urban masses into smaller communities, united by common interests and a common gossip, which the newspaper could then structure as it had done in the villages. But this, explained Park, had not made it possible to integrate the majority of the individuals in the large towns, especially as the journals of opinion had very quickly emerged as the organs of parties, their content based less on the spontaneous gossip of sympathizing publics than on serving the strategies of certain dominant political personalities.

The third and last stage was the 'independent' or 'mass circulation' press, which had taken fully into account the fact that times had changed. It completely redefined the function of the newspaper as compared with the old village gazette. The formula of Charles A. Dana, editor of the *New York Sun* in the 1880s, 'News is anything that will make people talk',[43] emerged as a counterpoint to the old mission, which had been to organize gossip. Whereas the old newspaper had imposed order on existing gossip, the new aimed to create speech where no one was speaking. It created conversation where there was none; it introduced, among the very different individuals who made up the urban masses, that minimal 'common' without which it is impossible to talk of a 'public'. The reign of the leader-writer was succeeded by that of the reporter, because the aim was no longer to select and discuss in print the 'stories' which were the stuff of oral gossip, but actually to make 'stories' exist. The popular press born in the 1830s in the United States had as its main objective making reality visible in the form of *stories*. It aimed, therefore, for what could interest the largest number; it banked on that great common denominator, *curiosity*, that is, what Park called 'human interest'.[44]

The main difference between this article of 1923 and Park's thesis of 1904 is the refusal now to treat this new stage with the contempt he had earlier displayed for it. The end of the article is an appeal to put moral judgements aside, an appeal based on the firm conviction that there was, in any case, no remedy.[45] More generally, it was Park's whole conceptualization that had changed. In 1904, the new mass public had been relegated from the start to the category of crowd, and urged to become at last, it is not clear how, a public; in 1923 Park implicitly recognized the naivety of envisaging a public where its first condition, that is, the existence of spontaneous collective gossip, an already 'active' curiosity, was not met. In trying to achieve this condition, was the popular press, which was enjoyable – its explicit aim was *entertainment* – and which 'made speak', perhaps, on the contrary, on the way to creating a 'public'?

Park was engaging in a theoretical U-turn. He gradually returned to a discussion of the concept of public, putting greater emphasis on the first requirement of its *integration*, and on the need for a communication which linked the individuals within it. The plurality of 'values' and the objectification of the 'facts' which resulted could only come about on the basis of an indispensable common foundation: a *shared curiosity* and, in consequence, a collective gossip, that is, a certain *cultural unity*. It was necessary, therefore, to relativize the plurality of values, initially attributed to the public, by emphasizing that this plurality only appeared on the basis of common, unifying cultural values: before a confrontation, there had to be something in common. In fact it seems that the conflicts which Park had in 1904 made central to his thinking on the public, so as to explain its characteristic respect for diversity, and which had at that period been perceived as spontaneously integrating (in line with the Simmelian conception of conflict), must now be subject to a condition: the existence of a *prior* socio-cultural integration.

This new theoretical direction is visible in the articles Park wrote in 1938–9, most notably 'Reflections on communication and culture'[46] and 'Symbiosis and socialization: a frame of reference for the study of society'.[47] In these two articles Park revised the central role he had attributed, in 1904, to *competition*; it lost its spontaneously integrating Simmelian function. Competition may well lead to the objectification of the 'facts' that are common to all, he said, but this is not enough to produce a sufficient unity for it to be possible to speak of a public. Competition is primarily a 'principle of individuation' in society; on its own it tends to bring the group closer to '*symbiosis*', a collection of rival and often utilitarian relations (for example a market), but which lacks the unity necessary to produce a truly united social group.

The real integrating and truly socializing principle, he now argued, was *communication*,[48] which was a process of a growth of mutual understanding, leading to the realization of a true 'cultural unit'.[49] Following in the footsteps of John Dewey,[50] Park even claimed that many relationships which, within a group, were not part of this 'integrating' communication were not, strictly speaking, 'social'. Which is to say that, for a public to be considered a true social unit, something more was needed than these inter-individual relations of exchange based on competition. In 'Symbiosis and socialization', he even argues that a public is characterized by an 'underlying and more or less unconscious unanimity of purpose and intent', which suggests that the notion of a plurality of values has been significantly watered down, even if he elsewhere maintains a distinction between the public and the 'complete unanimity' represented by a crowd.[51] Integration – Park sees this as little different from assimilation, even speaking of 'incorporation' – seemed to him an absolute necessity for the individual to be truly a member of the social group and not simply, for example, the stranger with whom one engages in a commercial transaction.

This conceptual revision encouraged a less unfavourable attitude to the mass journalism of the age of urbanization than that of 1904; by cultivating what is most common to the collective curiosity, and by seeking out 'human interest', this modern journalism promotes socio-cultural integration, 'acculturation', as Park calls it. In fact the mass press engages in a reintegration of individuals, against the backdrop of disintegration associated with urbanization. This is probably why his analysis of 1904, which viewed the mass public as a new crowd, now seemed to Park mistaken, in that it had amounted to describing an over-integration – this is really the definition of the crowd – where there was no more than a corrective trend starting from an initial situation of disintegration. Who knows, this labour of creating a 'common' between completely different individuals might actually be preparing the ground for the advent of a true public?

Nevertheless, though Park may now have believed that individualizing '*competition*' would never produce true integration, and that it was therefore necessary to add a more immediately unifying principle, that is, '*communication*', he had still not abandoned the Simmelian theory of conflict. What the alliance of competition and communication ought to produce was integrating conflict as defined by Simmel; Park had simply discovered that it was more difficult to make this happen (the principle of competition not being enough on its own).[52]

This point, which may seem a matter of detail, is in fact of great importance. It shows that Park, when he thought of the public as primarily an integrated group, had not altogether stopped seeing it as containing permanent conflict. Indeed it was what allowed him to hold on to his distinction between the public and the 'psychological crowd', even if he had meanwhile become much more flexible in his definition of the public. He had abandoned, most notably, the systematic contempt for mass journalism. However, it was equally important that the trend towards cultural integration and a homogenization of values through the search for 'human interest' and the writing of enticing 'stories' should not go too far, to the point where it killed off any possibility of conflict.

The mass public, a creation of modern journalism, was no longer, for Park, systematically an odious Le Bonian crowd. It was still necessary to study it in more detail, however, to establish whether it really did hold out the promise of becoming a public, that is, whether, through the integrating tendency that operated within it, it sufficiently prepared the way for the possibility of the conflict which remained, at the end of the day, an important characteristic of the public. For Park, this type of enquiry meant seeking a normative definition of journalism. The 'true' journalism, among all the reading matter offered to the mass public in the newspapers, was that which, beyond its tendency to unify or to integrate this public – a necessary condition – also prepared it to become a 'true' public, that is, *also* prepared it for conflict.

Preserving the possibility of conflict: the search for a normative definition of journalism

Park's caution is interesting. Even though he is increasingly inclined to valorize the 'integrating', socializing or 'acculturing' role of popular journalism, he is still careful not to lose sight of the distinction between a public – integrated, admittedly, and culturally unified – and a crowd – a sort of ultimate stage of unification. The question then becomes one of boundaries and balance. Journalism integrates, certainly, especially in the age of disintegration through mass urbanization, but the question remains: how far can it integrate without changing the nature of the public, without turning it into a crowd? The question can also be posed in the following terms: what is it, in what is published in the newspapers, that achieves this subtle balance and offers a type of gaze that treats its spectators as a public, that is, that allows a reception that is to some degree diversified and conflictual? And what is it, on the contrary, that is no more than a rite of unification, intended simply to merge the readers into a crowd? What is true journalism and what is simply a litany of homogeneous values, likely to fuse the cultural community of readers ever more closely together?

Park distinguishes *journalism* from the sort of reading matter, admittedly sometimes found in the newspapers themselves, that is no more than an unadulterated expression of the cultural homogeneity of the community. There are, he says, two different sorts of 'things' published in the newspapers:

> not everything printed in the newspapers is news. Much that is printed as news is read, at least, as if it were literature; read, that is to say, because it is thrilling and stirs the imagination and not because its message is urgent and demands action. Such, for example, are the 'human interest' stories, so called, which have been so influential in expanding and maintaining newspaper circulation. But human-interest stories are not news. They are literature.[53]

We should distinguish, therefore, between news, which is proper journalism, and human interest stories, that is, the anecdotes, sensational snippets, believe-it-or-not stories and tales of mystery and passion which fill the subsidiary pages of the newspapers. Their sole justification is their *human interest*; they are its 'pure' product. A disciple of Park, Helen M. Hughes, has drawn attention to the recurring features in these human interest stories, constants which reveal just how far they express the culture of the day. In the late nineteenth and early twentieth centuries, for example, she observed the frequency of animal stories and stories of lost children.[54] Park, in the passage just quoted, seems to believe that there is a fairly clear boundary between the news, which should be 'interesting', certainly, and the human interest stories, which may only be 'interesting'.

This is because news has an extra dimension: it satisfies the curiosity, but it is also 'knowledge', a knowledge that is often, Park observed, very useful to 'symbiotic' competition, in particular in commerce.[55] He took this argument further in the months that followed, notably in an article of 1940, 'News as a form of knowledge',[56] and in the Introduction he wrote for the book by Helen Hughes, *News and the Human Interest Story*.[57] What Park understood by 'knowledge' was a form of 'objectivity' that made the spectator-reader, when presented with it, feel that several judgements were possible. It seems that Park has returned here to his old Simmel-inspired theme of objectification, which had so preoccupied him in 1904. In contrast to pure human interest stories, the news demonstrated a clear concern to distinguish between 'facts' and 'values'. There was no longer any question, certainly, of thinking a simple distinction between facts and values in the public: 'a fact is only a fact in some universe of discourse',[58] he said, at the end of a passage asserting once again the extent to which news depended on a certain cultural condition of the collective curiosity. He chose as an example what has become a classic, still quoted in American schools of journalism: '"Dog bites man" – that is not news. But "Man bites dog" – that is.'[59] All news was subject to this norm of curiosity, to 'human interest'. Nevertheless, news had a special status among the many subjects which engaged the common curiosity. It had a sort of 'official', 'public' and 'authenticated' quality by the mere fact of its publication, the latter signifying that it had been 'exposed to the critical examination of the public'.[60] This is what distinguished it from rumour and gossip, which had little need of such authentication.[61] News, consequently, had an 'objective' dimension beyond its interesting and appealing nature. It was in this sense that, for Park, it constituted a 'knowledge'.

It was not a formalized and abstract knowledge, certainly, but it was knowledge none the less, practical and oriented towards action, analogous to that 'knowledge' which, at the level of 'the individual man', gave 'perception'.[62] One of the most important achievements of 'News as a form of knowledge' is to situate journalism (producer of news) within the continuum of the more formalized knowledge of the historian and the sociologist. The rooting in the present, in its priorities, interests, values and narrow or at least biased curiosity, did not preclude a form of 'objectivity', which Park defined, it is true, in a wholly relative manner, admitted as such. A journalistic 'fact' (contained in a piece of news), he explained, in his Introduction to the book by Helen Hughes, is defined by its quality of acceptability to actors who may interpret it differently, thus who are inspired by different values.[63] This is very relative, certainly, since it seems to accept that the conflicts and differences of values within a public emerge, in spite of everything, against a backdrop of common values. But it is still a form of 'objectivity' in the eyes of R. E. Park – I myself, in order to recall the link with Simmel, which is clear in these texts, prefer to call it 'objectification'.

Human interest stories, in contrast, are part of a different continuum, one which leads from fiction to literature. In them, 'the distinction between the news story and the fiction story tends to disappear'.[64] It appears, therefore, that two lines lead from human interest, that major journalist preoccupation. One, through the cult of human interest, ever stronger, ever less concerned with 'objective' reality, leads to art. The other maintains a balance between this concern for human interest and a desire for objectification; it leads to the social sciences. This balancing act specific to news, or this subtle mix, is described by Park as a compromise between the 'art of writing' and the 'art of reporting':

> It is the art of writing to tell a story in such a way as will permit the reader rather than the writer to have the appropriate emotions. It is the art of reporting to state the facts so that both parties to an issue will accept them as facts, though they may disagree as to the interpretation to be put upon them.[65]

The writing of human interest stories unbalances these skills to the benefit of the former, tempted as it is to overdramatize in a way that can endanger 'objectivity' – in the sense in which Park used the word. It is almost as if the human interest story destroys the last space, which some already saw as too small, which had still preserved, within the news, a relative diversity of judgements on the basis of a common factual foundation, that is, the minimal, residual distance which had still separated 'facts' and 'values'. In the human interest story, in contrast, there is something 'total'; its factuality is full of 'values' which leave no space to other values to interpret it; its meaning is given from the outset, in its entirety, in its factual texture. This is clear, for example, in a story of a lost child, where the emotion leaves little space for a diversity of opinions. By this lack of objectifying distance – which would assure the minimal plurality of interpretations necessary to claim to be dealing with a 'public' – the spectacle of the human interest story appears comparable to that 'contagious excitement' which Park believed characterized the mode of communication intrinsic to crowds.[66]

This feeling of plurality, preserved by the news, is for the spectator a feeling of being also an *actor*: reading the news is not only 'thrilling and stirs the imagination', it 'demands action'.[67] Park believed that in this way the news offered a type of spectacle that was *political*: 'The extent to which news circulates, within a political unit or a political society, determines the extent to which the members of such a society may be said to participate, not in its collective life – which is the more inclusive term – but in its political acts.' He went on to say that 'political action and political power, as one ordinarily understands these terms, are obviously based not merely on such concert and consensus as may exist in a herd or in a crowd'.[68]

Essentially, what Park understood by 'political' was two things at once, inextricably linked: both a relationship to action and the preservation of a certain (admittedly relative) plurality. The crowd was not 'political' because it consisted of a group of spectators who had lost the relationship to action, and who were as if merged – this was precisely the 'psychological crowd' of Le Bon. On the one hand, preservation of the spectator–actor link and preservation of differentiation; on the other, withdrawal from the link with action and loss of differentiation. But also, in the Parkian universe: on the one hand, a spectacle which remained pragmatic in outlook; on the other, a purely 'aesthetic' spectacle, cut off from any pragmatism of outlook – in fact pure cultural ritual.

It is thus the need for a minimum of objectification which constitutes the boundary between journalism strictly speaking and another sort of 'literature', which was present in the newspapers, admittedly, not to be despised in itself, and 'acculturizing', but which Park refused to recognize as journalism. It might also put it like this: it is a degree of respect for the reality/fiction divide, or a degree of concern to provide an 'objective' knowledge regarding reality, that constitutes the criteria by which to judge what is published in the newspapers, that is, by which to distinguish journalism from what, in spite of appearances, is not journalism (since in the human interest story reality is treated like fiction). This does not absolve journalism from its mission to entertain, but it requires it to be firmly linked to a mission to *inform* or to *instruct* regarding reality.

And yet, hardly has he provided this normative definition of journalism, that is, hardly has he constructed this distinction between the news and human interest stories, when Park appears to waver. One sign of this is his persistent interest in that strange phenomenon, the human interest story, which cannot perhaps quite so easily be separated from true journalism. It is as if the very nature of this 'literature', whose readers demand that it be interesting *but also* '*true*', holds him back from criticizing it for relinquishing all concern for factual accuracy. Thus Park also describes human interest stories as constituting 'a kind of popular literature for the entertainment and instruction of the proletarian public of the cities'.[69] The search for the most frenzied human interest, for 'contagious excitement', seems never properly to abandon the terrain of news.

In other words, the frontier that has to be held keeps retreating. Journalism seems to extend as far as the field of literature, as long as it remains this side of fiction, and this applies particularly to all the stories, sensational news items and tragic and exciting tales which fill the pages of the popular press, and which, sensational though they may be, have not (or not yet) been extracted by a novelist from their actuality, stripped of their reality, in a way, and transformed into eternal stories analogous to legends. As long as factual accuracy is respected, it is journalism.

Park was then led into ever greater indulgence towards mass circulation journalism. Was he uneasy about this? All he feared was a 'narrowing' of the collective curiosity:

> As tension arises, the limits of public interest narrows, and the range of events to which the public will respond is limited . . . this narrowing of the focus of public attention tends to increase the influence of the dominant person or persons in the community. But the existence of this dominance depends on the ability of the community, or its leaders, to maintain tension. It is in this way that dictators arise and maintain themselves in power.[70]

He remained confident in the ability of the modern public to demand something 'objective', something 'real', that is, an element of 'news' in all human interest stories, and thus to prepare for the moments of openness which would not fail to arise. Real danger could come only from a dictatorship which would totally reconstruct the real and thus deceive the public, deflecting its desire for 'reality' towards the 'fictive', without its being aware of it. But he considered such a situation to be both exceptional and too costly in energy for anyone who organized it to prove a lasting or serious threat.

A degree of democratic optimism

Helen M. Hughes, a disciple of Park, was perhaps even more indulgent towards human interest stories: yes, they are still journalism, she seems to say, as long as they continue to respect the 'real' – which on the whole they do. In fact it was the collective curiosity itself that was 'journalized' with the advent of modernity. Instead of the fictions of the past, urban communities wanted something 'true', something 'real', 'news', journalism. They wanted, spontaneously, in the very act of celebrating their cultural unity, in their way of stimulating their common curiosity, to be *publics* and not simply *crowds*. Contemporary cultural communities were thus closer than ever to becoming *political* communities, because their curiosity was now spontaneously oriented towards the real, rather than, as before, towards the legendary or the fictive.

This, says Hughes, constitutes the specificity of this new 'folklore' of modernity; it feeds on 'true' stories. Admittedly, she says, popular journalism seeks to re-forge, in the age of urbanization and the ensuing disintegration, the lost cultural link. In this way it takes the place of the legend and rumour of old, or generally of the old 'gossip'. It is thus analogous to the phenomena analysed by Robert Redfield, the recreation of 'folktales' and 'folkballads' at a time when the 'folk' (the village population, characterized by a closed local culture) had disappeared and been replaced by the *demos* (the population of the large cities). Hughes compares the popular journalism of human interest stories to the Mexican *corrido*, sung 'history', often published and sold, a symptom of nostalgia for the folklore lost in the age of urbanization.[71] But she is also careful to bring out the changes that accompany this labour of nostalgic recreation. Whereas the folk ballad was composed of legends and rumours, situated in a distant or imaginary past, and contained 'no news',[72] the *corrido* was a 'true' story of today; it was a 'news ballad' which portrayed 'living and contemporary persons'.[73] It performed the ancient folk ballad's function of entertainment and 'acculturation', while adding another: that of informing – a condition apparently now necessary to performing the first function itself. True to its name, which means 'event of the time', the *corrido* 'relates'; it is therefore 'a newspaper as well as an entertainment' and in this 'it departs from the folk ballad'.[74] The human interest stories which flourished from the end of the nineteenth century in the popular American newspapers were, in a way, the *corridos* of the American *demos*. They, too, were 'true' and so cannot be regarded as having broken with 'journalism' and its intrinsic requirement: to provide news.

A political dimension had thus been added to the old function of cultural unification performed by folklore. It now situates those who are entertained by it in their concrete actuality; it speaks to them of their world. In the second half of the nineteenth century, Hughes argues, 'the newspaper printed not only the kind of reading matter they had enjoyed in the ballads, but it also brought them some news of public affairs, and as much about political issues as they would give their attention to. This is, in the end, an accompaniment of expanding democracy.' And she adds, 'with reading, the *demos* little by little acquired a common body of knowledge and sentiment and began to develop into a public, and that means, eventually, that the political basis of the state becomes broader. Interest in the personal affairs which the ballads and then the penny papers made public may be said to be a stage of public opinion.'[75] One could hardly be clearer regarding the political consequences attributed to the fact of being entertained by *true* stories, not fictional ones.

From then on, Hughes is consistent: the only forms of 'journalism' which are to be condemned as pure entertainment, having split off from journalism, are those which do not respect this essential reality/fiction divide. She gives as an example the *New York Evening Graphic*, a newspaper founded in 1924, which relentlessly pursued a policy of extreme sensationalism. It was under pressure to do this because the press baron Randolph Hearst had just started a newspaper, the *Daily Mirror*, to compete with a scandal sheet which had been highly successful, the *New York Daily News*. Thus the *Graphic* was forced to fight for a place among an already existing gutter press. As a result, it overstepped the boundaries of journalism, that is, it ignored the reality/fiction divide, by inventing what was called at the time the 'composograph', the rigged photograph. The gutter press was then running stories about a particularly juicy scandal: a wealthy young man was seeking a divorce from his wife, a woman of mixed blood, whom he accused of having deceived him by leading him to believe she was white. The young woman's defence counsel got permission for her to undress to the waist, in court, to demonstrate that no such deception had been possible. The press had no hope of photographing the woman as she undressed, for fear of being sued for contempt of court. So the *Graphic* got a young woman to pose naked, her back turned, in front of some reporters, then replaced their faces with the faces of people who had been present in court. This rigged photo earned the *Graphic* record sales – and, says Hughes, the nickname the *Porno-Graphic*.

However, it also, according to Hughes, meant that the *Graphic* had abandoned journalism strictly speaking. For her, the infringement of the reality/fiction divide was the only real journalistic prohibition. In fact this idea still seems to be current today, in a more or less confused way, as shown by the scandals provoked by fake reporting. The gutter press can constantly juggle with reality, and dramatize it, but there is a line that apparently cannot be crossed without it endangering itself: the line beyond which it simply falsifies reality.

That said, Hughes's discussion of the affair of the *Graphic* led her to play down the danger of 'sensationalist elements' in modern journalism. In fact it was the offence committed by this newspaper, she says, that was the cause of its failure. The procedures it employed meant it gradually lost its anchorage in 'reality'. They might succeed once or twice, when they managed to render the 'fiction' particularly gripping, but, in the end, the paper cut itself off from the most powerful modern source of curiosity and 'sensation': the real. Also, it had to keep going ever further in order to compete with the newspapers which had not overstepped this mark. It needed to pull off a coup every day. If it failed, its readers turned to its rivals to satisfy their routine curiosity. The

Graphic fought the only way it knew how, with 'composographs' and invented celebrities (such as Edward 'Daddy' Browning and his child-bride 'Peaches'), to whom impossible things happened. But this 'cumulative hysteria' produced wild swings in sales, to which the paper eventually succumbed.[76]

Such a punishment inflicted by the public on a paper that had played fast and loose with factual accuracy, assuming it constitutes a universal rule, is very reassuring. The public wants something 'interesting' and spectacular, but it also wants something 'real'. In fact it wants 'true' journalism. In this sense, Hughes's book reveals a profound democratic optimism: respect for the reality/fiction divide increasingly prevails, it is part of the collective curiosity. In consequence, there is every chance that popular journalism will perform the role of politicizing the urban masses, which she describes with even greater conviction than Park.

But does this democratic optimism not ascribe too many virtues to the reality/fiction divide? Is the fact that journalistic spectacles focus on the real, and not on pure fiction, the fact that they always tell us something, at the same time as they entertain us, enough to allow us to conclude that, in their hands, the spectator does not entirely forget himself as actor and thus retains a 'political' gaze?

Can 'true' stories not be enjoyed like fictive stories? Park himself recognized that 'one may, in an idle moment, read the newspaper with the same interest that one looks out the window at the moving throng in a crowded street. One may read the newspaper without reference to the importance of the news.'[77] In which case, the difference between the various spectacles may lie less in their subjects – the 'real', the 'fictive' – than in the relationship the spectator establishes with them. It is far from certain that the divide between 'political' spectacle, on the one hand, and 'depoliticized' spectacle, on the other, echoes that between 'real' spectacle and 'fictive' spectacle. Instead of being satisfied with this latter divide, it might be better to ask what makes a spectacle 'political' – that is, what gives the spectators the feeling of their plurality and the desire to act.

Such an approach would retain much of the work of the Chicago sociologists, in particular the idea that what is essential, in order to think journalism in a critical fashion, is to explore the nature of the spectacle it offers: does it succeed in instituting a 'conflictual community'? This opportunity left to conflict and to the feeling of a minimal plurality, within the journalistic spectacle, might usefully define an 'ideal' journalism. But it means abandoning the democratic optimism that marks some of the work of these sociologists; it means being more demanding of journalism, less easily satisfied with the sole fact that its objects are 'real'; and it means asking, in particular, if there is a risk of 'depoliticizing' the objects put on display, even if these objects are 'real'.[78]

3. The risk of myth

'Mythical': journalism depoliticizes the relationship to the real (Roland Barthes)

How, exactly, does the journalistic spectacle designate the real as real? Does the way it does so enable it also to say: 'this concerns you, you the spectators, you who are also actors in this reality'? Or does it, on the contrary, entail a certain forgetfulness of their status of actors on the part of those the journalism addresses?

This 'forgetfulness' is central to the concept of 'myth' developed by Roland Barthes. Myth involves a sort of disengagement of the spectator, consumer of the myth, with regard to the actor which the spectator also is. Myth encourages its receivers to forget their status of actor. And myth is the stuff of journalism.

For Barthes, myth is a type of speech that creates a new semiological system (or metalanguage) over and above the ordinary linguistic system (or language-object).[79] In this new system, a signifier, while retaining its usual linguistic meaning, becomes the signifier, or 'form', of something else; it has a new, 'mythic' 'signification'. A rose, for example, which designates a particular flower, also signifies passion; a particular Latin sentence, over and above its meaning, signifies a grammatical example; a photograph of a black soldier standing to attention, at the time when Barthes was writing, had, alongside its immediate semiological meaning, another 'signification' in another semiological system: it signified that 'France is a great Empire'. The myth is thus a semiological system which constitutes a cultural, metalinguistic 'code'. It can 'say' things rapidly, above all conceptual things, ideas, notions, '-ities' or '-nesses' (such as 'Frenchness'). This is why myth goes beyond the reality/fiction divide; it can make it possible to express an idea, a '-ness', in any discourse, including a work of fiction.

Myth is frequently used to signify *the idea of the real*, 'real-ity' (as opposed to fiction). In an article of 1968 with the title 'The effect of the real' (or 'The reality effect') Barthes argued that it is the 'useless detail' which, in a would-be 'realist' text, has this status of signifier of the real. As well as its linguistic meaning – the detail in question designates the very object of which it is the signifier – it also 'signifies', in the sense this time of the mythic signification: 'this is real'. Barthes writes: 'Flaubert's barometer, Michelet's little door finally say nothing but this: we are the real; it is the category of "the real" (and not its contingent contents) which is then signified.'[80]

Thus Barthes implies that, in a discourse, the real is not 'represented' as such. Indeed it is probably the impossibility of this representation of the real itself, completely and in full – in person, dare I say – which explains the need to have recourse to myth. In his article of 1957, 'Myth today', Barthes had already said that it was because it cannot be represented that a concept is signified.[81]

This use of 'codes' to designate 'reality' is the source of Barthes's scorn for realist literature.[82] It is also the basis of his critique of journalism. For journalism revels in myths of all sorts, not only to say 'this is real', but more generally, in order to signify rapidly with regard to the large number of things that are difficult to represent in the time and with the means available to the media. 'The press', he writes, 'undertakes every day to demonstrate that the store of mythical signifiers is inexhaustible.'[83] The journalistic spectacle should be analysed, therefore, as a mythic spectacle. It uses a code which enables it to designate ideas and concepts with the same, generally accepted, 'evidence' as that with which the ordinary linguistic system designates objects; it becomes as natural for a rose to signify passion as for the word 'rose' to designate a flower.

Now, for Barthes, myth is a spectacle which prevents a *political* relationship with the things it presents, for two reasons which are exactly symmetrical with those which led the Chicago sociologists to say that journalism, on the contrary, 'politicized' the urban masses. Myth prevents you from experiencing the feeling of being an actor and, at the same time – the two things are connected, as they are for Park – from experiencing the feeling of belonging to a plurality of individuals. Myth is a fusional spectacle, which makes all its consumers, united in this common spectacle, lose the feeling of their diversity, and consequently cuts them off from their status as actors. In this sense, it is the favoured tool of a 'depoliticization' in relation to the real.

It could be said, adapting slightly a metaphor of Barthes, that myth 'robs' the spectators of their status of actor. The Barthesian metaphor of myth as 'language-robbery' refers back, admittedly, to a more general problem, that is, the distortion myth inflicts on the initial semiological system that is hijacked: 'What is characteristic of myth? To transform a meaning into form. In other words, myth is always a language-robbery.'[84] But it is undeniable that, for Barthes, one of the chief consequences of this robbery of language is the theft of the spectator's 'active', 'political' relationship to the real. Myth functions to the full, that is, has maximum effect, when the spectacle it produces makes it an 'innocent speech'.[85] The spectator then takes as natural fact, as a given and not as a construction, those links, semiological in origin, hence historic and contingent, which are instituted between a form (for example a rose) and a concept (for example passion). It kills off any thought about the concept, any openness to a plurality of appreciations and contents. 'Any semiological system is a system of values', he writes, 'now the myth-consumer takes the signification for a system of facts: myth is read as a factual system, whereas it is but a semiological system.'[86] In other words myth 'transforms history into nature',[87] because 'what myth gives in return is a *natural* image of this reality'.[88] And it is because it purports to 'state', when it actually fabricates, a signification that Barthes considers it 'depoliticized speech'.[89] In the case of the black soldier standing at attention who mythologizes 'French imperiality', for example, you forget 'the contingent, historical, in one word: *fabricated*, quality of colonialism . . . I am very near to finding that it is natural and *goes without saying*: I am reassured.'[90] Myth, declares Barthes, is 'trained to *celebrate* things and no longer to "*act* them"'.[91]

There is something irremediably tainted, therefore, in the mythic spectacle. Far from harmoniously dividing individuals into actors and spectators, as in the Kantian conception, this particular spectacle immediately institutes them as spectators cut off from their status as actor. The only 'salvation' envisaged, the only possibility of restoring a political relationship to things, seems to be, considering the radicality of the Barthesian analysis, to put an end to this spectacle, to emerge from it and emancipate oneself from its yoke, which cannot be reformed. For Barthes, nothing can be expected of the media 'products' served up to the spectators. There are no nuances or degrees to be distinguished. In other words, there are no more or less 'depoliticized', or more or less 'depoliticizing', myths. A critique of myth, especially journalistic myth, could only come from a complete conversion of the spectator, which consists, in essence, of a simple exit from the spectacle. In this regard, the Barthesian analysis does more than merely nuance the democratic optimism of the Chicago sociologists. They considered the spectacle that bore on 'reality' as *always* putting the spectator in the situation of actor; Barthes defines an opposite radical position, that of democratic pessimism: mythical evocations of reality *never* put the spectator in the situation of actor.

For Barthes, this severing of the spectators from their 'status' as actors is the corollary of the extreme, in fact fusional, integrating trend which operates in myth. Myth is what makes it possible to speak to everyone quickly, to create a common, fixed sense of things, on the model of our common linguistic system. In robbing language, it robs the possible plurality of words. In fact the same issues are found in the Barthesian analysis as in that of the Chicago sociologists, but the other way round. In the latter, the designation of the real by the journalistic spectacle enabled the spectators to think of themselves as also actors, *that is*, as relatively diverse in spite of this common or integrating spectacle. In Barthes, the same logic applies, but in reverse: the spectacle of the real, because it is mythical, makes them forget the status of actors, *that is*, it destroys the feeling of diversity in those who consume it. The politicization of the masses through journalism evoked by the Chicago sociologists is inverted, in Barthes, into certain depoliticization, effected by this fundamentally mythical spectacle.

With Barthes, therefore, we are plunged into a sombre approach to the journalistic act of integrating. No opportunity is left for conflict; the hopes of the Chicago sociologists will inevitably be disappointed. Unless, perhaps, we can imagine a journalism that is non-mythical.

The problem of the journalistic exit from 'myth'

To what extent is the Barthesian position a last dark word on journalism? Can it help us to think about a non-mythical and, therefore, an 'ideal' journalism?

We need to clarify further what Barthes means, at a general level, by the restoration or the construction of a political relationship to things. This problem, which we may call that of the emancipation from myth, was important to him, but we may wonder how far he succeeded in providing a logical solution. The difficulty is this: if the aim is to emerge completely from mythical language, we need to be assured that a non-mythical language exists, which is by no means clear. Perhaps what Barthes intended was simply an exit from language itself. In fact a close examination suggests he envisaged this possibility, since, when he discussed the nature of non-mythical, that is, political language, he emphasized the extent to which this language is constantly haunted by the fantasy of silence. This was the case with literary language, which he defined as an attempt to emerge from myth so as to achieve 'degree zero', and of which he observed that it was tormented by the temptation to end all language, that is, by the temptation of silence.[92] The ways by which one can leave myth, in order to restore a political relationship to the world, are thus problematic, even contradictory: language or non-language? Barthes praises, for example, the 'language of man as producer',[93] a language that is not mythical; but is it, one may ask, still a language? Is it not, rather, action without discussion, a totally silent *praxis*?

We encounter here, it should be noted, a difficulty which was also faced by Marx: if language is ideological, what is there that is non-ideological except total silence? And in particular: can journalism be 'saved', when it is by definition language happening on the stage of ideology? In fact Barthes's discussion of the myths conveyed by language, and especially by the language inherent to the public space of opinions, echoes the Marxian critique. Myth, for Barthes, like ideology for Marx, involves a failure to offer a gaze which touches the 'real' world, a world where things are always capable of being 'transformed', the world of praxis. In fact Barthes does no more than clarify, through his concept of 'myth', the tools of the Marxian ideology: it 'naturalizes' the real, it makes it a *given*, which looks at itself but does not communicate the idea of its transformation and hence does not lead on to a transcending of the social dominations which permeate it. It creates difficulties for the Kantian belief in the possibility of a serene division between the state of actor and the state of spectator, the one linked peaceably to the other, each enriching the other without any 'loss'. Against Kant, but like Marx, Barthes envisages spectators of the real completely cut off from their status as potential actors in a transformation of this real. And the unease of Marx with regard to the possibility of gaze that is not ideological, his temptation – not definitive – to celebrate a praxis resistant to all discourse, is also visible in Barthes. 'Politics' is perhaps a place which prevents any spectacle of itself, any discourse on itself; in short, it is perhaps a mute and 'invisible' action. In which case, perhaps journalism and, beyond it, all language and all gazes, are ultimately destined to remain mythical, hence depoliticizing.

Yet Barthes, in spite of the temptation which surfaces in his writing, refuses – once again like Marx – definitively to go down this road. He continues to assert that resistance to myth can be linguistic, and that a non-mythical speech is possible. In other words, his position varies. Sometimes he seems to feel that myth may be inherent to discursiveness; in which case he can only urge the 'spectators' to close their newspapers, switch off their radios and televisions, and leave this 'speaking' spectacle that is public space in order to reach 'another stage', on which 'politics' would have a quite different meaning: that of silent action. Sometimes, on the contrary, he claims that a non-mythical discursiveness is possible, that there *can* be a political *speech* there, which can be made to appear in place of the myths.

In the latter case, a non-mythical journalism is ultimately possible. But *how*? That is the question, which Barthes, some vague formulas notwithstanding, never really answers. One can hardly be satisfied with his peremptory and arbitrary claims that myth is basically right-wing, whereas the Left is capable of producing a true political language, 'revolutionary language proper'.[94] In reality the problem of non-mythical speech is, at best, the subject of all his work. Uncertainty remains, even so, with regard not only to a clear answer – the temptation of silence persists – but even more to a specific answer on the subject of journalism. It is even doubtful whether the idea of a non-mythical journalism had any meaning for Barthes.

There is nothing to stop us, however, from taking up this question ourselves. In which case, in order to escape from the Barthesian impasses, it may be more fruitful to admit the mythical character necessary to all speech, and then, instead of contemplating an impossible exit from myth, reflect on the possibility of a critique of myth in and through myth. Barthes himself sometimes advances an argument of this sort: what if an emancipating, 'political' speech consisted not of a complete abandonment of all myth, but of the critique of one myth by another, the destruction of one myth in order to replace it with another? 'Truth to tell,' he writes, 'the best weapon against myth is perhaps to mythify it in its turn, and to produce an *artificial myth*: and this reconstituted myth will in fact be a mythology. Since myth robs language of something, why not rob myth?'[95] Here he no longer seems to characterize literary labour as a complete exit from myth, but rather as the incessant, critical recreation of new myths against the imposed myths. For Barthes, Flaubert's *Bouvard et Pécuchet* constitutes just such an 'artificial mythology'; he defines Flaubertian speech not as a non-mythical speech but as a 'counter-mythical' speech.[96] This seems to recognize that we have to put up with myths, and that all we can do is change them. It is an admission that language, or discursiveness, cannot make a radical break with myth because it is integral to it, but that this does not mean it is necessary to flee to another stage, that of silent action; something like a critique of myth in and through myth remains possible.

Essentially, if we adopted this hypothesis, perhaps more wholeheartedly than Barthes himself – who once again seems to vacillate – it would mean that we could argue that a certain practice of myth can, after all, re-forge a more political relationship to the real, at any rate a less depoliticized relationship. In short, we could retain the scepticism of the Barthesian analysis, but not its deep pessimism: admittedly, the relationship to the real, to the extent that it is part of the discursive spectacle, is always mythical; admittedly, this carries the risk of a depoliticization of this relationship to the real; but perhaps all myths are not equally bad; perhaps some mythical spectacles are less prone than others to dissipate in the spectators their status as plural actors.

This hypothesis would also allow us to believe that, in certain sorts of spectacle, the Kantian to-ing and fro-ing between the state of spectator and the state of actor, that is, the fact that spectators are invited, in the course of the spectacle, to reflect on their status as actors, far from wholly forgetting it, remains possible. It would allow us to believe that the spectators and creators of spectacles *can* mediate action through the spectacle and prepare a return to it, far from wholly forgetting themselves as actors. It would thus refuse, through this – admittedly conditional – residue of Kantism, to tip over into an absolute denunciation of the fundamental and irreparable illusion of the spectacles which play out in public space.

Let us adopt this hypothesis. We then face the following question: what type(s) of journalism, in spite of the myths which it necessarily conveys in the way it signifies the real, could still preserve a political relationship to this real? This question takes us back to the very same issue of resistance to ideology, on ideology's own ground, that we detected and explored in Marx. However, because we are here introducing it as a counterpoint to the insights of the Chicago sociologists, it has acquired a new dimension. It boils down to this: 'integrating' as journalism necessarily is, offering a collective spectacle based on certain common myths on the subject of reality, is it still possible to forge in these assembled spectators a path towards action, which, by that very fact, reminds them of their diversity, or at least a degree of diversity?

In essence, Barthes enables us to reintroduce into the Chicago School's thinking on the journalistic process of integrating the political community an unease that is, if not 'Marxist', at least more sensitive to the question of domination and the difficulties of emancipation. However much the journalistic spectacle presents us with the 'real', it cannot do other, to signify this real, than utilize myths common to the democratic community. Now myth carries a risk, probably underestimated by R. E. Park and Helen M. Hughes: that of melding the spectators together in the contemplation of a real that is 'naturalized', fixed, closed to any possibility of action, and in this sense 'depoliticized'. So we need to retain Park's concern to think journalism, the 'true' journalism, as a 'conflictual unifying', that is, as a process which institutes a common while leaving an opportunity for conflict. However, we need to push this demand further than the democratic optimism of the Chicago sociologists allowed. We need to respond to the risk of myth in the Barthesian sense, and ask the following question: precisely how can journalism use myth, that is, this common code regarding the real, in part fixed and 'depoliticizing' but necessary to the creation of a collective spectacle, in a way that at the same time leaves space for a trend to repoliticize the real?

4. Towards a 'conflictual unifying': two journalistic acts

In short, we need to clarify exactly how the necessarily unifying spectacle that is the journalistic spectacle can work towards the creation of a *conflictual* community – instead of being content, as the Chicago sociologists seem sometimes to have been, with *banking on* this ultimate step, that of conflict, that it is assumed will emerge after the 'common' has been forged. In other words, and drawing on the work of the French philosopher Etienne Tassin, we need to define an 'ideal journalism' which would address its readers while concentrating from the outset on the two words which form the expression 'political community'.

In an article of 1991,[97] Tassin discussed the difficulty of thinking the notion of 'political community', given the different directions in which each of these two words pulls. The notion of 'community' suggests the need for integration, but the adjective 'political' assumes, unlike fusional forms of community, respect for a distance between individuals. In short, the 'political community', because it is political, lays down conditions for the community – which may even cast doubt on the possibility of such a thing. It is a dangerous balancing act: to be at the same time one and (relatively) plural. Or, to adopt a metaphor of Tassin's which is also, it seems to me, an implicit allusion to Claude Lefort: to be a body, but not just any body; to be an *incarnated* community, but not an *incorporated* community.[98] Applied to journalism, the problem becomes this: to what extent is the representation of the community which shows in the journalistic gaze that of a *political community*? If journalistic writing 'embodies' its readership through the gaze it offers, does it also know how to unbind what it binds? Does it show signs of stimulating plurality where it unifies? How does journalism achieve this delicate balance?

The crucial issue is the relationship journalism maintains with conflictuality.[99] The process of forging something 'common' is fairly obvious: journalism happens, by definition, on a stage which aspires to be common, and open to the whole of the political community; it needs to use common reference points, values which unify, in order to make itself immediately *visible* to the largest number. This is why it is the natural terrain of all sorts of myths, which it perpetuates and renews. The fundamental question, therefore, is this: how can journalists introduce conflictuality into the very process of unifying? Or better: exactly *what sort of* conflictuality can journalists make operate in their gaze?

It seems to me that there are two possible paths towards achieving this ideal-critique of 'conflictual unifying'; these two paths relate to two different conceptions of the democratic conflict.

Unifying through a test

The first path, that is, the first 'ideal' journalistic act, is to provide a gaze which fully embraces its desire to unify and to form a 'we' around it, and which in this sense defines a sort of centre for the democratic community, but which also bases this unifying process on the representation and deployment of a conflict within this 'we'. In other words, the appearance of the centre, with all its powers – its evident ability to unify – is presented through a necessary conflict. The journalist's gaze then says a 'we' ('this is what we see') which appears obvious, and yet this emphasis on these common values – this obvious 'common' which unifies – appears only in confrontation with enemies, that is, in a conflict in which it is itself at stake ('This is what we see, isn't it?'; 'We really are this "we", aren't we?'). The 'we' is revealed, *is experienced*, through a *test*. So I will call this first 'ideal' journalistic act *unifying through a test*.

This is not without echoes of the paradox which Nicole Loraux, in her work on Athenian democracy,[100] describes as the conflictual centre, or 'conflictual *meson*'. What allowed the Athenian city to unify, she says, and to be one, was division. In other words, the centre, far from being peaceful, was a scene of agitation and intense conflictuality, to the point where Loraux sees the search for the centre taking place in strange proximity to the desire to divide. She refers, for example, to the surprising praise by Solon of 'the man of the middle'. It is he who throws himself into the conflict. It is he, therefore, in a sense, who knows that it is in conflict that the centre is revealed, and that there is really no other way of reaching it. And in discussing these words of Solon, Loraux emphasizes that, in the end, it is difficult to distinguish between the citizen and the insurgent, since, to be a citizen, the individual must behave like an insurgent: 'nothing . . . distinguishes the gesture of the citizen from that of the insurgent, since it is precisely insofar as one is a citizen that one has the obligation to be an insurgent'.[101]

This paradox of the 'conflictual *meson*' crops up again in a metaphor borrowed from Heraclitus: 'Even the *kukeon* [a drink made of a mixture of water and barley flour] separates if it is not stirred.' In other words, unifying, which prevents disintegration, requires agitation. We rediscover here, she observes, the ambivalence of the Greek word *stasis*, which can mean being at rest and motionlessness as well as agitation or movement. She uses this word *stasis* to think unifying conflict, or what she calls 'the bond of division'. She refers also to the paradox of the verb *luo* ('to unbind'), which seems to say division ('I untie'), whereas given a prefix, and become *deluo*, it can also say reconciliation ('I reconcile').[102]

Loraux's discussion is part of a reflection on the specificity of democracy. Democracy is the system which achieves the ideal of a *political* community, that is, a community that is both one and conflictual,[103] but which also understands that the place where one can achieve the unification, the centre, the *meson*, only reveals itself in conflict. We may note that such a conception of democracy does not assume a perfect plurality. It is not Kantian, in the sense that it does not believe that the 'common' is forged peacefully, in confrontation between a plurality of constantly renewed points of view, continually improving the 'common' previously defined. The very fact of speaking of 'conflict' rather than of 'plurality' presupposes a fairly bumpy approach to the exchange of points of view; one has the feeling that the centre is victorious, then turns always against another camp, to become, once again, the subject of a new conflict. This process is also more reminiscent of a successive overthrow of dominations, through the interplay of resistances which never cease to reform and reorganize, than of the serenity of a plural exchange of points of view. For the same reasons, Nicole Loraux's argument here cannot be described as wholly 'Simmelian'; or if it is, it is in the sense in which the later R. E. Park is Simmelian, but not the Park of 1904 who made the Simmelian theory of 'integrating' conflict serve a happily plural vision of the public. Loraux is Simmelian in the sense that she sees in conflict a power to determine a centre to which all the warring parties ultimately contribute, but not in the sense that one has to think democracy as the harmonious alliance of the one and the plural. Democratic specificity means always leaving conflict a chance, not necessarily achieving a perfect plurality.

The major contribution of this analysis based on Nicole Loraux is that it enables us finally to put aside a mistrust in principle of the act of unifying. The real question, which should replace it, is *how*: how do journalists unify in and through their gaze? Does the community institute itself from the outset as a *political*, that is, a conflictual, community? Is there *a test* at the source of this unifying, or not? In other words, we need to stop thinking the act of unifying as an act of smoothing over conflicts and creating a consensus beyond a conflictuality ignored and/or suppressed. There is a way of creating the 'we' which is based on conflict, rather than on fighting against it. In this respect, there may be many sorts of so-called 'mass appeal' journalisms, as Park, too, suggests. There are certainly journalisms that might be called 'consensus' journalisms which avoid anything that causes conflict. But there may be journalistic ways of constituting a 'we' which inject conflictuality into this 'we' from the beginning. These *unifying journalisms*, which are not *consensus journalisms*, assume that the 'we' is only fully experienced when it is put to the test.

The modern figure of the reporter, born in the second half of the nineteenth century in the western democracies, is crucial to such a process. Reporters have from the beginning been combative figures, seeking for the truth – the 'facts' on which everyone can agree, hence 'unifying' facts – in confrontation and scandal; that is, by fighting an enemy, often some official body. Unlike the old journalists, who wrote under their own name, and expressed a personal opinion, reporters make themselves representatives of the 'we'. This does not mean that they never say 'I', but assumes that a more or less explicit bond is forged between this 'I' and the collectivity. I have elsewhere described this bond as a mandate instituting the reporter as 'witness-ambassador' on behalf of his or her public, and I have tried to analyse the permanence and the various forms assumed by this figure in the history of reportage.[104] It is clear that such a figure, in order to unify the 'we' behind it, likes to make it pass a test, a test set by the journalistic investigation itself.[105]

In other words, though it has often been diverted into an unimaginative quest for consensus, the act of achieving a *unification through a test*, that is, in conflict, has been part of modern journalism from the beginning. In which case, the question not only of the faithfulness of journalism to this founding act, but also of the different ways of achieving it, is perhaps rather more fruitful for a critical analysis than the habitual exasperation in the face of the homogeneity of media representations. And it at least makes the critique of journalism part of an explicit debate on democracy, its problems and its paradoxes – instead of lapsing into the lamentations and irritations which too often conceal a generalized hostility to democracy.

Decentring up to the limits of the bond

That said, we do not necessarily need, in order to think the ideal of a 'conflictual unifying' of the democratic community, to confine ourselves to Nicole Loraux's thinking on the 'conflictual *meson*'. This ideal-critique may have room for another journalistic act than that of unifying through a test.

Although we cannot wholly discount the thinking of Nicole Loraux on the Simmelian theory of conflict, it remains the case that it does not allow us, any more than Simmel, to envisage any other type of conflict than one that is 'integrating' or 'unifying'. Loraux refers, certainly, to the hypothesis that the democratic community may end up simply by disintegrating. But the paradox is that, in her argument, this situation is perceived essentially as the result of the absence of conflict: 'Even the *kukeon* separates if it is not stirred.' This disintegration, also sometimes called 'division', is *diastasis*, as opposed to *stasis*. Loraux makes this explicit in her discussion of Heraclitus. There is a law that 'requires the mixture to be stirred up in order to avoid division (*diistatai*, from which the noun *diastasis* is derived)';[106] that is, there has to be conflict, *stasis*, so as to avoid *diastasis*, the latter caused solely by the refusal or denial of confrontation. She does not allow for the possibility that certain types of conflict, different from *stasis*, might also contribute to the disintegration, to producing *diastasis*, rather than unify the community round a centre. In this sense, she never gets beyond a spontaneously unifying conception of conflict.

We may ask, however, if the ideal of 'conflictual unifying' can take a different, even an opposite, path from the one just described. This would be a path where the priority of the journalist was to inject conflict into the democratic community, but a conflict which, unlike that analysed by Nicole Loraux, did not move spontaneously towards the centre, that is, was not spontaneously imbricated into a process of integration. This would be, in short, a conflict that was centrifugal or, better, *decentring*, defying the 'centre', and which *a priori* set itself against the very possibility of unifying, against the very labour of constituting a 'we'.

This idea of *decentring* requires a different conception of conflict from that of Nicole Loraux. The 'decentring' journalist seeks, obviously, whatever shatters the 'common': an otherness of a type that will destroy the unity. This different conception of conflict is matched by a different conception of politics: the decentring journalist sees politics as a conflictuality which does not create any community, and which opposes precisely those communities which fix, reduce, tame and thereby misrepresent the intensity of the conflicts rife within them. The decentring journalist cultivates, in the expression 'political community', the requirements of the adjective to the point where they rebound on the noun. To put this in the vocabulary of Jacques Rancière,[107] decentring journalists are obsessed by the liberation of a true 'politics' against its distortion into 'police', and regard any institution of a 'common' as already policed and policing. They also contest the centred, integrating, over-organized character of the conflicts described as 'unifying'. They focus on the quest for an absolute alterity, which will put a stop to the 'we', which will reveal its constructed, false, malign character and designate it as a 'you' from which they themselves are already excluded, and whose identity is liable to crumble under a gaze coming from elsewhere.

Given the radicality of the conflict set in motion by the 'decentrers', what justifies us in incorporating them into the ideal-critique of 'conflictual unifying'? A paradox: the need to forge a bond, in spite of everything, between the warring parties – between the centre and what contests it. In fact journalism *acts* a conflict, it activates it on a stage of representations, not on a stage of actions. It necessarily assumes, therefore, a common, visible space, even if it is in order to undo the idea of the 'common'. The paradox of decentring is that it needs a bond in order to operate; and that, in the very act of operating, it forges a bond between what is decentred and what decentres. In short, whether it likes it or not, the conflict that is born of a journalist's gaze still needs, by its very nature, a common space in which to emerge.

That said, there remains a major difference between the conflict activated by the decentring journalist and the conflict presented by the unifying journalist described above. Decentring journalists forge a bond, certainly, but reject the possibility of establishing a centre. In fact they forge a bond almost in spite of themselves. Spontaneously, they would like to go further and act out an ever more serious, deeply divisive and irreparable conflict, demonstrate an absolute otherness, which would be there, wide open, within this falsely integrated 'we'. But there is something in the very fact of presenting or acting such a conflict on a stage *seen by all* that prevents them from carrying this process through. Nevertheless, it is still a bond that makes it possible to reject explicit unifications, stronger and more accepted bonds and constituted identities, defended and experienced as such; it is a bond which still reveals otherness, deep division, the differences and the disagreements it supposes. If this is a 'conflictual unifying', it has none of the energy of the unifications discussed earlier. The energy is instead employed in constantly undoing the centres and the 'we'.

It might be argued that this bond forged in spite of themselves by the decentrers, so that the decentring can take place, still has echoes of what Nicole Loraux called 'the bond of division'. Perhaps, but on condition that we retain from her work only the idea of a bond forged by the deployment of conflict, and that we reject her conclusion that the conflicts that bind gradually define a centre, a *meson*, in the political community. Decentring journalists activate these conflicts only in order to destroy the instituted centres and more effectively reject the attempts at 'recentring'. The bonds they assume are only there to demonstrate the impossibility of a triumphant, circumscribed and centred unification.

The history of journalism offers a number of examples of this process, though not without amply demonstrating its intrinsic difficulty. The 1960s and 1970s illustrated this quest for 'another' journalism, seeking out ignored alterities in order to denounce the illusory unifications of conventional journalism. The New Journalism movement in the United States and the launching of the daily paper *Libération* in France were expressions of this ambition.[108] It is significant that neither of these projects was ever able to deny that the single fact of presenting, in a common space, an otherness likely to 'decentre' the 'we' assumed that a bond would be forged with this otherness – hence they themselves, in a sense, became in their turn part of a process that was to some degree 'unifying'. The idea of the journalist as 'bond' between contradictory points of view, allowing them to express their oppositions, was an important element in the '*Libé*' project. It was articulated by Sartre (its first editor) at a press conference held on 4 January 1973, and it was present again in the expression 'bringing together of voices' which appeared on the readers' letters page on 18 April 1973. But it is clear that this idea bears no resemblance to that of unifying round a centre, a centre revealed and consolidated by a journalistic labour; the very phrase 'bringing together' is almost inappropriate to describe this labour of the encounter, a condition of the deployment of differences which resist the usual unifications.

Certainly, the fact that the act of *decentring* produces a 'common', in spite of everything, makes it permeable to that of *unifying through a test*. It can prepare for it and unmake a centre only to labour, ultimately, to replace it with another. The decentrer then heralds a new unifier, a sort of 'recentrer', and the conflictuality activated during the decentring turns out, in the end, to be simply a unifying conflictuality, which loses its radicality. In the *Libé* project, for example, there were times when the ambition to decentre, and to promote a generalized conflict, was supplanted by that to create a new community of 'the dominated'. It remains the case that this inherent temptation for the decentring journalists is not an essential element in their approach. It only signals its fundamental risk, its stumbling block, which has to be related to the very paradox of decentring: to forge a bond which unbinds, to create a common which delimits the common, to encounter in order to experience the radicality of otherness. It is understandable that 'simpler' temptations threaten such a tricky enterprise.

The vigilance of decentring journalists, if they are to escape these temptations, has to be tireless, because it leads only to a further deepening of the paradox in which they are caught: to seek an absolute otherness, one that is, dare I say, unintegratable, but an otherness that they must still make visible, present in the common space, hence, once again, *rebind* to this community which it nevertheless resists. Decentring journalists seek to make seen what will destroy the common gaze, but they still have to make it seen through the common gaze. In other words, they aim at a total rupture, but can only ever be on the edge of this total rupture. This is often their tragedy – what gives them a sense of failure, the impression of grasping only very 'tamed' alterities, alterities that *can be seen*. But it is also what allows me to incorporate them, once and for all, notwithstanding their trials and tribulations, in the ideal-critique I am describing here, that of 'conflictual unifying'. Whether they like it or not, they resist by placing themselves on the terrain of that which they resist. They *cannot*, therefore, make a complete break – even if it obsesses them and if this obsession is often fascinating to study.[109]

It seems that both of these journalistic acts essentially describe contrary movements – one moves towards the centre, the other seeks what prevents the very possibility of a centre – and yet belong to a same ideal-critique – they both in their own way suppose, and stimulate, in their 'public' the alliance of 'common' and 'conflict'; they create a *conflictual community*.

The fact is, decentring journalists may well implement a more radical and more disturbing conception of conflictuality, but they are stymied by the very nature of their activity. They act the conflict on a stage which is not that of actions; they represent or portray conflict, so have to make it seen by the very people who are affronted, undone and decentred. They refuse the position of 'unifier' or of 'witness-ambassador', which is associated with conflicts that create identity, that is, which present an 'other' in relation to which the 'we' experiences, rediscovers and reconstructs itself. They seek an 'other' which prevents the reconstruction of the 'we' and makes it possible to denounce its fraudulence. But they are still obliged to forge a bond between everyone, on that common stage where they introduce the 'other' and where they make it seen. Decentring journalists are rebels who remain on the terrain of what makes them rebel.

Here we rediscover certain features of the conflictual journalist, my second ideal-critique, which itself clarified my first, the figure of the journalist-flâneur. The act of decentring is the culmination of my reflection on journalism as a challenge to the dominant 'common'. This time, however, the point which remained rather obscure seems clearer: the act of decentring is itself trapped in the requirement to take place on a 'common' stage. This requirement, which was the source of the fundamental ambivalence of the flâneur – the conformist rebel – and also the enigma inherent to the Marxian attitude of resistance to ideology – since the resistance happened on the very same terrain as that which it resisted – is now explained: the conflictuality set in motion by the gaze of the journalist is necessarily frustrated in its quest for radicality.

At the same time, the fact of having distinguished two different journalistic acts, that of unifying through a test and that of decentring up to the limits of the bond, emphasizes that, while journalists can never escape the requirement to forge a 'common', there are more ways than one of meeting this requirement. The fact that journalists establish a bond does not mean that they necessarily construct a centre. It is perfectly possible to think a journalism of *decentring* (in the literal sense), even though it seems to be established that this act ought to remain visible on the common stage, hence linked, in one way or another, to the 'common' which it undoes. There is a real place for a journalism that is resolutely conflictual, firmly resistant with regard to the 'we' and what cements it, and concerned to make visible alterities that are too often forgotten; and this even though it has to make all this *visible*, hence, come what may, address this 'we' and remain *bound* to it.

Admittedly, no decentring journalist can be confident of not ultimately contributing to a new 'recentring'. This is a risk we have already noted when discussing the meaning of the journalism of Karl Marx: Marx fought against the ideology of the English public, on its own ground, perhaps ultimately helping to fabricate another ideology, that of the American public. It is only a short distance from the act that consists of giving a (subversive and decentring) visibility to *another* point of view to the process of constituting this 'other' as a new centre. It is only a short distance from the decentring journalist to the new witness-ambassador.

It is clearly this particular risk, that of contributing, in spite of their struggle, even by means of it, to the development of a new 'centred' and ultimately dominant unification, that is run by those who agree to fight on the terrain of journalism. The decentring journalist accepts a type of conflictuality which inevitably lacks the radicality of the conflicts taking place on another stage, that of actions. Hence the temptation, for those quick to denounce the inability of the public exchange of points of view to act a radical conflictuality, simply to desert public space and seek another stage, that of silent action. Not to desert carries a cost: it means accepting that you are bound to the very 'common' that you are contesting, and that you may be contributing to the manufacture of a new 'common' that will betray the radicality of the battle fought against the earlier 'common'; in fact it means accepting, quite simply, constraints specific to the principle of publicity, which is the very characteristic of democracy.

Democracy is a mutual exchange before taking action; it is representing a situation, holding a debate and making changes before passing to action. It is inevitably, therefore, the turning of conflicts, even the most radical, into conflicts that can be represented on a common stage. This is the constraint which is inherent to the idea of 'public space' and which causes so much anger, discouragement and despair. It is what sometimes leads to a renunciation of the search for an 'ideal' journalism, because it is only too clear that it will necessarily share some of the characteristics of the place in which it will happen and which it will help keep alive.

In fact, by characterizing it as a two-pronged movement, forging a common and injecting conflict, I have made it a frustrating activity, full of renunciations and dissatisfactions. But I have related it to the needs of democracy, to its inherent impurity, an alloy of 'common' and 'conflict'. Above all I have tried to show that such an alloy permits a variety of positions or 'acts', each permeable to the others: there is the act which creates unease, which allows for conflict of a type that will undo the constituted identities, and there is the act which re-forges identity by designating the adversary who had blurred it. There is the act of the decentrers and there is the act of the witness-ambassadors.[110] Both suppose a dynamic of conflict, but not the same one. Both suppose a 'common' in which conflict takes place, which also enables them, at a certain point, to meet. Nevertheless, they define two different journalistic, and democratic, attitudes, although the one is probably unimaginable without the other.

6

The limitations of the figure of the 'spectator', and what they tell us about democracy

The ideal-critique of 'conflictual unifying' refers back to the twofold tension that is the essence of democracy. It is this essence that journalism must try to realize as best it can. And it is because it provides a *spectacle* that journalism *can* realize this double process. The conflict that is shifted onto a stage of spectacle can go much further, without the community fragmenting, than when it is acted out. You can *see* more of it than you can live. The figure of the spectator is the key, allowing these two processes, at first sight contradictory, to take place together.

But the spectacle has its limits. Might there not, in spite of everything, be conflicts that cannot be seen? Radical forms of conflictuality which, in spite of the mediation of the spectacle, the 'we' cannot tolerate? It is perhaps because they know this only too well that there are some people who feel only a spontaneous scorn for and/or despair of public space: the conflict that is acted out there is insufficiently radical. But scorn is a barrier to thinking the limits in detail: at what point does the figure of the spectator fail? What are the limits of journalism, even ideal journalism?

1. The journalism of decentring as the search for the limits of 'seeing'

In fact, we are doing no more than return to our questions regarding the two journalistic acts likely to realize the ideal-critique of 'conflictual unifying'. Are they capable of showing a truly serious conflict? Decentring journalism is particularly tormented by this question: it is forever pushing back the boundaries, forever trying to decentre the 'we' even further. But how far can it go?

It certainly goes further than the journalism that has been dominant in the western democracies since the birth of reporting in the second half of the nineteenth century. This has primarily celebrated the figure of the reporter as the witness-ambassador of the public. The desire to unify has dominated the history of modern journalism, even if the figure of the witness-ambassador is no stranger to the tactic of also stimulating conflictuality in the public it addresses. But the conflict this figure sets out to activate fits the model of the *test*. In other words, it is a conflict that allows the 'we' to reconstruct itself better and experience itself better: the reporter shows that something 'is not right' and that the political community must fight this otherness which prevents it from being wholly itself. The idea of a *test* assumes a conflictuality that is guided and orchestrated by the reporter, culminating in the clear designation of an 'other' and the recentring of the political community.

In fact the reporter has many ways of administering a *test*, as I have shown elsewhere.[1] Indeed one could imagine a whole research programme devoted to identifying and analysing, in the history of reportage, the types of 'test' deployed by the journalistic gaze. The variety of media and contexts in no way detracts, it seems to me, from the relevance of this way of examining journalistic products, which I regard as essential to a truly *political* approach to journalism.

However, it is true that this concept of 'test' remains inadequate for thinking the conflictuality which journalists ought to be able to activate by their gaze. And it is this frustration that has been voiced by certain dissidents in the history of journalism: dissidents who have tried to disturb the 'we' more deeply, to undo its unity by introducing a much more radical conflictuality than that operative in the 'test', that is, dissidents who aspire to a *journalism of decentring*. A study of the history of journalism makes it possible to give substance to this new category; in particular, as has been said, the two decades of the 1960s and 1970s are invaluable for an exploration of the concrete methods of the journalistic act of decentring.

That said, there is in the decentring project, in spite of its demanding nature, an intrinsic difficulty, which I have already tried to articulate, and which needs further discussion, over and above its concrete manifestations. Decentring journalists seek a radical otherness which puts the 'we' into a more serious conflict. But they also need to make this 'other' *seen*, this other destined to reveal to the 'we' its hollowness, to unmake its fragile unity, to decentre it. Decentring journalists need to make seen the ignored marginalities and the 'other' viewpoints on the collective life, which reveal the immensity of the misunderstandings on which the development of a 'we' is based – this was a main aim, for example, of the New Journalism in the United States in the 1960s and

1970s. Or they need to make these 'others' see what 'our boys' become in violence, ruining our certainties regarding our identity – this was the aim of a representative of this journalistic movement, Michael Herr, sent to the front in the Vietnam War in 1967–9. It is the aim of every journalist anxious to apprehend the otherness that violence is. Thus a journalist like Seymour M. Hersh, who had few links with the New Journalism, became a 'decentrer' at the point when, eighteen months after the event, he tried to give an account of the My Lai massacre, an event that had caused a great stir in the United States, that is, the elimination, in March 1968, of a North Vietnamese village by Charlie Company.[2] Now, to *make seen* presupposes *binding to us* that which causes the 'we' to fragment. In other words, decentring journalists are inevitably trapped in the very thing they contest, the idea of a 'common' space, since, in practising journalism, they must also make visible, in this 'common' space, the very thing which is at the limit of the visible and at the limit of the 'common'. It is also what makes the decentring journalist not so very different from the preceding figure, that of the 'unifier through a test': decentring journalists may lead to this; they may set in motion, sometimes in spite of themselves, a 'recentring', reactivate a feeling of being a 'we', a revived and reconsolidated 'we', even though their aim had been to undo it much more thoroughly.

As a result, the consistent decentrer, who pushes this approach as far as it can go, is an extreme figure. Decentring journalists try to show something which is at the limit of the 'visible in common', at the limit of the bond; they push the encounter with otherness as far as is possible within journalistic constraints. In reality, what this journalism of the limits helps to show are the limits of journalism. There is an otherness that cannot be grasped by the journalist because it defies *visibility*. In other words, the problem raised by the decentring journalist is that of the limits of the *gaze*, of the structural limits of the figure of the *spectator*, the central importance of which to modern democracy this book has tried to show.

Some things are invisible, so that, at a certain point, failure is guaranteed; there is a boundary that cannot be crossed by the figure of the spectator that is the journalist. Nevertheless, precisely because of its imbrication in the democratic idea, it is not so easy calmly to turn one's back on this figure of the spectator, 'limited' though it may be. Here we rediscover the difficulty faced by the structural critiques of democratic public space: does their analysis justify a simple desertion? The abandonment, once and for all, of the question of journalism? What is important is not to deny the structural limits of the figure of the spectator, but to know what to do with it, what to deduce from it for our relationship with democracy. To the anti-democratic position of contempt, I myself prefer the lucid unease of the democrat, and the questions the democrat poses: can one, ultimately, push back the structural limits of collective 'seeing'? Can one try to introduce an alterity into public space other than by the *gaze*? To a serene exteriority with regard to journalism, I myself prefer the anxieties which arise from within journalism: what have the decentring journalists to tell us about the limits of their trade? In what direction, dare I say, do their impasses lead?

2. The Sartrean critique of the position of the spectator

The gaze that tames

In essence, the thought-systems that break with Kantian enthusiasm all, in their own way, describe the structural limitations of the political figure of the spectator. Marx and Barthes speak of a gaze which cannot see everything and so cannot act out, in its own space, a radical conflictuality – because this would require access to what remains structurally external to the common space of 'seeing'. (As will have become clear, I am not concerned here with the precise nature of this conflictuality according to these writers – that is, the class struggle – but only with its implications for a discussion of public space.)

Given that I have focused my discussion on the problem of the spectator, however, it is likely that nothing will throw more light on its limitations than those thought-systems which are interested in the *gaze*, which question, in particular, its capacity to apprehend a radical otherness, an otherness of a type that will thoroughly decentre the spectator and those with whom he or she shares the spectacle. The phenomenological tradition is essential here, because it is clear that the gaze is its preferred mode of access to the real. Its way of conceptualizing perception in general is deeply influenced, even in its vocabulary, by the sense of sight. So, in order to evoke the problems posed by the experience of the other, it chooses to study the issues and the difficulties inherent to the *gaze at the other*.

Within this tradition we find, in the person of Sartre, a denunciation of approaches to otherness that are too 'soft' and incapable of doing justice to a radical conflictuality, that conflictuality which the other represents for each of us. For Sartre, the traditional phenomenological thinking, that of Husserl in particular, conceptualized the gaze at the other in a way which, in a sense, tamed that other, that is, deprived it of what constituted its otherness. But what is particularly interesting in the Sartrean analysis, and pertinent to my own argument here, is that in making his critique, Sartre ultimately incriminates the *gaze*. It is the gaze that is the source of the domestication, hence betrayal, of the otherness; it is the gaze which irremediably forges a bond with what it touches, so is by definition incapable of apprehending that which disputes any bond: otherness.

Let us look more closely at the Sartrean critique. Its point of departure, in *Being and Nothingness*, is hostility with regard to the motif of the 'union of consciousnesses' which, according to Sartre, prevailed in phenomenological thinking, especially in that of Husserl, which was characterized by an intermonadic, or intersubjective, view of the world. This presupposition of the 'union of consciousnesses' was the explanation for the failure of phenomenology to think the other in all its radicality, because this would mean thinking it as fundamentally *separate* from the Ego. This Sartrean diagnosis is nicely summarized in an observation of Marcuse: 'in an excellent critique of Husserl and of Heidegger (and of Hegel) . . . [Sartre] shows that their attempts to establish the Being of the other as an independent ontological fact fail, that in all of them the existence of the other is more or less absorbed into the existence of the Ego'.[3]

It is certainly the case that in Husserl the experience of the other as *other* is at the same time the experience of a *bond*. In fact this bond is the condition that makes an experience of this otherness possible. This paradox derives, as noted by Paul Ricoeur in his discussion of Husserl's *Cartesian Meditations*,[4] from the way in which the question of the other is posed: Husserl wanted to be able to 'account for the originality, the specificity of the experience of the other, precisely because it is the experience of another than I'. But this is problematic, observes Ricoeur, a few lines later, 'for a philosophy which has set itself the task of understanding everything, of constituting everything, "in" and "on the basis of" *my* intentional life'.[5] It was this point that was to be attacked by Sartre.

To resolve this difficulty, it was necessary for Husserl to show that the bond between the other and me – a bond of the order of perception, since the other *appears* to me, enters my 'sphere of belonging' or 'sphere of ownness' (*Eigenheitssphäre*) – does not negate its otherness. This is a fundamental point in Husserlian thinking on the body: the body of the other, he says, appears to me both as a 'body-object' (*Körper*), which I perceive as any object, and as a 'flesh' (*Leib*), that is, as a completely novel object, which is still only an object, because it relates to the inaccessible world of the other and that other's own sensations, that is, that other's own 'sphere of belonging'. In this way the 'flesh' leaves me to imagine a whole invisible, inaccessible part of the other, which is not presented to me, but, says Husserl, 'appresented'. But Ricoeur shows that the original difficulty is still present, at every stage of Husserl's argument. It is by 'analogising apprehension' (or by 'apperceptive transfer') on the basis of what I, myself, am, a body-flesh, that I constitute the other: I perceive his body as flesh, I understand that the other is flesh, and by analogy with myself who am flesh, I deduce the existence of an *ego*, over there, analogous to what I am, here.[6]

According to Ricoeur, Husserl had been conscious of the weaknesses of his own argument, 'himself warning us against his own explanation'.[7] None of the grounds developed by Husserl – neither that of 'analogising apprehension', nor that of 'concordant behaviour', nor that of the 'imagination' of the 'if I were over there' – allows us to be sure that an other who really is *other* has been constituted.[8] Or, if we claim that this radical alterity of the other is not open to doubt, it is what has made it possible to constitute it that proves, in the end, totally enigmatic: how is it that the body of this other, so radically 'other', *shows* in my own sphere? That it is 'there' for him as much as for me, 'paired' to my body? The pivotal concept of Husserl in this 'meditation', that of 'pairing' (*Paarung*), is both the condition for the realization of the 'wager' (*gageur*) earlier evoked by Ricoeur to define the Husserlian project, and what, in the last analysis, constitutes its enigma.[9]

In many respects, the pairing belongs more, in Husserl, to the order of fact than to that of foundation. *In fact* – dare I say – 'it is a sole and same reality which belongs to my own sphere and which indicates another existence';[10] *in fact*, there is a 'twofold belonging of the body of the other to my system and to his'.[11] But it must then also be recognized that, *in fact*, the question arises of knowing if I am apprehending of the other, in reality, only what shows in this bond with me, and hence if I am reducing his alterity by thinking it in the context of a 'same aim' (*visée du même*).[12]

For Sartre, in any case, it is clear that the Husserlian approach leads to a denial of the radical nature of the alterity of the other; by making the other *perceptible*, that is, by supposing a *gaze* capable of apprehending this other, Husserl, in reality, only tames this 'other'. It is Husserl's way of describing this experience, that is, as a sensory experience, of which the *gaze* is the paradigm, that is criticized by Sartre. Husserl says, in short: I see that the other is also something that I do not see; there is a 'sphere of belonging', concealed from my view, which enables him to see me at the same time that I see him; but – I see this! Hence the failure of seeing is turned into a triumph of the gaze: my gaze really does apprehend an *other*. It was this triumph that Sartre challenged: for him, the gaze, face to face with the other, was impossible, in a way *prevented*, so radical and so elusive was the alterity with which it was confronted. There is not, as in Husserl, a gaze-encounter, by which I see and at the same time am seen (I see the other as a thing and apprehend him as a 'flesh' capable of 'seeing' me). For Sartre, this double experience, which was in Husserl what made this gaze at the other successful, signifying its ability to apprehend the other as other, broke down. There remained a stark alternative: either I *see* the other, as any object, that is, I 'reify' him, alienate him; or I *am seen* by him, and it is then I who am reified, alienated by him. In other words, either my gaze is deployed, but does not really see the other, it sees a 'tamed' other, reified by this very gaze – in particular it does not see the other's gaze at me, it does not see the reciprocal power of reification that the other also possesses with regard to me; or else my gaze suddenly apprehends, in a flash, that someone is looking at it, that it is itself 'reified', and then it is my gaze which yields, which is neutralized, seized by what Sartre calls 'shame', or the 'alienation of my own possibilities',[13] and it does away with itself. Either it is I who see, but an 'other' whose alterity is distorted since I deprive it of what constitutes its alterity, its gaze at me; or it is the other who sees me, which institutes it as a true other, as a subject, but I myself am deprived of my gaze, I no longer see him. This stark alternative is clear in this passage from *Being and Nothingness*: 'I am fixing the people whom I *see* into objects; I am in relation to them as the other is in relation to me. In looking at them I measure my power. But if the other sees them and sees me, then my look loses its power.'[14]

It is impossible, therefore, to see and to be seen at the same time, which foretells a 'life-or-death' competition between the gaze of the other and my own gaze, and which Sartre illustrates by the following example: 'It is never when eyes are looking at you that you can find them beautiful or ugly, that you can remark on their colour.'[15] Sartre did not believe that there was, in general, something like the 'double sensation' – touching and feeling touched, seeing and being seen. For him, the two types of phenomena 'are on different and incommunicable levels of being'.[16] In short, where you think there is a *bond* – that his 'inside' is my 'outside' and conversely, and that it is this complementarity that I experience when my look meets that of the other – it is actually necessary to think a radical conflict, which implies a fundamental solitude of each of the poles of this non-encounter. This may be the solitude of 'victory': my look absorbs and denies the other; this is the position which Sartre calls 'sadism'. Or that of 'defeat': it is the other who absorbs and denies me; this is the position of 'masochism'. In other words, either I am transcended by the other, or I make of him a 'transcendence transcended', in the Sartrean phrase. Accordingly, the use of the word 'bond' by Sartre is almost ironic, intended to reinforce the idea of separation, as in this sentence: 'Thus this Me which has been alienated and refused is simultaneously my bond with the other and the symbol of our absolute separation.'[17]

It is clear that only the position where the 'I' is absorbed by the other restores to the other his alterity, so gets the measure of the violence that he represents for me. Sartre speaks then of 'decentralization' of me by the other. But we need to understand what this implies. It is not a visual experience; on the contrary, 'decentralization' is the experience of the impossible, prevented gaze, because it is the other who is suddenly 'looking at me',[18] so that I myself no longer see him. For Sartre, if I suffer 'decentralization', it is because the gaze of the other has, in a sense, prevailed over mine: I am alienated, reified, in which case I can no longer see:

> Thus suddenly an object has appeared which has stolen the world from me. Everything is in place; everything still exists for me; but everything is traversed by an invisible flight in the direction of a new object. The appearance of the other in the world corresponds therefore to a fixed sliding of the whole universe, to a *decentralization* of the world which undermines the centralization which I am simultaneously effecting.[19]

It is clear, therefore, that Sartre was not thinking of something like a *gaze at the other*. For him, *to look at the other* was a contradiction in terms. It amounted to looking at him as he looked, that is, 'to look at the other's look',[20] but this confrontation clearly ended, for Sartre, in failure: it was a confrontation from which there emerged a victor and a vanquished. The result of the furtive exchange of looks between the other and me was the *blindness* of one or the other.[21] This is why Marcuse could say, in his remarks on *Being and Nothingness*, that failure was at bottom the most salient theme of Sartrean existentialism.[22] It is this theme – general in Sartrean philosophy, according to Marcuse – which is developed in Sartre's discussion of the possibility of a true *gaze at the other*. The result of this attempt is either his reification (sadism) or mine (masochism).[23] This failure signifies, Marcuse explains, that Sartre rejected the idea of a 'dialectic' in relations with the other, preferring that of a 'circle', since each of these two liberties 'is the death of the other; that is, the failure of the one motivates the adoption of the other'.[24]

The consequence, which can appear, from a certain point of view, paradoxical, is this: Sartre claimed to give full weight, in his way of conceiving the other, to a radical alterity, that is, radically conflictual with me, but I do not have *visual* experience of this conflictuality. Early in his chapter devoted to 'concrete relations with others' he says: 'The following descriptions of concrete behavior must therefore be envisaged within the perspective of conflict. Conflict is the original meaning of being-for-others.'[25] This is why he denounces the idea of 'community' between the other and me, why he criticizes the notions of 'being-with' (*Mitsein*) and the 'we', which correspond to a 'community alienation' due to the look of a third party who 'reifies' all of us together,[26] or else to a psychological experience which has no ontological basis and which only gives an illusion of denying the first ontological given, that is, 'the original conflict of transcendences'.[27] But the gaze cannot in any way act out or perform this conflict, since is supposes from the outset the victory of one or other of the two warring poles.

This Sartrean critique implies, therefore, that we abandon all hope of a *decentring gaze*, one that would be capable of seeing a radical alterity and, in giving it to us to see, of acting out an all-out conflict, of a type to unmake us. The supposedly decentring gazes are no more, from the Sartrean point of view, than gazes which tame otherness, soften it, in fact deny the deep conflict it represents. A poor sort of conflict, a poor sort of tamed alterity, a poor sort of decentring, turned, in reality, into 'reification' without knowing it. There can be no decentring gaze, because 'decentralization', in Sartre, literally, is not *seen*, and everything that might represent it, visually, necessarily falls well short of its violence.

Forging a bond, the only way to decentre

But to what exactly does real 'decentralization' correspond? To a non-visual experience? But of exactly what order? In truth, Sartre is enigmatic on the subject. He, too, is influenced by the phenomenological primacy of the sense of sight in thinking experience in general. In other words, as is suggested by the positions of 'sadism' and 'masochism', which concern all types of relationship with the other, it is not only the gaze at the other, but the relationship to the other in general which is considered by Sartre a negation of his otherness – or of me myself. Beyond his *invisible* character, the other is described by Sartre, more generally, as *incommunicable*:[28] his otherness defies *any* relationship. Thus it seems that 'decentralization' in Sartre does not happen *in any experience*, because it is, on the contrary, an obstacle to experience. In other words, and this time the paradox is patent, the other is radical conflict in relation to me, but this conflict has no terrain, neither the gaze nor communication in general, on which to be acted out, to take place.

This paradox is not without its reasons, from the Sartrean point of view: his philosophy is so anxious to think the other as beyond any bond with me that any relationship with him can appear only as a betrayal of what he is. Any communication, even potentially conflictual, is still something which forges a bond with him, hence tames him – or does away with me. But the consequences of such a position are stark. 'Decentralization' seems to be located, enigmatically, either beyond or short of all experience. And what we are left with, in the end, in, dare I say, our relationship to the other is still that impoverished decentring denounced by Sartre, that conflict which binds, so inevitably betrays the otherness. Sartre may well tell us that the gaze, and more generally the encounter, is structurally 'limited', but he is unable to describe another relationship to otherness which would itself be truly 'decentring' – precisely because any other relationship to otherness would still be a relationship, a bond, hence also condemned to miss the otherness. 'Decentralization' must therefore be a strange non-relationship, which still 'decentres', which is surprising because it is difficult to see how, situated beyond any relationship, it could have such an effect. Is it the brief and sudden moment, vertigo or nausea, as if falling short of any perception, which triggers the end of any experience of the other, which reveals the total absence of any point of intersection between his world and mine, to the point where any relationship can only be a construct, denying that which is other? But can there even be such a moment which, after all, requires something along the lines of an encounter?

In a way, the Sartrean critique suggests we return, if somewhat disillusioned, to the original Husserlian position: the bond with the other may betray the otherness of the other, but because no other relationship with this other is *possible*, we have to accept that this bond is the reality of experience of the other; without it the other would not even appear. The only decentring *possible* is that which forges a bond. It is probably well short of the radicality of the Sartrean 'decentralization', but that is in reality an abstraction which never actualizes in any experience.

In many respects, this return to Husserl, in spite, or perhaps because, of Sartre, is the path taken by Merleau-Ponty. There are certainly traces of the Sartrean argument in *The Visible and the Invisible*, in particular in the idea that the appearance of the other constitutes a 'catastrophe' beyond all 'spectacle': 'The other can enter into the universe of the seer only by assault, as a pain and a catastrophe; he will rise up not before the seer, in the spectacle, but laterally, as a radical casting into question of the seer.'[29] Merleau-Ponty emphasizes that the perception of the other *is not*, in a way, a perception: 'There is no perception of the other by me,' he writes, 'abruptly my ubiquity as a seer is belied, I feel myself seen – and the other is that X yonder which I do indeed have to think in order to account for the visible body that I suddenly feel myself to have.'[30] It is clear that he is trying, with greater clarity than Husserl, to posit the absolute otherness of the other by creating the notion of 'private landscape' which is beyond any analogizing perception.[31]

Nevertheless, Merleau-Ponty is still following in the footsteps of Husserl, against the Sartre of *Being and Nothingness*. Envisaging an other so radically other that no bond with me is possible, he says, is not only not necessary to thinking this 'catastrophe' that he represents, but is even an obstacle to thinking it. This is because it leads ultimately to a faceless other, without any point of intersection with my sphere of belonging, like a world of which I would have no trace, a sort of threat both absolute, because we exclude each other totally, the one from the other, and extraordinarily abstract:

> For the other to be truly the other, it does not suffice and it is not necessary that he be a scourge, the continued threat of an absolute reversal of pro and con, a judge himself elevated above all contestation, without place, without relativities, faceless like an obsession, and capable of crushing me with a glance into the dust of my world. *It is necessary and it suffices that he have the power to decenter me, to oppose his centering to my own* [my emphasis].

To which he adds: 'It is necessary and it suffices that the other's body which I see and his word which I hear, which are given to me as immediately present in my field, *do present to me in their own fashion what I will never be present to* [author's emphasis], what will always be invisible to me, what I will never directly witness – an absence therefore.'[32]

In these passages Merleau-Ponty gives us his own conception of the way in which the other *decentres* me, which is different from the Sartrean approach of 'decentralization'. In fact it is clearly argued here that the very possibility of this decentring is conditioned by the forging of a bond with the other. What was a problem for Sartre is resolved, in Merleau-Ponty, by the recognition that this bond probably constitutes a limited and, in a way, false access to the other, and the simultaneous conviction that it has to exist if one is to experience the presence of the other as a 'catastrophe': the bond may well not give me the totality of the otherness of the other, but it is nevertheless what decentres me. It is not 'absent' otherness that decentres me: that is beyond intersection, thus beyond any possible 'effect' on me. It is what binds me to the other which makes the decentring possible. This necessary condition for decentring appears very clearly in the sections I omitted from the passages quoted above, precisely so as to give them their full weight here. In them Merleau-Ponty emphasizes that it is because we both, that is, the other and I, have a different gaze at *the same world* that we each experience the decentring operated by the other: 'it is necessary and it suffices that he have the power to decenter me, to oppose his centering to my own', says the extract given above, which continues: 'and he can do so only because we are not two nihilations installed in two universes of the In Itself, incomparable, but two entries to the same Being, each accessible to but one of us, but appearing to the other as practicable by right, because they both belong to the same Being'.

It is true that this position is only tenable, according to Sartre, if it also recognizes that this bond is probably, in spite of everything, a betrayal of the otherness of the other, or at least that this point cannot be decided (how can it be verified, given that there is no access to this otherness beyond the bond?). Here Merleau-Ponty may perhaps, at one point, go too far in *The Visible and the Invisible*, or at least too far for his position to remain compatible with the critique of Sartre. This is when he considers the *absence* constituted by the other as 'a certain difference in terms of dimensions which are from the first common to us and which predestine the other to be a mirror of me as I am of him'.[33] This theme of 'intertwinings' (which I form with the other) returns to a pre-Sartrean position, suggesting a real union of our two consciousnesses. This theme is already outlined in the *Phenomenology of Perception*, in the idea of the body of the other as a 'miraculous prolongation' of my own and of a system where 'my body and the other person's are one whole'; he also says: 'we are collaborators for each other in consummate reciprocity. Our perspectives merge into each other, and we co-exist through a common world.'[34] This serene vision ought to calm the anxieties which had emerged earlier in his book in the form of juxtaposed questions, one of which is, 'whether [we know] my experience and that of another person can be linked in a single system of intersubjective experience?'[35]

In reality, one can continue to ponder these uneasy and essentially Sartrean questions without being convinced by the ultimate, serene answer of Merleau-Ponty. It is unnecessary, it seems to me, to adopt his theory of intersubjectivity in its entirety to be able to retain the idea already referred to that the 'decentring' effect of the other is felt only in the bond, even though this bond to some degree betrays the otherness which it constitutes. This is a way of holding on to Sartrean unease – is otherness not inevitably tamed by any experience you have of it, especially the gaze you direct at it? – while avoiding the various types of aporia to which it leads: what is the alternative? What can decentring resemble if there is no longer a bond, and no more 'common'? If the other is 'other' to the point that it scarcely appears to me, how can it decentre me?

Sartrean radicality leads, certainly, to major paradoxes, in particular this: ultimately, Sartre finds it easier to think the union of consciousnesses than the demonstration of their conflict – that is, easier to think the fusional bond than the conflictual bond.

This is particularly clear in his *What is Literature?* Here, Sartre poses the question, 'for whom does one write?', which includes journalism, since he says:

> Books are inert. They act upon those who open them, but they cannot open by themselves . . . so we must have recourse to other means. They already exist: the Americans have already adorned them with the name of 'mass media'; these are the real resources at our disposal for conquering the virtual public – the newspaper, the radio, and the cinema. Naturally, we have to quieten our scruples. To be sure, the book is the noblest, the most ancient of forms; to be sure, we will always have to return to it. But there is a *literary* art of radio, film, editorial work, and reporting.[36]

So, it is not 'addressing someone', or a potentially conflictual questioning that Sartre proposes as the main motive for writing. Against all expectations, it is rather the process of constituting a solid 'we': 'How shall we incorporate some of our potential readers into our actual public?', he asks.[37]

The Sartrean 'solution' to this enigma seems to lie in the thematic of choice. One can choose one's point of view, change it and then change it again. One can choose one's situation, therefore, and, in particular, decide to be more here (among the dominated) than there (among the dominant). The commitment constituted by such a choice is thus seen as a choice of *company*, that of all those who already, or will one day, share this point of view: 'the author's choice of a certain aspect of the world determines the reader and, vice versa . . . it is by choosing his reader that the author decides upon his subject'.[38] This argument is certainly difficult wholly to reconcile with the solitude of consciousnesses expounded in *Being and Nothingness*, and the Sartrean denunciation of the illusion represented by the 'we'; however, let that be. What is most surprising is that Sartre seems to find it easier to envisage 'company' than confrontation, the encounter-agreement than the encounter-conflict, the peaceful bond of the strongest unifying than the conflictual bond of 'decentring'. He finds it easier to imagine a writer who says 'we', and a 'we' with few internal disagreements, than a writer who says 'I say to you that . . .', addressing different persons, in order to present them with a conflictual speech.

In reality, this strange phenomenon relates to the impossibility, for the Sartrean philosophy, of thinking dialectical relations between beings, an interplay, an encounter in spite of the differences and disagreements. I can possibly amplify myself with a 'we' which has the same point of view as I do, but not confront other points of view: this is really how Sartre envisages commitment – rather like the choice to espouse a family without needing to interact with anyone else. The text which takes furthest the idea that the committed individual shares an experience with those he has chosen as companions, but does not in any way address those he opposes, is the Preface to Frantz Fanon's *The Wretched of the Earth*: 'He speaks of you often, never to you', he wrote;[39] and later: 'What does Fanon care whether you read his work or not? It is to his brothers that he denounces our old tricks, and he is sure we have no more up our sleeves. It is to them he says: "Europe has laid her hands on our continents, and we must slash at her fingers till she lets go".'[40]

Thus, when Sartre describes the 'committed writer' as a 'mediator' – 'The writer is, par excellence, a mediator and his commitment is to mediation'[41] – he is clearly thinking that it is the unconscious 'we', that of the dominated, that the writer 'mediatizes', that is, helps to constitute. As for engaging in dialogue with the dominant, or the conflictual relationship, this is seen as above all strewn with pitfalls. The 'public' of which Sartre speaks, all of those for whom the committed writer writes (such writers including, as we have said, journalists), is ultimately composed of those who are potentially with him and not against him. Sartre cites the case of the black American writer Richard Wright:

> To whom does Richard Wright address himself? Certainly not to the universal man . . . but neither can Wright think of intending his books for the white racialists of Virginia or South Carolina whose minds are made up in advance and who will not open them. Nor to the black peasants of the bayous who cannot read. And if he seems happy about the reception his books have had in Europe, still it is obvious that at the beginning he had not the slightest idea of writing for the European public. Europe is far away. Its indignation is ineffectual and hypocritical. Not much is to be expected from the nations which have enslaved the Indies, Indo-China, and the negro Africa. These considerations are enough to define his readers. He is addressing himself to the cultivated negroes of the North and the white Americans of goodwill (intellectuals, democrats of the left radicals, C.I.O. workers).[42]

In the end, the committed gaze seeks only to add to the troops behind it, not to combat its enemies. It is this that Merleau-Ponty never ceases to criticize in Sartre, especially in *Adventures of the Dialectic*: adopting only a single point of view, erected, according to the Sartrean reading of Marxism, into a 'true perspective' of history, and seeking to make it victorious, hence unifying around it, without allowing it to be disputed, without 'dialectically working it', by exposing it to those who might contradict it. It was 'to look at a man and society in their truth, that is to say, with the eyes of the least-favored'. And later:

> for Sartre, the relationships between classes, the relationships within the proletariat and finally those of the whole of history are not articulated relationships, including tension and the easing of tension, but are the immediate or magical relationships of our gazes. The truth of a society is seen through the eyes of its least-favored member.[43]

And there was no need for this 'true' point of view to be exposed to conflict with points of view that were not true.

For Merleau-Ponty, this conception of the gaze leads to a denial of what the gaze really is: a confrontation, a labour that brings many points of view into play at the same time, a truly dialectical investigation, a decentring based on exchange with an 'other'. Sartre, he believed, fled before the 'torments' inherent to contemplation, a contemplation which included, it should be noted, for Merleau-Ponty as for Sartre, journalism. 'Neither a government nor the [Communist Party] itself', he wrote,

> is obligated to have an opinion on the Soviet camps or, if they have one, to state it. The writer and the journalist must declare their position, for they *unveil*, their universe is a canvas upon which nothing exists unless it is represented, analyzed, and judged. The newspaper is the truth of the world; it acts by showing. As a result of this, there arise insoluble problems or illegitimate solutions which are not those of political action. The action of unveiling has its easy times and its torments, which are those of contemplation.[44]

In fact, according to Merleau-Ponty, Sartre's ultimate aim was a total closing down of the gaze at action.[45] He forgot that, whereas action makes choices and forges ahead, the gaze lags behind, plays the flâneur, is surprised, questions, confronts its point of view with others and works on its perspective.

This is hardly surprising. As we have seen, Sartre did not really believe in the 'dialectical' virtues of the gaze. The criticism articulated here by Merleau-Ponty, at the political level, relates to his disagreements at the phenomenological level, or to that 'failure' of Sartrean existentialism emphasized by Marcuse: a failure to show and deploy conflict, a failure to make perspectives merge into each other, a failure to engage in confrontation, because to do so would necessitate the *bond* that Sartre was trying to cut. 'In Sartre there is a plurality of subjects but no intersubjectivity', wrote Merleau-Ponty in his epilogue to the *Adventures of the Dialectic*.[46]

Here the whole paradox of the Sartrean position is laid bare: a position which keeps invoking the 'original conflict of transcendences', but which actually prevents this conflict from being shown, acted out or deployed. It is therefore an attitude which makes decentring – conceived of precisely as involving this presentation of conflict – impossible. Sartre still prefers to think the almost fusional 'we', solidarity with the point of view of 'the least-favored', with little introspection or dialectical elaboration, than to think the interaction of conflicting points of view. A strange situation indeed: he who wants too much, in the conception of otherness and conflict, emerges, in the end, as even more tempted by attitudes of empathic fusion, by the definitive choice of one 'camp' against others with whom the rift is so great that it produces no confrontation. To use the terminology of Max Scheler, the Sartrean position seems to be particularly threatened by the temptation of 'affective fusion' (*Einsfühlung*, *Einssetzung*) – that total empathy which Scheler distinguishes from 'sympathy', which requires, in contrast, a distance, that of confrontation and communication.[47] In denouncing the bonds of communication, which bear some resemblance to the 'sympathy' of Scheler, Sartre runs the risk of replacing them by the exclusive attitudes of 'affective fusion'. Conversely, it falls to those who think the bond and intersubjective communication to perfect the ability to think a decentring gaze, activating a conflict; and this in spite of the very 'Sartrean' unease they can arouse (do they sufficiently respect the otherness of the other? Do they not reduce the conflictuality by structuring it on the basis of the 'common' and the 'communicable'?).

In this way, even though the Sartrean critique denounces the unspoken prevalence of a thematic of unifying in many thinkers of decentring, since this 'other' who decentres me is still *bound* to me, it is not itself immune to a resurgence of this thematic of unifying, and in its most extreme form: failing to think the bond of encounter, of communication and of conflict, it is the fusional bond which resurfaces, a bond which excludes those who are not part of this 'we'. To them, it says only 'he speaks of you often, never to you'.

In the end, this philosophy did little to protect the *Libération* project from the temptations to which, according to this same Sartre, it succumbed in the 1970s.[48] Sartre was the first editor-in-chief of this daily newspaper, launched in 1973, and it was in this capacity that he spoke at a press conference on 4 January 1973, announcing the publication of the first issue for the following month. From the beginning, he warned the editors of *Libération* against the temptation of the 'leftist paper', that is, the 'sectarian spirit' which would result in it only ever offering the point of view of the dominated and stifling the 'contradictions' which characterized French society in general. He really seems to have been praising, against the excessively unifying tendencies which might tempt its founders, a journalism of *conflictual unifying*, perhaps even of *decentring*, at any rate one that would expose and activate conflicts. He was also insistent that disagreements within the editorial team should appear in the paper. He seems to have concluded, however, that his warnings had been in vain. In an interview in 1979,[49] he was hard on the early '*Libé*'. He criticized a style which tried to be 'of the workers', or 'in the style of *La Semaine de Suzette*', a famous popular magazine for girls, rather than 'speaking to a worker who read us as we would have spoken to him face-to-face'. His argument is not always clear, but one senses that he is challenging an excessively empathic gaze, exactly what he had tried to warn the editors against, and which had happily ended with the 'exit from leftism' operated by Serge July. But was this tendency Sartre criticized not, in the last analysis, remarkably Sartrean? It is significant that, when July praised the old *Libé* team in 1981, he spoke with a certain nostalgia about a 'group-in-fusion', in an allusion to Sartre.[50] And Sartre himself, in the 1979 interview, stated that there had been a price to be paid for this 'exit from leftism': 'The articles are better written. But you no longer sense the will behind them. There is good work, but you no longer sense rebellion. Many things have disappeared.' They looked more and 'acted' less, in a way! It is obvious that Sartre here has mixed feelings, which might well relate to his own philosophy and its temptation, as Merleau-Ponty had complained, to shut down the gaze at action. This philosophy had been, after all, the most obvious theorization of the 'leftism' and the empathic fusion with the dominated which Sartre claimed to reject.

In fact Sartre had great difficulty theorizing what he sometimes, it has to be said, advocated, as at this same press conference of 4 January 1973: a conflictual and not a fusional unifying, a mélange of conflict and bond. He spoke of 'contradictions and conflicts which should be publicly resolved in the newspaper, through articles which are in opposition to each other and which should lead, eventually, to an even stronger bond', contradicting some of his own philosophical assumptions. It could also be said that, in writing the Preface to *The Wretched of the Earth*, he was actually performing an act which ran counter to what he says in his text: his Preface is like a confession that, in spite of what he says about it, this book of Fanon is not content with creating a fusional 'we', closed to the dominant, but that it is also decentring. In fact, what he says is fairly contradictory:

> This book has not the slightest need of a preface, all the less so because it is not addressed to us. Yet I have written one, in order to bring the argument to its conclusion; for we in Europe too are being decolonized:

> that is to say that the settler who is in every one of us is being savagely rooted out. Let us look at ourselves, if we can bear to, and see what is becoming of us.[51]

The strength of Sartre's need to justify himself is striking. In fact he comes close to contradicting himself: Fanon's text is not addressed to us and yet at the same time it addresses us. And then, as if by chance, here he is rehabilitating the idea of a 'dialectic' of points of view that he objected to elsewhere. More than Fanon himself – who, once again, does not address us – it is Sartre who here elects himself a decentrer; it is he who, by his Preface, makes the 'impossible' conflict live, acts the invisible conflict, and thus confronts us with him who does not care about us – and this in order to decentre us. In which case, *The Wretched of the Earth*, this 'other' book, is perhaps not so very other after all. Perhaps it can be 'connected' to 'us', we are so very much outsiders to it. Sartre cannot escape. If he accepts the position of the decentrer, he 'reintroduces' a bond.

But it is clear that these observations are marginal in relation to the essential philosophy of Sartre, which they largely contradict. It is a sort of confession, against Sartrean existentialism, that it is not true that there is only the terrible alternative of sadism or masochism, of a gaze that reifies or a non-gaze. There is also a gaze that encounters and activates conflict, a gaze that may well tame – not everything about the 'damned' is accessible to us, and it is probably that which is least other in them that we are able to encounter – but that still has a major impact on our identity, which unmakes us and decentres us. It is in spite of himself that Sartre finds something which is closer to decentring as formulated by Merleau-Ponty than to his own conception of 'decentralization'.

The only Sartrean dimension which remains in this acceptance of decentring as the forging of a bond is the recognition that a part of what decentres probably remains completely inaccessible – that is, beyond the bond. In other words, the decentring operates only by bringing that which is 'other' into the common space of 'seeing', which assumes, admittedly, that part of this otherness is probably lost in the process.

3. From the gaze to listening: Jean Hatzfeld on the Rwandan genocide

Thoughtful decentrers are inevitably conscious of this limitation. Even they, who seek to play out, in their gaze, a more radical conflict than the 'unifiers', and so expose an otherness much more threatening to the identity of the 'we,' are destined to at least partial failure. They can, after all, only represent what can be represented. They must necessarily skip over that which, in the 'other' they show, is beyond all visibility. They are subject to the limitations inherent to the figure of the spectator.

Journalism can fight against these structural limitations of the figure of the spectator, it can try to distance itself ever further from them, but it cannot make them go away. But where does this struggle take it? How can journalism be taken further? Such questions suppose that we address the problem of the limits of journalism by starting from journalism itself, not from a position from the outset external to it, sure of itself and proud of its exteriority – a position common in the social sciences when they see themselves as having nothing in common with journalism, confident of reaching what Foucault called 'the hidden'.

To try to respond to this question we could return to a hypothesis I formulated earlier, in my discussion of the Sartrean critique of the gaze: if the bond which the gaze forges with the object looked at is by nature reductive, other types of bond may be more fruitful. This hypothesis is not, as I have said, enriched by the arguments of Sartre, because his notion of 'gaze' is, in the last analysis, a paradigm for thinking perception in general, experience and the relationship to the other. Sartre never poses, for example, the question of *listening* and the differences it involves as compared with the gaze, so preoccupied is he with listing all the forms of 'communication' with the other which always forge a bond and hence betray the 'incommunicable' character of the otherness.

It is an interesting question, nevertheless, and an important one for any discussion of journalism. It does not necessarily mean envisaging a space for listening entirely autonomous in relation to that of 'seeing'. In many respects, listening also helps to 'see', like writing in general. Words describe, they produce visualization. It is not only television that makes people *see*; newspapers and the radio do so too. In any case, when we say that the figure of the spectator in politics was born with Kantism, we are evoking a person who writes, a spectator whose gaze is *put into words* so that it is shared with all the other spectators. In fact we need to begin by asking how certain types of writing can enlarge the space of 'seeing', in particular in relation to images, but also in relation to ordinary journalistic writing of every type.[52] But we need also to ask if, by seeking to enlarge the gaze, there is a risk that we end up aiming at an access to the real which is no longer dependent on 'seeing', in short which goes beyond the journalistic requirement of 'showing'.

Journalistic writing faces a double problem, which risks imprisoning it and blocking the gaze it offers: that of its temporality, the present, and that of the access if offers to a reality (in fact a problem of all writing).

It has perhaps been too hastily assumed that the first problem, the anchorage in the present, is the main one, and that it is this that limits access to the real. This is not necessarily the case. The immediacy of writing also enables it to touch certain realities, sometimes to apprehend the presence of things in an exceptional way. If Albert Londres described the bombardment of the cathedral of Reims, in September 1914, in the way he did, giving the reader such a strong sense of being there, it is probably because he was writing so close in time to the actual event.[53] Grasping the present – the presence – can even be a literary challenge within an approach which still calls itself journalistic. This was the case with Michael Herr in Vietnam. Herr wanted to catch the violence in progress, the violence lived, and it was clear to him that, to do this, there had to be a simultaneity of writing and experience, that is, a journalistic approach. The 'holes' in a writing in the present, its blindnesses and its incomprehensions, are also part of its truth; it is precisely because it does not see everything that it describes the present of an event. Think, for example, of Orwell's writing on the front during the Spanish War, for instance his description of being hit by a bullet. The inability to 'see' the violence in the writing of Michael Herr, his admission of defeat, the feeling of being overwhelmed, 'blanketed' by the war, is in another sense a sign of his success; he had truly grasped the *present of the violence*, that moment when the violence becomes strange, invisible, almost absent, so strongly do you protect yourself from it.[54]

Writing in the present, journalistic writing, thus has its own resources as well as its limitations, and writing at a distance has them too. In other words, it is certainly not my intention to claim that the latter resolves the aporias of the former – that journalists can only accede to the reality that interests them by standing back, by abandoning journalism in favour of writing at a distance. My chapter on flânerie, following in the footsteps of Walter Benjamin, where I discussed the search for 'shock' as both a journalistic and an artistic aim, should already have suggested that I am hardly likely to attack what in journalism so often puts people off, that is, the anchorage in the present, the desire to give the 'presence' of things, including in their sudden traumatic eruption. On the contrary, this seems to me of great interest, suggesting, 'ideally', a true labour of writing, by the text or the image.

In reality, what is gained by writing after a lapse of time is often access to something other than what is aimed at by writing in the present, that is, another aspect of reality. It is less focused on its sudden appearance, on the lived immediacy it implies; it approaches it differently, it digs deeper, it explores it in a way that is impossible for the journalist who works in the present moment – even if it means certain aspects are lost, especially the feeling of the 'present'. Thus writing at a distance enlarges what can be 'seen', not in the sense that it at last makes visible what journalism has failed to penetrate, but by opening up other spaces. When the same Michael Herr, ten years after his reporting from the front, republished his articles in book form, in *Dispatches*, he broadened the gaze though without correcting the gaze of the past: the 'visions' which surfaced afterwards, in his nightmares, only confirmed the strange blindness inherent to the present of violence.

At the same time, in this same example, one sees that to write after the event is a major temptation for the journalist. It is a delay that relieves the gaze of the imperative to give its recipient a *presence*, so as to reveal other aspects of a reality. There have been times in the history of journalism when newspapers have welcomed ventures of this sort. The affair of the My Lai massacre was revealed to the wider public, a year and a half after the events, by a journalist who had never been to Vietnam. In his articles of November 1969, in which he presented his interviews with the GIs responsible for the killing, it was the 'logic' of this massacre, rather than its 'presence', that Seymour M. Hersh tried to piece together. As a general rule, there is no fixed, essential definition of 'journalism' which prohibits extending the concerns of journalism to 'seeing' further than the legitimate concern to give the public the 'presence' of the world. The journalists who work after the event, when they publish their work in book form, far from proclaiming a venture quite other than that of the journalist, are often the first to regret that they have not been published where it would have been appropriate for them to be.

That said, it remains true that a journalism of afterwards can only really happen by operating on the margins of journalism as it has been constructed in our political modernity. This is because its purpose is no longer exclusively to 'show'. It extends the gaze, certainly, but it does more. It opens up to a different relationship to the real from that of *visibility*. It is not aimed only at the imagination which forms images. But nor is it aimed primarily at judgement, as, for example, in the case of the leader-writer who develops a 'point of view', and who is consequently still involved in the desire to 'show'. Its search for meaning often goes well beyond this need to judge. It seeks a 'sense' of the event which is, in fact, a 'sentiment' of the event; it wants to make it *felt*, beyond the impression that its presence has been able to give, beyond images that are readily available, beyond its visibility, which is often already very real. It extends the process of decentring, which forged a bond in order sometimes to 'show' the unimaginable, the most unexpected otherness, by forging a bond of another type: by the quest for a voice more than a vision.

Words do not convey the whole of the otherness that is expressed in them, either, but they open up to other dimensions of an event from the approach that consists of making it *visible*. They do not get rid of the limitations, they alter them. They are often sought after by those very 'decentring' journalists whose aim is to confront us with *something other*, but when they find them, it can be said, in a way, that they invent another journalism beyond that of the 'gaze'.

It is probably the work of Jean Hatzfeld on the Rwandan genocide that best illustrates this search for *a voice* – a voice that reports that very otherness that constitutes the event. Six years after the massacre of Tutsis which had taken place in the commune of Nyamata (in April–May 1994), Hatzfeld published a first book, *Into the Quick of Life: The Rwandan Genocide: The Survivors Speak*,[55] which largely consisted of the statements of survivors he had met on the spot. Three years later, in another book, *Machete Season: The Killers in Rwanda Speak*,[56] he recorded the voices of their killers. Voices, the voices of violence, violence suffered and violence perpetrated: at the heart of Hatzfeld's writing, it was these he had searched for during the long months of interviews. Voices in which there appears, at least sketchily, that enigmatic, appalling otherness that is genocide. Hatzfeld gently complements them, clarifies them and reveals his own incomprehensions and questions. But it is the voices that matter.

This search for a *voice* supposes both forging a bond, 'encountering' the violence and showing the limits of the bond, since all of them, survivors and executioners, remain, in a sense, incomprehensible, forever remote from us. In this regard, it is truly the process of decentring that we encounter here: creating a bond which decentres, but by suggesting that this bond gives only a limited access to this otherness and does not claim to grasp the whole of it. Yet it is not a decentring *gaze* that Hatzfeld offers us; it is *words*, which do little to help us see the massacre, but which give us the terrible 'sentiment' of it. And these words take up a lot of space, clearly exceeding the habitual formats of journalism – which is not to say that a brave newspaper could not have published extracts. There is a rhythm in these books which in itself constitutes a world, a unity in which you go round and round, trapped in these words, which never stop *saying what we cannot see*. This way of situating oneself as if beyond the visible, hence of the journalism which wants to 'show', is explicit in Hatzfeld. He writes:

> The most telling explanation I have heard so far (food for thought for those who, at every human tragedy, wonder aloud about the usefulness of information and eyewitness testimony) comes from Claudine Kayitesi, a farmer and survivor on the hill of Ntarama, when she says, reversing our proverb: 'Whites do not want to see what they cannot believe, and they could not believe a genocide, because that is a killing that overwhelms everyone, them as much as the others.' So they left.[57]

There is a limit to the 'I saw', a limit which relates to our conception of the 'common', excluding what this woman describes as 'beyond everyone's understanding'. Hatzfeld begins where the 'I saw' stops.

It is to another decentring than that operated by the *gaze*, then, that he introduces us, even if the process is analogous: forging a bond to a reality by suggesting that much of it remains beyond the bond. So, when he says he is trying to 'establish a link with the past', he uses this expression while suggesting, straightaway, his failure to understand everything of what he links himself and links us to. In fact this expression appears in the last chapter of *Machete Season*, after the author has described the following scene: one morning in August 1994 he was driving through the forest of Nyungwe in western Rwanda. The road was teeming with fleeing Hutus hoping to cross the river separating them from the camps of the Congo. Turning off onto a path, Hatzfeld and his companions discover about a dozen men crouching round a fire in a clearing; they are *interahamwe*, that is, former members of the extremist Hutu militia. They spend a few moments with them, then several of the *interahamwe* rise, machetes in hand, and begin to surround them; they flee. Hatzfeld says that these killers may have been members of the gang he questioned a few years later in a penitentiary. And he adds: 'I wonder now if, unconsciously, I didn't go to the penitentiary, among other reasons, expecting to find those same expressions of unfathomable hatred, to compare them to my memories and establish a link with the past.'[58] What is interesting here is that Hatzfeld says that he had never again seen this expression on any of the faces of his interlocutors; if he had, he suggests, he might not have been able to continue with these interviews: 'If the ferocity glimpsed in the forest of Nyungwe had ever surfaced in any of their faces, would we have stopped the interview? I really don't know.'[59] In other words, it may only have been possible to forge this bond with an effectively 'reduced' or 'tamed' otherness, leaving its core, its profound enigma, inaccessible. Hatzfeld makes us access 'them', but without ever solving the enigma that constitutes them. He does not claim to have understood them or explained them to us. It is for this reason that this voice, which emerges from an abyss we never completely penetrate, disturbs us and decentres us even more deeply than a 'vision' could do.

This way of saying the inaccessible in the very process of creating access had been an essential characteristic of Hatzfeld's first book, on the Tutsi survivors. How can one not read into the statement of a social worker as she explains how she managed to make the other survivors speak, and 'forge a bond' with them, an implicit reference to Hatzfeld's own labour and situation in relation to them? The shared experience of this survivor and her interlocutors, she says, helped these words to come. Nevertheless, it is striking that she refuses to think something like a 'communion' of suffering. She herself is in a situation that is out of kilter with that of the survivors who spoke to her; once she had told them of her own past, she appeared only 'less strange'. So, the issue for her is the bond, not the feeling of 'community', which seems impossible. And this bond, she says, will be even slower to be forged between the survivors and those who have not lived through it (Hatzfeld? 'us'?): 'Those who have not lived the genocide see nothing. If they try hard, then one day they will be able to acknowledge the secret pain we feel. But it will take a long time, even if these people are Tutsis from Rwanda or Burundi, even if they lost families and close relations during the killings.'[60] Hatzfeld's work seeks this bond which the young woman also forges, a bond that does not create a true 'common'. And these are its voices, voices that do not deny, at the same time, the incommunicable.

The incommunicable – the gulf that remains in spite of the bond forged by words – appears with particular clarity in the story of another woman:

> One day, in my watery hiding place, I got caught. That morning, I had run off behind an old woman I knew. We were hunkered down in the water in silence. The killers sprang her first. They hacked her before my very eyes, without going to the trouble of pulling her out of the water. Then they meticulously searched the undergrowth because they knew all too well that a woman never hid alone, and they found me. I was holding my child in my arms. They slew it. I asked to be let up onto the grass and not die in the mire of blood where the woman already lay. There were two men, of their faces I have not forgotten a single feature. They dragged me through the papyrus, and they laid me out with a blow full in the forehead, they did not chop off my neck. Often, they left wounded people in the mud for a day or two, before coming back to finish them off. In my case, I believe they simply forgot to come back that way, which is why there is some work they left undone.
>
> I lay in a dead faint for a long time: then Théophile and some other runaways found me there at death's door and restored me with water . . .
>
> Four months after the genocide I married Théophile. We acted as though nothing had changed between us, despite what had happened. In this way we came back to each other again, saying quietly what needed

> to be said quietly, saying aloud what could be said aloud. We live in a three-room clay-brick house with a sheet metal roof with our two children and four orphans. *As for the orphans, there is no more point in talking to them of the genocide; they have seen reality at its worst. My two little children will later learn the necessary truth about the genocide. That said, I think that a gulf of understanding now separates those who lay down in the marsh and those who did not; between you and me for instance.*[61]

The end of the passage (the emphasis is mine) tells us that, in spite of what the beginning had 'shown', we see nothing, can see nothing. This is precisely what words can do: they can destroy the feeling of seeing that they create, and in this way make us understand something else, beyond the 'vision': the feeling of incomprehension, of the gulf revealed by the bond and by the voices. Words get further in the approach to the otherness than the story which 'shows', even if they are no better than the decentring gaze at enabling us to comprehend this otherness in its entirety.

In *Machete Season*, the book on the killers, we again encounter this labour to unlock words, which nevertheless does not reduce the impossibility of understanding in those who receive them (beginning with Hatzfeld himself). On the contrary, they make something irredeemably 'other' heard. The book is full of words which seem, in a sense, *impossible*. Take, for example, the analogies between killing the Tutsis and killing chickens or goats:

> ELIE: . . . in the end, a man is like an animal: you give him a whack on the head or the neck, and down he goes. In the first days someone who had already slaughtered chickens – and especially goats – had an advantage, understandably. Later, everybody grew accustomed to the new activity, and the laggards caught up.[62]

Or between wielding a machete and wielding a ballpoint pen:

> FULGENCE: . . . if you and me are given a ballpoint pen, you will prove more at ease with writing work than me, no jealousy on my part. For us, the machete was what we knew how to use and sharpen.[63]

Or between the killings and the routine of work in the fields:

> LÉOPORD: Killing was less wearisome than farming. In the marshes, we could lag around for hours looking for someone to slaughter without getting penalized. We could shelter from the sun and chat without feeling idle. The workday didn't last as long as in the fields. We returned at three o'clock to have time for pillaging. We fell asleep every evening safe from care, no longer worried about drought. We forgot our torments as farmers. We gorged on vitamin-rich foods.[64]

IGNACE: . . . for the simplest farmers, it was refreshing to leave the hoe in the yard. We got up rich. We went to bed with full bellies, we lived a life of plenty. Pillaging is more worthwhile than harvesting, because it profits everyone equally.[65]

ALPHONSE: . . . at first the activity was less repetitive than sowing; it cheered us up, so to speak. Afterwards it became the same every day. More than anything, we missed going home to eat at noon. At noon we often found ourselves deep in the marshes; that is why the midday meal and our usual afternoon naps were forbidden us by the authorities.[66]

And then there are the 'logics', coolly expressed, as obvious truths or rationalizations come who knows where from:

LÉOPORD: . . . we had sessions with girls who were raped in the bush. Nobody dared protest that. Even those who were edgy about it, because they had received blessings in church for example, told themselves *it would change nothing since the girl was marked for death anyway.*[67]

IGNACE: . . . we thought that since this job was meeting no opposition, it was because it really had to be done.[68]

ALPHONSE: Saving the babies, that was not practicable. They were whacked against walls and trees or they were cut right away. But they were killed more quickly, because of their small size and because their suffering was no use. They say that at the church at Nyamata they burned children with gasoline. Maybe it's true, but that was just a few in the first-day turmoil. Afterwards that did not last. In any case I noticed nothing more. The babies could not understand the why of the suffering, it was not worth lingering over them.[69]

ELIE: . . . we no longer counted up what we had killed but what it would bring us.[70]

ADALBERT: In town we would recount the exploits of the day. Some exaggerated their score, hoping to get a more fertile plot eventually or a field in a better location.[71]

It is when he interviews the killer Joseph-Désiré Bitero that Hatzfeld most clearly expresses his incomprehension, his feeling of dealing with a radical other, even when he meets him, gets him to talk and literally understands his words. Bitero is a former leader of the *interahamwe* of the commune where Hatzfeld had done his research; he had been condemned to death. It is clear that it is he, above all, who poses the problem of the proximity of the 'ordinary' and the massacre. It is this proximity he makes heard, as an incomprehensible statement of the obvious. He says: 'We had lived with Tutsi friends without noticing it, and we became contaminated by ethnic racism without noticing it.' To which Hatzfeld adds: 'Then he finally says something that reveals the abyss of incomprehension lying between us: "If a divine miracle were to help me to return to my hill, my family, and a job, people would see that I can become an ordinary person again".'[72]

In general Hatzfeld never stops tracking down 'other' statements of the obvious which he hears and makes heard – for example the obvious truth, for these killers, that to ask for a pardon, which inevitably humiliated them, ought to be enough for them to be pardoned.[73] The book constantly poses this problem of their strangeness, their remoteness even when the author *encounters* them and ends up by conceiving with regard to them, by his own telling, a feeling, if not of sympathy, at least of accessibility (as, for that matter, do we): 'But as time passes, a kind of perplexity creeps in, which makes the Kibungo gang not more likable but less unpleasant to spend time with – under the acacia tree, anyway. This is awkward to admit, but curiosity wins out over hostility.'[74] In reality, it is the problem of this place, 'under the acacia tree', which is posed here: it is a sort of non-place, or 'place outside' – outside him and us, and outside them – which is precisely where words can come. These words remind us always of what separates 'them' and 'us', but they create, after all, a point of intersection. Hatzfeld refers explicitly to this condition of the voice which is to create a 'place outside', like the prison, in its own way: 'subsequent visits confirmed my hunch that only an *imprisoned* killer, a killer who has not yet lived at liberty, can or will tell his story. Clearly, the freer the Hutus were on their land, the less free they were with their words.'[75]

It is because a place is created where words become possible that they offer a true visibility with regard to the otherness that is expressed in them. Even including for those who speak, what is said often remains opaque. Strangely, the voices readily utter, whether an obvious fact or an enigma, but do not really clarify. The counterpoint to the statements of Bitero is these words of Léopord, a confession of a complete invisibility as to the enigma which had come about in him: 'This gentleman I killed at the marketplace, I can tell you the exact memory of it because he was the first. For others, it's murky – I cannot keep track anymore in my memory. I considered them unimportant; at the time of those murders *I didn't even notice the tiny thing that would change me into a killer*.'[76] In many respects, it is an analogous invisibility that is revealed by the escaped Tutsis, with regard to the gulf produced in them by the violence – with the difference, Hatzfeld says, that they were less at peace with their memories than the killers with theirs.[77] Invisibility is sometimes more, sometimes less difficult to live with.

It is not exactly a comprehension of the event, therefore, that Jean Hatzfeld gives: 'When the killings begin, you find it easier to ply the machete than to be stabbed by ridicule and contempt. This truth is impossible to understand for anyone who was not there beside us.'[78] In making them talk, Hatzfeld tries to go beyond the frontiers of 'seeing', that of the imagination or that of the intellect. He seeks a voice, which offers this truth without necessarily making it possible to understand it. He 'decentres' our identity as human beings by describing what human beings can also produce, and how far it goes; but by voices, not by a gaze.

It would be ridiculous to see this approach as literally an *exit from* journalism. For that we would need to have a closed, unchanging definition of journalism. However, it is true that, since its birth, journalism, in modern democracies, has been a labour to *show*, that it is the figure of the *spectator* that journalism illustrates, defends and incarnates in a democracy, and that it is the limits inherent to this figure that we find in journalistic practice. Democracy remains, for the present, strongly marked by the need to *see together*, and journalism remains subject to the constraints this implies. In forging other bonds with the real than that of the gaze, some journalistic approaches engage in journalism by other means. They labour to make democratic public space itself evolve, towards a more complex grasp of the real. They forge new bonds with an invisible otherness, which they try to introduce into a common space of exchanges which is not exclusively a space of 'seeing'. They show that such a development of the idea of public space, whether one regards it as well or badly occupied till now, is possible, conceptually at least.

Epilogue

Journalism does not have a good press, and there are good reasons for the anger it arouses. But there are good reasons also for vigilance, and a rejection of trivial criticism that is ignorant of its problems. It is my hope that this book will have helped to clarify the questions posed by journalism in our modern democracies – in other words, how we might engage in a serious debate about its political role, and formulate ambitious if anxious expectations for it, instead of drowning it in facile sarcasms.

I have tried to show that a rational political analysis of journalism requires a return to the question of the status of the spectator in a democracy. Modern democracy has been constructed by clearing, alongside the stage of actions, a place where the people can observe itself, a place where the people becomes a 'public'. We need to understand, therefore, what requirements the democratic ideal needs us to formulate for those who are now leaders of opinion in this place.

My own answer has been to reject two extremes: on the one hand, the ideal of a perfect plurality of points of view, which journalism ought to protect and stimulate; on the other, renunciation or desertion in the face of a homogeneity of opinions and gazes seen as structural to democratic public space. I have tried to find an 'ideal-critique' of journalism which in reality reveals my own conception of democracy: a mélange of conflict and bond, a curious, precarious and fragile mélange, which there are several ways of achieving, and no doubt also of betraying. This complex mélange, if it is to come about and survive, needs a stage on which society represents itself. This is why it is on journalism, which makes visible, which shows, that the safeguarding, or perpetual recreation, of the 'democratic enigma' has devolved.

I have developed my 'ideal-critique' of journalism through a series of auto-corrections. I see the journalist-flâneur as the culmination of the Kantian apologia for an infinitely curious gaze, in love with diversity, ready to enrich the 'common' with an undreamed-of 'new'. But the greatest flâneurs never denied the pitfalls of a diversity that was, in the end, limited. Their occasional anger at needing always to woo this 'common' that they wanted to open up to other gazes, their inability to break with it and the need to act out their rebellion in the very place which had provoked it, all emphasize the ambiguity contained within flânerie. This ambiguity begged only to be further explored. The ideal of the conflictual journalist, as illustrated by Marx, allowed me to radicalize my approach to the space of 'seeing' as a space of tensions between domination(s) and resistance(s). At this point my discussion abandoned the Kantian confidence in plurality, a confidence which had already been eroded by the very figure of the flâneur to which it had led. The problem of 'ideal' journalism now presented itself in these terms: how to preserve the possibility of conflict.

The idea that this conflict could only come to the surface by remaining, in one way or another, imbricated in the 'common' that it challenged, and caused to be reformulated, had already emerged in my discussion. It seemed necessary, however, to think journalism more clearly as a two-pronged movement: that of introducing conflict and that of forging a common. This is how I ended up with an 'ideal-critique' that I have called the 'conflictual unifying' of the democratic community. I have described two paths to achieving this ideal, two paths which I believe are clearly visible in the history of journalism since the second half of the nineteenth century. These two paths are on the one hand that of *unifying through a test*, and on the other that of *decentring up to the limits of the bond.*

This approach has led me to put the question of conflict at the heart of my discussion of democracy. In fact what these two journalistic approaches illustrate are the two forms which conflictuality can take in a democracy. The second attempts to go further in the radicality of the conflict it tries to act out. Like the first, however, it remains trapped in the democratic requirement to take place in a common space. There can be no doubt that this requirement limits the conflictuality that can operate in the gaze of the journalist. It relates to the structural limits of democratic public space. Nevertheless, it still leaves journalists with real room for manoeuvre. They can do many things. They can act out in many ways the alliance of the common and conflict. All they need is an analysis capable of revealing the subtlety of the acts – political acts – which they achieve in their texts, the products they offer their public.

But there remain, it will be said, the limits inherent to the very position of the spectator. Yes, but it would be perverse to brandish these as confirmation that little can be expected of journalism. These limits do not in any way justify systematic hostility to journalism, that hatred tinged with anti-democratism which Michel Foucault so convincingly denounced. The limits inherent to the function of *representing* are not a justification for being satisfied with a world where this function is in danger, or even abolished. Even the dangers of an omnipotent 'seeing' should not make us forget that seeing, seeing together, is an essential precondition for democracy. But I have also argued that journalism itself is capable of reflecting on the limits of the role that consists of 'showing'. Within journalism there are journalists who are attempting to forge a bond of a different kind with these things, these events and these traumas, which they struggle to introduce into our public space. Rather than expend so much energy on polemical criticism of bad journalism, we might do better to think more deeply about this question, which has been abandoned for the time being to a handful of writer-journalists, a handful of 'decentrers', who are, sadly, too cut off from the public debate. It is a question that is vital if we are to make democracy evolve, so that it will of itself start to push back its own boundaries: how to act and how to write so that this world in which we live *speaks* to us?

Notes

Introduction

1. T. W. Adorno and M. Horkheimer, *Dialectic of Enlightenment: Philosophical Fragments* [Amsterdam, 1947], trans. John Cumming (London: Allen Lane, 1973; Verso, 1997); see also trans. Edmund Jephcott, *Dialectic of Enlightenment: Philosophical Fragments* (Stanford: Stanford University Press, 2002).
2. Stéphane Haber, 'Les Formes de la connaissance du présent dans les sciences sociales: une introduction au concept de modernité', Unpublished thesis, University of Franche-Comté (December 1996).
3. Ibid., ch. 3.
4. See in particular Rolf Lindner, *The Reportage of Urban Culture: Robert Park and the Chicago School*, trans. Adrian Morris with Jeremy Gaines and Martin Chalmers (Cambridge: Cambridge University Press, 1996); Pierre Saint-Arnaud, *Park, Dos Passos, metropolis: regards croisés sur la modernité urbaine aux Etats-Unis* (Quebec and Toulouse: Presses de l'Université de Laval and Presses Universitaires du Mirail, Toulouse, 1997).
5. Many books have been written on the New Journalism. I have myself discussed it in: Géraldine Muhlmann, *A Political History of Journalism*, trans. Jean Birrell (Cambridge: Polity, 2008).
6. See in particular T. Ferenczi, *L'Invention du journalisme en France* (Paris: Payot, 1993).
7. Emile Zola, 'Préface pour *La Morasse*, volume collectif de nouvelles', in *Oeuvres complètes*, ed. Henri Mitterand (Paris: Ed. Claude Tchou, 1966–70), vol. 3, pp. 643–6.
8. P. Assouline, *Albert Londres: vie et mort d'un grand reporter, 1884–1932* (Paris: Balland, 1989), p. 90 (cited by Ferenczi, *L'Invention du journalisme*, p. 39).

9. Wolf Lepenies, *Between Literature and Science: The Rise of Sociology* [1985], trans, R. J. Hollingdale (Cambridge: Cambridge University Press, 1988), p. 47.
10. See Michel Foucault, 'La philosophie analytique de la politique' [1978], in *Dits et écrits 1954–1988*, eds D. Defert and F. Ewald, with J. Lagrange (Paris: Gallimard, 1994), vol. 3, pp. 534–51, at pp. 540–1.
11. See in particular Jay Rosen, *What are Journalists For?* (New Haven and London: Yale University Press, 1999); Theodore L. Glasser (ed.), *The Idea of Public Journalism* (New York and London: Guilford Press, 1999); Anthony J. Eksterowicz and Robert N. Roberts (eds), *Public Journalism and Political Knowledge* (Boston: Rowman & Littlefield, 2000).
12. See in particular J. Herbert Altschull, *From Milton to McLuhan: The Ideas Behind American Journalism* (New York: Longman, 1990); Steven R. Knowlton and Patrick R. Parsons (eds), *The Journalist's Moral Compass: Basic Principles* (Westport: Praeger, 1995); John Durham Peters, *Courting the Abyss: Free Speech and the Liberal Tradition* (Chicago and London: University of Chicago Press, 2005).
13. The heritage of Walter Lippmann and John Davey is alive and well in the United States. As shown in masterly fashion by James Carey (*Communication as Culture: Essays on Media and Society* (New York and London: Routledge, 1992)), they can be regarded as the 'fathers' of two different trends in work on the press, which in itself suggests a certain fruitfulness, including in their disagreements. See also Herbert J. Gans, *Deciding What's News* (New York: Pantheon Books, 1979); Gans, *Democracy and the News* (Oxford: Oxford University Press, 2003).
14. Christopher Lasch, 'Mass culture reconsidered', *Democracy* (October, 1981), pp. 7–22.
15. Lasch refers in particular to Herbert Gans, *Popular Culture and High Culture: An Analysis and Evaluation of Taste* (New York: Basic Books, 1974; revised edn 1999).
16. Christopher Lasch, *The New Radicalism in America 1889–1963: The Intellectual as a Social Type* (New York and London: W. W. Norton, 1965), ch. 8.
17. Muhlmann, *Political History of Journalism*, ch. 4.
18. Isaac Bashevis Singer, *A Little Boy in Search of God* (1976), in *Love and Exile: The Early Years – A Memoir* (Harmondsworth: Penguin, 1986), p. 21.
19. M. Mouillaud and J.-F. Tétu, *Le Journal quotidien* (Lyon: PUL, 1989), p. 23.
20. This is the summary given, with scarcely controlled anger, by the media specialist Michael Schudson of E. S. Herman and Noam Chomsky's *Manufacturing Consent: The Political Economy of the Mass Media* (New York: Pantheon Books, 1988); it is brutal but not inaccurate: Michael Schudson, *The Power of News* (Cambridge, MA: Harvard University Press, 1995), p. 4.
21. Muhlmann, *Political History of Journalism*.
22. Thesis submitted in 2001 to the University of Paris 7-Denis Diderot.

Chapter 1

1. Edward S. Herman and Noam Chomsky, *Manufacturing Consent: The Political Economy of the Mass Media* (New York: Pantheon Books, 1988), p. xv.
2. 'The great media also depend on the government for more general policy support. All business firms are interested in business taxes, interest rates, labor policies, and enforcement and nonenforcement of the anti-trust laws': ibid., p. 13.
3. Serge Halimi, *Les Nouveaux chiens de garde* (Paris: Liber, 1997).
4. Paul Nizan, *The Watchdogs: Philosophers of the Established Order*, trans. Paul Fittingoff (New York and London: Monthly Review Press, 1972).
5. For a critique of the perverse effects of an excessive distrust of authorities on the part of 'watchdog journalism', see, for example, H. Eugene Goodwin and Ron F. Smith, *Groping for Ethics in Journalism* (Ames: Iowa State University Press, 1983; 3rd edn 1994), ch. 7, 'The government watch'.
6. Halimi, *Les Nouveaux chiens de garde*, p. 13.
7. Herman and Chomsky, *Manufacturing Consent*, p. 29.
8. Karl Marx and Frederick Engels, *The German Ideology* [1845–6], repr. in *Karl Marx, Frederick Engels. Collected Works*, vol. 5: *Marx and Engels: 1845–47* (London: Lawrence & Wishart, 1976), pp. 19–539, at p. 59. Similarly, when Serge Halimi denounces what he calls *la pensée unique* (literally, 'single' or 'uniform thought') of French journalists, he defines it in a way that evokes the Marxian concept of ideology, although he cites not Marx himself but another journalist at *Le Monde diplomatique*, Ignacio Ramonet: *la pensée unique*, Halimi says, 'is the translation "*in ideological terms with a pretension to universality of the interests of international capital*", of those who are called "the markets", that is, the great financiers': Halimi, *Les Nouveaux chiens de garde*, p. 46 (the quotation in italics is taken from the article by Ignacio Ramonet, 'La Pensée unique', *Le Monde diplomatique*, January 1995).
9. See Chapter 4 below.
10. Marx and Engels, *The German Ideology*, p. 59.
11. 'This whole appearance, that the rule of a certain class is only the rule of certain ideas, comes to a natural end, of course, as soon as class rule in general ceases to be the form in which society is organized, that is to say, as soon as it is no longer necessary to represent a particular interest as general or the "general interest" as ruling': ibid., p. 61.
12. See, in particular, for the subtlety of the way the media 'frames' individual representations: S. Iyengar and D. Kinder, *News That Matters: Television and American Opinion* (Chicago: University of Chicago Press, 1987); S. Iyengar, *Is Anyone Responsible? How Television Frames Political Issues* (Chicago: University of Chicago Press, 1991). For a synthesis on the problem of reception, see the works of Brigitte Le Grignou, especially her latest book, *Du côté du public: usages et réceptions de la télévision* (Paris: Economica, 2003).

13. Pierre Bourdieu published Serge Halimi's *Les Nouveaux chiens de garde* in his 'Liber' series for Seuil.
14. Pierre Bourdieu, *On Television and Journalism*, trans. P. P. Ferguson (London: Pluto, 1998), p. 17.
15. Ibid., p. 39.
16. Ibid., pp. 16–17.
17. P. Champagne, *Faire l'opinion: le nouveau jeu politique* (Paris: Minuit, 1990), pp. 279–80.
18. Ibid., p. 280.
19. Bourdieu, *On Television and Journalism*, p. 28.
20. Ibid., p. 18 (p. 16 of French edition).
21. Ibid., p. 14.
22. Ibid., p. 20.
23. Daniel Cornu, *Journalisme et vérité: pour une éthique de l'information* (Geneva: Labor et Fidès, 1994), p. 216.
24. Pierre Nora, 'L'événement monstre', *Communications*, 18 (Paris: Seuil, 1972).
25. Pierre Bourdieu, J.-C. Chamboredon and J.-C. Passeron, *The Craft of Sociology: Epistemological Preliminaries*, trans. Richard Nice (Berlin and New York: Walter de Gruyter, 1991).
26. Bourdieu, *On Television and Journalism*, p. 18 (and p. 17 of French edition).
27. Ibid., p. 44.
28. Ibid., p. 51.
29. Pierre Bourdieu, *The Political Ontology of Martin Heidegger*, trans. Peter Collier (Cambridge: Polity, 1991).
30. Bourdieu, *On Television and Journalism*, p. 21.
31. Ibid., p. 60.
32. He refers, in particular (pp. 60–2), to an article by Gisèle Sapiro on the intellectuals of the inter-war years, which he summarizes in a fairly crude way: the more an intellectual or cultural field is autonomous, that is, the less it cares about commercial success or recognition by the wider public, preferring the recognition of its peers alone, the less it is inclined to collaborate with the powers that be, for example with Vichy. The article in question is: Gisèle Sapiro, 'La raison littéraire: le champ littéraire français sous l'Occupation (1940–1944)', *Actes de la Recherche en Sciences Sociales* (March 1996), reprinted (after the appearance of Bourdieu's book) in Gisèle Sapiro, *La Guerre des écrivains: 1940–1953* (Paris: Fayard, 1999). There are plenty of counter-examples; one thinks in particular of those university circles, by no means open to the wider public, which, as in the case of the legal profession, were hardly distinguished for their courage: see D. Lochak, 'La doctrine sous Vichy ou les mésaventures du positivisme', in *Les Usages sociaux du droit* (Paris: CURAPP-PUF, 1989). However, Sapiro's discussion is much more subtle than it appears in the crude summary given by Bourdieu.
33. Bourdieu, *On Television and Journalism*, pp. 63–4.

34. Ibid., pp. 64–5.
35. Ibid., p. 66.
36. Ibid.
37. Ibid., p. 57.
38. Ibid., p. 33.
39. The analogies between 'critical thought' defined by Kant, under the aegis of 'publicity', and the attitude of Socrates are firmly emphasized by the philosopher Hannah Arendt, who wrote: 'Critical thinking, according to Kant and according to Socrates, exposes itself to "the test of free and open examination", and this means that the more people participate in it, the better': Hannah Arendt, *Lectures on Kant's Political Philosophy*, ed. Ronald Beiner (Brighton: Harvester Press, 1982), p. 39.
40. Bourdieu, *On Television and Journalism*, p. 28.
41. Ibid., pp. 65–6.
42. Ibid., p. 23.
43. The presenters 'turn themselves into representatives of the public at large: "I have to interrupt you here, I don't understand what you mean." What comes across is not that the [presenter] is dumb – no [presenter] will let that happen – but that the average viewer (dumb by definition) won't understand. The [presenter] appears to be interrupting an intelligent speech to speak for the "dummies". In fact, as I have been able to see for myself, it's the people in whose name [the presenter] is supposedly acting who are the most exasperated by such inference.' Ibid., pp. 32–3.
44. Ibid., p. 36.
45. Ibid., p. 47.
46. Pierre Bourdieu, 'Questions aux vrais maîtres du monde', *Le Monde*, 14 October 1999.
47. Bourdieu, *On Television and Journalism*, p. 26.
48. Jürgen Habermas, *The Structural Transformation of the Public Sphere: An Enquiry into a Category of Bourgeois Society* (Cambridge: Polity, 1989).
49. Bourdieu, *On Television and Journalism*, p. 43.
50. For discussion of this question, see Craig Calhoun (ed.), *Habermas and the Public Sphere* (Cambridge, MA: MIT Press, 1992).
51. Bourdieu, *On Television and Journalism*, p. 29.
52. Ibid., p. 61.
53. Ibid., p. 55.
54. Michael Schudson, *The Power of News* (Cambridge, MA: Harvard University Press, 1995), p. 14.
55. Ibid., p. 16.
56. See in particular Theodore L. Glasser (ed.), *The Idea of Public Journalism* (New York and London: Guilford Press, 1999); Jay Rosen, *What are Journalists For?* (New Haven and London: Yale University Press, 1999).
57. Rosen, *What are Journalists For?*, p. 135.
58. Ibid., p. 143.

59. John Dewey, *The Public and its Problems* (New York: H. Holt, 1927; repr. Athens, OH: Swallow Press, 1954).
60. James W. Carey, *Communication as Culture: Essays on Media and Society* (Boston and London: Unwin Hyman, 1989; repr. New York and London: Routledge, 1992).
61. Michael Schudson, 'What Public Journalism knows about journalism but doesn't know about "public"', in Glasser, *The Idea of Public Journalism*, pp. 118–33. See also Michael Schudson, *Discovering the News: A Social History of American Newspapers* (New York: Basic Books, 1978).
62. These questions are discussed in the final section of ch. 4 of my earlier book: Géraldine Muhlmann, *A Political History of Journalism*, trans. Jean Birrell (Cambridge: Polity, 2008).
63. See his detailed critique of the partial and ignorant coverage of the Soviet revolution by American newspapers: Walter Lippmann and Charles Merz, 'A test of the news', *New Republic*, 4 August 1920, pp. 1–40.
64. James W. Carey, 'In defense of Public Journalism', in Glasser, *The Idea of Public Journalism*, pp. 49–66. Carey recognized that Public Journalism deserved some of the criticisms levelled against it. But he saw it as recognition, at last, of the crisis affecting the old model, a product of the Progressive Era, which remained confined within a centralized vision of power, structured by a confrontation between the 'elites of power' and the 'People'. Public Journalism tried to tap into the vitality of small decentralized communities, and the (Jeffersonian?) virtues of local democracy. For Carey, in spite of its defects, it was 'the only movement around that at least provides some oppositional force to the next wave in the global concentration of power and the tyranny of the market': ibid., p. 64.
65. Schudson, 'What Public Journalism knows about journalism but doesn't know about "public"'.
66. Ibid., p. 130.
67. There is clearly an element of romanticism in this project, which, like romanticism itself, can be suspected of an anti-modern dimension, a desire to limit individual freedom and erect boundaries under cover of providing markers. In fact this romanticism is explicit in the Public Journalism movement, proclaimed even by Jay Rosen: Rosen, *What are Journalists For?*, p. 23.
68. Muhlmann, *Political History of Journalism*, ch. 4.
69. Ibid., ch. 5.
70. John Durham Peters, 'Public Journalism and democratic theory', in Glasser, *The Idea of Public Journalism*, pp. 99–117.
71. Ibid., p. 114.
72. Michel Foucault, 'The masked philosopher', repr. in *Ethics: Subjectivity and Truth*, ed. Paul Rabinow, trans. Robert Hurley et al., *Essential Works of Michel Foucault, 1954–1984*, vol. 1 (New York: New Press, 1997; repr. Harmondsworth: Penguin, 2000), pp. 321–8, at p. 325, trans. slightly amended.

73. See the discussion of Park in Chapter 5 below.
74. Michel Foucault, 'La philosophie analytique de la politique' [1978], in *Dits et écrits 1954–1988*, vol. 3, pp. 534–51, esp. pp. 540–1.
75. Michel Foucault, 'La fonction politique de l'intellectuel', *Politique-Hebdo*, 29 November–5 December 1976, pp. 31–3; trans. Colin Gordon, 'The political function of the intellectual', *Radical Philosophy*, 17 (1977), pp. 12–14, also Foucault, 'Truth and power', in *Power/Knowledge: Select Interviews and Other Writings 1972–1977*, ed. Colin Gordon (New York and London: Harvester Wheatsheaf, 1980), pp. 109–33.
76. Michel Foucault, 'La scène de la philosophie' (interview with M. Watanabe 22 April 1978), *Sekai* (July 1978), pp. 312–32.
77. *I, Pierre Riviere, Having Slaughtered My Mother, My Sister, and My Brother . . . : A Case of Parricide in the 19th Century*, ed. Michel Foucault, trans. Frank Jellinek (New York: Pantheon Books, 1975; repr. Lincoln, NE: University of Nebraska Press, 1982).
78. *Blow-up* was a film by Michelangelo Antonioni (1966); Foucault and he discussed their respective methods of work.
79. Michel Foucault, 'Le retour de Pierre Rivière' (interview with G. Gauthier), *La Revue du cinéma*, 312 (December 1976), repr. in *Dits et écrits 1954–1988*, vol. 3, pp. 117–18.
80. Bourdieu, *On Television and Journalism*, p. 15.
81. 'An interview with Stephen Riggins', repr. in Foucault, *Ethics: Subjectivity and Truth*, pp. 121–35, at p. 132 (very slightly amended).
82. 'Entretien avec M. Foucault', *Il Contributo*, 1 (January–March 1980), pp. 23–84, repr. in *Dits et écrits 1954–1988*, vol. 4, pp. 41–95, at p. 47.

Chapter 2

1. John Locke, *Second Treatise on Civil Government*, ch. 11, §138.
2. Eric Barendt, *Freedom of Speech*, 2nd edn (Oxford: Oxford University Press, 2005), ch. 1.
3. This concept was developed most notably by the jurist Oliver Wendell Holmes Jr (1841–1935), Supreme Court judge 1902–32, who strongly distanced himself from his colleagues in the famous decision in *Abrams v. US* of 1919: by this decision the Court forbade certain discourses critical of the government, failing to see this as a contradiction of the First Amendment, whereas Holmes defended total freedom of opinion. Brandeis joined Holmes in this dissenting opinion. Among their sources, Barendt emphasizes the importance of John Stuart Mill. But the historical source for the concept of the 'marketplace of ideas', which valorizes 'participation' in ideas, minimizes its harmful effects and emphasizes its virtues in 'rationalization', also dates back to the century of Enlightenment. All this has echoes, in particular, of the principle of publicity formulated in 1784 by Kant, in his 'An answer to the question: "What is Enlightenment?"': in Hans Reiss (ed.), *Kant: Political Writings* (Cambridge: Cambridge University Press, 1970; 2nd edn 1991), pp. 54–60.

4. J. D. Peters, *Courting the Abyss: Free Speech and the Liberal Tradition* (Chicago and London: University of Chicago Press, 2005).
5. This idea did not appear historically until later, in the eighteenth century for the concept of 'publicity', and probably later still for the theory of the 'marketplace of ideas'. John Durham Peters believes that the theory of the 'marketplace of ideas' did not really appear until the twentieth century: Peters, *Courting the Abyss*, p. 69, where he refers to an earlier article of his: 'The marketplace of ideas: history of a concept', in Andrew Calabrese and Colin Sparks (eds), *Toward a Political Economy of Culture: Capitalism and Communication in the Twenty-First Century* (Boulder, CO: Rowman & Littlefield, 2004), pp. 65–82.
6. 'Call him radical, call him Puritan, call him Republican, but do not call Milton (neo-) liberal': Peters, *Courting the Abyss*, p. 72.
7. For these beginnings in seventeenth-century England, which have been neglected, particularly by Habermas in his discussion of the conditions for the historic appearance of the 'bourgeois public sphere', see also David Zaret, 'Religion, science and printing in the public spheres in seventeenth-century England', in Craig Calhoun (ed.), *Habermas and the Public Sphere* (Cambridge, MA: MIT Press, 1992), pp. 212–35.
8. John Milton, *Areopagitica: A Speech for the Liberty of Unlicenc'd Printing*, in *Areopagitica and Other Political Writings of John Milton* (Indianapolis: Liberty Fund, 1999, p. 15.
9. Ibid., p. 18.
10. Ibid., pp. 17–18.
11. John Carey, *Milton* (New York: Arco, 1970), p. 68, quoted by Peters, *Courting the Abyss*, p. 78.
12. Peters, *Courting the Abyss*, p. 76.
13. Ibid., p. 87.
14. See the editorial of 24 June 2002 in the *New Republic*, quoted by Peters, *Courting the Abyss*, p. 96.
15. Quoted by Peters, *Courting the Abyss*, p. 144.
16. Milton, *Areopagitica*, p. 37.
17. Ibid.
18. Ibid., p. 38.
19. Ibid., p. 43.
20. See the four successive points developed by Locke in his *Essay Concerning Toleration*: John Locke, *An Essay Concerning Toleration: And Other Writings on Law and Politics, 1667–1698*, eds J. R. Milton and Philip Milton (Oxford: Clarendon, 2006), pp. 278–80.
21. Ibid., p. 285.
22. Ibid., pp. 290ff.
23. *A Letter Concerning Toleration*, eds J. Horton and S. Merdus (London and New York: Routledge, 1991), pp. 47–8.
24. Thomas Hobbes, *Leviathan* (London and New York: J. M. and E. P. Dutton, 1914; repr. 1934), p. 92 (my emphasis).
25. John Locke, *Second Treatise on Civil Government*, ch. 7, §93 (pp. 52–3 of Prometheus Books edn (Amherst, New York: 1986).

26. Ibid., ch. 14, §168 (p. 93 of Prometheus Books edn).
27. Ibid., ch. 19, §223 (p. 120 of Prometheus Books edn).
28. Ibid.
29. Ibid., ch. 14, §§241, 168, 210 (pp. 131, 93, 113–14 of Prometheus Books edn).
30. Kant, 'Answer to the question: "What is Enlightenment?", p. 55.
31. Ibid.
32. The word 'scholar' here does not, clearly, mean a competence reserved to a few.
33. Kant, 'Answer to the question: "What is Enlightenment?"', p. 56.
34. Ibid.
35. Ibid., pp. 57–8.
36. Hannah Arendt, *Lectures on Kant's Political Philosophy*, ed. Ronald Beiner (Brighton: Harvester Press, 1982), p. 55.
37. Ibid., p. 54.
38. Ibid.
39. Immanuel Kant, *The Conflict of the Faculties*, in Hans Reiss (ed.), *Kant: Political Writings*, 2nd edn (Cambridge: Cambridge University Press, 1991), pp. 181–2.
40. Michel Foucault, 'Qu'est-ce que les Lumières?', *Magazine littéraire*, 207 (May 1984), pp. 35–9 (extract from lecture of 5 January 1983 at the Collège de France), repr. in *Dits et écrits 1954–1988*, eds D. Defert and F. Ewald, with J. Lagrange (Paris: Gallimard, 1994), vol. 4, pp. 679–88, at p. 685.
41. Ibid.
42. Letter to Marcus Herz, 7 June 1771, quoted in Arendt, *Lectures on Kant's Political Philosophy*, p. 42.
43. Ibid.
44. Kant wrote in 1883, 'Every philosophical work must be susceptible of popularity; if not, it probably conceals nonsense beneath a fog of seeming sophistication'; quoted in Arendt, *Lectures on Kant's Political Philosophy*, p. 39. It is in this section of her book that Arendt likens Kant to Socrates.
45. Hannah Arendt. 'The crisis in culture: its social and its political significance', in *Between Past and Future: Six Exercises in Political Thought* (London: Faber, 1961), pp. 197–226, at p. 219.
46. Immanuel Kant, *Critique of the Power of Judgment*, ed. Paul Guyer, trans. Paul Guyer and Eric Matthews (Cambridge: Cambridge University Press, 2000), §40, pp. 173–4.
47. 'Eine erweiterte Denkungsart': Kant, *Critique of the Power of Judgment*, §40. The expression is discussed by Arendt, 'The crisis in culture', p. 220.
48. The idea of the beautiful as 'subjective universality' appears in §6 of Kant, *Critique of the Power of Judgment* (p. 97 of Guyer edn).
49. For Kant, judgements of taste were considered as 'universally communicable without the mediation of a concept': *Critique of the Power of Judgment*, §40 (p. 175 of Guyer edn).

50. Arendt, 'The crisis in culture', p. 220.
51. This paradigm of aesthetic judgement as a way of conceiving other forms of judgement, in particular moral judgement, was explored more fully by some readers of Kant, most notably Friedrich von Schiller, *On the Aesthetic Education of Man in a Series of Letters* [1794], eds and trans. Elizabeth M. Wilkinson and L. Willoughby (Oxford: Clarendon, 1982).
52. Kant, 'Answer to the question: "What is Enlightenment?"', p. 55 (my emphasis).
53. Foucault, 'Qu'est-ce que les Lumières?', p. 679. In the (English) version of the text published with the title 'What is Enlightenment?' (in *Ethics: Subjectivity and Truth*, ed. Paul Rabinow, trans. Robert Hurley et al., *Essential Works of Michel Foucault, 1954–1984*, vol. 1 (New York: New Press, 1997; repr. Harmondsworth: Penguin, 2000), pp. 303–19), Foucault says: 'It is in the reflection on "today" as difference in history and as motive for a particular philosophical task that the novelty of this text appears to me to lie' (p. 309).
54. Foucault, 'What is Enlightenment?', p. 310.
55. Kant, 'Answer to the question: "What is Enlightenment?"', p. 54.
56. Foucault, 'Qu'est-ce que les Lumières?', p. 687.
57. Ibid., p. 680.
58. Ibid., p. 682.
59. Ibid., pp. 683–4.
60. Ibid.
61. To use the words of John Durham Peters (*Courting the Abyss*, p. 115).
62. This figure has been used in contemporary work on the relationship of the media to suffering – what they say about it, how they represent it – in particular in work which asks questions about the type of 'impartial spectator' which, in so doing, the media suggest to the public: see for example Luc Boltanski, *Distant Suffering: Morality, Media and Politics*, trans. G. Burchell (Cambridge: Cambridge University Press, 1993).
63. Peters, *Courting the Abyss*, p. 119.
64. Ibid., p. 122.
65. The trial of Zenger was the occasion for a confrontation between a position favourable to limitations on press freedom (represented by Andrew Bradford, founder of the *New England Courant* in 1721) and a more radical position, that of the Philadelphia lawyer Andrew Hamilton, who successfully defended Zenger at the trial. The precise legal problem posed by this case was the possibility of condemning a journalist for libel in the event that the attacks he had made were *true*, which they were. This verdict was the first in history where 'truth' was accepted as a proper defence against the charge of libel.
66. For the Founding Fathers and the press, see in particular J. Herbert Altschull, *From Milton to McLuhan: The Ideas Behind American Journalism* (New York: Longman, 1990); Steven R. Knowlton and Patrick R. Parsons

(eds), *The Journalist's Moral Compass: Basic Principles* (Westport: Praeger, 1995).

67. See Elisabeth Zoller, 'La Cour Suprème des Etats-Unis et la liberté d'expression', in *La liberté d'expression aux Etats-Unis et en Europe* (Actes du colloque des 18–19 janvier 2008 à l'Université Paris II) (Paris: Dalloz, 2008), pp. 253–88.
68. See *Police Department of the City of Chicago v. Mosley* (1972).
69. See *Considerations on the Government of Poland* (1772): restriction through electoral mandates defined by electoral colleges, frequent re-election, prohibition on repeated re-election.
70. For the filiation of Hobbes to Rousseau, see Robert Derathé, *Jean-Jacques Rousseau et la science politique de son temps* (Vrin, 1970; new edn 1974), esp. ch. 5 (on the theory of sovereignty).
71. B. Bachofen, *La Condition de la liberté: Rousseau, critique des raisons politiques* (Paris: Payot, 2002), p. 191.
72. Ibid., p. 188.
73. Bruno Bernardi, *La Fabrique des concepts: recherches sur l'invention conceptuelle chez Rousseau* (Paris: Champion, 2006), p. 515.
74. Ibid., p. 519.
75. Since 'what enlightens the general will is the very process by which it is formed': ibid.
76. Derathé, *Jean-Jacques Rousseau et la science politique*, ch. 5.
77. Stephen Holmes, *Benjamin Constant and the Making of Modern Liberalism* (New Haven and London: Yale University Press, 1984), p. 3.
78. Benjamin Constant, 'The liberty of the Ancients compared with that of the Moderns', in *Political Writings* 317 (Cambridge: Cambridge University Press, 1988), esp. p. 328.
79. Holmes, *Benjamin Constant*, p. 75.
80. Constant, 'The liberty of the Ancients compared with that of the Moderns', esp. pp. 326–8
81. Camille Desmoulins, *Le Vieux Cordelier* [1793], ed. Pierre Pachet (Paris: Belin, 1987), p. 38.
82. Quoted in Claude Bellanger, Jacques Godechot, Pierre Guiral and Fernand Terrou (eds), *Histoire générale de la presse française*, vol. 1: *Des origines à 1814* (Paris: PUF, 1971), pp. 424–5.
83. Desmoulins, *Le Vieux Cordelier*, p. 58.
84. See Jean-Claude Bonnet, 'Les rôles du journaliste selon Camille Desmoulins', in Pierre Rétat (ed.), *La Révolution du journal 1788–1794* (Paris: CNRS, 1989), pp. 179–85.
85. C. Labrosse and P. Rétat, *Naissance du journal révolutionaire, 1789* (Lyon: PUL, 1989), pp. 104–5.
86. Ibid., p. 215.
87. Ibid., p. 197.
88. Roger Chartier, *Les Origines culturelles de la Révolution française* (Paris: Seuil, 1990), p. 54.
89. Labrosse and Rétat, *Naissance du journal révolutionaire*, pp. 79–83.

90. Quoted in Bellanger et al., *Histoire générale de la presse française*, vol. 1: *Des origines à 1814*, p. 425.
91. *Le Cri du Peuple*, the paper Vallès founded during the Commune, in 1870, pushed to the limit this theme of a writing adding a new 'we' and helping it to emerge; it even abandoned signed articles. See Roger Bellet, *Jules Vallès: journalisme et révolution, 1857–1885* (Tusson, Charente: Ed. du Lérot, 1987); also the sections on Séverine and Vallès in Géraldine Muhlmann, *A Political History of Journalism*, trans. Jean Birrell (Cambridge: Polity, 2008), ch. 2.
92. R. E. Park, 'The crowd and the public (Masse und Publikum)', trans. Charles Elsner, in *The Crowd and the Public and Other Essays* (Chicago: University of Chicago Press, 2005), pp. 3–81.
93. Gustave Le Bon, *The Crowd: A Study of the Popular Mind* (London: Ernest Benn, 1952, 20th edn), pp. 61–2.
94. Ibid., p. 63.
95. Gustave Le Bon, *The Psychology of Peoples* [1894] (London: Fisher Unwin, 1899; New York: Arno Press, 1974), esp. the preface written by Le Bon in May 1916, pp. 6–8.
96. Ibid., p. 11.
97. Ibid., p. 138.
98. Le Bon, *The Crowd*, p. 14.
99. Ibid., p. 18.
100. The quotations in this paragraph are all ibid., pp. 149–50.
101. See in particular Alexis de Tocqueville, *Democracy in America* [1835], in *Democracy in America and Two Essays on America*, trans. Gerald E. Bevan (London: Penguin, 2003), vol. 2, part 2, ch. 5.
102. Ibid., vol. 1, part 2, ch. 4, p. 226.
103. Ibid., vol. 1, part 2, ch. 6, p. 601.
104. Ibid., p. 603.
105. Ibid., vol. 1, part 2, ch. 3, p. 210.
106. Ibid., pp. 212–13.
107. The quotations in this paragraph are all ibid., pp. 218–19.
108. Agnès Antoine, *L'Impensé de la democratie: Tocqueville, la citoyenneté et la religion* (Paris: Fayard, 2003), p. 88.
109. Holmes, *Benjamin Constant*.
110. This is brought out by the media specialist Michael Schudson in the article on Public Journalism discussed in Chapter 1 above: Michael Schudson, 'What Public Journalism knows about journalism but doesn't know about "public"', in Theodore L. Glasser (ed.), *The Idea of Public Journalism* (New York and London: Guilford Press, 1999).
111. Nicole Loraux, *The Divided City: On Memory and Forgetting in Ancient Athens*, trans. Corinne Pache with Jeff Fort (New York: Zone Books, 2002), p. 66.
112. Ibid., p. 70.
113. Ibid.
114. Ibid., p. 97.

115. Ibid., p. 67.
116. M. Gauchet and C. Lefort, 'Sur la démocratie: le politique et l'institution du social', *Textures*, 2–3 (1971), pp. 7–78.
117. Ibid., p. 9.
118. Arendt, 'The crisis in culture', pp. 220ff.
119. Antoine de Baecque, *Le Corps de l'histoire: métaphores et politique (1779–1800)* (Paris: Calmann-Lévy, 1993).

Chapter 3

1. Michel Foucault, 'What is Enlightenment?', in *The Foucault Reader*, ed. Paul Rabinow (Harmondsworth: Penguin, 1991), pp. 38–9.
2. Charles Baudelaire, 'The painter of modern life', trans. Jonathan Mayne, in *The Painter of Modern Life and Other Essays* (London and New York: Phaidon Press, 1964; repr. 2001), pp. 1–41, at p. 12.
3. Ibid.
4. Foucault, 'What is Enlightenment?', pp. 40–1 (translation slightly amended).
5. Baudelaire, 'The painter of modern life', p. 12.
6. Foucault, 'What is Enlightenment?' p. 41.
7. Immanuel Kant, *Critique of the Power of Judgment*, ed. Paul Guyer, trans. Paul Guyer and Eric Matthews (Cambridge: Cambridge University Press, 2000), §50, p. 197.
8. The quotations in the following paragraphs are all from Baudelaire, 'The painter of modern life', pp. 7–11.
9. See, for example, C. Romano, *L'Evénement et le monde* (Paris: PUF, 1998), esp. pp. 272–84), which are far more Heideggerean than Benjaminian in their failure to engage, beyond a handful of quotations, with the complexity of Benjamin's critique of journalism. The passages in this book which deplore the inauthenticity of the relationship to the event, as in journalistic news, based on shock, reveal a total insensitivity to the thinking of Benjamin; for Benjamin, modernity having seen the disappearance of the 'aura', shock had become the only *possible* relationship to the event.
10. See, in particular, how one of Benjamin's heirs, Theodor W. Adorno, waged war on the notion of authenticity and its principle proponent, Heidegger: Theodor W. Adorno, *The Jargon of Authenticity*, trans. Knut Tarnowski and Frederic Will (London: Routledge and Kegan Paul, 1973); also the first part of his *Negative Dialectics*, trans. E. B Ashton (New York: Seabury Press, 1973; repr. New York: Continuum, 1983; London: Routledge, 1990); also his *Lectures on Negative Dialectics: Fragments of a Lecture Course 1965/1966* (Cambridge: Polity, 2008).
11. Walter Benjamin, 'Karl Kraus', *Frankfurter Zeitung*, 10, 14, 17 and 18 March 1931; repr. in *Walter Benjamin: Selected Writings*, eds Michael

W. Jennings, Howard Eiland and Gary Smith, vol. 2: *1927–34* (this article trans. Edmund Jephcott) (Cambridge, MA, and London: Harvard University Press, 1999), pp. 433–58.

12. Walter Benjamin, *The Paris of the Second Empire in Baudelaire*, in *Charles Baudelaire: A Lyric Poet in the Era of High Capitalism*, trans. Harry Zohn (London: New Left Books, 1973), p. 34.
13. Ibid., p. 20.
14. Ibid., p. 23.
15. Ibid., p. 24.
16. As a general rule, the ambivalences noted here echo, and perhaps help to explain, Benjamin's sibylline formulation, 'Extremes meet': 'Paralipomènes et variantes de L'Oeuvre d'art à l'époque de sa reproduction mécanisée' [1936], in *Ecrits français*, ed. J.-M. Monnoyer (Paris: Gallimard, 1991), p. 178.
17. Benjamin, *The Paris of the Second Empire in Baudelaire*, p. 33.
18. Quoted ibid.
19. Ibid., p. 26.
20. Ibid., p. 29.
21. Ibid., p. 37.
22. Ibid.
23. Ibid., p. 40.
24. Ibid., pp. 43–4.
25. Ibid., p. 43.
26. Ibid., p. 45.
27. Benjamin, 'Notes sur les *Tableaux parisiens* de Baudelaire', in *Ecrits français*, pp. 242–3.
28. Benjamin, *The Paris of the Second Empire in Baudelaire*, p. 55.
29. Ibid.
30. 'Central Park', trans. Lloyd Spencer, *New German Critique*, 34 (Winter, 1985), pp. 32–58, at p. 40.
31. Jean-Pierre Richard, *Poésie et profondeur* (Paris: Seuil, 1955), pp. 92–162.
32. Ibid., p. 133.
33. Benjamin, *The Paris of the Second Empire in Baudelaire*, p. 69.
34. Ibid., p. 97.
35. Ibid., p. 96.
36. Walter Benjamin, *Some Motifs in Baudelaire*, in *Charles Baudelaire*, p. 112.
37. 'Central Park', p. 41. An example of auratic experience or response to the gaze is given in *The Work of Art in the Age of Mechanical Reproduction*: it is the experience of the man who leaves urban modernity (or is not yet/still there), when, 'on a summer afternoon, you follow with your eyes a mountain range on the horizon or a branch which casts its shadow over you, you experience the aura of those mountains or that branch': Walter Benjamin, *The Work of Art in the Age of Mechanical Reproduction*, in *Illuminations*, ed. Hannah Arendt, trans. Harry Zorn (London: Pimlico, 1999), p. 216 (pp. 224–5 of Fontana Collins edn).

38. See Benjamin, *Some Motifs in Baudelaire*; also *The Storyteller*, which has this observation near the beginning: 'Experience has fallen in value': Walter Benjamin, *The Storyteller*, in *Walter Benjamin: Selected Writings*, vol. 3: *1935–1938* (Cambridge, MA, and London: Harvard University Press, 2002), pp. 143–66, at p. 143.
39. Benjamin, *The Work of Art in the Age of Mechanical Reproduction*, p. 232 (p. 239 of Fontana Collins edn).
40. Benjamin, *Some Motifs in Baudelaire*, p. 117.
41. Ibid., p. 148.
42. Ibid. pp. 138ff.
43. Ibid., p. 141.
44. Ibid.
45. Ibid., p. 142.
46. Ibid., pp. 142–3.
47. Ibid., p. 143.
48. Walter Benjamin 'A propos de quelques motifs baudelairiens', in *Ecrits français*, p. 245.
49. 'To perceive the aura of an object we look at means investing it with the ability to look at us in return': Benjamin, *Some Motifs in Baudelaire*, p. 148.
50. Ibid., p. 149.
51. Benjamin, 'A propos de quelques motifs baudelairiens', p. 245.
52. Benjamin, *Some Motifs in Baudelaire*, pp. 122ff; 'Notes sur les *Tableaux parisiens* de Baudelaire', p. 236.
53. 'A propos de quelques motifs baudelairiens', pp. 244–5.
54. Benjamin, *Some Motifs in Baudelaire*, pp. 153–4.
55. Ibid., p. 132.
56. Pierre Pachet, *Le Premier venu: essai sur la politique baudelairienne* (Paris: Denoël, 1976), p. 103, where Pachet cites in particular this passage from *My Heart Laid Bare*: 'It is impossible to glance through any newspaper, no matter what the day, the month or the year, without finding on every line the most frightful traces of human perversity, together with the most astonishing boasts of probity, clarity and benevolence and the most brazen statements regarding the progress of civilisation . . . I am unable to comprehend how a man of honour could take a newspaper in his hands without a shudder of disgust.' Charles Baudelaire, *Intimate Journals*, trans. Christopher Isherwood (London and New York: Blackamore Press and Random House, 1930), pp. 95–6.
57. Benjamin, *The Storyteller*, p. 143.
58. Ibid., p. 146.
59. Ibid.
60. Ibid., pp. 147–8.
61. Ibid., p. 156.
62. Michael Herr, *Dispatches* (New York: Knopf, 1977; new edn New York: Vintage International, 1991).
63. For a detailed study of the journalism of Michael Herr, see Géraldine Muhlmann, *A Political History of Journalism*, trans. Jean Birrell (Cambridge: Polity, 2008), ch. 7.

64. Karl Kraus, 'Heine and the consequences', *Die Fackel*, 329/30 (1910).
65. Benjamin, 'Karl Kraus', p. 434.
66. Kraus, 'Heine and the consequences' (quoted in Harry Zohn, *Karl Kraus* (New York: Twayne, 1971), p. 55).
67. Benjamin, 'Karl Kraus', p. 435.
68. Karl Kraus, *The Last Days of Mankind*, in particular Act 3, Scene 2.
69. See, for example, the monologue in Act 4, Scene 5: ibid.
70. G. Simmel, *Mélanges de philosophie relativiste: contribution à la culture philosophique*, French trans. A Guillain (Paris: 1912), pp. 26–7, cited in Benjamin, *The Paris of the Second Empire in Baudelaire*, p. 151.
71. Most notably: 'On language . . .'. One commentator, Stéphane Mosès, attributes a central place, in his reading of Benjamin, to these writings on language: Stéphane Mosès, *L'Ange de l'histoire* (Paris: Seuil, 1992), esp. p. 107.
72. Elias Canetti, 'Karl Kraus: école de la Résistance', trans. E. Kaufholz, in *Karl Kraus: la littérature démolie*, trans. Y. Kobry (Paris: Rivages, 1993).
73. Ibid., p. 27.
74. Ibid.
75. Ibid.
76. Ibid., p. 28.
77. Kraus said that every language 'caused eloquence and turmoil like a woman', but that the German language was a very special woman, 'who only creates and thinks for he who is capable of giving her children': Kraus, 'Heine and the consequences'.
78. Ibid., p. 164.
79. Benjamin, 'Karl Kraus', p. 441.
80. Ibid., p. 442.
81. Ibid.
82. Ibid., pp. 447–8.
83. Ibid., p. 450.
84. Ibid., p. 452.
85. Karl Kraus, 'Apocalypse' [1909].
86. Ibid.
87. Ibid.
88. Ibid.
89. Karl Kraus, 'The beaver coat', *Die Fackel*, 305/306 (1909), repr. in *In These Great Times: A Karl Kraus Reader*, ed. Harry Zohn (Manchester: Carcanet Press, 1976/84), pp. 58–63.
90. Karl Kraus, 'The world of posters', *Die Fackel*, 283/284 (June 1909), repr. in *In These Great Times: A Karl Kraus Reader*, pp. 42–7.
91. Jacques Bouveresse, 'Kraus, Spengler et le déclin de l'Occident', in *Karl Kraus et son temps*, eds G. Krebs and G. Stieg (Asniéres: Publications de l'Institut d'allemand, Université de la Sorbonne nouvelle, 1989), pp. 231–41, at p. 241. It is to be regretted that Bouveresse no longer shows this sensitivity to the complexity of Kraus in his more recent book:

Schmock ou le triomphe du journalisme: la grande bataille de Karl Kraus (Paris: Seuil, 2001). Here, far from bringing out the love–hate relationship to public space and journalism which characterizes Kraus, Bouveresse comes close to a polemic against the press, which crushes the richness of the person in whose name he claims to speak. Admittedly, he does not go to the extent of rehabilitating censorship, but he asserts that 'this concept of press freedom cannot be linked, loosely or closely, to any fundamental right and does not correspond to anything that previous epochs knew, imagined or claimed in the name of "liberty"': ibid., p. 47. And he seems to be calling for increased state control: 'In view of the results so far, one may ask if, in effect, to bank on the supposed capacity of the guardians to guard themselves is not, all things considered, even more naïve than to count on the assistance of the law and the state': ibid., p. 55. Quite apart from the question of faithfulness – or not – to Kraus, these words seem to me unacceptable as things stand. It is clear that, in this book at least, Bouveresse breaks with the requirements of the Kantian principle of publicity, whereas Kraus, in my view, remains always on the point of making such a break, which is much more interesting.

92. Pierre Bourdieu, 'A propos de Karl Kraus et du journalisme', intervention at the colloquium 'L'Actualité de Karl Kraus', Le Centenaire de *Die Fackel* (Le Flambeau – 1899–1936), Paris, 4–6 November 1999, repr. in *Actes de la Recherche en sciences socials*, 131–2: 'Le Journalisme et l'économie' (March, 2000), pp. 123–6.
93. As Adorno says, 'the core of Benjamin's philosophy is the idea of the salvation of the dead': Theodor W. Adorno, 'A portrait of Walter Benjamin', in *Prisms*, trans. Samuel and Shierry Weber (Cambridge, MA: MIT Press, 1967), pp. 227–41, at p. 241.
94. Miguel Abensour, 'Le Choix du petit', *Passé Présent*, 1 (1982), repr. as postscript to Theodor W. Adorno, *Minima moralia: réflexions sur la vie mutilée* [1951] (Paris: Payot, 1980, new edn 1991), pp. 231–43, at p. 234.

Chapter 4

1. Paul Ricoeur, *Lectures on Ideology and Utopia*, ed. George H. Taylor (New York: Columbia University Press, 1986), p. 8.
2. Maximilien Rubel, *Karl Marx: essai de biographie intellectuelle* (Paris: Ed. Marcel Rivière, 1971), p. 68.
3. Karl Marx, 'Comments on the latest Prussian censorship instruction', *Anekdota*, vol. 1 (1843), repr. in *Karl Marx, Frederick Engels. Collected Works*, vol. 1: *Karl Marx: 1835–43* (London: Lawrence & Wishart, 1975), pp. 109–31, at pp. 111–12.
4. Karl Marx, 'Proceedings of the Sixth Rhine Province Assembly. First article. Debates on the freedom of the press and publication of the

proceedings of the Assembly of the Estates', *Rheinische Zeitung*, 125 (5 May 1842), supplement, repr. in *Collected Works*, vol. 1, pp. 132–81, at p. 158.

5. Ibid., p. 159.
6. Ibid., pp. 164–5.
7. Karl Marx, 'The supplement to nos 335 and 336 of the Augsburg *Allgemeine Zeitung* on the Commissions of the Estates of Prussia', *Rheinische Zeitung*, 345 (11 December 1842), repr. in *Collected Works*, vol. 1, pp. 292–306, at p. 292.
8. Karl Marx, 'The leading article in no. 179 of the *Kölnische Zeitung*', supplement to the *Rheinische Zeitung*, 191, 193 and 195 (10, 12 and 14 July 1842), repr. in *Collected Works*, vol. 1, pp. 184–202, at p. 195.
9. Rubel, *Karl Marx*, p. 34; he is here referring to paragraph 319 of Hegel's *Philosophy of Right*.
10. Ibid., p. 39.
11. Bernard Groethuysen, 'Les Jeunes Hégéliens et les origins du socialisme contemporain en Allemagne', *Revue philosophique*, 5–6 (May–June 1923), vol. 95, pp. 381–402, at p. 382.
12. G. W. F. Hegel, 'Introduction', in *Lectures on the History of Philosophy*, Part 3, 'Modern philosophy', trans. E. S. Haldane (London: Kegan Paul, Trench, Trübner, 1896), vol. 3, p. 159.
13. Alexandre Koyré, *Etudes d'histoire de la pensée philosophique* (Paris: A. Colin, 1961; new edn Paris: Gallimard, 1971), p. 176.
14. G. W. F. Hegel, *Elements of the Philosophy of Right* [1821], ed. Allen W. Wood, trans. H. B. Nisbet (Cambridge: Cambridge University Press, 1991), p. 23.
15. Aphorism 32: 'The morning reading of the newspaper is a kind of realistic morning prayer. One orients one's attitude toward the world with respect to God or with respect to what the world is. The latter provides the same security as prayer, in that one knows where one stands', quoted in Joachim Ritter, *Hegel and the French Revolution: Essays on the Philosophy of Right*, trans. Richard Dien Winfield (Cambridge, MA, and London: MIT Press, 1982), p. 106.
16. Hegel, *Elements of the Philosophy of Right*, pp. 20–1.
17. Hannah Arendt, *Lectures on Kant's Political Philosophy*, ed. Ronald Beiner (Brighton: Harvester Press, 1982), p. 35.
18. Ibid.
19. Jacques d'Hondt, *Hegel: philosophe de l'histoire vivante* (Paris: PUF, 1966), p. 155.
20. Ibid., p. 157.
21. Ibid., p. 167.
22. Ritter, *Hegel and the French Revolution*, pp. 106–8.
23. Hegel to Niethammer, Bamberg, 30 May 1807, repr. in *Hegel: The Letters*, trans. Clark Butler and Christiane Seiler (Bloomington: Indiana University Press, 1984), pp. 130–1 (translation slightly amended).
24. Miguel Abensour, 'Marx: quelle critique de l'utopie?', *Lignes*, 17 (October 1992), pp. 43–65, at p. 53.

25. August von Cieszkowski, *Prolegomena to Historiosophy* [1838], in *Selected Writings of August Cieszkowski*, trans. André Liebich (Cambridge: Cambridge University Press, 1979), p. 77.
26. Karl Löwith, *From Hegel to Nietzsche: The Revolution in Nineteenth-Century Thought* [1941], trans. David E. Green (London: Constable, 1965) (first published New York: Holt, Rinehart and Winston, 1964), p. 214. Earlier, Löwith had compared the Hegelian conception of 'the spirit of the age' to the figure of Münchhausen, in the work of Immermann – that baron 'in whom the Lord God enclosed all the "winds of the age"'. In Immermann, he says 'there still lives Hegel's consciousness that beneath the dazzling surface of the age there pulses an eternal world spirit which is only waiting to break through the shell in order to achieve present existence . . . this ambiguous sense of time, which separates the present into temporal and eternal components, as surface and depth, was lost in the Young Hegelians, together with the conservative aspect of Immermann's revolutionary criticism of the age', p. 205.
27. Ludwig Feuerbach, *Principles of the Philosophy of the Future*, §24.
28. Ibid., §28, p. 42.
29. Ibid., §29.
30. Ibid., §22.
31. Ibid., §29.
32. Löwith, *From Hegel to Nietzsche*, p. 207.
33. The expression is that of Löwith: ibid., p. 84.
34. Ibid., p. 79.
35. See, for example, §25 of the *Principles of the Philosophy of the Future.*
36. Ibid., §51.
37. Arnold Ruge, article first published in the *Annales franco-allemandes* (*Deutsch-französische Jahrbücher*), January 1843.
38. Letter to Ruge, September 1843, in *Collected Works*, vol. 3: *Marx and Engels: 1843–44*, pp. 141–5, at p. 144.
39. Karl Marx, 'On the Jewish question', in ibid., pp. 146–74, at p. 165.
40. Karl Marx, 'Contribution to the critique of Hegel's Philosophy of Law. Introduction', in ibid., pp. 175–87, at p. 181.
41. Ibid.
42. Ibid., p. 178.
43. Ibid., p. 177.
44. Ibid., pp. 177–8.
45. Ibid., p. 178.
46. Ibid., pp. 184, 186.
47. Ibid., pp. 183–4.
48. Ibid., p. 185.
49. Ibid., p. 184.
50. Ibid., p. 182.
51. Ibid., p. 182.
52. Ibid., p. 183.
53. To use the language of the French philosopher Jacques Rancière, the 'politics' that appeared in the newspapers was seen by Marx as a 'police',

and in this sense denounced, because, far from expressing the real struggles, it contained and concealed them: Jacques Rancière, *Disagreement: Politics and Philosophy*, trans. Julie Rose (Minneapolis: University of Minnesota Press, 1998).

54. Marx, 'Contribution to the critique of Hegel's Philosophy of Law', p. 186.
55. Karl Marx, 'Critical marginal notes on the article "The king of Prussia and social reform. By a Prussian"', *Vorwärts!*, 60, in *Collected Works*, vol. 3, pp. 189–206, at p. 199.
56. It is one of the central themes of the *Prolegomena to Historiosophy* of August von Cieszkowski (see n. 25 above) to turn Hegelianism into a philosophy both anchored in and oriented towards practice. 'The main agent in this transformation was not to be thought, as in Hegel's philosophy, but will, which was the motive force for that synthesis of thought and action for which Cieszkowski coined the term, so influential later, of "praxis"': D. McLellan, *The Young Hegelians and Karl Marx* (London: Macmillan, 1969), p. 10.
57. Marx, 'Critical marginal notes', p. 203.
58. 'Their *political* understanding deceived their *social* instinct', wrote Marx of the workers of Lyon who were in revolt: ibid., p. 204.
59. Ibid., pp. 191–2.
60. It was the same criticism that Marx formulated against Bruno Bauer in 1845, that is, that critical criticism makes it own 'Mass': *The Holy Family*, in *Collected Works*, vol. 4: *Marx and Engels: 1844–5*, pp. 5–211.
61. This idea that he who looks from his point of anchorage in praxis (even if it is an anchorage of 'dominant') always sees more (even if it is a partial and distorted vision) than he who seeks a vantage point, the understanding of disinterested perception, outside praxis, was to be prominent in the article Marx wrote on suicide in January 1846. In it he discusses the memoirs of Jacques Peuchet, of the Parisian police, which he reckoned more enlightening and more profound than the views of the 'Socialist' and 'Communist' thinkers who talked about society in an abstract fashion: Karl Marx, 'Peuchet: on suicide', in *Collected Works*, vol. 4, pp. 597–612.
62. Marx, 'Critical marginal notes', p. 204.
63. Ibid., p. 202.
64. Ibid.
65. Ibid., p. 201.
66. Karl Marx, *The German Ideology* [1845–6], repr. in Marx and Engels, *Collected Works*, vol. 5, pp. 19–539, at p. 30. It may be noted that the word 'phrases' (or 'jargon') was also later used by Kraus to denounce the journalism of his day (see Chapter 3 above).
67. See Chapter 1 above.
68. 'The existence of revolutionary ideas in a particular period presupposes the existence of a revolutionary class': Marx, *The German Ideology*, p. 60; this was a theme taken up in the *Preface to the Contribution to the Critique of Political Economy* [1859], in the formulation: 'Mankind thus inevitably sets itself only such tasks as it is able to solve.'

69. Marx, *The German Ideology*, p. 54: 'it does not explain practice from the idea but explains the formation of ideas from material practice'.
70. Ibid., p. 56.
71. Etienne Balibar, *Masses, Classes, Ideas: Studies on Politics and Philosophy Before and After Marx*, trans. James Swenson (London and New York: Routledge, 1993), pp. 181–2, 244–5.
72. Ibid.
73. Karl Marx and Frederick Engels, *The Communist Manifesto*, in *Collected Works*, vol. 6: *Marx and Engels: 1845–48*, pp. 477–517, at p. 493.
74. Balibar, *Masses, Classes, Ideas*, pp. 101–2.
75. Ibid., p. 101.
76. Karl Korsch, *Marxism and Philosophy*, trans. Fred Halliday (London: New Left Books, 1970).
77. Ibid., p. 83.
78. Georg Lukacs, *History and Class Consciousness: Studies in Marxist Dialectics*, trans. Rodney Livingstone (London: Merlin Press, 1971), pp. 19–20.
79. Lukacs gives the example of the change in the way of seeing a black worker and a machine for spinning cotton: in order that, against the ideology which prevents seeing what is really there, the former can appear as a slave, and the latter as capital, there has to be both an anchorage in social struggles and, at the same time, a proper labour of the gaze. The correction of the vision is not a sudden conversion but a dialectical leap, which supposes that one first espouses what one will later reject: it is necessary first to have seen simply a negro and a machine for spinning cotton before one can later see, through successive corrections, capital and a slave: ibid., p. 13.
80. Marx, 'Critical marginal notes', p. 201.
81. Marx, *The German Ideology*, p. 236.
82. 'Thus we must never overlook the distance that separates the consciousness of even the most revolutionary worker from the authentic class consciousness of the proletariat . . . the proletariat must not shy away from self-criticism': Lukacs, *History and Class Consciousness*, pp. 80–1.
83. Saul K. Padover (ed.), *The Karl Marx Library, Vol. 2: On America and the Civil War* (New York, St Louis and San Francisco: McGraw-Hill, 1972).
84. The loss of income resulting from the reduction in the number of his articles published in the *Tribune* caused Marx, from October 1861, to write for another newspaper, *Die Presse*, a paper with a middle-class readership in Vienna.
85. Padover, *The Karl Marx Library*, pp. 53–61.
86. My emphasis.
87. Marx published many articles on the *Trent* affair, both in *Die Presse* and in the *New York Daily Tribune*. I refer here to the article of 30 November 1861, published in the *Tribune* on 19 December: Padover, *The Karl Marx Library*, pp. 125–9.
88. See James M. McPherson, *Battle Cry of Freedom: The Civil War Era* (Oxford: Oxford University Press, 1988; repr. Harmondsworth: Penguin, 1990), esp. pp. 389–91 on the *Trent* affair, and ch. 18.

89. It is probable that Marx, in writing for *Die Presse*, was similarly without illusions regarding his European readers.
90. Article of 7 December 1861, published in the *New York Daily Tribune* of 25 December 1861 (my emphasis).
91. Article of 11 January 1862, published in the *New York Daily Tribune* of 1 February 1862, with the title 'English public opinion'.

Chapter 5

1. See Chapter 2 above.
2. Gabriel Tarde, *L'Opinion et la foule* [1901] (Paris: PUF, 1989), p. 38.
3. Ibid., p. 32.
4. 'The crowd is the social group of the past; after the family, it is the oldest of all the social groups': ibid., p. 37.
5. Ibid., p. 122; see also G. Tarde, *Les lois de l'imitation* [1890], new edn ed. B. Karsenti (Paris: Kimé, 1993), p.55.
6. Tarde, *L'Opinion et la foule*, p. 92.
7. Ibid., p. 85.
8. Ibid., pp. 35–6.
9. Ibid., p. 37.
10. Ibid., p. 129.
11. Ibid., p. 43.
12. Ibid., p. 33.
13. Ibid., pp. 32–3.
14. Ibid.
15. 'The influence which the publicist exercises on his public, though it may be much less intense at any given moment, is, by its continuity, much more powerful than the brief and fleeting impulse imprinted on the crowd by its leader': ibid., p. 40.
16. Ibid., p. 102.
17. Ibid., p. 42.
18. Ibid., p. 55.
19. Ibid., p. 46.
20. Ibid.
21. Ibid., p. 48.
22. Ibid., pp. 101–2.
23. Dominique Reynié, *Le Triomphe de l'opinion publique: l'espace public français du XVIe au XXe siècle* (Paris: Odile Jacob, 1998).
24. Ibid., p. 314.
25. Ibid., p. 312.
26. This was the reasoning of deputé Dussolier: 'That the press has nothing in common with seditious cries, the wearing of certain badges or organized gatherings in the public highway is clear. I do not believe that the relationship between the newspaper and the poster is any greater. Like the book, the newspaper is offered for sale, and the public is ignorant of it or aware of it depending on whether it buys it or opens it. The bill or

the poster strikes the eye, it violently forces itself on one's attention': Chamber of deputies, 1884, quoted by Reynié, *Le Triomphe de l'opinion publique*, pp. 315–16.

27. 'It was the idea that the publication of an opinion was capable of inducing in whoever became aware of it a sort of behaviour he would not have engaged in without this publication': ibid., pp. 320–1.
28. Tarde, *L'Opinion et la foule*. p. 47.
29. Ibid.
30. Ibid., pp. 43–4
31. Ibid., p. 44.
32. Ibid., pp. 41–2.
33. R. E. Park, 'The crowd and the public (Masse und Publikum)', trans. Charles Elsner, in R. E. Park, *The Crowd and the Public and Other Essays* (Chicago: University of Chicago Press, 2005), pp. 3–81, at p. 50.
34. Park referred in particular to a text of Simmel: 'Ueber soziale Differenzierung' [1892], in *Gesamtausgabe. Band 2* (Frankfurt: Suhrkamp, 1989), pp. 109–205. Simmel's work on conflict appeared from 1903 on in Germany and the United States, republished in his *Soziologie* of 1908, ch. 4 of which is entitled 'Conflict'.
35. Park, 'The crowd and the public', pp. 43–4.
36. For objectification and the notion of 'form' in Simmel, see his *Grundfragen des Soziologie* (1918); the analogies between Simmel's theory of forms and the Kantian aesthetic are strong.
37. Park, 'The crowd and the public', p. 61.
38. Ibid., p. 57.
39. Ibid., pp. 59–60.
40. R. E. Park, 'Natural history of the newspaper', *American Journal of Sociology*, 29, 3 (November, 1923), pp. 273–89; repr. in *The Collected Papers of R. E. Park*, vol. 3: *Society*, ed. E. C. Hughes (New York: Arno Press, 1974), pp. 89–104.
41. Park, 'Natural history of the newspaper', p. 277.
42. Ibid., p. 278.
43. Ibid., p. 285.
44. Ibid., p. 278.
45. Ibid., p. 289.
46. R. E. Park, 'Reflections on communication and culture', *American Journal of Sociology*, 44 (September, 1938), pp. 187–205; repr. in *Collected*, vol. 1: *Race and Culture*, ed. E. C. Hughes (Glencoe, IL: Free Press, 1950), pp. 36–52.
47. R. E. Park, 'Symbiosis and socialization: a frame of reference for the study of society', *American Journal of Sociology*, 45 (1939), pp. 1–25; repr. in *The Crowd and the Public*, pp. 117–42.
48. Park, 'Reflections on communication and culture', pp. 192–4.
49. Ibid., p. 191.
50. See, in particular, John Dewey, *The Public and its Problems* (New York: H. Holt, 1927; repr. Athens, OH: Swallow Press, 1954).
51. Park, 'Symbiosis and socialization', p. 11.

52. As shown, in particular, in Park, 'Reflections on communication and culture', pp. 192–3.
53. Ibid., p. 204.
54. Helen M. Hughes, *News and the Human Interest Story*, intro. R. E. Park (Chicago: University of Chicago Press, 1940; new edn New York: Greenwood Press, 1968), esp. ch. 8.
55. Park, 'Reflections on communication and culture', pp. 200–1.
56. R. E. Park, 'News as a form of knowledge', *American Journal of Sociology*, 45, 5 (March 1940), pp. 669–86; repr. in *Collected Papers*, vol. 3, pp. 71–88.
57. Park's Introduction was reprinted with the title 'News and the human interest story' in *Collected Papers*, vol. 3, pp. 105–14 (cited here).
58. Park, 'News as a form of knowledge', p. 679.
59. Ibid., p. 678.
60. Ibid., p. 679.
61. Ibid.
62. Ibid., p. 677.
63. Park, 'News and the human interest story', p. 108.
64. Ibid., p. 113.
65. Ibid., p. 108.
66. Park, 'News as a form of knowledge', p. 682. Park is here speaking of the 'herd' rather than the 'crowd', but what he says is entirely analogous to what he says about the 'crowd' elsewhere.
67. Park, 'Reflections on communication and culture', p. 204.
68. Park, 'News as a form of knowledge', p. 677.
69. Park, 'News and the human interest story', p. 112.
70. Park, 'News as a form of knowledge', pp. 683–4.
71. Hughes refers to Robert Redfield, *Tepoztlan: A Mexican Village* (Chicago: University of Chicago Press, 1930).
72. Hughes, 'News and the human interest story', p. 108.
73. Ibid., p. 124.
74. Ibid., p. 110.
75. Ibid., p. 149.
76. Ibid., p. 242.
77. Park, 'News and the human interest story', p. 111.
78. The connection made by the Chicago School between interest in the 'real' and the 'politicization' of the spectators is based on philosophical premises which are in themselves debateable. This way of thinking is surely related to the influence of pragmatism on the Chicago sociologists; a 'knowledge' of the real encourages the practical and hence political consciousness. A perspective spontaneously more concerned to link the political consciousness to the imaginary would not so readily make this connection between 'knowledge' of the real and the consciousness of being a political actor.
79. Roland Barthes, 'Myth today', in *Mythologies*, trans. Annette Lavers (London: Vintage, 1993), p. 115 (and for the rest of this paragraph, pp. 113, 115–17).

80. Roland Barthes, 'L'Effet de réel', *Communications*, 11 (1968).
81. Barthes, 'Myth today', p. 127.
82. Ibid., pp. 136–7.
83. Ibid., p. 127.
84. Ibid., p. 131.
85. Ibid.
86. Ibid.
87. Ibid., p. 129.
88. Ibid., p. 142.
89. Ibid., p. 143.
90. Ibid.
91. Ibid., p. 144.
92. Ibid., pp. 134–5.
93. Ibid., p. 146.
94. Ibid. The Stalinism of certain passages is frankly creepy: 'what can be more meagre than the Stalin myth?', he dares to ask: ibid., p. 148.
95. Ibid., p. 135.
96. Ibid., p. 136.
97. Etienne Tassin, 'Espace commun ou espace public? L'antagonisme de la communauté et de la publicité', *Hermès*, 10 (1991), pp. 23–37.
98. For the notion of 'incorporation' in Lefort, see Claude Lefort, 'The image of the body and totalitarianism', in *The Political Forms of Modern Society: Bureaucracy, Democracy, Totalitarianism*, ed. John B. Thompson (Cambridge: Polity, 1986), pp. 292–306.
99. More generally, beyond the question of journalism, Tassin is moving towards a discussion of the specificity of political conflictuality; see his latest book: Etienne Tassin, *Un monde commun: pour une cosmo-politique des conflits* (Paris: Seuil, 2003).
100. Nicole Loraux, *The Divided City: On Memory and Forgetting in Ancient Athens*, trans. Corinne Pache with Jeff Fort (New York: Zone Books, 2002). I refer in what follows especially to ch. 4, pp. 93–122.
101. Ibid., pp. 102–3.
102. Ibid., pp. 108, 95–6, 104.
103. See Chapter 2 above.
104. Géraldine Muhlmann, A *Political History of Journalism*, trans. Jean Birrell (Cambridge: Polity, 2008).
105. For this notion of the test, see ibid., ch. 3.
106. Loraux, *The Divided City*, p. 108.
107. Jacques Rancière, *Disagreement: Politics and Philosophy*, trans. Julie Rose (Minneapolis: University of Minnesota Press, 1998), especially the chapter entitled 'Wrong: politics and police', pp. 21–42.
108. See ch. 5 of my *Political History of Journalism*.
109. It is particularly an obsession of reporters who encounter violence. They feel they are confronted by an otherness which they sense that they miss in the very labour of bringing it to 'us', of making us see it. The writing of Michael Herr, sent to the front line during the Vietnam War, is typical of this sense of permanent failure.

110. These two categories provide the underlying structure for my *Political History of Journalism*.

Chapter 6

1. Géraldine Muhlmann, *A Political History of Journalism*, trans. Jean Birrell (Cambridge: Polity, 2008).
2. Ibid., ch. 7.
3. Herbert Marcuse, 'Existentialism: remarks on Jean-Paul Sartre's *L'Etre et le Neant*', *Philosophy and Phenomenological Research*, 8 (3) (March 1948), pp. 309–36, at p. 316.
4. Edmund Husserl, 'Fifth meditation', in *Cartesian Meditations: An Introduction to Phenomenology*, trans. Dorion Cairns (The Hague: Martinus Nijhoff, 1960).
5. Paul Ricoeur, 'Edmund Husserl: la cinquième méditation cartésienne', in *A l'école de la phénoménologie* (Paris: Vrin, 1993), pp. 197–225, at p. 200.
6. Ibid., p. 206. See also the discussion of Didier Franck in his *Chair et corps: sur la phénoménologie de Husserl* (Paris: Minuit, 1981), esp. p. 167.
7. Ricoeur, 'Edmund Husserl: la cinquième méditation cartésienne', p. 212.
8. For this problem, see Franck, *Chair et corps*, ch. 13.
9. Ricoeur, 'Edmund Husserl: la cinquième méditation cartésienne', p. 212.
10. Ibid., p. 214.
11. Ibid.
12. Ibid., p. 216.
13. Jean-Paul Sartre, *Being and Nothingness*, trans. Hazel E. Barnes (London: Methuen, 1958), pp. 262–3.
14. Ibid., p. 266.
15. Ibid., p. 258.
16. Ibid., p. 305.
17. Ibid., p. 285.
18. Ibid., p. 260.
19. Ibid., p. 255 (my emphasis).
20. Ibid., p. 379.
21. Ibid., pp. 380–2.
22. Marcuse, 'Remarks on Jean-Paul Sartre's *L'Etre et le Neant*', p. 315.
23. Ibid., p. 318.
24. Sartre, *Being and Nothingness*, p. 363.
25. Ibid., p. 364.
26. Ibid., pp. 414–15.
27. Ibid., p. 425.
28. The other, for Sartre, 'is the concrete pole (though out of reach) of my flight, of the alienation of my possibles, and of the flow of the world

toward another world which is the same world and yet lacks all communication with it': Marcuse, 'Remarks on Jean-Paul Sartre's *L'Etre et le Neant*', p. 269.

29. Maurice Merleau-Ponty, *The Visible and the Invisible*, ed. Claude Lefort, trans. Alphonso Lingis (Evanston: Northwestern University Press, 1968), p. 78.
30. Ibid.
31. Ibid.
32. Ibid., p. 82.
33. Ibid.
34. Maurice Merleau-Ponty, *Phenomenology of Perception*, trans Colin Smith (London: Routledge & Kegan Paul, 1962), 1967 edn, p. 354.
35. Ibid., p. 220.
36. Jean-Paul Sartre, *What is Literature? and Other Essays*, intro. Steven Ungar (Cambridge, MA: Harvard University Press, 1988), p. 216.
37. Ibid.
38. Ibid., p. 73.
39. Sartre, 'Preface', in Frantz Fanon, *The Wretched of the Earth*, trans. Constance Farrington (London: Macgibbon & Kee, 1965; Penguin, 1967; repr. 1990), p. 9.
40. Ibid., p. 11.
41. Sartre, *What is Literature?*, p. 77.
42. Ibid., p. 79.
43. Maurice Merleau-Ponty, *Adventures of the Dialectic*, trans. Joseph Bien (Evanston: Northwestern University Press, 1973; London: Heinemann Educational, 1974), pp. 147, 153–4.
44. Ibid., p. 177.
45. Ibid., pp. 177–8.
46. Ibid., p. 205.
47. Max Scheler, *The Nature of Sympathy*, trans. Peter Heath (London: Routledge & Kegan Paul, 1954).
48. This is discussed in greater detail in ch. 5 of Muhlmann, *A Political History of Journalism*.
49. 'Comment Sartre voit le journalisme aujourd'hui: un entretien avec François-Marie Samuelson', *Les Nouvelles Littéraires*, 15–22 November 1979.
50. Serge July, 'C'était quoi *Libération*? Une équipe', *Libération*, 23 February 1981.
51. Fanon, *The Wretched of the Earth*, p. 21.
52. In general, my notion of 'writing' here refers to the written word. But I believe it would be possible to expand it to include the audiovisual, which it is of great interest also to apprehend in terms of 'writing'. See, for example, A. Gaudreault, *Du littéraire au filmique: système du récit* (Paris: Méridiens Klincksieck, 1989).
53. The article was published on 19 September 1914 in *Le Matin*. It is reproduced in P. Assouline, *Albert Londres: vie et mort d'un grand reporter 1884–1932* (Paris: Balland, 1989), pp. 12–15.

54. For Orwell and Herr, see, respectively, chs 6 and 7 of Muhlmann, *A Political History of Journalism*.
55. Jean Hatzfeld, *Into the Quick of Life: The Rwandan Genocide: The Survivors Speak*, trans. Gerry Feehily (London: Serpent's Tail, 2005).
56. Jean Hatzfeld, *Machete Season: The Killers in Rwanda Speak*, trans. Linda Coverdale (New York: Farrar, Straus and Giroux, 2005).
57. Ibid., p. 83.
58. Ibid., p. 223.
59. Ibid., p. 226.
60. Testimony of Sylvie Umubyeyi, aged 34, social worker, Nyamata Gatare, in Hatzfeld, *Into the Quick of Life*, p. 158.
61. Testimony of Francine Niyitegeka, aged 25, shopkeeper and farmer, Colline de Kibungo, ibid., pp. 25–6 (my emphasis).
62. Hatzfeld, *Machete Season*, p. 32.
63. Ibid., p. 33.
64. Ibid., p. 56.
65. Ibid., p. 58.
66. Ibid., p. 54.
67. Ibid., p. 89 (my emphasis).
68. Ibid., p. 218.
69. Ibid., p. 123.
70. Ibid., p. 76.
71. Ibid., pp. 80–1.
72. Ibid., p. 165.
73. Ibid., ch. 32, pp. 191–5.
74. Ibid., p. 228.
75. Ibid., p. 119.
76. Ibid., p. 23 (my emphasis).
77. See the words of Clémentine, ibid., pp. 152–3.
78. Ibid., p. 213.

Bibliography

Abensour, Miguel, 'Le Choix du petit', *Passé Présent*, 1 (1982), repr. as postscript to Theodor W. Adorno, *Minima moralia: réflexions sur la vie mutilée* [1951] (Paris: Payot, 1980, new edn 1991), pp. 231–43

Abensour, Miguel, 'Marx: quelle critique de l'utopie?', *Lignes*, 17 (October 1992), pp. 43–65.

Abensour, Miguel, *La Démocratie contre l'etat: Marx et le moment machiavélien* (Paris: PUF, 1997).

Adorno, Theodor W, 'A portrait of Walter Benjamin', in *Prisms*, trans. Samuel and Shierry Weber (Cambridge, MA: MIT Press, 1967), pp. 227–41.

Adorno, Theodor W., *The Jargon of Authenticity* [1964], trans. Knut Tarnowski and Frederic Will (London: Routledge and Kegan Paul, 1973).

Adorno, Theodor W., *Negative Dialectics* [1966], trans. E. B Ashton (New York: Seabury Press, 1973; repr. New York: Continuum, 1983; London: Routledge, 1990).

Adorno, Theodor W., *Lectures on Negative Dialectics: Fragments of a Lecture Course 1965/1966* (Cambridge: Polity, 2008).

Adorno, T. W. and M. Horkheimer, *Dialectic of Enlightenment: Philosophical Fragments* [Amsterdam, 1947], trans. John Cumming (London: Allen Lane, 1973; Verso, 1997); trans. Edmund Jephcott, *Dialectic of Enlightenment: Philosophical Fragments* (Stanford: Stanford University Press, 2002).

Altschull, J. Herbert, *From Milton to McLuhan: The Ideas Behind American Journalism* (New York: Longman, 1990).

Antoine, Agnès, *L'Impensé de la democratie: Tocqueville, la citoyenneté et la religion* (Paris: Fayard, 2003).

Arendt, Hannah, 'The crisis in culture: its social and its political significance', in *Between Past and Future: Six Exercises in Political Thought* (London: Faber, 1961), pp. 197–226.

Arendt, Hannah, *Lectures on Kant's Political Philosophy*, ed. Ronald Beiner (Brighton: Harvester Press, 1982; Chicago: University of Chicago Press, 1982, 1989).

Assouline, P., *Albert Londres: vie et mort d'un grand reporter, 1884–1932* (Paris: Balland, 1989).

Bachofen, B., *La Condition de la liberté: Rousseau, critique des raisons politiques* (Paris: Payot, 2002).

Balibar, Etienne, *La Crainte des masses: politique at philosophie avant et après Marx* (Paris: Galilée, 1997), trans. James Swenson, *Masses, Classes, Ideas: Studies on Politics and Philosophy Before and After Marx* (London and New York: Routledge, 1993).

Barendt, Eric, *Freedom of Speech*, 2nd edn (Oxford: Oxford University Press, 2005).

Barthes, Roland, 'Myth today', in *Mythologies* [1957], trans. Annette Lavers (London: Cape, 1972; London: Vintage, 1993).

Barthes, Roland, 'L'Effet de réel', *Communications*, 11 (1968), repr. in T. Todorov and G. Genette (eds), *Littérature et réalité* (Paris: Seuil, 1982), pp. 81–90.

Baudelaire, Charles, 'Le Peintre de la vie moderne', *Le Figaro*, 26 and 29 November, 3 December 1863, trans. Jonathan Mayne, 'The painter of modern life', in *The Painter of Modern Life and Other Essays* (London and New York: Phaidon Press, 1964; repr. 2001), pp. 1–41.

Baudelaire, Charles, *Intimate Journals*, trans. Christopher Isherwood (London and New York: Blackamore Press and Random House, 1930).

Bellanger, Claude, Jacques Godechot, Pierre Guiral and Fernand Terrou (eds), *Histoire générale de la presse française*, vol. 1: *Des origines à 1814* (Paris: PUF, 1971).

Bellet, Roger, *Jules Vallès: journalisme et révolution, 1857–1885* (Tusson, Charente: Ed. du Lérot, 1987).

Benjamin, Walter, 'Karl Kraus', *Frankfurter Zeitung*, 10, 14, 17 and 18 March 1931; repr. in *Walter Benjamin. Selected Writings*, eds Michael W. Jennings, Howard Eiland and Gary Smith, vol. 2: *1927–34* (this article trans. Edmund Jephcott) (Cambridge, MA, and London: Harvard University Press, 1999).

Benjamin, Walter, *Illuminations*, ed. Hannah Arendt, trans. Harry Zorn (New York: Harcourt, 1968; London: Cape, 1970; Fontana Collins, 1973, repr. 1979; London: Pimlico, 1999) (text quoted: *The Work of Art in the Age of Mechanical Reproduction*).

Benjamin, Walter, *Oeuvres, I*: 'Mythe et violence' (Paris: Denoël, 1971); contains in particular 'Sur le langage en général et sur le langage humain' (written in Munich in November–December 1916, *Schriften*, II, pp. 401–19).

Benjamin, Walter, *Charles Baudelaire: A Lyric Poet in the Era of High Capitalism*, trans. Harry Zohn (London: New Left Books, 1973) (texts quoted: *The Paris of the Second Empire in Baudelaire*; *Some Motifs in Baudelaire*).

Benjamin, Walter, 'Central Park', trans. Lloyd Spencer, *New German Critique*, 34 (Winter, 1985), pp. 32–58.

Benjamin, Walter, *Ecrits français*, ed J.-M. Monnoyer (Paris: Gallimard, 1991) (texts quoted: 'Paralipomènes et variantes de L'Oeuvre d'art à l'époque de sa reproduction mécanisée' [1936]; 'Notes sur les *Tableaux parisiens* de Baudelaire'; 'A propos de quelques motifs baudelairiens' [1937–9]).

Benjamin, Walter, *The Storyteller*, in *Walter Benjamin: Selected Writings*, vol. 3: *1935–1938* (Cambridge, MA, and London: Harvard University Press, 2002), pp. 143–66.

Benrekassa, G., 'Camille Desmoulins, écrivain révolutionnaire: "Le Vieux Cordelier"', in J.-C. Bonnet (ed.), *La Carmagnole des Muses: l'homme de lettres et l'artiste dans la Révolution* (Paris: A. Colin, 1988), pp. 223–41.

Bernardi, Bruno, *La Fabrique des concepts: recherches sur l'invention conceptuelle chez Rousseau* (Paris: Champion, 2006).

Boltanski, Luc, *La Souffrance à distance* (Paris: Métailié, 1993), trans. G. Burchell, *Distant Suffering: Morality, Media and Politics* (Cambridge: Cambridge University Press, 1993).

Bonnet, Jean-Claude, 'Les rôles du journaliste selon Camille Desmoulins', in Pierre Rétat (ed.), *La Révolution du journal 1788–1794* (Paris: CNRS, 1989), pp. 179–85.

Bourdieu, Pierre, *L'Ontologie politique de Martin Heidegger* (Paris: Minuit, 1988), trans. Peter Collier, *The Political Ontology of Martin Heidegger* (Cambridge: Polity, 1991).

Bourdieu, Pierre, *Sur la télévision* (Paris: Liber, 1996), trans. P. P. Ferguson, *On Television and Journalism* (London: Pluto, 1998).

Bourdieu, Pierre, 'Questions aux vrais maîtres du monde', *Le Monde*, 14 October 1999.

Bourdieu, Pierre, 'A propos de Karl Kraus et du journalisme', intervention at the colloquium 'L'Actualité de Karl Kraus', Le Centenaire de *Die Fackel* (Le Flambeau - 1899–1936), Paris, 4–6 November 1999, repr. in *Actes de la Recherche en sciences socials*, 131–2: 'Le Journalisme et l'économie' (March, 2000), pp. 123–6.

Bourdieu, Pierre, J.-C. Chamboredon and J.-C. Passeron, *Le Métier de sociologue* (Paris: Mouton, Bordas, 1967; 4th edn Paris, The Hague and New York: EHESS, 1980), trans. Richard Nice, *The Craft of Sociology: Epistemological Preliminaries* (Berlin and New York: Walter de Gruyter, 1991).

Bouveresse, Jacques, 'Kraus, Spengler et le déclin de l'Occident', in *Karl Kraus et son temps*, eds G. Krebs and G. Stieg (Asniéres: Publications de l'Institut d'allemand, Université de la Sorbonne nouvelle, 1989), pp. 231–41.

Bouveresse, Jacques, *Schmock ou le triomphe du journalisme: la grande bataille de Karl Kraus* (Paris: Seuil, 2001).

Cabestan, P., 'La Constitution du corps selon l'ordre de ses apparitions: la conception satrienne du corps', in M. Abensour and E. Tassin (eds), *Revue EPOKHE*, 6 'L'Animal politique' (Grenoble: Ed. Jérôme Million, 1996), pp. 279–98.

Calhoun, Craig (ed.), *Habermas and the Public Sphere* (Cambridge, MA: MIT Press, 1992).

Canetti, Elias, 'Karl Kraus: Ecole de la Résistance', trans. E. Kaufholz, in Karl Kraus, *La Littérature démolie*, ed. Y. Kobry (Paris: Rivages, 1993).

Carey, James W., *Communication as Culture: Essays on Media and Society* (Boston and London: Unwin Hyman, 1989; repr. New York and London: Routledge, 1992).

Champagne, P., *Faire l'opinion: le nouveau jeu politique* (Paris: Minuit, 1990).

Chartier, Roger, *Les Origines culturelles de la Révolution française* (Paris: Seuil, 1990), trans. Lydia G. Cochrane, *The Cultural Origins of the French Revolution* (Durham, NC, and London: Duke University Press, 1991).

Cieszkowski, August von, *Prolegomena to Historiosophy*, in *Selected Writings of August Cieszkowski*, trans. André Liebich (Cambridge: Cambridge University Press, 1979).

Constant, Benjamin, 'The liberty of the Ancients compared with that of the Moderns' [1819], in *Political Writings* 317 (Cambridge: Cambridge University Press, 1988).

Cornu, Daniel, *Journalisme et vérité: pour une éthique de l'information* (Geneva: Labor et Fidès, 1994).

De Baecque, Antoine, *Le Corps de l'histoire: métaphores et politique (1770–1800)* (Paris: Calmann-Lévy, 1993).

Derathé, Robert, *Jean-Jacques Rousseau et la science politique de son temps* (Paris: Vrin, 1970, new edn 1974).

Desmoulins, Camille, *Le Vieux Cordelier* [1793], ed. Pierre Pachet (Paris: Belin, 1987).

Dewey, John, *The Public and its Problems* (New York: H. Holt, 1927; repr. Athens, OH: Swallow Press, 1954).

Eksterowicz, Anthony J. and Robert N. Roberts (eds), *Public Journalism and Political Knowledge* (Boston: Rowman & Littlefield, 2000).

Ferenczi, T., *L'Invention du journalisme en France* (Paris: Payot, 1993).

Feuerbach, Ludwig, *Principles of the Philosophy of the Future*, trans. Manfred Vogel (Indianapolis: Bobbs-Merrill, 1966; new edn Hacket, 1986).

Foucault, Michel (ed.), *Moi, Pierre Riviere, ayant égorgé ma mère, ma soeur at mon frère . . . Un cas de parricide au XIXe siècle présenté par Michel Foucault* (Paris: Gallimard, 1973), trans. Frank Jellinek, *I, Pierre Riviere, Having Slaughtered My Mother, My Sister, and My Brother . . . : A Case of Parricide in the 19th Century* (New York: Pantheon Books, 1975, repr. Lincoln, NE: University of Nebraska Press, 1982).

Foucault, Michel, 'La fonction politique de l'intellectuel', *Politique-Hebdo*, 29 November–5 December 1976, pp. 31–3; trans. Colin Gordon, 'The political function of the intellectual', *Radical Philosophy*, 17 (1977), pp. 12–14.

Foucault, Michel, 'Le retour de Pierre Rivière' (interview with G. Gauthier), *La Revue du cinéma,* 312 (December 1976), repr. in *Dits et écrits 1954–1988*, vol. 3, pp. 117–18.

Foucault, Michel, 'La scène de la philosophie' (interview with M. Watanabe, 22 April 1978), *Sekai* (July 1978), pp. 312–32.

Foucault, Michel, 'La philosophie analytique de la politique' [1978], in *Dits et écrits 1954–1988*, vol. 3, pp. 534–51.

Foucault, Michel, 'Entretien avec M. Foucault', *Il Contributo,* 1 (January–March 1980), pp. 23–84, repr. in *Dits et écrits 1954–1988*, vol. 4, pp. 41–95.

Foucault, Michel, 'Le philosophe masqué' (interview with C. Delacampagne, February 1980), *Le Monde*, 6 April 1980; 'The masked philosopher', repr. in *Ethics: Subjectivity and Truth*, vol. 1, pp. 321–8.

Foucault, Michel, 'Truth and power', in *Power/Knowledge: Select Interviews and Other Writings 1972–1977*, ed. Colin Gordon (New York and London: Harvester Wheatsheaf, 1980), pp. 109–33.

Foucault, Michel 'An interview with Stephen Riggins' (Toronto, 22 June 1982), repr. in *Ethics: Subjectivity and Truth*, pp. 121–35.

Foucault, Michel, 'Qu'est-ce que les Lumières?', *Magazine littéraire*, 207 (May 1984), pp. 35–9 (extract from lecture, 5 January 1983, Collège de France), repr. in *Dits et écrits 1954–1988*, vol. 4, pp. 679–88. Also appeared in an English version, 'What is Enlightenment?', in *Ethics: Subjectivity and Truth*, vol. 1, pp. 303–19; also in *The Foucault Reader*, ed. Paul Rabinow (New York: Random House, 1984; repr. Harmondsworth: Penguin, 1991), pp. 38–9.

Foucault, Michel, *Dits et écrits 1954–1988*, eds D. Defert and F. Ewald, with J. Lagrange (Paris: Gallimard, 1994).

Foucault, Michel, *Ethics: Subjectivity and Truth*, ed. Paul Rabinow, trans. Robert Hurley et al., *Essential Works of Michel Foucault, 1954–1984*, vol. 1 (New York: New Press, 1997; repr. Harmondsworth: Penguin, 2000).

Franck, Didier, *Chair et corps: sur la phénoménologie de Husserl* (Paris: Minuit, 1981).

Gans, Herbert J., *Deciding What's News* (New York: Pantheon Books, 1979).

Gans, Herbert J., *Democracy and the News* (Oxford: Oxford University Press, 2003).

Gauchet, M. and C. Lefort, 'Sur la démocratie: le politique et l'institution du social', *Textures*, 2–3 (1971), pp. 7–78.

Gaudreault, A., *Du littéraire au filmique: système du récit* (Paris: Méridiens Klincksieck, 1989).

Glasser, Theodore L. (ed.), *The Idea of Public Journalism* (New York and London: Guilford Press, 1999).

Goodwin, H. Eugene and Ron F. Smith, *Groping for Ethics in Journalism* (Ames: Iowa State University Press, 1983; 3rd edn 1994).

Groethuysen, Bernard, 'Les Jeunes Hégéliens et les origins du socialisme contemporain en Allemagne', *Revue philosophique*, 5–6 (May–June 1923), vol. 95, pp. 381–402.

Haber, Stéphane, 'Les Formes de la connaissance du présent dans les sciences sociales: une introduction au concept de modernité', Unpublished thesis, University of Franche-Comté (December 1996).

Habermas, Jürgen, *The Structural Transformation of the Public Sphere: An Enquiry into a Category of Bourgeois Society* (Cambridge: Polity, 1989).

Halimi, Serge, *Les Nouveaux chiens de garde* (Paris: Liber, 1997).

Hamilton, Alexander, James Madison and John Jay, *The Federalist Papers* (Harmondsworth: Penguin, 1987).

Hatzfeld, Jean, *Dans le nu de la vie: récits des marais rwandais* (Paris: Seuil, 2000), trans. Gerry Feehily, *Into the Quick of Life: The Rwandan Genocide: The Survivors Speak* (London: Serpent's Tail, 2005).

Hatzfeld, Jean, *Une saison de machettes: récits* (Paris: Seuil, 2000), trans. Linda Coverdale, *Machete Season: The Killers in Rwanda Speak* (New York: Farrar, Straus and Giroux, 2005); also published as *A Time for Machetes: The*

Rwandan Genocide: The Killers in Rwanda Speak (London: Serpent's Tail, 2005).

Hegel, G. W. F., *Lectures on the History of Philosophy*, Part 3, 'Modern philosophy', trans. E. S. Haldane (London: Kegan Paul, Trench, Trübner, 1896).

Hegel, G. W. F., *Hegel: The Letters*, trans. Clark Butler and Christiane Seiler (Bloomington: Indiana University Press, 1984).

Hegel, G. W. F., *Elements of the Philosophy of Right*, ed. Allen W. Wood, trans. H. B. Nisbet (Cambridge: Cambridge University Press, 1991).

Herman, E. S. and Noam Chomsky, *Manufacturing Consent: The Political Economy of the Mass Media* (New York: Pantheon Books, 1988).

Herr, Michael, *Dispatches* (New York: Knopf, 1977; new edn New York: Vintage International, 1991).

Hobbes, Thomas, *Leviathan* (London and New York: J. M. Dent and E. P. Dutton, 1914; repr. 1934).

Holmes, Stephen, *Benjamin Constant and the Making of Modern Liberalism* (New Haven, CT, and London: Yale University Press, 1984).

Hondt, Jacques d', *Hegel: philosophe de l'histoire vivante* (Paris: PUF, 1966).

Hughes, Helen M., *News and the Human Interest Story*, intro. R. E. Park (Chicago: University of Chicago Press, 1940; new edn New York: Greenwood Press, 1968).

Husserl, Edmund, 'Fifth meditation', in *Cartesian Meditations: An Introduction to Phenomenology*, trans. Dorion Cairns (The Hague: Martinus Nijhoff, 1960).

Iyengar, S., *Is Anyone Responsible? How Television Frames Political Issues* (Chicago: University of Chicago Press, 1991).

Iyengar, S. and D. Kinder, *News That Matters: Television and American Opinion* (Chicago: University of Chicago Press, 1987).

July, Serge, 'C'était quoi *Libération*? Une équipe', *Libération*, 23 February 1981.

Kant, Immanuel, 'An answer to the question: "What is Enlightenment?" [1784], in Hans Reiss (ed.), *Kant: Political Writings* (Cambridge: Cambridge University Press, 1970; 2nd edn 1991), pp. 54–60.

Kant, Immanuel, *Critique of the Power of Judgment* [1790], ed. Paul Guyer, trans. Paul Guyer and Eric Matthews (Cambridge: Cambridge University Press, 2000).

Kant, Immanuel, *The Conflict of the Faculties* [1798] in Hans Reiss (ed.), *Kant: Political Writings*, 2nd edn (Cambridge: Cambridge University Press, 1991).

Knowlton, Steven R. and Patrick R. Parsons (eds), *The Journalist's Moral Compass: Basic Principles* (Westport: Praeger, 1995).

Korsch, Karl, *Marxism and Philosophy* [1923], trans. Fred Halliday (London: New Left Books, 1970).

Koyré, Alexandre, *Etudes d'histoire de la pensée philosophique* (Paris: A. Colin, 1961; new edn Paris: Gallimard, 1971).

Kraus, Karl, 'The world of posters', *Die Fackel*, 283/284 (June 1909), repr. in *In These Great Times*, pp. 42–7.

Kraus, Karl, 'The beaver coat', *Die Fackel*, 305/306 (1909), repr. in *In These Great Times*, pp. 58–63.

Kraus, Karl, 'Heine and the consequences', *Die Fackel*, 329/30 (1910).

Kraus, Karl, *In These Great Times: A Karl Kraus Reader*, ed. Harry Zohn (Manchester: Carcanet Press, 1984).

Labrosse, C. and P. Rétat, *Naissance du journal révolutionaire, 1789* (Lyon: PUL, 1989).

Lasch, Christopher, *The New Radicalism in America 1889–1963: The Intellectual as a Social Type* (New York and London: W. W. Norton, 1965).

Lasch, Christopher, 'Mass culture reconsidered', *Democracy* (October, 1981), pp. 7–22.

Le Bon, Gustave, *Lois psychologiques de l'évolution des peuples* [1894] (Paris: Les Amis de Gustave Le Bon, 1978), trans. as *The Psychology of Peoples* (London: Fisher Unwin, 1899; New York, Arno Press, 1974).

Le Bon, Gustave, *Psychologie des foules* [1895] (Paris: PUF, 1988), trans. as *The Crowd: A Study of the Popular Mind* (London: Ernest Benn, 1952, 20th edn).

Lefort, Claude, 'L'Image du corps et le totalitarisme', *Confrontation*, 2 (Autumn 1979), repr. in Claude Lefort, *L'Invention démocratique: les limites de la domination totalitaire* (Paris: Fayard, 1981; rev. edn 1994), pp. 159–76, trans. as 'The image of the body and totalitarianism', in *The Political Forms of Modern Society: Bureaucracy, Democracy, Totalitarianism*, ed. John B. Thompson (Cambridge: Polity, 1986), pp. 292–306.

Le Grignou, Brigitte, *Du côté du public: usages et réceptions de la télévision* (Paris: Economica, 2003).

Lepenies, Wolf, *Between Literature and Science: The Rise of Sociology* [1985], trans, R. J. Hollingdale (Cambridge: Cambridge University Press, 1988).

Lindner, Rolf, *The Reportage of Urban Culture: Robert Park and the Chicago School* (first pub. in German, Frankfurt: Suhrkamp, 1990), trans. Adrian Morris with Jeremy Gaines and Martin Chalmers (Cambridge: Cambridge University Press, 1996).

Lippmann, Walter and Charles Merz, 'A test of the news', *New Republic*, 4 August 1920, pp. 1–40.

Lochak, D., 'La doctrine sous Vichy ou les mésaventures du positivisme', in *Les Usages sociaux du droit* (Paris: CURAPP-PUF, 1989).

Locke, John, *An Essay Concerning Toleration* [1667], in *An Essay Concerning Toleration: And Other Writings on Law and Politics, 1667–1698*, eds J. R. Milton and Philip Milton (Oxford: Clarendon, 2006), pp. 278–80.

Locke, John, *A Letter Concerning Toleration* [1674], eds J. Horton and S. Merdus (London and New York: Routledge, 1991).

Locke, John, *Second Treatise on Civil Government* (Oxford: Blackwell, 1966; Amherst, New York: Prometheus Books, 1986).

Loraux, Nicole, *La Cité divisée: l'oubli dans la mémoire d'Athènes* (Paris: Payot, 1997), trans. Corinne Pache with Jeff Fort, *The Divided City: On Memory and Forgetting in Ancient Athens* (New York: Zone Books, 2002).

Löwith, Karl, *From Hegel to Nietzsche: The Revolution in Nineteenth-Century Thought*, trans. David E. Green (New York: Holt, Rinehart and Winston, 1964; London: Constable, 1965).

Lukacs, Georg, *History and Class Consciousness: Studies in Marxist Dialectics* [1923], trans. Rodney Livingstone (London: Merlin Press, 1971).

Mann, Michael, *The Insider* (film) 1999.
Marcuse, Herbert, 'Existentialism: remarks on Jean-Paul Sartre's *L'Etre et le Neant*', *Philosophy and Phenomenological Research*, 8 (3) (March 1948).
Marx, Karl, 'Proceedings of the Sixth Rhine Province Assembly. First article. Debates on the freedom of the press and publication of the proceedings of the Assembly of the Estates', *Reinische Zeitung,* 125 (5 May 1842), supplement, repr. in Marx and Engels, *Collected Works*, vol. 1, pp. 132–81.
Marx, Karl, 'The leading article in no. 179 of the *Kölnische Zeitung*', supplement to the *Reinische Zeitung,* 191, 193 and 195 (10, 12 and 14 July 1842), repr. in Marx and Engels, *Collected Works*, vol. 1, pp. 184–202.
Marx, Karl, 'The supplement to nos 335 and 336 of the Augsburg *Allgemeine Zeitung* on the Commissions of the Estates of Prussia', *Reinische Zeitung,* 345 (11 December 1842), repr. in Marx and Engels, *Collected Works*, vol. 1, pp. 292–306.
Marx, Karl, Letter to Ruge, September 1843, repr. in Marx and Engels, *Collected Works*, vol. 3, pp. 141–5.
Marx, Karl, 'Comments on the latest Prussian censorship instruction', *Anekdota*, vol. 1 (1843), repr. in Marx and Engels, *Collected Works*, vol. 1, pp. 109–31.
Marx, Karl, 'On the Jewish question', repr. in Marx and Engels, *Collected Works*, vol. 3, pp. 146–74.
Marx, Karl, 'Contribution to the critique of Hegel's Philosophy of Law. Introduction', repr. in Marx and Engels, *Collected Works*, vol. 3, pp. 175–87.
Marx, Karl, 'Critical marginal notes on the article "The king of Prussia and social reform. By a Prussian"', *Vorwärts!*, 60, repr. in Marx and Engels, *Collected Works*, vol. 3, pp. 189–206.
Marx, Karl, *The Holy Family*, repr. in Marx and Engels, *Collected Works*, vol. 4, pp. 5–211.
Marx, Karl, 'Peuchet: on suicide', in Marx and Engels, *Collected Works*, vol. 4, pp. 597–612.
Marx, Karl and Frederick Engels, *The German Ideology* [1845–6], repr. in Marx and Engels, *Collected Works*, vol. 5, pp. 19–539.
Marx, Karl and Frederick Engels, *The Communist Manifesto*, in Marx and Engels, *Collected Works*, vol. 6, pp. 477–517.
Marx, Karl and Frederick Engels, *Karl Marx, Frederick Engels. Collected Works*, Vol. 1: *Karl Marx: 1835–43*, Vol. 3: *Marx and Engels: 1843–44*, Vol. 4: *Marx and Engels: 1844–45* (London: Lawrence & Wishart, 1975).
Marx, Karl and Frederick Engels, *Karl Marx, Frederick Engels. Collected Works*, Vol. 5: *Marx and Engels: 1845–47*, Vol. 6: *Marx and Engels: 1845–48* (London: Lawrence & Wishart, 1976).
McLellan, D., *The Young Hegelians and Karl Marx* (London: Macmillan, 1969).
McPherson, James M., *Battle Cry of Freedom: The Civil War Era* (Oxford: Oxford University Press, 1988; repr. Harmondsworth: Penguin, 1990).
Merleau-Ponty, Maurice, *Phénoménologie de la perception* (Paris: Gallimard, 1945), trans. Colin Smith, *Phenomenology of Perception* (London: Routledge & Kegan Paul, 1962, 1967).

Merleau-Ponty, Maurice, *Les Aventures de la dialectique* (Paris: Gallimard, 1955), trans. Joseph Bien, *Adventures of the Dialectic* (Evanston: Northwestern University Press, 1973; London: Heinemann Educational, 1974).

Merleau-Ponty, Maurice, *Le Visible et l'invisible* (Paris: Gallimard, 1964), trans. Alphonso Lingis, *The Visible and the Invisible*, ed. Claude Lefort (Evanston: Northwestern University Press, 1968).

Milton, John, *Areopagitica: A Speech for the Liberty of Unlicenc'd Printing*, in *Areopagitica and Other Political Writings of John Milton*, foreword John Alvis (Indianapolis: Liberty Fund, 1999).

Mosès, Stéphane, *L'Ange de l'histoire* (Paris: Seuil, 1992).

Mouillaud, M. and J.-F. Tétu, *Le Journal quotidien* (Lyon: PUL, 1989).

Muhlmann, Géraldine, *Une Histoire politique du journalisme XIXe–XXe siècle* (Paris: PUF, 2004; new edn, Paris: Seuil 'Points', 2006), trans. Jean Birrell, *A Political History of Journalism* (Cambridge: Polity, 2008).

Nizan, Paul, *Les Chiens de garde* (Paris, 1932; new edn Paris: Maspéro, 1960), trans. Paul Fittingoff, *The Watchdogs: Philosophers of the Established Order* (New York and London: Monthly Review Press, 1972).

Nora, Pierre, 'L'événement monstre', Communications, 18 (Paris: Seuil, 1972).

Pachet, Pierre, *Le Premier venu: essai sur la politique baudelairienne* (Paris: Denoël, 1976).

Padover, S. K. (ed.), *The Karl Marx Library, Vol. 2: On America and the Civil War* (New York, St Louis and San Francisco: McGraw-Hill, 1972).

Park, Robert E., 'The crowd and the public (Masse und Publikum)' [1904], trans. Charles Elsner, in *The Crowd and the Public*, pp. 3–81.

Park, Robert E., 'Natural history of the newspaper', *American Journal of Sociology*, 29, 3 (November, 1923), pp. 273–89; repr. in *Collected Papers*, vol. 3, pp. 89–104.

Park, Robert E., 'Reflections on communication and culture', *American Journal of Sociology*, 44 (September, 1938), pp. 187–205; repr. in *Collected Papers*, vol. 1, ed. E. C. Hughes (Glencoe, IL: Free Press, 1950), pp. 36–52.

Park, Robert E., 'Symbiosis and socialization: a frame of reference for the study of society', *American Journal of Sociology*, 45 (1939), pp. 1–25; repr. in *The Crowd and the Public*, pp. 117–42.

Park, Robert E., 'News as a form of knowledge', *American Journal of Sociology*, 45, 5 (March 1940), pp. 669–86; repr. in *Collected Papers*, vol. 3, pp. 71–88.

Park, Robert E., 'News and the human interest story', introduction to *News and the Human Interest Story*, repr. in *Collected Papers*, vol. 3, pp. 105–14.

Park, Robert E., *The Collected Papers of R. E. Park*, vol. 1: *Race and Culture*, ed. E. C. Hughes (Glencoe, IL: Free Press, 1950).

Park, Robert E., *The Collected Papers of R. E. Park*, vol. 3: *Society*, ed. E. C. Hughes (New York: Arno Press, 1974).

Park, Robert E., *The Crowd and the Public and Other Essays* (Chicago: University of Chicago Press, 2005).

Peters, John Durham, *Courting the Abyss: Free Speech and the Liberal Tradition* (Chicago and London: University of Chicago Press, 2005).

Plato, *Protagoras and Meno* (Harmondsworth: Penguin, 2006).

Popkin, J. D. *Revolutionary News: The Press in France 1789–1799* (Durham, NC, and London: Duke University Press, 1990).

Rancière, Jacques, *La Mésentente* (Paris: Galilée, 1995), trans. Julie Rose, *Disagreement: Politics and Philosophy* (Minneapolis: University of Minnesota Press, 1998).

Redfield, Robert, *Tepoztlan: A Mexican Village* (Chicago: University of Chicago Press, 1930).

Rétat, Pierre (ed.), *La Révolution du journal 1788–1794* (Paris: CNRS, 1989).

Reynié, Dominique, *Le Triomphe de l'opinion publique: l'espace public français du XVIe au XXe siècle* (Paris: Odile Jacob, 1998).

Richard, Jean-Pierre, *Poésie et profondeur* (Paris: Seuil, 1955) (esp. the text 'Profondeur de Baudelaire').

Ricoeur, Paul, *Lectures on Ideology and Utopia*, ed. George H. Taylor (New York: Columbia University Press, 1986).

Ricoeur, Paul, 'Edmund Husserl: la cinquième méditation cartésienne', in *A l'Ecole de la phénoménologie* (Paris: Vrin, 1993), pp. 197–225.

Ritter, Joachim, *Hegel and the French Revolution: Essays on the Philosophy of Right*, trans. Richard Dien Winfield (Cambridge, MA, and London: MIT Press, 1982).

Romano, C., *L'Evénement et le monde* (Paris: PUF, 1998), trans. as *Event and World* (Ashland, OH: Fordham University Press, 2009).

Rosen, Jay, *What are Journalists For?* (New Haven and London: Yale University Press, 1999).

Rousseau, Jean-Jacques, *The Social Contract* [1762], trans. Maurice Cranston (Harmondsworth: Penguin, 1968).

Rubel, Maximilien, *Karl Marx: essai de biographie intellectuelle* (Paris: Ed. Marcel Rivière, 1971).

Ruge, Arnold, 'Une autocritique du libéralisme: bilan de l'année précédente des Annales', first pub. in *Annales franco-allemandes* (*Deutsch-französische Jahrbücher*), January 1843, repr. in S. Mercier-Josa, *Théorie allemande et pratique française de la liberté* (Paris: L'Harmattan, 1993), pp. 245–68.

Saint-Arnaud, Pierre, *Park, Dos Passos, metropolis: regards croisés sur la modernité urbaine aux Etats-Unis* (Quebec and Toulouse: Presses de l'Université de Laval and Presses Universitaires du Mirail, Toulouse, 1997).

Sapiro, Gisèle, 'La raison littéraire: le champ littéraire français sous l'Occupation (1940–1944)', *Actes de la Recherche en Sciences Sociales* (March 1996), repr. in *La Guerre des écrivains*.

Sapiro, Gisèle, *La Guerre des écrivains: 1940–1953* (Paris: Fayard, 1999).

Sartre, Jean-Paul, *L'Etre et le neant* (Paris: Gallimard, 1943), trans. Hazel E. Barnes, *Being and Nothingness* (London: Methuen, 1958).

Sartre, Jean-Paul, *Qu'est-ce que la littérature?* (Paris: Gallimard, 1948), trans. as *What is Literature? and Other Essays*, intro. Steven Ungar (Cambridge, MA: Harvard University Press, 1988).

Sartre, Jean-Paul, 'Preface', in Frantz Fanon, *Les Damnés de la terre* (Paris: Maspéro, 1961), trans. Constance Farrington, *The Wretched of the Earth* (London: Macgibbon & Kee, 1965; London: Penguin, 1967; repr. 1990).

Sartre, Jean-Paul, 'Comment Sartre voit le journalisme aujourd'hui: un entretien avec François-Marie Samuelson', *Les Nouvelles Littéraires*, 15–22 November 1979.

Scheler, Max, *The Nature of Sympathy*, trans. Peter Heath (London: Routledge & Kegan Paul, 1954).

Schiller, Friedrich von, *On the Aesthetic Education of Man in a Series of Letters* [1794], eds and trans. Elizabeth M. Wilkinson and L. Willoughby (Oxford: Clarendon, 1982).

Schudson, Michael, *Discovering the News: A Social History of American Newspapers* (New York: Basic Books, 1978).

Schudson, Michael, *The Power of News* (Cambridge, MA: Harvard University Press, 1995).

Simmel, Georg, 'Ueber soziale Differenzierung' [1892], in *Gesamtausgabe. Band 2* (Frankfurt: Suhrkamp, 1989), pp. 109–205.

Simmel, Georg, *Soziologie* [1908].

Simmel, Georg, *Grundfragen des Soziologie* [1918].

Singer, Isaac Bashevis, *Love and Exile: The Early Years – A Memoir* (Harmondsworth: Penguin, 1986).

Smith, Adam, *Theory of Moral Sentiments* [1759], eds D. D. Raphael and A. L. Macfie (Oxford: Clarendon, 1976; repr. Indianapolis: Liberty Press, 1982).

Tarde, Gabriel, *Les Lois de l'imitation* [1890], new edn ed. B. Karsenti (Paris: Kimé, 1993).

Tarde, Gabriel, *L'Opinion et la foule* [1901] (Paris: PUF, 1989).

Tassin, Etienne, 'Espace commun ou espace public? L'antagonisme de la communauté et de la publicité', *Hermès*, 10 (1991), pp. 23–37.

Tassin, Etienne, *Un monde commun: pour une cosmo-politique des conflits* (Paris: Seuil, 2003).

Tocqueville, Alexis de, *Democracy in America and Two Essays on America*, trans. Gerald E. Bevan (London: Penguin, 2003).

Zaret, David, 'Religion, science and printing in the public spheres in seventeenth-century England', in Calhoun, *Habermas and the Public Sphere*, pp. 212–35.

Zohn, Harry, *Karl Kraus* (New York: Twayne, 1971).

Zola, Emile, 'Préface pour *La Morasse*, volume collectif de nouvelles', in *Oeuvres complètes*, ed. Henri Mitterand (Paris: Ed. Claude Tchou, 1966–70), vol. 3, pp. 643–6.

Zoller, Elisabeth, 'La Cour Suprème des Etats-Unis et la liberté d'expression', in *La liberté d'expression*, pp. 253–88.

Zoller, Elisabeth (ed.), *La liberté d'expression aux Etats-Unis et en Europe* (Actes du colloque des 18–19 janvier 2008 à l'Université Paris II) (Paris: Dalloz, 2008).

Index